The Price of Knowledge 2004
Access and Student Finance in Canada

The Price of Knowledge 2004
Access and Student Finance in Canada

Written by:
Sean Junor
Alex Usher

Canada Millennium Scholarship Foundation
Millennium Research Series

Published in 2004 by
The Canada Millennium Scholarship Foundation
1000 Sherbrooke Street West, Suite 800, Montreal, QC, Canada H3A 3R2
Toll Free: 1-877-786-3999
Fax: (514) 985-5987
Web: www.millenniumscholarships.ca
Email: millennium.foundation@bm-ms.org

To order:
Renouf Publishing Company Limited
www.renoufbooks.com
(888) 551-7470

National Library of Canada Cataloguing in Publication

Junor, Sean 1974–
The Price of Knowledge 2004: Access and Student Finance in Canada
Sean Junor, Alex Usher

Includes bibliographical references.
ISBN 0-9730495-2-9

1. College students—Canada—Economic conditions. 2. Student aid—Canada. 3. Student loan funds—Canada
4. Postsecondary education—Economic aspects—Canada. I. Usher, Alexander, 1970- II. Canada Millennium
Scholarship Foundation. III. Title.

Cover Design: Manifest Communications
Layout Design: Charlton + Company Design Group

Acknowledgements

The authors fully admit to being interpreters, rather than creators, of most data. Virtually all of the data in this book was generated by and/or with others, and so we owe a debt of gratitude to many people, including:

Susan Galley of Ekos Research, whose patience and forbearance in putting together *Making Ends Meet* and its soon-to-be released sequel have been greatly appreciated; Garth Wannan, Alan Vladicka and Kerry Dangerfield, whose remarkable work in organizing and developing the annual Undergraduate and College Student Surveys has vastly increased our knowledge of the college and university student populations. In the same vein, Rod Skinkle of Acumen Research has over the years contributed enormously to improving our understanding of the decision-making process of both university and—more recently—college applicants.

At the Canada Millennium Scholarship Foundation, the usual suspects deserve credit and thanks. Robert Hamel, Natasha Sawh, Andrew Parkin and Fred Hemingway for their focus on detail and useful comments. Also, much appreciation for Joey Berger's good humour and keen eye for sentence structure. Finally, the Foundation's Board of Directors and especially its executive director, Norman Riddell, deserve credit for generously supporting research work in general and this publication in particular. Also, the Foundation's various summer students dedicated long hours in the pursuit of institutional and government data which is not always an easy task. Naomi Agard, Melissa McDowell, Ester Middleton, Johanne Nadeau and Stephanie Watt deserve a tip of the cap for their ability to find and analyze data.

At the Educational Policy Institute, Amy Cervenan was responsible for collecting and analyzing much of the data that appears in Chapter 4, and provided helpful comments on the rest of the text as well.

On the editing front, David Dalgleish (in Japan) brought the Foundation's work to a whole new time zone with his rapid-fire turnout, finally allowing us to achieve the round-the-clock, just-in-time work schedule we've been aiming for all these years. Denis Poulet oversaw the revision of the French text precisely and efficiently.

Dianne Looker, Lesley Andres, Robert Clift, Ross Finnie, Herb O'Heron, Paul Grayson, Ken Snowdon and Glen Jones provided expert advice and helpful comments on the text of this book. In particular, Herb has been a friend, colleague and mentor for both of us. He had done this for more years than any of us (or probably Herb, for that matter) care to count and the influence of his work and comments can be seen throughout the text.

Closer to home, Benjamin Deller-Usher was always available for consultation, and his assistance in ensuring an undefeated season for Arsenal Football Club has been greatly appreciated by at least one of the authors. In Montreal, Johanna Galarneau is due a huge thank-you for all her patience and understanding for my limited availability over the course of the winter and spring. She never complained and for that I am grateful.

Finally, this book is for Franca (Alex) and Charlotte, Jan Nijman and Don Junor—my grandparents who taught me right from wrong (Sean).

Data Sources Used in This Publication

Canadian College Student Finance Survey 2002 and 2003

The target population of this survey is the student population of participating institutions. Institutions with more than 1,500 students surveyed 450 students, and institutions with fewer than 1,500 students 300. Overall, 9,878 valid questionnaires were received. Technically, survey results are only generalizable to the institutions at which the survey was conducted. Given both the large sample size, and the number and diversity of the institutions taking part, it is probably a very good reflection of the Canadian student body, or at least that portion of it that lies outside the province of Quebec, where coverage is somewhat weak.

In 2003, 27 colleges participated in the survey, which was filled out in class by students. The classes in which the survey was administered were chosen so as to create a stratified sample for the institution. Institutions participating in the 2003 survey were Aurora (NT), Capilano (BC), Baie Comeau (QC), Gaspé (QC), Sainte-Foy (QC), Champlain (QC), Outaouais (QC), Edouard-Montpetit (QC), North Atlantic (NL), Merici (QC), Confederation (ON), George Brown (ON), Grande Prairie (AB), Grant MacEwan (AB), Humber (ON), John Abbott (QC), Keyano (BC), Langara (BC), NBCC Bathurst (NB), Nova Scotia Community College, Red Deer (AB), Red River (MB), Saskatchewan Institute of Applied Sciences and Technology (SK), Seneca (ON), Sir Sandford Fleming (ON), Fraser Valley (BC) and Yukon College (YT).

Canadian Undergraduate Survey Consortium's *Survey of First-Year University Students 2001*, *Survey of Undergraduate Students 2002* and *Graduating Student Survey 2000* and *2003*

The Canadian Undergraduate Survey Consortium (CUSC) is a co-operative research group involving a collection of Canadian universities. Begun in 1994, CUSC now rotates its survey subject each year between first-year students, graduating students and all undergraduate students. The Consortium's membership varies from year to year; in 1997, there were nine Canadian universities involved, while in 2001 the number had increased to 26. The survey is co-coordinated by the University of Manitoba's Department of Housing and Student Life.

Each participating university distributes a survey package consisting of a cover letter, questionnaire and postage-paid return envelope. Different institutions may use different means to pursue follow-up contact with survey recipients in order to increase the response rate. Technically, survey results are only generalizable to the institutions at which the survey was conducted. Given both the large sample size, and the number and diversity of the institutions taking part, it is probably a very good reflection of the Canadian student body, or at least that portion of it that lies outside the province of Quebec, where coverage is somewhat weak.

In 2001, each participating university sent surveys to 600 randomly selected first-year students in a first-level Bachelor's degree program. Only students who entered university from high school or CEGEP were eligible—i.e., students who had no previous post-secondary experience other than the current academic year. Independent and special students were excluded. If an institution did not have 600 first-year students who met the criteria, all eligible first-year students were surveyed. The total number of surveys distributed was 14,972, of which 7,093 were completed and returned (a response rate of 47%). The participating institutions in 2001 were: Brandon, Carleton, Concordia, Dalhousie, Lakehead, Lethbridge, McMaster, Memorial, Nipissing, Ontario College of Art and Design, Queen's, Ryerson, Saint Mary's, Simon Fraser, Trent, Trinity Western, Wilfrid Laurier, Alberta, British Columbia, Manitoba, Montréal, New Brunswick (Saint John), Ottawa, Regina, Saskatchewan, Toronto (Scarborough Campus), Windsor and Winnipeg.

In 2002, each participating university sent surveys to 1,000 randomly selected undergraduate students. In all 31,000 surveys were mailed out and 12,695 were returned, for a response rate of 42.3%. Thirty universities across Canada participated in the study. Universities participating in this survey were: Alberta, British Columbia, Calgary, Carleton, Concordia, Dalhousie, Lakehead, Lethbridge, Manitoba, McMaster, Montréal, Mount St. Vincent, New Brunswick (Saint John and Fredericton), Nippissing, Ontario College of Art and Design, Ottawa, Queen's, Regina, Ryerson, Saskatchewan, Saint Mary's, Simon Fraser, Trent, Trinity Western, Toronto (Scarborough), Waterloo, Wilfrid Laurier, Windsor and Winnipeg.

In 2003, each participating university sent surveys to 1,000 randomly selected graduating students. Where an institution had fewer than 1,000 students graduating, surveys were distributed to all graduating students. In all 22,922 surveys were mailed out and 11,224 were returned, for a response rate of 49.0%. Twenty-six universities across Canada participated in the study. Universities participating in this survey were: Alberta, British Columbia, Calgary, Carleton, Concordia, Dalhousie, Lakehead, Lethbridge, Manitoba, McMaster, Montréal, New Brunswick (Saint John and Fredericton), Nippissing, Ontario College of Art and Design, Regina, Ryerson,

Saskatchewan, Saint Mary's, Simon Fraser, Trinity Western, Toronto (Scarborough), Wilfrid Laurier, Windsor, Winnipeg and Victoria.

Community College Student Information Survey (Statistics Canada)

The *Community College Student Information Survey* is an annual Statistics Canada survey that collects data on enrolment and graduates of post-secondary programs at community colleges and related institutions. The data are used by Human Resources and Skills Development Canada and the Secretary of State to analyze the labour force supply; by educational associations for studies of the education system; and by individual researchers to study the participation of special groups, such as foreign students and women.

The types of program included in the survey are career and university transfer/university-level programs at community colleges, CEGEPs, technical institutes and university colleges.

Career programs consist of certificate and diploma programs offered at community colleges and similar institutions. Completion of secondary school or the equivalent is the normal prerequisite for entry into the program. The length of the program can range from one to several years, with one-year programs leading to a certificate and longer ones to a diploma.

University transfer programs at community colleges and university colleges provide a student with a standing equivalent to the first or second year of a university degree program; the student can then apply for admission to subsequent senior years at a degree-granting institution.

The "général" program at Quebec institutions, the completion of which is a prerequisite for entry into universities, is included in this classification.

The survey was discontinued in 2001 so that the Expanded Student Information Survey, which collects data on both college and university students, could replace it. However, problems in the implementation of this survey have resulted in an inability to obtain data on college students since that time.

Expanded Student Information Survey (Statistics Canada)

The *Expanded Student Information Survey (ESIS)* brings together and enhances three existing surveys—the University Student Information System (USIS), the Community College Student Information System (CCSIS) and the Trade and Vocational Survey (TVOC). It was introduced as a pilot program in the three maritime provinces in 1999 and the entire country in 2001. Continuing implementation problems have meant that data from this source are still incomplete in many respects, not simply from 2001 onwards but from 1999 onwards. Data on university enrolment from 2000 to 2002 were released in the summer of 2004. Data on college enrolment over the period 1999 onwards remain unreleased.

Labour Force Survey (Statistics Canada)

The *Labour Force Survey (LFS)* conducted by Statistics Canada provides the most current monthly labour market statistics. Each month, approximately 50,000 Canadians are interviewed as part of the *LFS*.

Data which can be derived from the *LFS* include: labour force characteristics by age and sex (this includes working-age population, labour force, employment, full-/part-time employment, unemployment, participation rate, unemployment rate, employment rate, and part-time rate); employment by class of worker (public, private and self-employed) and by industry; labour force characteristics by province, by metropolitan area and by economic region; average usual hours and wages of employees by age and sex, union coverage, job permanency and occupation groups; and regional unemployment rates used by the Employment Insurance Program.

National Graduate Survey 1982, 1986, 1990, 1995 and 2000 (Statistics Canada)

This survey, which began in 1984, was designed to determine factors such as the relationship between post-secondary graduates' programs of study and the employment subsequently obtained by them;

graduates' job and career satisfaction; the rates of under-employment and unemployment; the type of employment obtained related to career expectations and qualification requirements; and the influence of post-secondary education on occupational achievement. The information is directed towards policymakers, researchers, educators, employers and young adults interested in post-secondary education and the transition from school to work for trade/vocational, college and university graduates.

Respondents to this survey are contacted two and five years after their graduation. Thus, graduates from the class of 1982 were interviewed in 1984 and 1987; graduates from 1986 were interviewed in 1988 and 1991; graduates from 1990 were interviewed in 1992 and 1995; graduates from 1995 were interviewed in 1997 and 2000. Approximately 50,000 graduates are included in each survey. This publication does not make use of the five-year surveys, nor does it make use of the 1984 survey of 1982 graduates. Only the 1988 survey of the class of 1986, the 1992 survey of the class of 1990, the 1997 survey of the class of 1995 and the 2002 survey of the class of 2000 were used.

The sample frame for NGS 2000 consists of all persons graduating from a recognized Canadian post-secondary institution who completed an eligible program or obtained their diploma during the 2000 calendar year. This does not include graduates of private post-secondary educational institutions (e.g., computer training schools or commercial secretarial schools); individuals completing courses via continuing education courses at a university or college (unless these led to a degree or diploma); individuals who took part-time trade courses (e.g., adult education evening courses) while employed full-time; persons who completed vocational training programs lasting less than three months or programs not offered in the skilled trades (e.g., basic training or skill development programs) or persons in apprenticeship programs.

The NGS sampling methodology is based on a stratification of the graduate population by province of institution, education level and major field of study. The province of institution can be any of

Canada's ten provinces or three territories. Education levels include five classes: trade/vocational training, college, Bachelor's degree or its equivalent, Master's degree or its equivalent and doctorate or its equivalent. Major fields of study, which number either eight or nine depending on the education level, group together study programs according to the associated codes, based on the Classification of Instructional Programs. (Note that this classification is new for 2000 and as a result, NGS 2000 data is frequently incompatible with data from earlier versions of the survey.) Approximately 60,000 graduates were sampled; the unweighted response rate was approximately 70%.

Ontario *College Applicant Survey* (Acumen Research)

The Ontario *College Applicant Survey (CAS)* is an annual survey carried out by the Acumen Research Group with the assistance of the Canada Millennium Scholarship Foundation, Ontario College Application Services (OCAS) and the Association of Colleges Applied Arts and Technology in Ontario (ACAATO). OCAS selects a random sample of applicants for the study and oversees the distribution and collection of all surveys. Each individual is mailed a package that includes a covering letter explaining the nature of the survey, a questionnaire and a postage-paid return envelope. The covering letter explains the voluntary nature of the questionnaire and outlines the prizes available to participants.

In 2003, 12,000 applicants to Ontario colleges were selected for the College Applicant Survey. Of the approximately 133,000 applicants applying to the fall term to an Ontario College, 9,500 English-speaking applicants were randomly selected from the English-speaking pool and 2,500 French-speaking applicants were selected from the French-speaking pool. This represents an over-sampling of French-speaking applicants as they represent only 3% of the total college applicant pool. This over-sampling was necessary to ensure an adequate number of responses from this important segment of the population.

Ontario *University Applicant Survey* (Acumen Research)

The Ontario *University Applicant Survey (UAS)* is an annual survey carried out by the Acumen Research group with the assistance of the Ontario University Application Centre (OUAC). OUAC selects a random sample of applicants for the study and oversees the distribution and collection of all surveys. Each individual is mailed a package that includes a covering letter explaining the nature of the survey, a questionnaire, and a postage-paid return envelope. The covering letter explains the voluntary nature of the questionnaire, and outlines the prizes available to participants.

The study includes a sample of 10,000 applicants who are randomly selected from the total population of applicants to Ontario universities (approximately 90,000 at the time of the survey). In 2001, the survey was distributed in both English (9,000) and French (1,000), and of the 10,000 surveys distributed 1,845 were correctly completed and returned. This provided an overall response rate of 19%. The majority of respondents were from the province of Ontario (88%), and the remainder were almost evenly divided between Eastern Canada (5%) and Western Canada (7%).

Post-Secondary Education Participation Survey (Statistics Canada)

The *Post-Secondary Education Participation Survey (PEPS)* was administered by Statistics Canada on behalf of Human Resources Development Canada in February 2002 to a sub-sample of dwellings involved in Statistics Canada's Labour Force Survey. The target population of this survey is Canadian youth aged 18–24 (in Quebec: 17–24). Response rate to the survey was just under 80%; 5,141 questionnaires were completed. Some questionnaire items—particularly those involving continuous variables—had high non-response rates.

Of those completing surveys, approximately two-thirds either were or had been students at the time of the survey. The sample size for "students" in this survey is therefore approximately 3,400 and the sample size for "non-students" (i.e., those who may have had a "barrier") is approximately 1,700.

Post-Secondary Education: Cultural, Scholastic and Economic Drivers (COMPAS)

The *Post-Secondary Education: Cultural, Scholastic and Economic Drivers* project was a parental survey conducted by COMPAS Research Inc. for the Canada Millennium Scholarship Foundation. A national, representative sample of 1,000 parents with at least one child aged 12–17 was interviewed in November 2003. The purpose of the project was to provide the Foundation with a better understanding of how families perceive and prepare for the post-secondary education options of their children

In this report, COMPAS reports relationships that are valid in a statistically significant sense. Unless the report specifically says that a relationship or difference is nominal or suggestive rather than statistically significant, any observation of a relationship can be assumed to meet the requirements of statistical significance. For example, COMPAS tested each demographic variable against all perceptual questions. Where no significant relationships or patterns were found, results of the correlations are not reported.

School Leavers Survey (Statistics Canada)

The *School Leavers Survey (SLS)* was conducted in 1991 by Statistics Canada on behalf of Human Resources Development Canada (at the time known as Employment and Immigration). The primary objectives of the 1991 SLS were to establish high school leaving rates and to compare secondary school students who had successfully completed high school ("graduates") with those who were still attending ("continuers") and those who had left school before graduating ("leavers"). The SLS was conducted between April and June 1991.

The SLS target population consisted of young people aged 18 to 20 (as of April 1, 1991) from the ten provinces (Yukon and the Northwest Territories were excluded). The original SLS sampling frame was formed from five years (1986–1990) of Family Allowance files. These files were employed because it was thought that they provided the most complete listing of young persons under 15 in Canada at the time.

The SLS sample consisted of 18,000 individuals from the ten provinces who were selected using a stratified design. There were 9,460 interviews completed with Canadians aged 18 to 20.

School Leavers Follow-Up Survey (Statistics Canada)

The *School Leavers Follow-Up Survey (SLF)* was conducted between September and December 1995 by Statistics Canada on behalf of Human Resources Development Canada. The *SLF* gathered information on school-to-work transitions of young adults by focusing on education and work activities beyond high school. The *SLF* re-interviewed the same young Canadians who participated in the *SLS*, now aged 22 to 24.

The *SLF* was conducted in the fall to better gauge activities of individuals (going back to high school, pursuing post-secondary education, working, etc.) which would be more easily discernible at that time of year. In addition, a more accurate count of the number of graduates was possible, as many individuals complete the requirements for a high school diploma in June or during the summer. The *SLF* sample began at 9,460 but was reduced to 9,431, as a number of individuals elected not to participate in the follow-up survey.

Student Income and Expenditure Survey
(EKOS Research Associates and the Canada Millennium Scholarship Foundation)

EKOS Research Associates and the Canada Millennium Scholarship Foundation conducted a monthly national study of the finances of post-secondary students from September 2001 to May 2002. The study was designed to capture the expenses and income of students on a monthly basis, in order to profile the financial circumstances of Canadian post-secondary students and the adequacy of available funding. The Web-based *Student Financial Survey* provided accurate, quantifiable results for the first time on such issues as the incidence and level of assistance, the level of debt from outstanding bank loans, personal lines of credit and credit cards. The study also yielded up-to-date information on student assets (such as automobiles, computers and electronics), student earnings, time usage and types of expenses incurred.

The survey featured a panel of 1,524 post-secondary students from across the country, who participated in a very brief monthly survey, either via Internet or telephone. Students were required to complete a longer baseline wave of the survey in order to participate. The baseline survey asked a number of questions concerning summer income and existing debt, including credit card debt.

Survey of Approaches to Educational Planning 1999 and 2002 (Statistics Canada)

The *Survey of Approaches to Educational Planning (SAEP)*, conducted by Statistics Canada in partnership with Human Resources Development Canada, is the first household survey to collect detailed information on how Canadians prepare for their children's post-secondary education.

The survey was first conducted in October 1999 as a supplement to the *Labour Force Survey*. Data were collected concerning 20,353 children aged 18 years or under in 1999. The *SAEP* collected detailed information focusing on children and the two key ways in which their parents prepare for their post-secondary education:

- *Financial preparation:* This includes whether savings are being set aside for their children's post-secondary education; awareness of the cost of post-secondary schooling; types of savings vehicles used; and expectations regarding other means of financing post-secondary studies, including potential demand for student loans.

- *Non-financial preparation:* This includes, for example, communicating their aspirations and expectations concerning participation in post-secondary studies to their children; the extent of their involvement in their children's learning and schooling; and attitudes and practices concerning homework and television viewing.

Detailed information was collected for both children and households, allowing analysis by such characteristics as children's age, gender, grade in school, academic performance, number of children in the family, household income, and parental education, occupation, and labour force status.

The second edition of the survey was conducted in October 2002. Data were collected concerning just over 10,000 children aged 18 and under. This report is organized around central themes. The first two sections consider context and abilities while the last three sections examine savings, financial planning, amounts saved by October 2002, and amounts parents expect to have saved by the time their children become eligible for postsecondary enrolment.

The first section explores parental perceptions towards education in general and post-secondary education more specifically. The second section looks at children's grades in light of meeting post-secondary admission requirements. It also includes information on children's attitudes towards school and overall general performance in school.

Section three examines the many factors that may play a role in whether or not savings are being put aside for children's postsecondary education. The analysis examines parents' current, future or non-saving status by parental perceptions of post-secondary education, parental educational aspirations for children and children's academic abilities and attitudes to school. Section four examines the anticipated use of other sources of funding for post-secondary schooling that are considered by parents. The final section looks at the amounts saved to date, and contributions made to savings in 2001, including amounts saved and contributed to Registered Education Savings Plans (RESP) by selected demographic characteristics.

Survey of Labour and Income Dynamics (Statistics Canada)

The *Survey of Labour and Income Dynamics (SLID)* is a longitudinal panel survey designed to understand the economic well-being of Canadians by measuring the economic shifts in Canadian households over an extended period of time. The first *SLID* panel began in 1993 and lasted until 1998. Each panel consisted of approximately 15,000 households, including about 30,000 adults.

A preliminary interview took place at the beginning of each panel to collect background information. Each of the six years had a split-interview format, with labour-related topics covered in January and income-related topics covered in May. In both cases, questions refer to the previous calendar year. The income-related interview took place in May in order to coincide with the end of the income tax period, when respondents were more familiar with their records. In addition, many respondents allowed Statistics Canada to consult their income tax file and avoided the interview.

University Student Information System (Statistics Canada)

The *University Student Information System (USIS)* is a national database containing pertinent, up-to-date information on student participation in Canadian degree-granting institutions. USIS contains a large amount of information, only a portion of which is made available to the public in a published format. Enrolment data are available from the 1972–73 academic year to 2001. Degree data are available from 1970 to 2001.

Youth in Transition Survey (Statistics Canada)

The *Youth in Transition Survey (YITS)* is a longitudinal survey developed through partnership between Human Resources Development Canada and Statistics Canada. The preliminary report presents findings from the first cycle of the *YITS*. Between January and April 2000, more than 22,000 Canadian youth participated in the survey.

The survey is designed to examine key transitions in the lives of young people as they move from high school to post-secondary education and from schooling to the labour market. The preliminary report examines the situation of youth (18 to 20 years old) with respect to both their participation in education and attainment, as well as their labour market participation, as of December 1999.

In addition to the survey of 18- to 20-year-olds, *YITS* also collected information from a cohort of 15-year-olds in the spring of 2000. These youth were involved in the Programme for International Student Assessment (PISA). Youth from both the 15-year-old and 18- to 20-year-old cohorts will be surveyed again in 2002, and asked about changes in their family situation, participation in education and labour market activity.

Table of Contents

Acknowledgements ——————————— i
Data Sources Used in This Publication —— iii
Introduction ——————————————— 1

Chapter 1 — Deciding to Go to Post-Secondary

1.I — Introduction ————————— 3
1.II — Parental Aspirations for
Post-Secondary Education—————— 5
1.III — The Decision to Pursue
Post-Secondary Education ————— 9
1.IV — Financial Preparation for
Post-Secondary Education ————— 19
1.V — Institutional Choice ————— 25

Chapter 2 — A Profile of the Student Body

2.I — Introduction—Participation in
Post-Secondary Education ————— 31
2.II — Enrolment ————————— 33
2.III — Participation Rates ————— 47
2.IV — Socio-Economic Background —— 53
2.V — Visible Minorities —————— 57
2.VI — Students With Disabilities —— 59
2.VII — Aboriginal Students ———— 61
2.VIII — Students With Dependants —— 69
2.IX — Students From Rural Areas —— 71
2.X — Student Mobility —————— 75
2.XI — International Mobility ———— 79
2.XII — Dropouts, Persistence and Stop-Outs —— 87

Chapter 3 — Barriers to Access and Participation

3.I — Introduction ———————— 91
3.II — Survey Data on Barriers to
Post-Secondary Education ————— 93
3.III — Academic Barriers ————— 97
3.IV — Financial Barriers ————— 103
3.V — Motivation/Interest Barriers —— 109
3.VI — Conclusion ———————— 113

Chapter 4 — Costs and Resources

4.I — Introduction ———————— 115
4.II — Tuition Rates ——————— 117
4.III — Ancillary Fees —————— 123
4.IV — Textbooks ———————— 127
4.V — Supplies and Equipment ——— 129
4.VI — Housing ————————— 135
4.VII — Childcare Costs —————— 139
4.VIII — Transportation —————— 141
4.IX — Miscellaneous Expenditures—— 145
4.X — Family Contributions ———— 149
4.XI — Employment Income ———— 153
4.XIa — Student Time Usage ———— 161
4.Xib — Employment and Academic
Performance ———————————— 165
4.XII — Income From Student Assistance
Programs ———————————— 167
4.XIII — Miscellaneous Student Income —— 173
4.XIV — Student Perceptions of their Finances —— 177

Chapter 5A — Student Aid in Canada

5A.I — Introduction — How Student
Assistance Works ———————— 181
5A.II — Eligibility ———————— 183
5A.III — Need Assessment ————— 187
5A.IV — Available Aid —————— 195
5A.V — Portability ———————— 203
5A.VI — In-School Interest Subsidy —— 205
5A.VII — Debt Reduction ————— 207
5A.VIII — Repayment —————— 211
5A.IX — Total Aid Available to Students —— 215

Chapter 5B — Sources of Student Assistance

5B.I — Introduction ——————— 219
5B.II — Institutional Assistance ——— 221
5B.III — Student Employment Programs —— 225
5B.IV — Tax Benefits —————— 231
5B.V — Private Borrowing and Credit Cards —— 237
5B.VI — Other Assistance Programs —— 243

Chapter 5C — Government Expenditures on Student Assistance

5C.I — Introduction — Government Expenditures on Students ———— 249

5C.II — Government Expenditures on Student Assistance ———— 251

5C.III — Tax Expenditures and Canada Education Savings Grants ———— 255

5C.IV — Student Employment Program Expenditures ———— 261

5C.V — Expenditures on Post-Secondary Institutions ———— 263

5C.VI — Aggregate Post-Secondary Expenditures ———— 269

Chapter 6 — Student Outcomes

6.I — Introduction ———— 273

6.II — Time to Completion ———— 275

6.III — Graduation and Attainment Rates ———— 277

6.IV — Student Debt at Graduation ———— 281

6.V — Student Loan Repayment ———— 287

6.VI — Pursuing Further Studies ———— 293

6.VII — Transition to the Labour Force ———— 297

6.VIII — Graduate Earnings ———— 307

6.IX — Graduate Mobility ———— 313

6.X — Benefits of Post-Secondary Education to Individuals and Society ———— 321

Tables and Figures ———— 329

Bibliography ———— 339

Appendix A — Additional Data ———— 347

Introduction

The benefits of today's globalized information economy accrue primarily to those with high levels of education. Equality of access to post-secondary education is therefore a key mission of governments everywhere. Without such access, societies will become fractured along class lines, just as they were in the industrial age. The distinction will no longer be between capital and labour but between the knowledge-rich and the knowledge-poor.

Canada has a problem when it comes to ensuring equal access to the knowledge economy for all its citizens. Despite years of attempting to change the situation, there remains a serious gap in post-secondary participation between children from upper- and lower-income backgrounds. That this situation is not getting any worse over time is somewhat encouraging, but it is by no means a cause for celebration. Canada's record in providing equal post-secondary education access is no worse than any other nation, and it could be a point in our favour, but this should not blind us to the remaining work that is required to make equal access a reality.

Canada's record in providing equal post-secondary education access is no worse than any other nation, but this should not blind us to the remaining work that is required to make equal access a reality.

This volume is the second edition of *The Price of Knowledge*. When the first edition was published in 2002, the state of research on students and access to education in Canada was generally poor and certainly inferior to that available in other countries. Statistical data were weak, scattered and frequently years out of date. In short, the country lacked the basic tools to properly diagnose—let alone attempt to cure—its post-secondary education access problems. The purpose of the first volume was therefore to remedy some of these data deficiencies through the creation of a central reference work on all aspects of access to education and student finance.

Two years later, the research scene in Canada has improved tremendously, thanks largely to the appearance of several new Statistics Canada surveys related to post-secondary education and several years of investment in research and data gathering by the Canada Millennium Scholarship Foundation. The new data-rich environment has had a profound impact on the way this edition of *The Price of Knowledge* was written. In the first edition, data were not filtered much—there were generally so few quality data available that almost anything in the public domain was included in the book. Today, conversely, we are almost inundated with data. Although this volume for the most part follows the same format as the first edition, in almost every section readers will find that the text offers more information and deeper analysis. In addition to being a compilation of data from a variety of sources, this work also contains a large amount of secondary analysis and even some original research, particularly with respect to student living standards and data on college students—two large data lacunae in the past.

We have also tried to respond to some of the helpful comments and constructive criticism regarding the first edition, which have in particular led to two major changes in the design of the book. The first is an increase in the amount of raw data made available to readers. For this edition, all the graphs in the book are also available online in Excel format, and a number of helpful data tables are available in an appendix. These modifications enable interested readers to peer "behind the data" should they wish to perform their own analyses.

The second major change is an increase in the amount of analysis regarding barriers to post-secondary education. Some readers told us that the first version of the book—while useful as a data compendium—could have benefitted from greater synthetic analysis of issues that cut across the narrow borders of individual chapters, notably with respect to barriers to post-secondary education. A new chapter (Chapter 3) has therefore been included in order to integrate much of this material and provide a critical analysis of various theories of barriers to access.

There is no single storyline linking the various sections of this book. Students, policies and the institutions that affect them are too diverse to be easily summarized. There are very few areas of access and student finance where cause and effect are linked in an easy or straightforward manner. There are, however, a few themes which emerge from the data in this volume.

The first is that most of the news on access and student finance is good. Nearly all parents are aspiring to a post-secondary education for their children and savings for education are increasing in both incidence and amount. Enrolment is increasing —dramatically so at the university level. Low-income students are accessing post-secondary education in ever greater numbers. Nearly all students have summer jobs, and the incidence and amount of work for university students is not increasing. Most students appear to have adequate means of support. Need-based grants to students are at an all-time high. Government student loan borrowing has been decreasing since 1997, total debt at graduation has stabilized and possibly begun to fall since 2000, and low interest rates mean that the loan repayment burden has eased considerably over the last five years. Finally, graduates are doing much better in the labour market in the early part of this decade than they were in the latter half of the previous one.

Nevertheless, there are still some problems. Grants to universities and colleges are nowhere near as generous as they were a decade ago. Tuition fees continue to rise, and average debt is considerably higher than it was ten years ago. The decline in borrowing mentioned above is not entirely benign— it also reflects the fact that student assistance limits are not as generous as they used to be, although this may change in the wake of the 2004 Federal Budget. The academic bar is being set ever higher for entrance to educational institutions, and students with weaker grades (a situation correlated with lower family income) are finding it more difficult to pursue university education. Educational attainment rates among Aboriginal Peoples are still too low, and at least one province (Saskatchewan) seems to be going backwards in terms of post-secondary education participation rates. There is a significant group of students which has trouble making ends meet on a daily basis, and fees—especially equipment costs— in certain professional programs are astonishingly high. Lastly, graduates are taking much longer to repay their debts than they used to.

In short, Canada's record on access to post-secondary education is generally a positive one, but much work remains to be done. Barriers to education remain, and for the most part those barriers are income-related. These barriers are not just a matter of insufficient finances; they also reflect serious deficiencies in social and cultural capital among young people from lower-income families. These are problems that cannot be solved simply by writing a cheque; they require constant interventions beginning at a fairly young age. Unfortunately, Canadian governments and school boards currently show little sign of engaging with these "non-financial" issues in a serious way.

As always, feedback from readers will be important in improving subsequent editions. Readers with comments on data sources, interpretation of data or the layout and organization of the book are encouraged to contact the authors by email at sjunor@bm-ms.org or ausher@educationalpolicy.org.

Chapter 1

Deciding to Go to Post-Secondary

Chapter 1

Deciding to Go to Post-Secondary

I. Introduction

The decision to obtain a post-secondary education is unlike any other. It is not simply a purchase of services. Depending on the type of education one chooses, it is a decision about how to spend one, two, four, or more years of one's life. In a larger sense, it is also a choice about one's entire future and the range of jobs that one wishes to pursue. In many cases, it is not even an individual decision; the decision to pursue post-secondary education is almost always influenced by the values and attitudes of family members and peers. It cannot be reduced to a simple equation about supply and demand, dollars and cents.

A post-secondary education carries with it numerous benefits both for the individual and society. Increasing levels of education are associated with greater potential for higher earnings and employment stability, increased levels of literacy, more positive perceptions of personal health, and greater participation in volunteering and higher levels of charitable contributions. Despite all this, not everyone chooses to pursue post-secondary education. The purpose of this chapter is to explain some of the factors at work when young Canadians make their choices about post-secondary education. A related discussion on barriers to education will take place in Chapter 3, following a discussion of the composition of the student body in Chapter 2.

The decision to obtain a post-secondary education is a choice about one's entire future. It is unlike any other.

Section II of this chapter focuses on *parental aspirations* for children's education. While not necessarily decisive, parental expectations are nonetheless a major determinant of children's decisions to pursue post-secondary education. The best available evidence shows that Canadian parents have absorbed the labour market's message about the returns of higher studies. Almost without exception, they hope that their children will pursue a post-secondary education, and a large majority hope that their children will attend university.

Section III examines the *decision to pursue post-secondary education*. The best available data suggest that children's expectations and desires with respect to education are highly conditioned by their parent's expectations and desires. Parental desires tend to change over time, however, in response to observations about their child's ability. Hence, as time passes, there is a gradual downward shift in parental educational desires. Among secondary school students, there appears to be very little "shifting" of educational aspirations; the desire to go to university or college seems to be "locked in" as early as the sixth grade and does not vary substantially after that. Perceptions of barriers to the desired level of education do, however, change with academic barriers slowly being pre-empted by financial ones as completion of secondary school approaches, especially among children who must move in order to obtain a post-secondary education.

Having decided to pursue one's studies, some degree of *financial preparation for post-secondary education* must be undertaken. Section IV looks at patterns of education savings and expectations for future financing options. The latest data from Statistics Canada provide few surprises: richer, better-educated Canadians have larger-than-average nest eggs for their children, and there are few noteworthy geographic variations in savings patterns. Parents continue to overestimate their children's ability to obtain merit-based financial scholarships and underestimate the need for non-government loans as their child progresses through post-secondary education.

Finally, Section V looks at the two forms of *institutional choice*—namely, how a student picks an institution and how an institution picks a student. College- and university-bound students appear to have fundamentally different ways of choosing an institution. College-bound students tend to look for a program of studies that interests them and only subsequently choose an institution; university-bound students, on the other hand, appear to choose an institution prior to making a decision on their course of studies. With respect to how institutions select students (an effect which really only occurs at the university level), selection procedures appear to have become more rigorous in recent years. According to data collected for *Maclean's* annual report on universities, the average entering grade of university students across the nation has increased from 74% in 1996 to nearly 84% in 2003. It is unclear from the data, however, whether this increase reflects an increase in demand for a fixed number of places, grade inflation at the secondary school level or revisions in the way universities report their data to *Maclean's*.

II. Parental Aspirations for Post-Secondary Education

Despite the rising cost of post-secondary education, Canadian families continue to have high educational aspirations for their children. In 2002, Statistics Canada conducted a major survey called the *Survey of Approaches to Educational Planning (SAEP)*. It found that over 93% of Canadian parents of children aged 0 to 18 hope that their children will receive some kind of post-secondary education. While there are some differences in aspirations based on family income, parental education and geography, the most startling fact is that the desire for post-secondary education has become almost universal.

Considering that just forty years ago the majority of the working-age population had not even attended high school, this is an absolutely fundamental change in Canadians' attitudes to formal education.

There is a small but noticeable positive relationship between aspirations and household income. Aspirations for children attending post-secondary education rise by between one or two percentage points for $10,000 of additional family income. Figure 1.II.1 shows parental post-secondary education aspirations by household income.

Figure 1.II.1 — Parental Post-Secondary Education Aspirations by Household Income

Source: Statistics Canada's 2002 *Survey of Approaches to Educational Planning.*

Figure 1.II.2 — Parental Aspirations by Type of Education

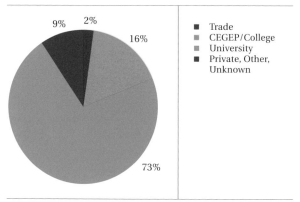

In terms of the type of education desired, parents' aspirations for their children lean heavily towards university; over 70% of all parents who hope their children will pursue post-secondary studies hope they will do so at a university. Only 2% hope their children will pursue trade or vocational studies. Figure 1.II.2 shows parental post-secondary aspirations by type of education.

Source: Statistics Canada's 2002 *Survey of Approaches to Educational Planning.*

Figure 1.II.3 — Parental Aspirations by Highest Education Attained

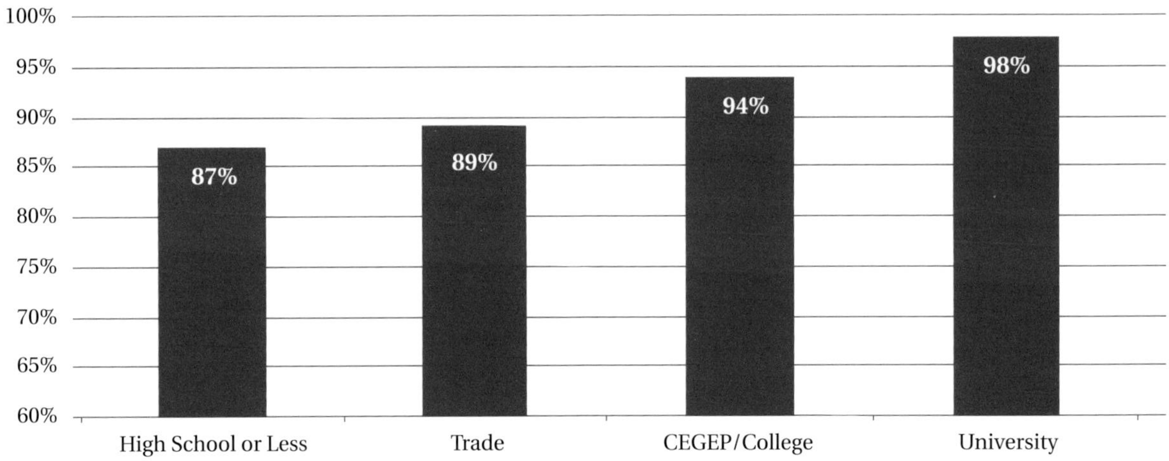

Source: Statistics Canada's 2002 *Survey of Approaches to Educational Planning.*

There is a small but positive correlation between parental educational attainment and parental aspirations. Figure 1.II.3 shows parental post-secondary education aspirations by highest level of parental education.

There is some regional variation in parental aspirations for their children's post-secondary education. At one extreme, over 96% of Ontario parents report hoping that their children will attend post-secondary education, while at the other end of the scale fewer than 88% in Saskatchewan report the same desire. Similarly, the percentage of parents who hope their children will attend university varies slightly by province. At the extremes, almost 80% of Prince Edward Island parents aspire to a university education for their child, while in neighbouring New Brunswick the figure is 67%.

While much of this provincial variation is statistically trivial, two points deserve special attention. The province where "college" is most frequently cited as the highest level of aspiration is Quebec, which has a CEGEP (college) system that begins a year earlier than the rest of the country (typically, at age 17 instead of 18), is required for students to pursue university studies and is free. In this case, it is likely that parental aspirations are influenced by the structure of the system in Quebec. Also, Alberta and B.C. have a formal system of articulation between community colleges and universities. This system allows students to complete the first two years of their university program at a community college, and then transfer to a university for the latter part of their program; this can be an attractive option, especially for students in rural areas. The four Atlantic provinces, Saskatchewan, Manitoba and Ontario have no such formal system; rather, transfers are negotiated on a case-by-case basis.[1] Figure 1.II.4 shows parental aspirations for children's post-secondary education by province of residence.

---

1.   Andres and Looker, "Rurality and Capital."

Figure 1.II.4 — Parental Aspirations by Province of Residence and by Type of Education

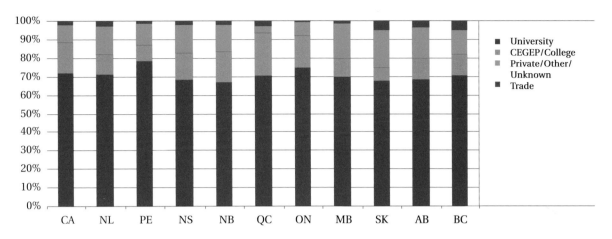

Source: Statistics Canada's 2002 *Survey of Approaches to Educational Planning.*

The *SAEP* reveals some slight differences in aspirations between parents in rural and urban Canada. Urban parents (96%) are more inclined to hope their children will pursue post-secondary studies than their rural counterparts (90%). There is also a small difference in the type of education rural and urban parents hope their children will attend. Parents from rural areas are more likely than their urban counterparts to report aspiring to a community college education for their child. This may be due to the fact that rural Canadians tend to live closer to community colleges/CEGEPs than universities, and colleges are thus a more familiar (not to mention cheaper) educational option. Figure 1.II.5 shows rural and urban parents' educational aspirations for their children.

Figure 1.II.5 — Parental Aspirations for Rural and Urban Families

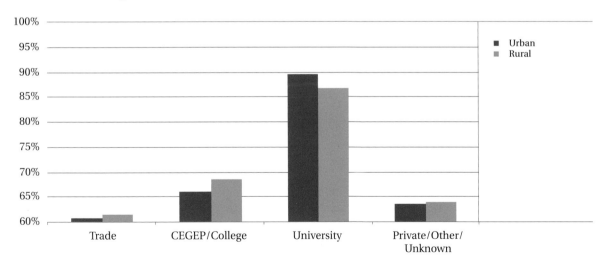

Source: Statistics Canada's 2002 *Survey of Approaches to Educational Planning.*

Finally, there is also a slight difference in parental aspirations by gender. More parents hope their daughters will pursue university education than their sons. Conversely, more parents hope that their sons will end their education at the secondary level. Figure 1.II.6 shows parental aspirations by gender and type of education.

Figure 1.II.6 — Parental Aspirations by Gender and Type of Education

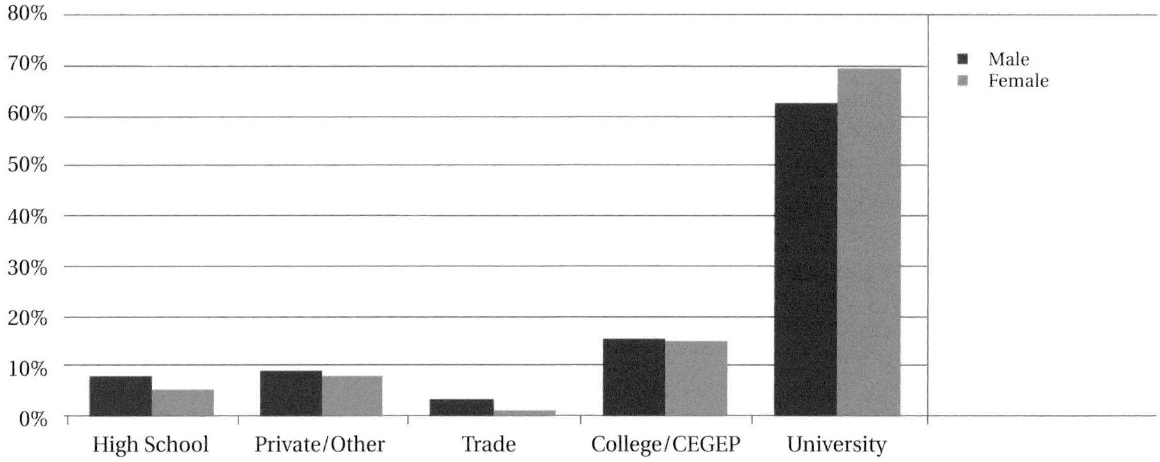

Source: Statistics Canada's 2002 *Survey of Approaches to Educational Planning.*

III. The Decision to Pursue Post-Secondary Education

Despite a near-universal *desire* among parents to see their children receive some form of post-secondary education, *participation* is far from universal. There are a number of stages which need to be passed before aspirations turn into participation, and at each of these stages some youth choose a lifepath that does not include post-secondary education. Figure 1.III.1 illustrates the stages of the educational decision pathway for young people.

Figure 1.III.1 — Youth Educational Decision Pathway for 18- to 20-Year-Olds

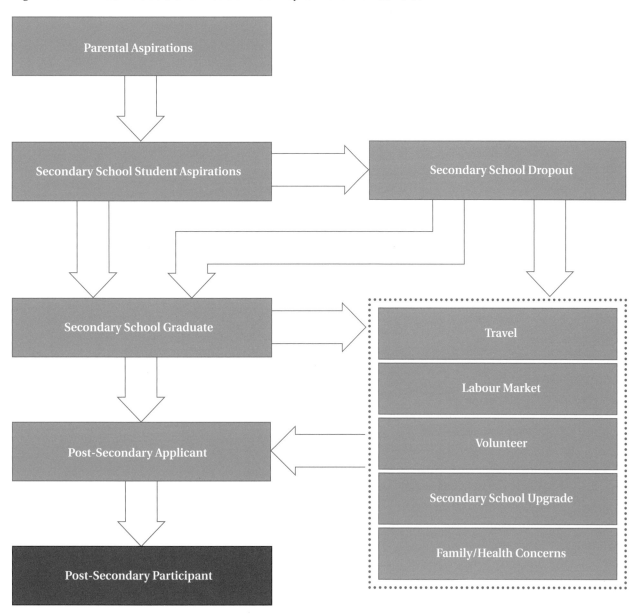

Figure 1.III.2 — Parental Aspirations for Children Expected to Finish High School by Age of Child

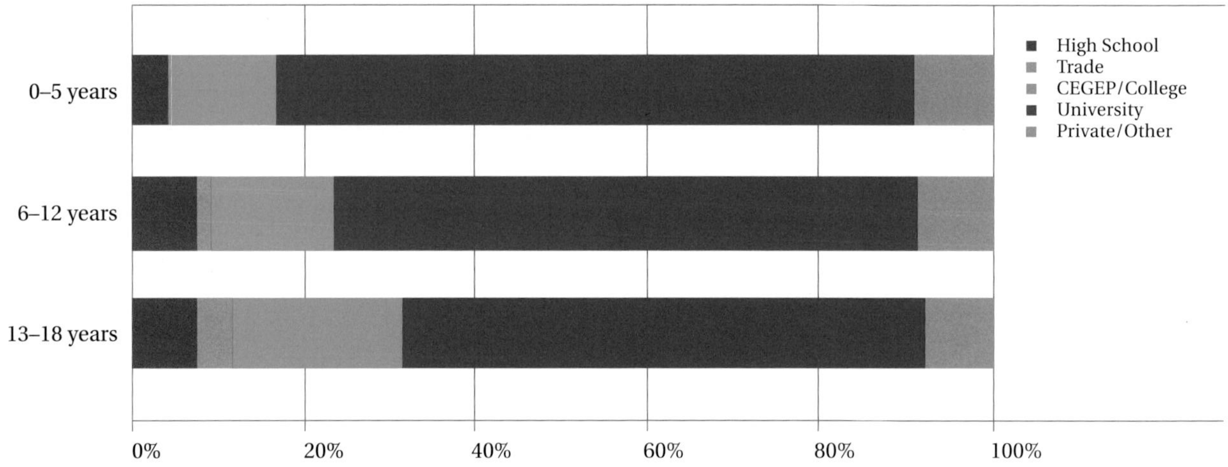

Source: Statistics Canada's 2002 *Survey of Approaches to Educational Planning.*

As children grow into adolescence, a significant shift occurs in parental aspirations regarding their children's post-secondary future. Generally speaking, as time passes parents become considerably less confident about the likelihood of their children gaining a university level education and somewhat less confident about their chances in post-secondary education generally. Figure 1.III.2 shows the changes in parental aspirations by child's age.

Much of this change in parental aspirations over time could be attributed to parents' increased ability to gauge their child's interests and abilities as their child grows older. Parents may see that their children are not performing as well as hoped in school or that their interest in school is fading. Some intriguing evidence in this respect is provided by a 2003 COMPAS Research survey done for the Canada Millennium Scholarship Foundation in part to examine how parents perceive their children's educational futures, as shown in Figure 1.III.3.

Parents who were not optimistic about the education prospects of their children were asked to rate various reasons for their pessimism on a five-point

Generally speaking, as time passes parents become considerably less confident about the likelihood of their children gaining a university level education.

scale (where 1 indicates disagreement and 5 indicates agreement). Half of the parents rated the following reason as either 4 or 5: "child does not have good enough grades to enter university." By comparison, only one-quarter gave a score of 4 or 5 to the statement that their children will likely not go on to college or university because it would be "too expensive." In other words, according to parents of teenagers believed unlikely to continue to higher studies, abilities and interests ("Grades not good enough," "Job child wants doesn't require university") appear to be the most salient factors. Cost is also an important factor, but less so than barriers related to ability and interest.

Broadly speaking, secondary students themselves seem to hold the same views about their educational futures as their parents. According to the 2003–04 *Pan-Canadian Secondary School Survey,* nearly 90% of students in Grades 6 to 12 expect to complete some form of post-secondary education. Between 55% and 60% of students say they expect to complete a university education (compared to 60% of parents with children aged 12 to 18 in the *SAEP*),

Figure 1.III.3 — Parents' Perceptions of Barriers Preventing Their Children From Attending University[a]

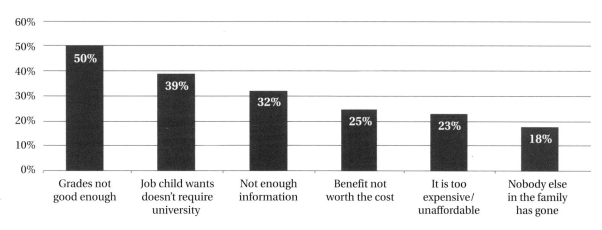

Source: COMPAS Research's *Post-Secondary Education: Cultural, Scholastic and Economic Drivers.*

Note: [a] Among respondents reporting that they do not believe their children will pursue post-secondary only.

and approximately 23% say they will complete a college degree (compared to 20% of parents with children aged 12 to 18 in the *SAEP*). The *Pan-Canadian Secondary School Survey* also asked questions about what secondary students *thought* their parents' expectations were with respect to their educational future. As it happens, in just over 90% of cases, the students' own expectations matched what they believed their parents' expectations to be. This evidence attests to the powerful role played by parental expectations in determining students' post-secondary destinations. However, these data should

be interpreted with caution, as students may in fact be simply projecting their own educational expectations onto their parents.

One striking detail in the *Pan-Canadian Secondary School Survey* data is how little change there is in student expectations from Grade 6 through Grade 12, as presented in Table 1.III.1. This is a clear indication that educational expectations are established early in one's life. In fact, it is very likely that some secondary school students report post-secondary aspirations simply to legitimize their parents' expectations.

Table 1.III.1 — Secondary Student Educational Expectations by Secondary School Grade

	Grade 6	Grade 7	Grade 8	Grade 9	Grade 10	Grade 11	Grade 12
Complete secondary school	9.9%	11.3%	11.6%	11.3%	10.6%	7.5%	8.8%
Complete a university degree	57.9%	55.3%	57.2%	60.6%	55.5%	56.0%	53.8%
Complete an apprenticeship program	7.1%	7.1%	6.8%	6.3%	10.4%	10.7%	10.6%
Complete a college or technical institute diploma/certificate	22.4%	22.3%	22.4%	19.8%	21.4%	23.9%	25.7%
No response	.6%	4.1%	2.0%	2.0%	2.0%	1.8%	1.2%

Source: Prairie Research Associates' *Pan-Canadian Secondary School Survey* (forthcoming).

Students appear to be less likely than parents to cite poor marks as a potential barrier to education. The *Pan-Canadian Secondary School Survey* asked secondary school students to identify up to 12 potential "barriers" to education. Table 1.III.2 shows that no single factor predominates as a potential barrier to education. Roughly one-quarter of all secondary students report poor marks as a "major" or "significant" barrier to obtaining education beyond the high school level, and this proportion does not change substantially from Grade 8 onwards. In contrast, the percentage of secondary students citing insufficient money grows steadily over time, more than doubling from 16.2% in Grade 6 to 34.4% in Grade 12. This seems to be especially relevant for students who must travel in order to attend post-secondary education, since the proportion declaring "having enough money" to be a major barrier seems closely tied to the proportion reporting that "having enough money to live away from home" is a significant obstacle. The relation-

ship between "having enough money" and "fear of debt," on the other hand, seems somewhat weaker.

The progressively greater emphasis on finances as a perceived barrier as secondary school students approach completion is a reflection of two factors. The first has to do with the way in which secondary students approach educational planning. Acumen (2003) has shown that 60% of university applicants do not begin discussing educational finances with their parents until after Grade 10. Clearly, financial barriers cannot become an issue unless educational finances have been considered, and since this is not the case for the majority of students prior to Grade 11, lower levels of concern about finances in lower grades should not come as a surprise.

The second, less obvious factor is sample bias. Many of those for whom academic barriers might have presented a problem will have dropped out of school prior to Grade 12, increasing the likelihood that other barriers will come to the fore as completion of secondary school draws near.

Table 1.III.2 — Secondary School Students' Perceptions of Barriers to Education After High School

	Grade 6	Grade 7	Grade 8	Grade 9	Grade 10	Grade 11	Grade 12
Not having enough money	16.2%	17.5%	22.9%	22.3%	26.7%	32.3%	34.4%
Poor school marks	19.4%	21.6%	25.0%	22.3%	24.9%	26.7%	26.3%
Parents don't encourage it	10.4%	11.6%	11.2%	8%	8.6%	7.0%	6.7%
Friends don't encourage it	8.7%	7.3%	10.3%	6.9%	7.5%	5.8%	4.3%
Lack of interest/motivation	N/A	N/A	N/A	15.6%	18.2%	16.2%	16.3%
Family obligations	N/A	N/A	N/A	7.9%	10.0%	6.8%	9.1%
Not knowing what careers are available	N/A	N/A	N/A	14.6%	17.4%	14.3%	17.2%
Not knowing what to do	N/A	N/A	N/A	21.9%	23.4%	22.2%	27.2%
Having to pay to move	N/A	N/A	N/A	21.7%	26.5%	28.9%	32.5%
Having to leave friends	N/A	N/A	N/A	27.6%	25.9%	24.8%	22.3%
Want to get a job	N/A	N/A	N/A	14.1%	15.4%	15.7%	15.9%
Don't believe it will pay off in the long run	N/A	N/A	N/A	12.6%	13.3%	10.6%	12.9%
Fear of debt	N/A	N/A	N/A	21.7%	23.1%	21.4%	27.0%

Source: Prairie Research Associates' *Pan-Canadian Secondary School Survey* (forthcoming).

Figure 1.III.4 — Average Age at Which Students Decide to Attend College or University

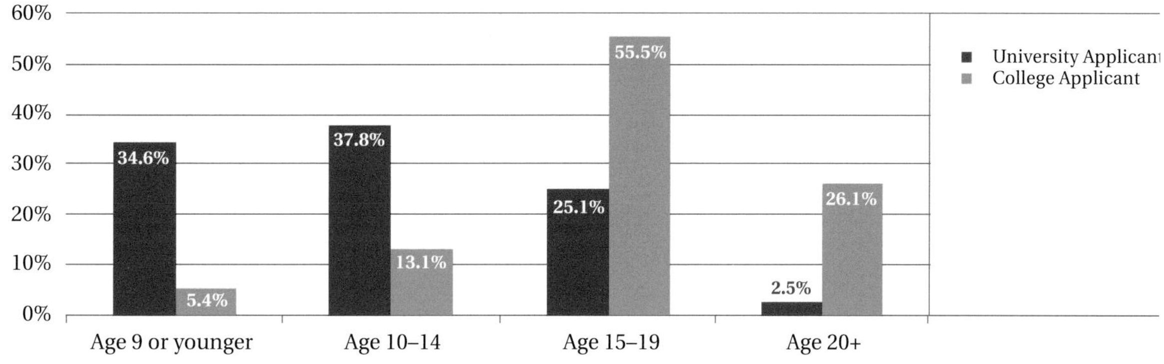

Source: Acumen Research's 2003 *University Applicant Survey* and 2003 *College Applicant Survey.*

Decision Making: Students Who Continue to Post-Secondary Education

In general, the age at which young Canadians make decisions about their post-secondary education is correlated with gender (i.e., female students seem to decide to attend post-secondary studies at an earlier age than males) and grades (i.e., the higher the secondary school marks, the earlier the decision).

The best available evidence on this subject comes from the 2003 *University Applicant Survey (UAS)* and the 2003 *College Applicant Survey (CAS)*, conducted by Acumen Research. There are, however, two notable caveats regarding data from these studies: 1) they rely heavily on a retroactive self-assessment of attitudes, and 2) they are solely based on the results of applications to Ontario colleges and universities.

The *UAS* asked applicants to indicate the age at which they decided they would attend university. Of the 5,380 respondents, a majority of students reported making the decision before the age of 14. In fact, nearly 73% of students who choose to attend university make the decision to do so before reaching upper secondary school (Grade 9). Not surprisingly, the college applicant data show a

different result. According to the *CAS*, less than 19% of applicants decided on college before the age of 14. Figure 1.III.4 compares the age at which applicants decide to attend college or university.

There is a marked difference in the age at which 2003 applicants decided to attend university compared with the 2001 and 2002 *UAS*. Previously, about two-thirds of applicants stated that they made the decision prior to age 14, but in 2003 this jumped to nearly 73%. A possible explanation for this discrepancy is the change of curriculum in Ontario requiring all students entering Grade 9 to decide between work-bound, college-bound or university-bound courses. If the change in results is indeed curriculum driven, it is unlikely that a similar shift has occurred in other provinces.

Female students appear to make the decision to attend college and university at an earlier age than their male counterparts. According to the *UAS*, nearly 76% of females make the decision to attend university by the age of 14, compared to only 68% of males. This gender difference was also evident in the college applicant data. Nearly 22% of female applicants decided on college before the age of 14, compared to just 12% of males. This gender gap is consistent with numerous studies (most notably *Pan-Canadian Education Indicators in Canada*, published by the Council of Ministers of Education, Canada), which show that females display higher organizational ability and achieve higher academic scores in primary and secondary school than males in almost every subject. Figure 1.III.5 shows the breakdown by gender for the age at which students decide to go to college and university.

It is perhaps salient at this point to call into question the notion of "decision making." To most, "choice" refers to a conscious procedure involving a weighing of alternatives which leads to a rational selection of a particular option. One may have legitimate doubts about the consciousness of the procedure that leads students under 14 to make a "choice" about university. For the one-third of university applicants who say that they made a

"choice" at age 9 or less, these doubts become outright incredulity. In effect, what the *UAS* results really suggest is that a university education is not something most students choose, but rather something they have been socialized to desire from childhood—if not from birth.

The correlation between secondary school marks and plans to attend university is even more pronounced than those between gender and planning. Almost 90% of students with marks of 95% or more in secondary school reported that they made their decision to study at university prior to the age of 14. Conversely, only 56% of those with average marks of 75% or less reported that they made their decision to attend university before the age of 14. Figure 1.III.6 displays the differences in the age at which students decide to attend university, sorted by reported secondary school grade average.

Figure 1.III.5 — Average Age at Which Students Decide to Attend College and University by Gender

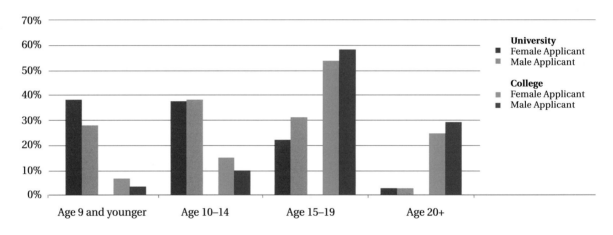

Source: Acumen Research's 2003 *University Applicant Survey* and 2003 *College Applicant Survey*.

Figure 1.III.6 — Average Age at Which Students Decide to Attend University by Secondary School Average

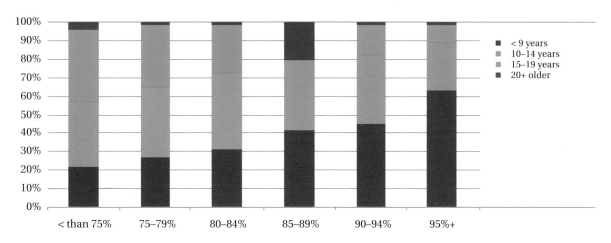

Source: Acumen Research's 2003 *University Applicant Survey* and 2003 *College Applicant Survey.*

With respect to college applicants, the relationship between high school grades and the age of decision is the inverse of the relationship observed among university applicants. Younger college applicants tend to have poorer high school marks than their university counterparts. However, community colleges are also a destination for students with some post-secondary education; in fact, nearly 70% of college applicants over the age of 25 already possessed a university degree.[2] As a result, overall, high secondary school marks are positively correlated with age at community colleges. Figure 1.III.7 shows the age and secondary school average when an applicant decided to attend college.

Figure 1.III.7 — Average Age at Which Students Decide to Attend College by Secondary School Average

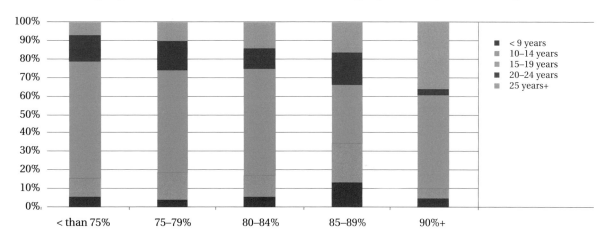

Source: Acumen Research's 2003 *College Applicant Survey.*

2. The total number of respondents over the age of 25 was 438.

Figure 1.III.8 — Grade in Which University Applicants Learned About Academic Requirements

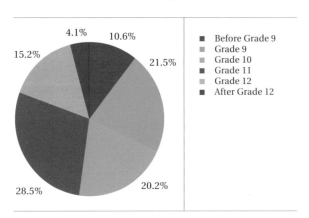

Source: Acumen Research's 2003 *University Applicant Survey.*

It is unclear from the data presented above whether the decision to attend university at an early age is a cause or an effect of high academic achievement. The 2003 *UAS*, in an attempt to clarify this relationship, added some new questions— e.g., it asked applicants when they first learned of university academic requirements. The evidence, as it turns out, leans strongly to the side of the decision being a *cause* of high academic achievement rather than an effect. Figure 1.III.8 shows the grade in which applicants first learned about academic requirements.

As previously seen in Figure 1.III.4, 72% of all university applicants make the decision to go at age 14 or younger. Yet only 10.6% of students say that they learned about university entrance requirements before Grade 9. In other words, students make the decision to go to university long before they know the entrance requirements. Since this decision is tightly correlated to academic grades (Figure 1.III.6), it suggests that students do not become high achievers in order to go to university; rather, high-achieving students decide to go to university *because* they are high achievers.

Further evidence in favour of this hypothesis is shown in Figure 1.III.9. While there is a relationship between an applicant's secondary school marks and the grade in which he or she first learned of institutional academic requirements, the link is a fairly weak one. University applicants with extremely high marks (i.e., over 95%) do learn about university entrance requirements earlier than students with lower marks: 62% of students with marks over 95% learned of academic entrance requirements prior to Grade 11, compared to only 45% of students with marks under 80%. However, the relationship breaks down at lower levels of academic achievement, suggesting once again that students do not change their behaviour in order to get to university, but rather get to university on the basis of their existing behaviour.

Figure 1.III.9 — Grade in Which University Applicants Learned about Academic Requirements, by Academic Achievement

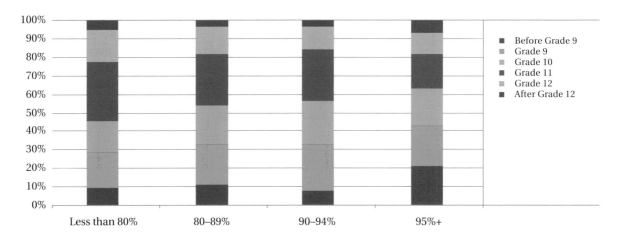

Source: Acumen Research's 2003 *University Applicant Survey.*

Decision Making: Students Who Do Not Go to Post-Secondary Education

As noted previously in Figure 1.III.1, there are three main reasons why people might not make a direct transition to post-secondary education. First, they might not be academically prepared for post-secondary education in the very basic sense that they did not complete secondary school. Second, they may prefer to enter the labour market. Finally, they may prefer to "stop out" of the educational system by taking a "gap" year to travel or study. While all these routes stray from the path of post-secondary education, they are not one-way streets. From each of these three routes out of the educational system, there are ways back in.

With respect to secondary school dropouts, the *2003 Education Indicators in Canada* indicates that the high school graduation rate stands at 78%.[3] Since much of the country's post-secondary system requires completion of secondary school as a pre-requisite to entry, this suggests that at least 20% of Canadians aged 18 to 20 are simply not academically qualified to pursue post-secondary education. This is a major—numerically, the most important—reason why not all students who aspire to post-secondary education receive it.

Yet while this group may be temporarily ineligible for post-secondary education, it is important not to dismiss them completely. Because of open admissions policies at Canadian community colleges, the pool of individuals eligible for post-secondary studies includes individuals who have not completed secondary school. This is important because surveys show that the majority of secondary school dropouts still aspire to some form of post-secondary education. According to the *Youth in Transition Survey*, nearly three-quarters of high school dropouts wish to pursue some form of post-secondary education in the future. Figure 1.III.10 shows the educational aspirations of secondary school dropouts.

Another reason why not all young people continue on to post-secondary education is the lure of the labour market. In Alberta, for example, the robust oil

Figure 1.III.10 — Educational Aspirations of Secondary School Dropouts

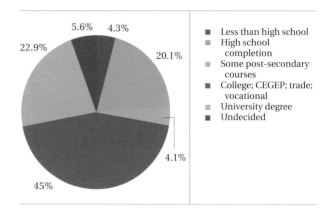

Source: Statistics Canada's *Youth in Transition Survey.*

and gas sector entices high school graduates (predominantly males) to enter the labour market directly from secondary school. According to the *Youth in Transition Survey*, nearly 86% of secondary school graduates not in post-secondary education (n=270,967, or 26%) are working either full- or part-time.[4] The employment rate may appear to be quite high—but it is important to note that more than one-third of these individuals are working part-time. As well, there is a sizable gender gap; specifically, the full-time participation rate of males was 16 percentage points higher than that of females. The relatively poor showing of females with only a high school education could be related to females' relatively higher participation rates in post-secondary education.

A final reason why students may not proceed immediately to post-secondary education is that some secondary school graduates want to take advantage of their "gap" year. After completing 13 years of compulsory schooling, for some people the appeal of another two or four years in formal education is limited. As a result, some graduates head abroad for a few months to enjoy new countries and cultures. Others take advantage of volunteer programs such as Katimavik and Canada World Youth.

---

3.   The graduation rate is calculated from administrative data provided by provincial Ministries of Education and from population estimates provided by the Demography Division at Statistics Canada. Administrative data tend to underestimate the true graduation rate since they do not include people who complete high school outside the regular secondary school systems. Data on graduates from some secondary programs are not uniformly available across all jurisdictions, and General Education Diplomas (GEDs), adult basic upgrading and education, and graduation from adult day schools, which take place outside regular secondary school programs, are in most instances not included.

4.   Bowlby and McMullen, *At a Crossroads.*

IV. Financial Preparation for Post-Secondary Education

Families play an important role in financial preparation for their children's post-secondary education. This section will examine the multiple financial tools that families rely on to assist their children in pursuing post-secondary education.

According to the 2002 *Survey of Approaches to Educational Planning*, half of the parents of children expected to complete high school were already putting money aside for their post-secondary studies ("current savers"). This is notably higher than the total recorded in the 1999 *SAEP*, which suggests that Canadians' saving habits have changed markedly in the past few years. A further 30% of parents reported that they intend to start saving in the future ("future savers"), while the remaining 19% said they did not plan to save for their child's post-secondary education ("non-savers").

The relationship between income and reported savings is both positive and noteworthy. According to the 2002 *SAEP*, less than 30% of families with incomes below $25,000 are saving for their children's

> *Half of the parents of children expected to complete high school were already putting money aside for their post-secondary studies.*

education. The proportion is more than two and a half times greater (69%) among families with incomes above $85,000. Unsurprisingly, the percentage of families identifying themselves as future savers or non-savers (i.e., no plans to save at all) is highest amongst lower-income Canadians.

Figure 1.IV.1 shows the patterns of post-secondary expectations and savings for post-secondary education.

The disparity in savings rates between high- and low-income parents is not surprising given the lack of disposable income available to low-income Canadians.[5] However, it is important to note that the number of low-income parents saving for their children's education has increased considerably in recent years. The 1999 *SAEP* found that nearly 19% of parents with incomes of less than $30,000 were saving for their child's post-secondary education; three years later, the figure had risen to just over 26%. This increase is likely a result of the maturation of the Canada Education Savings Grant (CESG) program; details on the CESG may be found

Figure 1.IV.1 — Parental Saving Status by Household Income

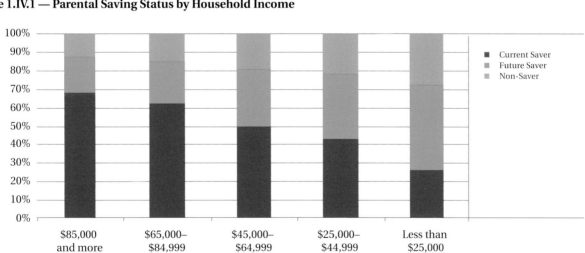

Source: Statistics Canada's 2002 *Survey of Approaches to Educational Planning.*

---

5.   The Government of Canada has taken steps to address this in the 2004 Federal Budget by introducing changes to the Registered Education Savings Plan and creating a Learning Bond for low-income families.

in Section 5B.VI. The 2002 *SAEP* also found a signifi-cant positive correlation between the highest level of parental education and saving patterns. Parents who have a university education themselves are four times more likely to be saving for their children's education than parents who did not complete high school. Figure 1.IV.2 shows parental post-secondary edu-cation saving status by highest level of education.

There is little regional variation in parental saving habits for their children's post-secondary education. There are, however, a few deviations from the national average of 50% for current savers. Nearly 59% of Saskatchewan parents are current savers, compared to less than 41% in Quebec. The explanation for the Quebec results seems relatively straightforward: colleges in Quebec are basically free, while at the university level, tuition is the lowest in the country and the province's standard three-year degree is one of the country's shortest. The low savings rate is there-fore likely a reflection of provincial policies designed to keep private educational expenditures low. Figure 1.IV.3 shows the percentage of parents who are currently saving for their children's post-secondary education by province of residence.

Figure 1.IV.2 — Parental Saving Status by Highest Level of Education

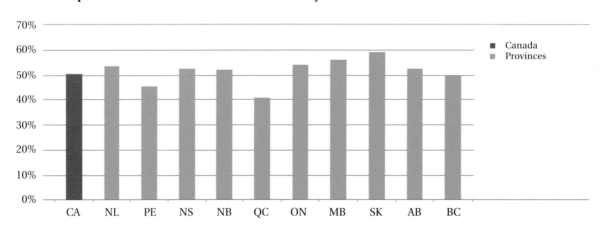

Source: Statistics Canada's 2002 *Survey of Approaches to Educational Planning.*

Figure 1.IV.3 — Proportion of Parents Who Are Current Savers by Province of Residence

Source: Statistics Canada's 2002 *Survey of Approaches to Educational Planning.*

Figure 1.IV.4 — Proportion of Parents Who Are Current Savers by Residential Status and Province

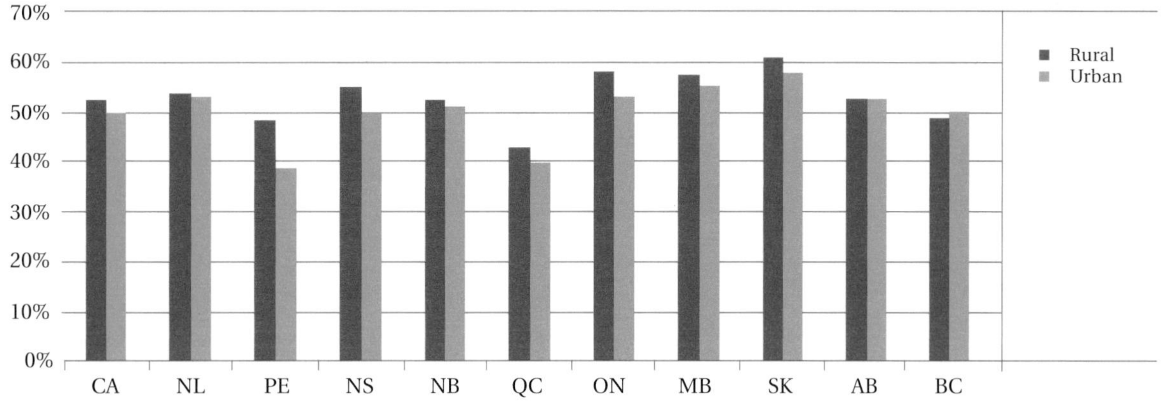

Source: Statistics Canada's 2002 *Survey of Approaches to Educational Planning.*

Parents in rural Canada appear to save more for their children's education than their urban counterparts. This result is not surprising, given that almost all Canadian universities are located in urban Canada, and, as a result, prospective students from rural areas must move to attend one, thereby incurring substantial living costs. In addition, Statistics Canada studies indicate that rural Canadians in general tend to save more than their urban counterparts. Figure 1.IV.4 shows the percentage of parents who are currently saving for their children's post-secondary education in rural and urban areas.

Current savers reported a total accumulation of $32 billion dollars for their children's post-secondary education by 2002. This is almost double the $17 billion of accumulated savings reported in the 1999 *SAEP.* The median amount saved to date in 2002 was $5,000 per child, an increase of $1,500 since 1999. These significant increases are almost certainly a result of heavier use of the CESG program and heightened parental awareness about the cost of post-secondary education.

Savings, of course, involve sacrificing present consumption in order to facilitate future purchases. COMPAS (2004) provides some interesting insight

into the sacrifices currently being made by parents to fund their children's education. For example, parents say they have spent less money on major purchases, reduced spending in general and paid down their mortgage faster than originally planned (this may not appear to be a present sacrifice, but the act of paying the mortgage down is what is considered). These are perhaps normal and relatively easy sacrifices. Somewhat more disquieting is the fact that 21% of parents say they delayed retirement in order to save for their children's education, 17% report taking a second job and 9% went as far as remortgaging their house. These sacrifices are self-reported and thus should be taken with a grain of salt, because of the tendency of respondents in surveys to over-report beliefs or behaviours that are socially desirable. Figure 1.IV.5 shows the various financial preparations taken by parents for their children's education.

Savings are not the only possible source of funds parents will use to support their children's post-secondary education. The 2002 *SAEP* also showed that over 84% of parents who are saving for their children's education still intend to support their children from their current income once they enter post-secondary studies; over 70% expect to provide

Figure 1.IV.5 — Parents' Reported Trade-Offs to Save for Children's Education

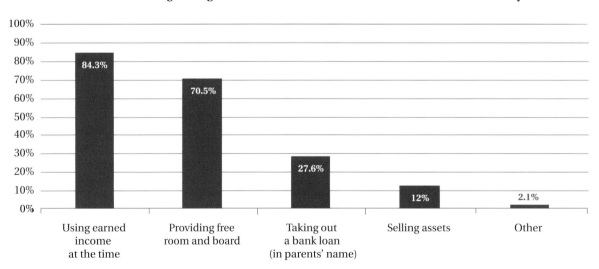

Source: COMPAS Research's *Post-Secondary Education: Cultural, Scholastic and Economic Drivers.*

free room and board to assist their children; and just over one-quarter expect to provide assistance to their children by taking out loans. This last figure is particularly interesting, since it suggests that existing student debt numbers provide only a partial portrait of total borrowing for education and that there is an entire "hidden world" of borrowing for education. This hidden world is unseen by policy-makers because it is both the family as well as the

student who is incurring debt. Figure 1.IV.6 shows the alternative financing strategies parents plan to use to meet their child's post-secondary costs.

The majority of parents believe their children will contribute to the funding of their own education through a variety of sources, including employment income, bursaries, loans and scholarships. The results from the 2002 *SAEP* indicate that parents possess a better sense of funding sources available to

Figure 1.IV.6 — Alternative Financing Strategies Parents Plan to Use to Meet Children's Post-Secondary Costs

Source: Statistics Canada's 2002 *Survey of Approaches to Educational Planning.*

Table 1.IV.1 — Parents' Expected Sources of Children's Contributions to Post-Secondary Costs

	1999 Results	2002 Results
Work before PSE	72%	80%
Work during PSE	86%	66%
Work interrupting PSE	5%	8%
Academic scholarships	65%	40%
Need-based grants and bursaries	34%	29%
Government loans	92%	36%
Non-student loans	22%	11%

Source: Statistics Canada's 1999 and 2002 *Survey of Approaches to Educational Planning.*

students than was the case three years earlier. While parents in 1999 appeared to be overly optimistic about the various funding sources available to their children—particularly with respect to government student loans and academic scholarships—parents in 2002 were much more realistic. In fact, the difference between the two surveys is so striking that one suspects that in at least one of the two surveys there was a significant error in data reporting. Table 1.IV.1 shows the differences in expected sources of funding in the 1999 and 2002 *SAEP*.

The 2002 *PEPS* survey results allow for a comparison to be drawn between parental perceptions and the reality faced by students. *PEPS* asked full-time post-secondary students aged 18 to 24 to provide information on what sources they were using to fund their current academic year.

Just over three-quarters of *PEPS* respondents had worked before starting post-secondary studies and were using savings from their past earnings to fund their current studies. Also, about two-thirds (64%) were working during their current academic year. Just over one-quarter of *PEPS* respondents (26%) had received a government student loan for the current year. These figures were very close to the 2002 *SAEP* figures for each of these funding sources, although it should be noted that the 2002 *SAEP* looks at financing strategies throughout an entire program of post-secondary studies, while *PEPS* looks at strategies used for the current academic year only. This is noteworthy because the use of specific financial resources may vary according to the year of post-secondary studies.[6] One of the more interesting points emerging from the data comparison is the substantial gap in expected and actual funding with respect to both scholarships and bursaries.

Figure 1.IV.7 — Parents' Expected Sources of Funding and Children's Actual Sources of Funding for Post-Secondary Education

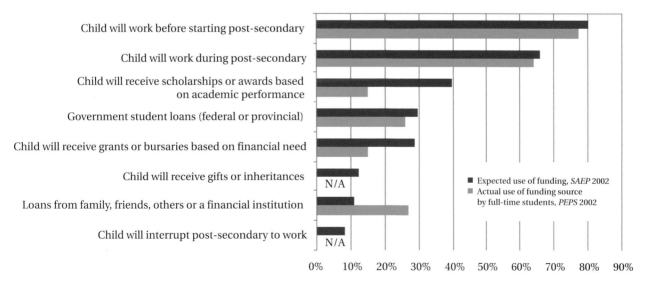

Source: *Statistics Canada's 2002 Survey of Approaches to Educational Planning* and *Post-Secondary Education Participation Survey.*

6.   Shipley, Ouellette and Cartwright, Planning and Preparation.

It appears that students compensate for this gap, at least in part, through alternative loans—primarily lines of credit at financial institutions. Figure 1.IV.7 shows parental expectations for various sources of funding for their children's' education and actual usage of those funding sources.

Not all parents are saving for their children's post-secondary education. For the most part, this reflects not neglect, but the struggle of many families to make ends meet. According to the 2002 *SAEP*, over 60% of parents who identified themselves as "future savers" and over half of parents who are "non-savers" simply lack the disposable income to save for their children's post-secondary studies.

Most parents contribute more than money to the post-secondary education planning process. In addition to saving for their children's education, parents participate in the selection of programs and institutions. Figure 1.IV.8 shows parental activities prior to their children's post-secondary education.

Figure 1.IV.8 — Parental Activities Prior to Children's Post-Secondary Education

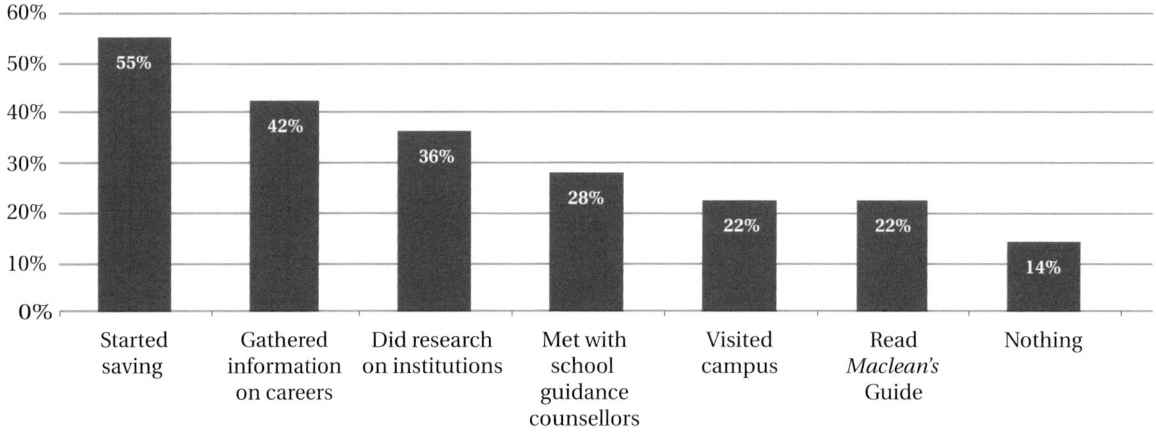

Source: COMPAS Research's *Post-Secondary Education: Cultural, Scholastic and Economic Drivers.*

V. Institutional Choice

Having decided to pursue post-secondary education, individuals must still select one or more institutions to which they will apply. Individuals examine program offerings, weigh the financial implications of studying (at home or away, college or university), and research the entrance requirements of prospective institutions. Once these factors have been examined, the next step for students is the application process.

Choosing a Type of Education

The first step in choosing an institution is to choose the *type* of education one wishes to pursue. The evidence suggests that there is no substantial overlap between students who choose college and universities. In effect, there are two very separate "markets" for post-secondary education in Canada, and prospective students make their choice between these markets prior to applying for admission. The best available data on this subject come from Acumen Research's *University Applicant Survey* and *College Applicant Survey*, as well as the Canadian Undergraduate Survey Consortium's *Survey of First-Year University Students*. The Acumen data, although limited to Ontario only, provide valuable insight into the choices faced by applicants.

According to the *Survey of First-Year University Students*, only 15% of first-year university students applied for college, and, similarly, the *University Applicant Survey* found that only 14% of applicants considered college when investigating post-secondary options. Applying for college was strongly and negatively correlated with secondary school grades, as shown in Figure 1.V.1. Since very few students are actually able to enter university with a grade below 75%, the increase in college application rates that occurs once grades sink below 80% can best be seen as a form of post-secondary "insurance"—i.e., a back-up plan in case university application does not work out.

Among college students, 10% of Ontario applicants (the only ones for whom data are available) said they had also applied to a university, again indicating very little overlap between university and college applicants. This group was evenly split between those who said that, given the choice, they would prefer to attend university and those who said they would prefer to attend college.

Figure 1.V.1— University Applicant Consideration of College by Grade Average

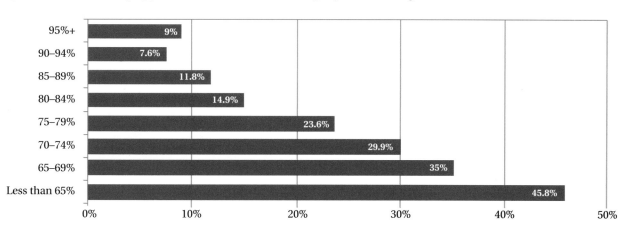

Source: Acumen Research's 2003 *University Applicant Survey.*

Figure 1.V.2 – Reasons for Choosing University

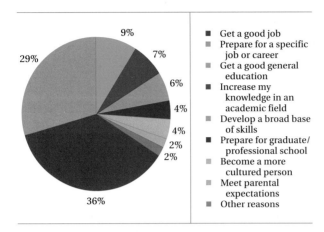

- Get a good job
- Prepare for a specific job or career
- Get a good general education
- Increase my knowledge in an academic field
- Develop a broad base of skills
- Prepare for graduate/professional school
- Become a more cultured person
- Meet parental expectations
- Other reasons

9%
7%
6%
4%
4%
2%
2%
29%
36%

Source: Canadian Undergraduate Survey Consortium's 2001 *Survey of First-Year University Students.*

The reasons why people choose their type of education are difficult to ascertain. While existing surveys do show that university and college students cite very different reasons for wishing to attend their "type" of post-secondary education, these surveys typically measure this desire with closed questions, and, as a result, the individual is limited to a few pre-selected responses. It is therefore unclear if different results actually reflect a different set of reasons or simply different survey designs.

Figures 1.V.2 and .3 display data from the *Survey of First-Year University Students* and the *College Applicant Survey* with respect to reasons for choosing a type of institution.

University students by and large appear to have occupational concerns on their minds when they apply for university. Nearly two-thirds (65%) say they are attending university in order to "get a good job" or "preparing for a specific career." This rises to over 70% of respondents if we include those saying they applied to "develop a broad base of skills." While all students no doubt have either general or specific academic interests, only 16% of students said that their *primary* aim was to "get a good general education" or "increase my knowledge in an academic field."

Nearly all college applicants cite an employment-related reason for wanting to attend college. Only one-eighth of applicants cited a reason unrelated to employment—namely, "preparing for university" (which may in fact be considered an employment-related decision) and "other." However, given the limited choices available in answering this question—unlike the *Survey of First-Year University Students*, there were no answers such as "general academic interest," etc.—readers should be wary of drawing definite conclusions from these data.

Figure 1.V.3 — Reasons for Applying to College

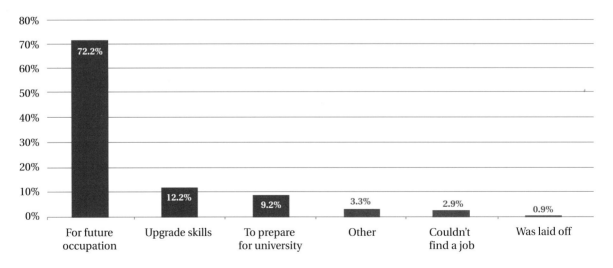

Source: Acumen Research's 2003 *Ontario College Applicant Survey.*

Figure 1.V.4 — Decision to Attend First-Choice Institution Among University Applicants

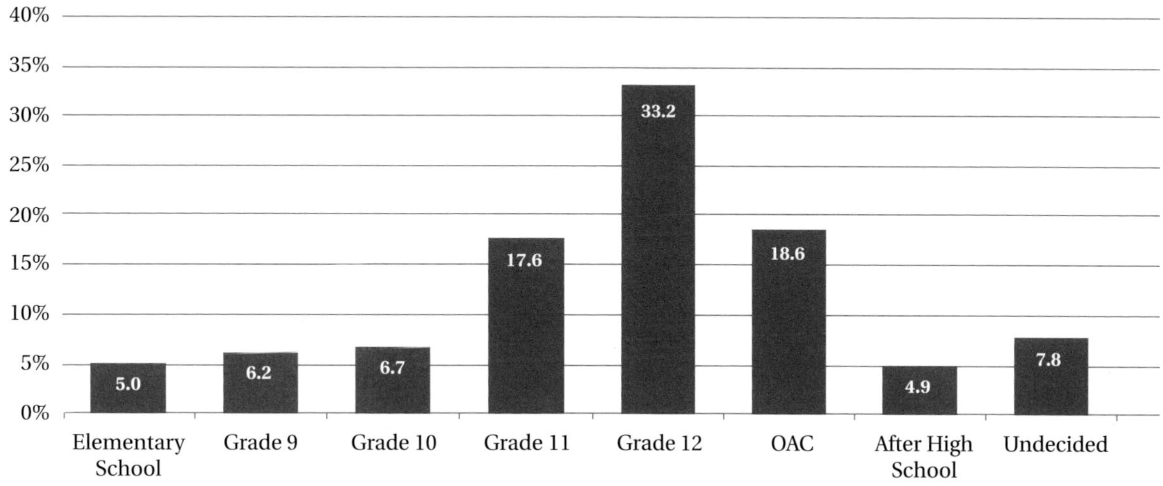

Source: Acumen Research's 2003 *University Applicant Survey*.

Choosing an Institution

The age at which a student selects a preferred university appears to happen quite late in his or her studies. According to the 2003 *University Applicant Survey*, over 50% of students choose their preferred institution in Grade 12 or later. Figure 1.V.4 illustrates the breakdown by year of study. College applicants tend to make their decision later than university applicants. This is unsurprising, given that nearly 70% of college applicants take at least one year off between ending high school and starting college.

College students tend to select their program of interest and then search for an institution offering that program. According to the *College Applicant Survey*, nearly three-quarters of college applicants indicated that their program of interest led them to consider certain colleges. In fact, the top five college characteristics chosen by applicants were the following: 1) program offering, 2) program reputation, 3) college reputation, 4) instructional quality and 5) proximity to home. Over 50% (n=1,574) of applicants saw all five of these reasons as

Over 50% of students choose their preferred institution in Grade 12 or later.

having "very much" influence on their decision. Figure 1.V.5 shows the top five factors in the final selection of college.

Potential university students, on the other hand, tend to select their institution first and then proceed to choose their program. According to the 2003 *University Applicant Survey*, the five most important factors in a potential university student's decision are: 1) employment outcomes, 2) academic reputation of school, 3) tuition costs, 4) proximity to home, and 5) availability of scholarships. These findings are consistent with those of the 2001 *Survey of First-Year University Students*, which found that the five most influential factors were: 1) specific career-related program, 2) quality of academic programs, 3) desire to live close to home, 4) institutional reputation and 5) financial assistance/scholarships. Given that university programs are longer and more costly than college programs, it is no surprise that university students are likelier than college students to accord greater importance to program cost and funding sources in the institutional selection process.

Figure 1.V.5 — Top Five Factors in the Selection of College

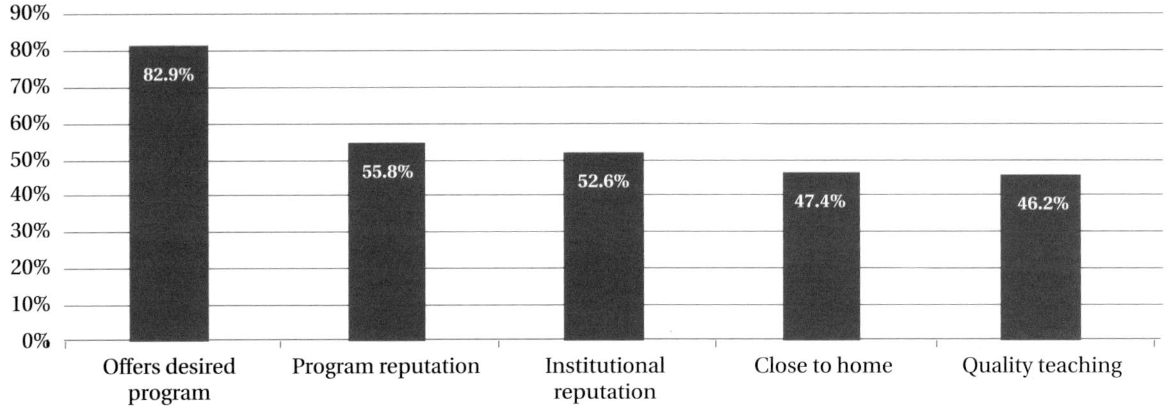

Source: Acumen Research's 2003 *Ontario College Applicant Survey.*

The decision to attend a specific university is made with the assistance of many resources. According to the *Survey of First-Year University Students,* the single most important factor is visiting the campus. Table 1.V.2 illustrates the most important resources accessed by students when making their decision to attend a specific university.

Table 1.V.1 — Single Most Important Information Source in the Decision to Attend a Specific University

Information Source	Percentage
Campus visit	26%
Brochures or pamphlets	17%
Visit by a representative to high school or CEGEP	13%
University Web site	9%
Maclean's magazine	7%
Calls from faculty or students of the university	4%
Meeting with university admissions officer on campus	3%
Letters from university rep to high school or CEGEP	2%
Media reports	2%
CD-ROM	<1%
Other reason	9%
Don't know/No response	9%

Source: Canadian Undergraduate Survey Consortium's 2001 *Survey of First-Year University Students.*

As was the case for university applicants, a visit to the campus proved to be the most important factor for college applicants when choosing a particular institution. Web sites also played an important role in influencing college applicants' choices. Figure 1.V.6 shows the most influential factors for these individuals.

Being Selected by an Institution

The majority of this section has dealt with the individual's choice of institution. In many cases, however, this is only half the story. The desire to study at a particular institution or pursue a specific program is no guarantee of admittance. For the most part, this is not an issue in the Canadian community college sector, as community colleges are for the most part "open access" institutions, requiring only a high school diploma to gain admittance.[7] Universities, on the other hand, ration spaces on the basis of academic merit; in many programs, this rationing is done on the basis of high school marks.

Institutional selectivity is a difficult quality to measure. As reported in the first edition of *The Price of Knowledge,* outside Ontario (where required entrance averages actually change over time), published university entrance requirements are

7.   This distinction is not true for all community college programs. There are some college programs that have academic requirements that are at least as restrictive as Canadian university programs.

Figure 1.V.6 — Ten Most Influential Recruitment and Marketing Activities for College Applicants

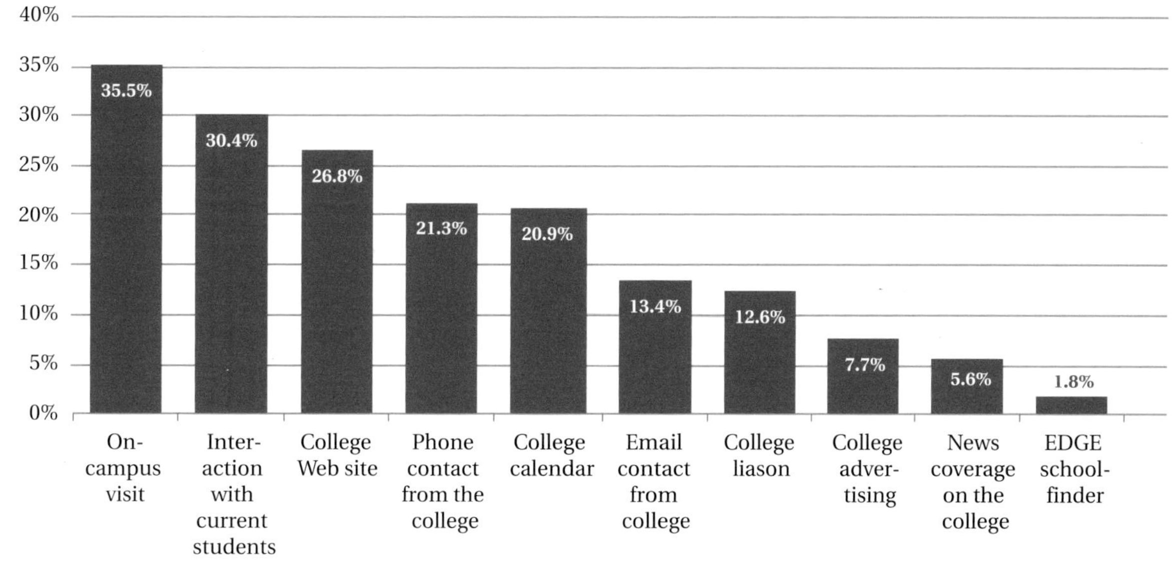

Source: Acumen Research's *2003 Ontario College Applicant Survey.*

frequently little more than a polite fiction. Major research universities such as the University of Calgary and the University of British Columbia still publish their "minimum" entrance requirements as being a secondary school average of 65%—even though no student with a 65% average has graced their classrooms for several years.

Institutional entrance averages are similarly an inadequate method of measuring selectivity. The average marks of an entering class says something about the degree of selectivity of an institution (that is, a higher average implies greater selectivity), but it does not tell us how high the "bar" is for students wishing to enter, because it still sheds no light on the minimum marks required to enter.

In fact, the best available method of measuring selectivity in Canadian institutions is to examine both average institutional entering marks and minimum entering marks. The best proxy for minimum entering grades for which data are available would appear to be the percentage of students entering with average high school marks over 75%. Both this figure

and the average entering grade can be obtained from 1994 onward, using information from *Maclean's* annual university rankings.

Figure 1.V.7 shows national average entering marks and minimum entering marks over the past decade. *Maclean's* institutional data have been weighted to take into account enrolment and to derive national averages. The average includes virtually all institutions in the country, with the exception of the Université du Québec system, which does not participate in the *Maclean's* exercise.

Generally speaking, what Figure 1.V.7 shows is that higher grades are required to enter university now than ten years ago. It is unclear to what extent this is due to grade inflation and to what extent it is due to increased competition and selectivity. It is likely a combination of the two: increased selectivity can certainly serve as fuel for grade inflation. At least superficially, there appears to be an increase in selectivity at Canadian universities. Given that selectivity acts as an impermeable entrance screen, it would not be an exaggeration to say that the

Figure 1.V.7 — Average Entering Grades and Proportion of Students With Entering Grades Above 75% Across Canada From 1994 to 2003

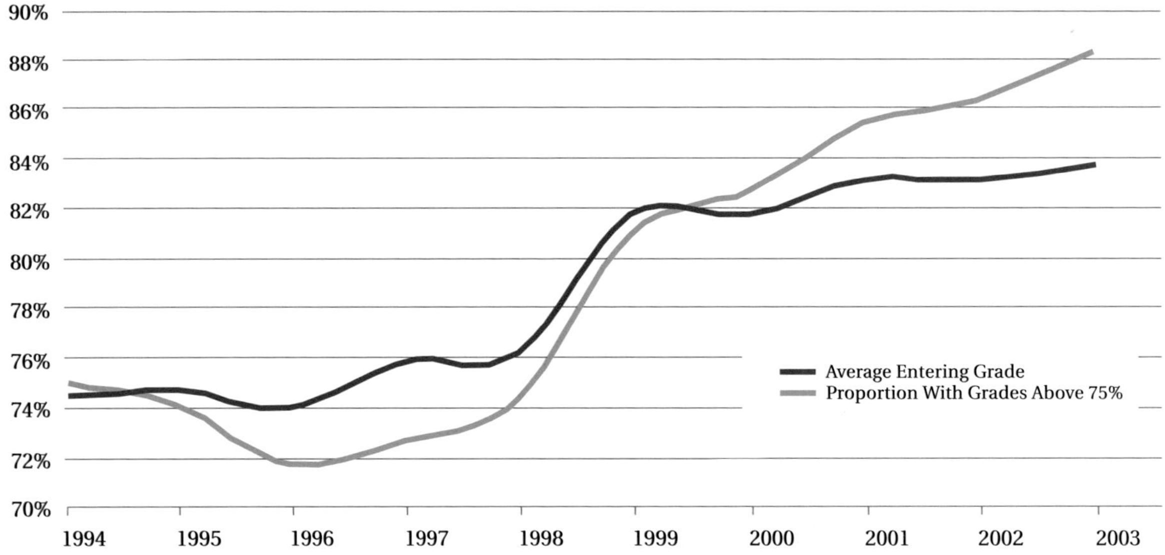

Source: *Maclean's* rankings (1994–2003) and authors' calculations.

academic barriers to post-secondary education, based on this evidence, have increased over the past ten years.

There is, however, a third possible explanation: the change may simply be due to changes in the way institutions report data to *Maclean's*. Many institutions have made "technical" changes in the way they report data over the past decade, such as calculating the entering average based on a student's strongest five secondary-level courses instead of on all his or her courses, or excluding from the calculation special admission programs for specific groups of students. These small changes can have a substantial effect on institutional ranking, and so there is a clear incentive for institutions to portray data in this more flattering manner.

Interestingly, while both selectivity indicators show an upward trend, the effect is stronger on the indicator that is more susceptible to institutional manipulation. Between 2000 and 2003, there was a six percentage-point increase in the level of minimum selectivity (proportion of students entering with grades above 75%), with no corresponding increase in the average entering grade. This suggests that a large number of people are being nudged over the 75% "line" without the overall average increasing that much. Given that this figure accounts for 12% of the final *Maclean's* ranking, it would not be surprising to find a certain entrepreneurial streak in the way institutions report their enrolment data.

Chapter 2

A Profile of the Student Body

Chapter 2

A Profile of the Student Body

I. Introduction—Participation in Post-Secondary Education

In 2002–2003 there were just under 1.7 million Canadians enrolled in courses leading to degrees, diplomas and certificates at universities, colleges and technical institutes across the country. Post-secondary students, therefore, represent just over 5% of the Canadian population as a whole. There are more students in Canada than there are Manitobans or Saskatchewanians, and their total number rivals the entire population of the Maritimes. The country's full-time farmers, fishers, miners, forestry workers, utility workers, oil and gas workers, and construction workers *combined* are not as numerous as the country's student population.

Much more is known about Canadian students than was the case two years ago, when the original *Price of Knowledge* was written. At that time, most of the available data were for aggregate student populations. But as a result of extensive survey research undertaken by Statistics Canada, the Canada Millennium Scholarship Foundation, the Canadian Undergraduate Student Survey Consortium and the Canadian College Student Survey Consortium a much more detailed picture of the Canadian student population can now be drawn.

Section II of this chapter begins with the most basic facts: the number of students, the level of education they are pursuing and various trends in *enrolment*, including changes in the gender, age and registration status of Canadian students. In terms of age and gender, the composition of the student body has not altered much in recent years; rather, the key

Post-secondary students represent just over 5% of the Canadian population as a whole.

trend in recent years is that, after a decade of relative stagnation, university enrolment has increased sharply since the turn of the millennium, a phenomenon that can only partially be attributed to Ontario's double cohort.

While the overall numbers are important, rising enrolment must be viewed within the context of the overall youth population. Section III therefore concentrates on the all-important participation rate—that is, the proportion of the nation's total youth population enrolled in post-secondary education.

In keeping with rising enrolment, the nation's *participation rate* is also rising. Regionally, participation rates are highest in Quebec and Nova Scotia and lowest in the three Prairie provinces.

Participation rates do not tell the entire story about access to post-secondary education. While it is important to know how many people are accessing post-secondary studies, it is also necessary to consider who is accessing post-secondary education. Data on the *socio-economic background* of students, which are examined in Section IV, suggest that the situation is not ideal, with students from higher-income families continuing to attend university in greater numbers than students from lower-income families. However, family education seems to be a more important factor than family income in determining post-secondary pathways, and there appears to be little evidence to suggest that educational inequality is increasing over time. In fact, if inequality is measured by the proportion of students from lower-income backgrounds enrolled in post-secondary studies, there is considerable evidence to suggest that inequality has actually been decreasing over time.

A vast amount of new data on specific student sub-populations has recently become available. *Visible minority* students (Section V), *students with disabilities* (Section VI), *Aboriginal students* (Section VII), *students with dependants* (Section VIII) and *rural students* (Section IX) are all examined in detail. Students with disabilities appear to be slightly over-represented in the student population compared to the population as a whole, although this may simply be the result of a greater willingness to identify "learning disabilities" as a disability. Students from rural areas and visible minority students both appear to attend post-secondary education in numbers roughly proportional to their share of the population. Aboriginal students have made enormous strides in educational attainment in the past 25 years, but while Aboriginal college attainment rates are now equal to those of non-Aboriginal students, their attainment rates at the university level continue to lag significantly behind those of other students.

Section X looks at patterns of *student mobility* within Canada. Many students, particularly at the university level, move away from their home towns to study. Few university students and virtually no college students, however, appear to leave their home province to study. Inter-provincial mobility is most prominent in the Atlantic region, but less so in the West, Ontario and Quebec.

Section XI, on *international mobility*, examines Canada's "trade" in students with the rest of the world. The most recent data show that Canada receives about twice as many students from other countries as it sends abroad. Students come to Canada from a great number of countries, and no single country dominates our student "imports." While international students come primarily from Asian countries, there are significant numbers of American and French students present as well. Canadian students abroad, on the other hand, are less eclectic in their choice of destination—more than three-quarters of these students head south of the border to the United States.

Access to post-secondary education is, however, only part of the story. Simply gaining access to post-secondary education is only half the battle; persisting through to completion is equally, if not more, important. The final section of this chapter therefore looks at what is known about *dropouts, persistence* and stop-outs in post-secondary education. Data in this section show that while system-level retention rates are fairly good in Canada, institutional retention rates are less so, with many students apparently changing institutions at least once before finishing a degree.

II. Enrolment

Reliable enrolment data are difficult to obtain in Canada. Statistics Canada, which for decades has been the "official" source of statistics, has in recent years switched student data tracking systems and experienced large problems. These problems are not attributed solely to Statistics Canada since colleges and universities across the country have made the data problems, in some cases, worse. As a result, Statistics Canada has not been able to release enrolment data in a timely fashion. Therefore, the most recent "official" data date from 1999–2000 for the college sector and 2000–01 for the university sector. In the absence of official data, other sources—notably the Association of Universities and Colleges of Canada (AUCC) and various provincial governments—must be used to estimate more recent enrolment trends.[1]

After very strong growth in enrolment throughout the 1980s, enrolment in the 1990s was extremely stable. There was a small drop in university enrolment over the decade, which was due entirely to a drop in enrolment rates among older adults pursuing part-time university studies. At the turn of the decade, however, enrolment growth began again in the university sector (but not in the college sector). In 2002–03, the last year for which reasonably complete data are available, just under 1.7 million Canadians were enrolled in university and college programs leading to a degree, certificate or diploma—the highest total ever.[2] Although no college figures are available for 2003–04, it is expected that this year will surpass the previous year, if only because this is the year that Ontario's "double cohort" graduated to the post-secondary level. Figure 2.II.1 shows trade-vocational, college and university enrolment trends in Canada since 1990.[3]

Despite relatively stable enrolment at the national level, there have in fact been major shifts at the provincial level which, in sum, have tended to offset each other. Increases in university enrolment have

Figure 2.II.1 — Post-Secondary Enrolment in Canada From 1990–91 to 2003–04

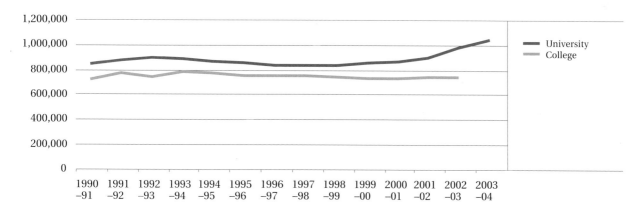

Source: Statistics Canada's University Student Information System and Community College Student Information System, AUCC's annual enrolment estimates, provincial government records and authors' calculations.

1. Non-Statistics Canada sources tend to use slightly different definitions of what constitutes a "student" for statistical purposes. Therefore, it is impossible simply to add AUCC and provincial data to the existing Statistics Canada time-series data. What the authors have done instead is to index the changes in AUCC/provincial data to the last year of existing Statistics Canada data and then apply the index to the Statistics Canada figures available that year. The logic behind this method of estimation is that, despite differences in methodology between Statistics Canada and non-Statistics Canada sources, *changes* in non-Statistics Canada data are likely reflective of changes in underlying realities, and so applying the change trend to existing numbers is likely to provide a reasonably accurate estimate of current enrolment levels.

2. The previous edition of *The Price of Knowledge* used slightly higher figures for total enrolment in the 1990s. These data have been revised downwards slightly in this edition following an advisory from Statistics Canada that data on part-time trade-vocational enrolment are unreliable. These figures have therefore been excluded from the data in this section, leading to slightly lower overall figures. Regardless of whether these students are included or excluded, 2002–03 is still the year with the highest ever national enrolment level.

3. The enrolment data in this section are head count data and not full-time equivalent or full-time data.

Figure 2.II.2 — Changes in Enrolment by Province (1990–91 = 100%)

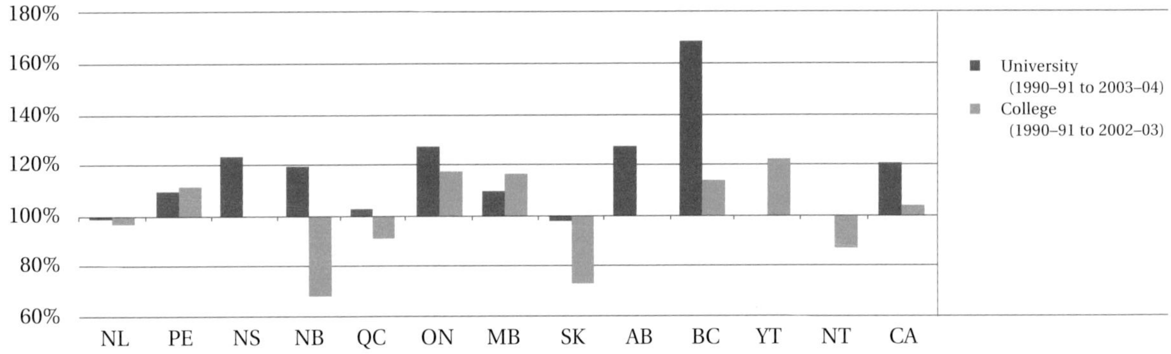

Source: Statistics Canada's University Student Information System and Community College Student Information System, AUCC's annual enrolment estimates, provincial government records and authors' calculations.

been the most spectacular in B.C., where enrolment at universities has increased by 70% since 1990; this increase would be even more pronounced if one included students at university colleges. Ontario, New Brunswick, Nova Scotia and Alberta have also registered important gains in university enrolment. Enrolment increased only modestly in Prince Edward Island and Manitoba, stagnated in Newfoundland and Labrador and Quebec, and declined slightly in Saskatchewan. At the college level, five jurisdictions registered increases, four registered decreases, while the rest in effect reported no change. Figure 2.II.2 shows changes in enrolment by province.

University Enrolment

Between 1980 and 1992, enrolment in Canadian universities increased by nearly 40% to 885,000 students. Growth then stopped and reversed quite suddenly in the mid-1990s. This change was due to two trends that began more or less simultaneously: 1) flat-lined enrolment for the full-time student population, and 2) a sudden decline in the number of part-time students in all provinces except B.C. and Alberta. Neither phenomenon is particularly well understood, although many explanations have been proposed. Since both events coincided with a general rise in the price of tuition, financial factors have frequently been cited as the reason for the decline. However, the evidence presented in

Chapter 3 of this book tends to undermine this explanation. Another explanation holds that rising enrolment standards, such as those shown in Chapter 1.V, were responsible for the levelling off of full-time enrolment, if not the decline in part-time students. A third explanation acknowledges the role of rising academic cut-offs, but suggests that the real cause was declining institutional revenue in the wake of government cutbacks. This explanation posits that rising academic standards were simply the institutions' way of keeping enrolment growth under control during a time of shrinking resources.

The decline in part-time enrolment has also been linked by some to gender enrolment patterns. For most of the 1970s, 1980s and early 1990s, female post-secondary students tended to increase their academic qualifications and upgrade their skills in order to participate in the changing labour market; they were therefore less likely to enroll in full-time university studies. Also, since it takes considerably longer to complete a credit part-time, this likely reinforced the growth. Since 1992, however, there has been a decline in female part-time enrolment, largely due to the fact that their educational qualifications are now roughly equivalent to those of males and they have thus "caught up" in the labour market.[4]

Whatever the reasons for the decline in enrolment, enrolment levels reached a trough in 1997–98 and began rising thereafter. At first, the increase was slow, but the pace quickened at the turn of the decade. Full-time enrolment is now at an all-time

4. Drews and O'Heron 1999.

Figure 2.II.3 — Canadian University Enrolment by Registration Status

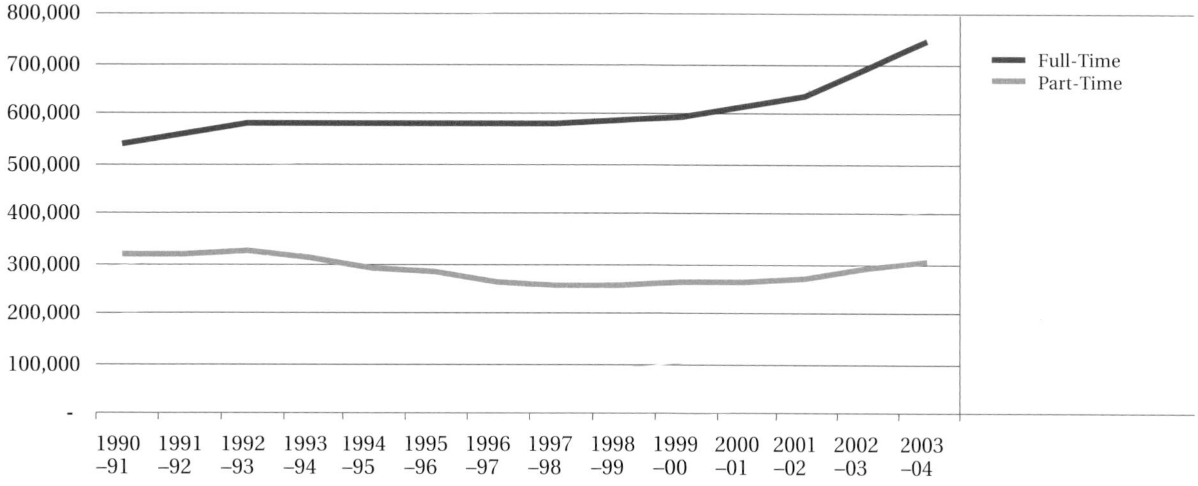

Source: Statistics Canada's University Student Information System and AUCC's annual enrolment estimates.

high and part-time enrolment is increasing again, though it still remains some ways off of former levels. Figure 2.II.3 shows total enrolment numbers for full-time and part-time university students since 1990.

The steep increase in Canadian university enrolment between 1999–2000 and 2003–04 was unprecedented in the country's history. In just three years, the university population jumped by 155,000 students, which represents an 18% increase. This increase, from the perspective of the year 2000, is equivalent to adding the entire university population of Newfoundland and Labrador, New Brunswick, Prince Edward Island, Nova Scotia, Manitoba and Saskatchewan *combined*, plus the student body of McGill University. Some of this increase can certainly be attributed to the one-time effect of the "double cohort" in Ontario, but this is by no means the entire story. Over the three-year period in question it was in fact British Columbia that experienced the largest increase in enrolment (despite massive tuition increases of nearly 70% during the same span), while Manitoba, which had a tuition freeze in place during this period, recorded an impressive 29% increase in enrolment. Of the remaining provinces, Quebec and the Maritime provinces all recorded enrolment increases of 10% or

more. Newfoundland and Labrador's 8% increase is remarkable considering it came despite a falling youth population.

Alberta's small growth appears to be the result of a reporting error at Athabasca University in the base year (1999-2000); the true growth figure is likely between 12-15%. Only Saskatchewan saw a drop in total student numbers and even here the drop was entirely due to a decline in part-time enrolment; full-time enrolment actually rose slightly. Changes in provincial university enrolment from 1999–2000 to 2003–04 are shown below in Figure 2.II.4.

Age

As mentioned in Cervenan and Usher (2004), there has been little change in the average age of Canadian university students in the past 40 years. These findings are consistent with Statistics Canada's enrolment data, which likewise show that the age of the full-time university student population has, on the whole, remained remarkably constant. In fact, despite the creation of substantial lifelong learning initiatives, the age of the full-time student body has barely moved. There are more students over the age of 30 in the university system,

Figure 2.II.4 — Changes in University Enrolment by Province From 1999-2000 to 2003–04

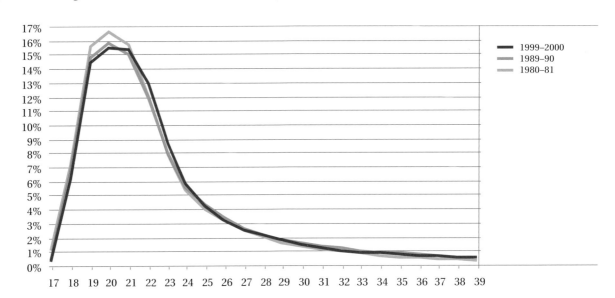

Source: Statistics Canada's University Student Information System and AUCC's annual enrolment estimates.

Figure 2.II.5 — Age Distribution of Full-Time University Students in 1980–81, 1989–90 and 1999–2000

Source: Statistics Canada's University Student Information System.

Figure 2.II.6 — Mean Age of Full-Time University Students by Province in 1998–99

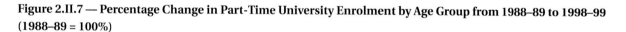

Source: Statistics Canada's University Student Information System.

but that growth has been mitigated by expansion among the younger cohort. In 1999, the average age of full-time university students was 22, compared to 21 two decades earlier. In fact over the 1990s the average age of students declined as enrolment growth was driven by younger students. Figure 2.II.5 shows the age distribution of full-time university students for 1980, 1989 and 1999.

There are some slight differences in the age breakdown by province at the university level. Figure 2.II.6

shows the mean age of full-time university students by province in 1998–99.

Part-time university enrolment, as mentioned previously, is on the rise again. It appears that younger students are driving this growth. Although the majority of part-time students in Canadian universities are still over the age of 30, the average age of part-time students is falling. The only age group in which the number of part-time students grew during the 1990s was the 18- to 21-year-old

Figure 2.II.7 — Percentage Change in Part-Time University Enrolment by Age Group from 1988–89 to 1998–99 (1988–89 = 100%)

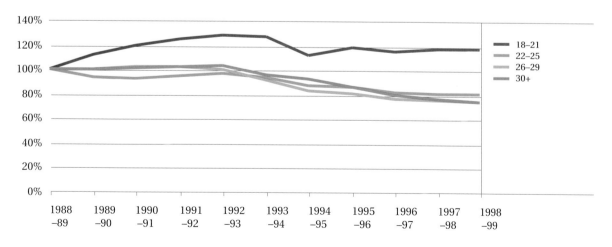

Source: Statistics Canada's University Student Information System and AUCC's annual enrolment estimates.

group. The 22- to 25-year-old age group ended the decade at more or less the same level at which it began, while the number of 26- to 29-year-olds enrolled in part-time university studies decreased by approximately 20%. The most significant decrease in the number of part-time university students was observed in the largest age cohort: by the end of the decade, the number of part-time students aged 30 or over had decreased by almost a third from its 1992 peak level. Enrolment in all three of these groups appeared to have levelled off at the turn of the century. Figure 2.II.7 shows the percentage change in part-time university enrolment by age group over the past decade.

Gender

The major trend in the past three decades concerning gender in Canadian post-secondary education has occurred almost exclusively within the university sector. Female students accounted for approximately three-quarters of the growth in full-time enrolment during the 1980s and 1990s; as a result, their share of the entire full-time university population increased from 45% to 55%. Female enrolment still lags behind male enrolment in a few select fields of study, such as the physical sciences and engineering, but in most fields of study females are now the majority. Since

enrolment for both genders is on the rise male enrolment, which was declining in the late 1990s, is at its highest level in the past six years. This growth has nevertheless been overshadowed by the larger growth among female students.

There are striking patterns in part-time enrolment when examined by gender. It is clear that both the initial growth and subsequent decline in the number of part-time students were largely female-driven. While male students contributed to the growth and decline in part-time enrolment, they did so to a much lesser extent than females. It is worth mentioning that after a decade of declining part-time enrolment (female and male), this trend has started to reverse. Figure 2.II.8 shows female university enrolment as a percentage of total university enrolment over the past two decades.

There are some slight differences in the gender breakdown by province at the university level. Programs offered at the various institutions in a province can help explain the majority of these differences. For example, the University of Prince Edward Island (the only university in the province) has relatively few students in traditionally male-dominated fields such as math, physical science and engineering. Figure 2.II.9 shows the university gender breakdown by province in 2000–01.

Figure 2.II.8 — Female University Enrolment as a Percentage of Total University Enrolment From 1980–81 to 2000–01

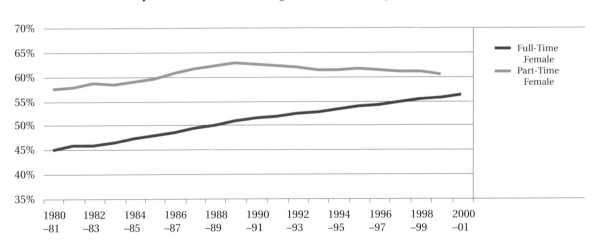

Source: Statistics Canada's University Student Information System and Community College Student Information System.

Figure 2.II.9 — University Students by Gender and Province in 2000–01

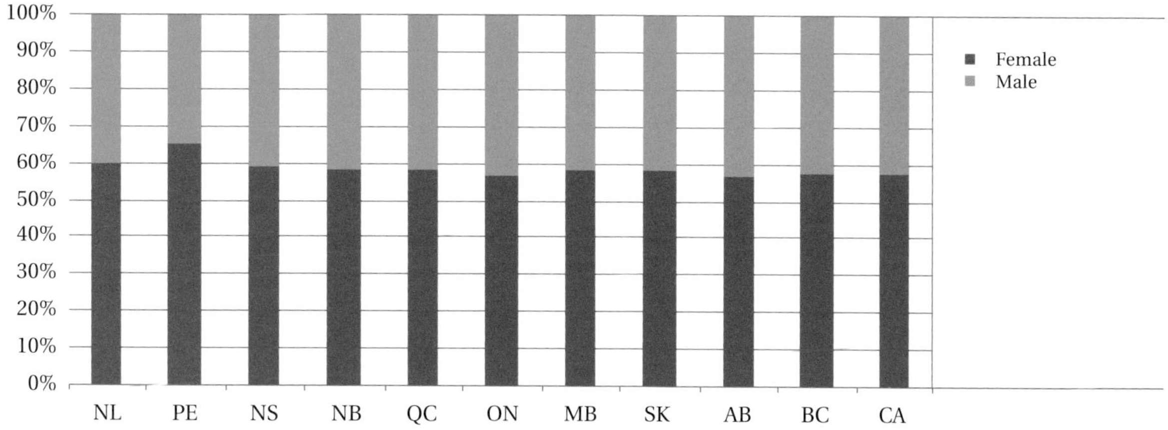

Source: Statistics Canada's University Student Information System.

Location of Study

The geographical distribution of Canadian university students does not differ significantly from that of the population as a whole; the majority of Canadian university students (and Canadians) live in the Quebec City—Windsor corridor. According to Statistics Canada enrolment numbers for 2001–2002 (the last year for which data is available), over two-thirds of the country's university students were studying in either Ontario or Quebec. As befits an increasingly urban nation, the majority of university students study at institutions in large urban centres. At the university level, students are concentrated very heavily at a handful of large institutions; as Table 2.II.I shows, over 616,000 of the nation's 886,000 university students (approximately 69% of the university students) attend just twenty institutions. Table 2.II.1 shows the country's largest universities, by enrolment.

College Enrolment

Accurate data on college enrolment are very difficult to obtain. For statistical purposes, college enrolment is divided into "college" and "trade-vocational." Data quality are barely adequate for the former and poor for the latter. Reporting for the sector as a whole is, as a result, uneven.

The division made by Statistics Canada between "college" and "trade-vocational" is based primarily on program requirements. Specifically, "college" programs require a secondary school diploma. "College" students are primarily studying in degree or diploma programs of a general or professional nature (such as business, commerce or health sciences). "Trade-vocational" programs, on the other hand, do not require secondary school completion. These programs are primarily career-oriented (e.g., machining, secretarial studies, plumbing, hairdressing, etc.), but the category also includes

Table 2.II.1 — Top 20 Canadian Universities by Enrolment in 2001–2002[5] (Full-Time and Part-Time)[a,b]

Institution	Location	Full-Time	Part-Time	Total Number of Students
University of Toronto	Toronto, Ontario	44,060	14,940	59,000
Université de Montréal	Montreal, Quebec	34,165	18,520	52,685
York University	Toronto, Ontario	30,465	9,110	39,575
Université du Québec à Montréal	Montreal, Quebec	18,545	18,640	37,185
University of British Columbia	Vancouver, British Columbia	28,900	7,095	35,995
Université Laval	Quebec City, Quebec	23,715	11,495	35,210
University of Alberta	Edmonton, Alberta	27,675	4,775	32,450
McGill University	Montreal, Quebec	22,735	7,415	30,150
University of Western Ontario	London, Ontario	25,220	4,430	29,650
University of Calgary	Calgary, Alberta	22,725	4,660	27,385
Concordia University	Montreal, Quebec	16,755	10,200	26,955
University of Ottawa	Ottawa, Ontario	19,275	7,290	26,565
University of Manitoba	Winnipeg, Manitoba	18,075	6,195	24,270
Ryerson University	Toronto, Ontario	11,370	12,070	23,440
University of Waterloo	Waterloo, Ontario	19,780	2,935	22,715
Simon Fraser University	Vancouver, British Columbia	11,010	9,390	20,400
University of Saskatchewan	Saskatoon, Saskatchewan	15,395	4,730	20,125
Carleton University	Ottawa, Ontario	14,075	4,390	18,465
McMaster University	Hamilton, Ontario	14,920	3,530	18,450
Queen's University	Kingston, Ontario	15,260	2,965	18,225

Source: Statistics Canada's University Student Information System.

Note: a Includes full- and part-time students, at both the graduate and undergraduate levels.

       b Numbers have been rounded to the nearest 0 or 5.

Figure 2.II.10 — Canadian Full-Time College Enrolment by Type of Program From 1990–91 to 1999–2000

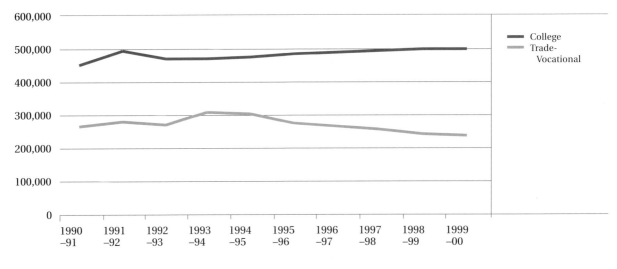

Source: Statistics Canada's Community College Student Information System.

5.   Due to the new format of data reporting the total enrolments for each university include enrolments for the entire institution including affiliated colleges, etc.

students in a variety of other types of programs, such as pre-employment, pre-apprenticeship, registered apprenticeships, skills upgrading, language training, special contract training, job readiness training, academic upgrading and preparatory training. Many of these latter types of students—who comprise nearly a third of all trade-vocational students—are in programs that would in almost all circumstances not be considered post-secondary. For instance, many students in this category would be ineligible to receive government student assistance because the course was too short or of a pre-tertiary nature.

College enrolment data indicate that full-time enrolment increased by over 25% in the 1990s. On the other hand, trade-vocational full-time enrolment declined by just over 10% in the same time period. Figure 2.II.10 shows the evolution of full-time college and trade-vocational enrolment in Canada from 1990–91 to 1999–2000.

Because data on part-time trade-vocational students are not reliable, it is not possible to portray the full-time/part-time status of college students as a whole. Among those in "college" programs, roughly 83% were studying full-time in 1999–2000, compared to about 75% in 1990–91. Thus, according to the most recent Statistics Canada data (1999–2000), there are roughly 90,000 part-time college students across the country. This figure is substantially lower than the 1.5 million part-time college students commonly referred to in the college community. The main reason for this discrepancy is that Statistics Canada's data include only those individuals pursuing post-secondary studies and do not include those individuals who are taking non-credit (e.g., English as a second language) or non-post-secondary courses (e.g., community education or life skills programs) at a college.

Age

The average age of Canadian college students is almost identical to that of their university counterparts. According to Statistics Canada's 1998–99 enrolment data, the average age of a Canadian college student is 22.[6] This finding is similar to the average age (23) in the Canadian College Student Survey Consortium's past three general surveys (2001–2003). Figure 2.II.11 shows the age distribution of full-time college students in the 1990s.

Figure 2.II.11 — Age Distribution of Full-Time College Students in 1990–91, 1994–95 and 1998–99

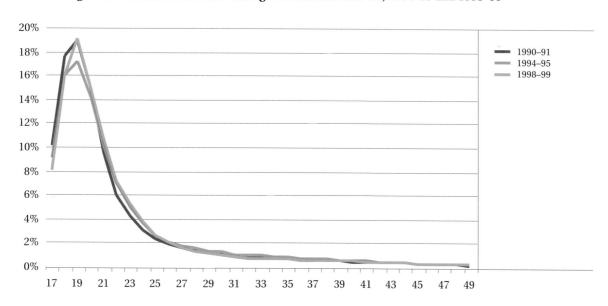

Source: Statistics Canada's Community College Student Information System.

---

6.   The average age increases to 23 if CEGEP enrolment in Quebec is not included.

There are some slight differences in the age break-down by province at the college level. The average age of full-time college students is youngest in Quebec (19.6) and oldest in Nova Scotia (24.7). The age difference by region is explained by the fact that students in Quebec are entering the college system earlier (typically at 17 years old) than students in the rest of Canada. Figure 2.II.12 shows the mean age of full-time college students by province in 1998–99. It is important to note that the number for Canada as a whole (CA) includes CEGEP enrolment in Quebec, while the figure for the rest of Canada (ROC) does not.

As mentioned previously, data on part-time college enrolment need to be viewed with extreme caution. Due to data reporting problems, part-time enrolment levels by institution and age are difficult to calculate. Nevertheless, complete data are available from about 50% of institutions in the country, which, while not a full census, at least provide a large sample.

Although the majority of part-time students in Canadian colleges are still over the age of 30, the average age of part-time students appears to be falling. The only age group in which the number of part-time students grew during the 1990s is the 18- to 21-year-old group. The number of 22- to 25-year-olds enrolled in part-time college studies decreased

by approximately 20%. The most significant decrease in the number of part-time college students was observed in the broadest age cohort: by the end of the decade, the number of part-time students aged 30 or over had decreased by nearly 40% from the 1992 peak level. Enrolment for all of these groups appeared to have leveled off at the turn of the century. Figure 2.II.13 shows the percentage change in part-time college enrolment by age group over the past decade.

Gender

While the number of female students enrolled on a full-time basis in the college system has increased, their share of overall enrolment remains more or less unchanged over the period in question. Thus female full-time students continue to slightly outnumber male full-time students in the college sector. In the trade-vocational sector, as one would expect given the programs offered, male students outnumber their female counterparts (60% to 40%), and these percentages have remained more or less the same for the past decade. Figure 2.II.14 shows female college enrolment as a percentage of total college enrolment over the past decade.

Figure 2.II.12 — Mean Age of Full-Time College Students by Province in 1998–99[7]

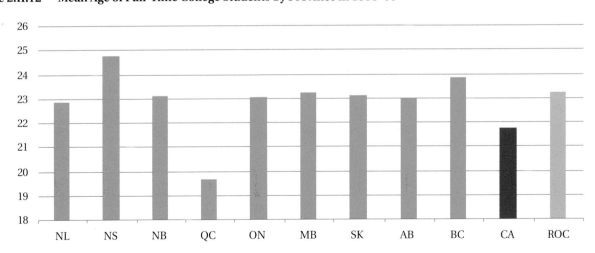

Source: Statistics Canada's Community College Student Information System.

7. Data for Prince Edward Island were unavailable.

Figure 2.II.13 — Percentage Change in Part-Time College Enrolment by Age Group From 1988–89 to 1998–99 (1988–89 = 100%)[8]

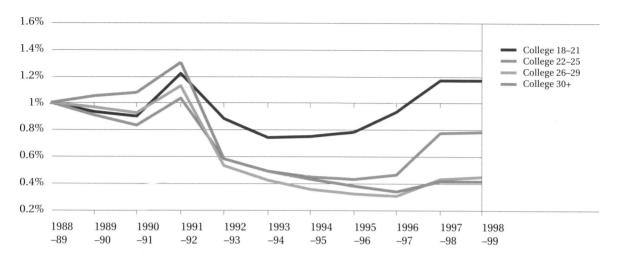

Source: Statistics Canada's University Student Information System.

Figure 2.II.14 — Female College Enrolment as a Percentage of Total College Enrolment From 1990–91 to 1999–2000

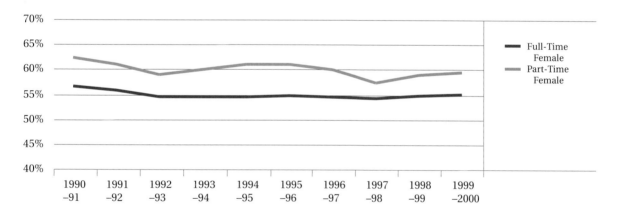

Source: Statistics Canada's Community College Student Information System.

8. Data calculations are based on a 50% sample..

There are some slight differences in the gender breakdown by province at the college level. As is also the case for universities, the type of programs offered at the various colleges in each province can account for most of these differences. Figure 2.II.15 breaks down community college enrolment by gender and jurisdiction in 1999–2000.

Location of Study

The geographical distribution of Canadian college students does differ significantly from that of the population as a whole. As mentioned previously, the majority of Canadians (and university students) live in the Quebec City-Windsor corridor. This pattern,

however, does not hold true for college students. At the college level, students are not concentrated as heavily at a handful of large institutions; as Table 2.II.2 shows, only 253,000 of the nation's 725,000 college students (approximately 33%) attend the largest twenty institutions. This is largely a function of the wide geographical distribution of Canadian colleges. Another function of this geographical distribution is that the majority of Canadians live closer to a college than to a university, therefore increasing the likelihood of students being able to study at a college close to home (see Section 2.IX for details). Table 2.II.2 shows the country's largest colleges, by enrolment.

Figure 2.II.15 — Community College Gender Breakdown by Jurisdiction in 1999–2000

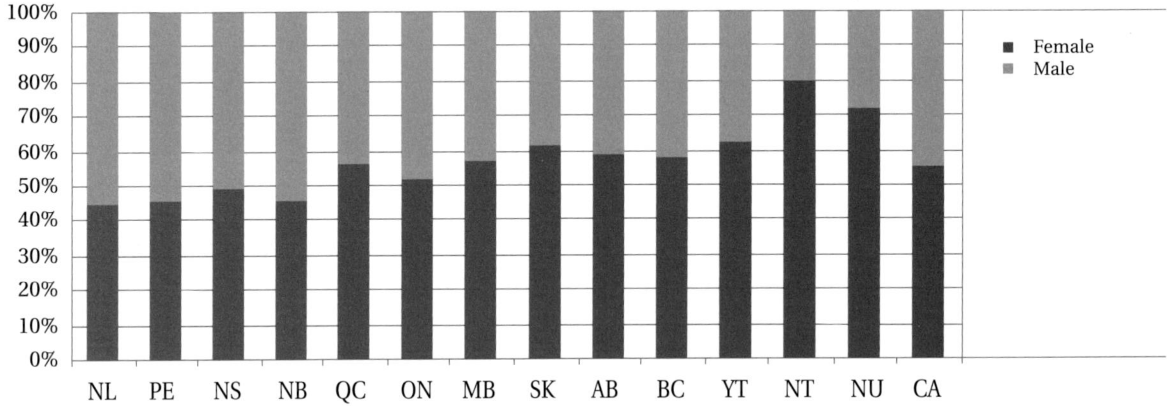

Source: Statistics Canada's University Student Information System.

Table 2.II.2 — Largest 20 Canadian Colleges by Enrolment (including Trade and Vocational) in 1999–2000

Institution	Location	Full-Time College	Part-Time College	Trade and Vocational[a]	Total Number of Students
Seneca College of Applied Arts and Technology	Toronto, Ontario	12,677	2,173	5,103	19,683
Algonquin College of Applied Arts and Technology	Ottawa, Ontario	10,966	999	6,095	18,060
British Columbia Institute of Technology (BCIT)	Vancouver, British Columbia	4,725	5,737	6,778	17,240
Northern Alberta Institute of Technology (NAIT)	Edmonton, Alberta	6,107	3,056	7,382	16,545
Centennial College of Applied Arts and Technology	Toronto, Ontario	10,556	1,262	3,198	15,016
New Brunswick Community College	Saint John, New Brunswick[b]	3,376	100	10,989	14,465
Southern Alberta Institute of Technology (SAIT)	Calgary, Alberta	4,649	4,394	5,128	14,171
George Brown College of Applied Arts and Technology	Toronto, Ontario	9,069	334	4,541	13,944
Humber College of Applied Arts and Technology	Toronto, Ontario	11,090	592	2,283	13,965
Sheridan College of Applied Arts and Technology	Oakville, Ontario	10,014	355	1,718	12,087
Fanshawe College of Applied Arts and Technology	London, Ontario	9,378	449	2,583	12,410
Mohawk College of Applied Arts and Technology	Hamilton, Ontario	7,448	556	3,655	11,659
Kwantlen University College	Surrey, British Columbia	3,403	5,576	2,515	11,474
Saskatchewan Institute of Applied Science and Technology (SIAST)	Saskatoon, Saskatchewan[c]	2,910	131	6,490	9,531
Open Learning Agency	Burnaby, British Columbia	0	9,270	154	9,424
Douglas College	New Westminster, British Columbia	3,163	5,032	1,075	9,270
College of the North Atlantic	Stephenville, Newfoundland and Labrador[d]	6,002	821	2,401	9,224
Red River College	Winnipeg, Manitoba	3,264	2,127	3,447	8,838
Camosun College	Victoria, British Columbia	2,794	2,727	2,570	8,091
Nova Scotia Community College	Halifax, Nova Scotia[e]	5,317	187	3,086	8,590

Source: Statistics Canada.

Note: [a] Trade and Vocational enrolment includes both full-time and part-time data.

[b] The administrative office for New Brunswick Community College is located in Saint John; however, there are campuses throughout the province.

[c] The administrative office for the Saskatchewan Institute of Applied Science and Technology is located in Saskatoon; however, there are 3 other campuses in the province.

[d] The administrative office for the College of the North Atlantic is located in Stephenville; however, there are campuses throughout the province.

[e] The administrative office of Nova Scotia Community College is located in Halifax; however, there are campuses throughout the province.

III. Participation Rates

When studying trends in post-secondary enrolment, it is important to examine not just total enrolment but also the number of enrolled students vis-à-vis the size of the general population. The ratio of the student population to the general population of the same age is known as the "participation rate." In the preceding section, we looked at the size of the student population. In this section, we will consider broader population trends and then examine student enrolment data in light of these trends.

Figure 2.III.1 shows changes in Canada's youth population over the past 20 years. The 18- to 21-year-old section of the population hit its peak at slightly less than 2 million in 1982, while the 22- to 25-year-old population hit its peak at just over 2 million five years later. In the language of demographer David Foot (Stoffman & Foot, 1997), this was the tail-end of the baby boom ("Generation X") passing through the system. The overall 18- to 25-year-old population was at its largest in 1982, at 3.97 million, a number which dropped nearly 20% over the next 15 years to its eventual trough of 3.23 million in 1996, as the

When studying trends in post-secondary enrolment, it is important to examine not just total enrolment but also the number of enrolled students vis-à-vis the size of the general population.

"Baby Bust" generation aged. In 1996, the "Echo" generation began reaching adulthood and the cohort size began increasing once again.

Naturally, this drop in cohort size did not occur uniformly across the entire country. It was most pronounced in Atlantic Canada and Quebec, less so in the Prairies and Ontario, and in British Columbia the youth cohort has actually grown. Figure 2.III.2 shows province-by-province changes in the size of youth population during the past two decades.

Most of the decline in the youth cohort occurred in the 1980s; in the 1990s the cohort size was more or less stable. As seen in the previous section, however, the same cannot be said of post-secondary enrolment. The 1980s were a period of enrolment growth, the 1990s were a period of stagnation, and the first decade of the new century—thus far—has seen strong increases in enrolment like those in the 1980s. As a result, the participation rate increased significantly in the 1980s and 2000s, but was flat in the 1990s.

Internationally, the 18- to 21-year-old age group tends to have the highest participation rate in

Figure 2.III.1 — Youth Cohort Sizes in Canada From 1980 to 1999

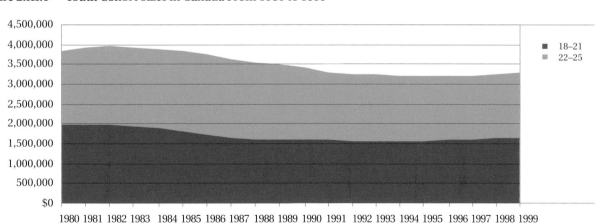

Source: Statistics Canada's annual population estimates.

Figure 2.III.2 — Changes in the 18- to 25-Year-Old Population by Province From 1980 to 1999

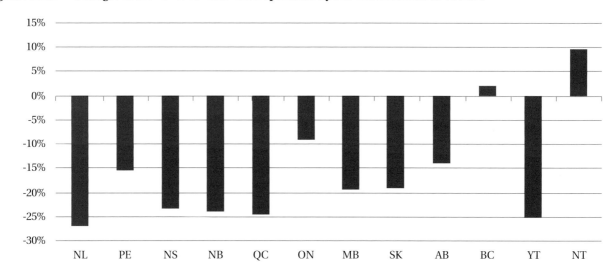

Source: Statistics Canada's annual population estimates.

post-secondary education and is therefore used as the "standard" measurement of participation. Figure 2.III.3, which displays university participation rates of 18- to 21-year-olds by province from 1989–90 to 2003–04, shows that university participation rates differ significantly across the country. While the national participation rate for 18- to 21-year-olds was just under 21% in 1998–99, provincial participation rates for the same academic year varied from 39% in Nova Scotia to 13.5% in B.C.

Figure 2.III.3 shows some notable results. Full-time university participation rates for 18- to 21-year-olds in all four Atlantic provinces are above the national average. Nova Scotia's participation rate—which is nearly double the national average—is somewhat inflated by the presence of a large number of out-of-province students, but even without these "imports," Nova Scotia's participation rate for 18- to 21-year-olds would be over 30% and still likely the country's highest. The high university participation rates in Atlantic Canada are explained in part by the fact that, until very recently, the college systems in these provinces were extremely small. While the college systems in these provinces are now beginning to expand, it is not yet clear if their growth will, over time, reduce university participation rates to levels comparable to those seen in other provinces.

Data from Figure 2.III.3 on the Western provinces show a mixed picture. Participation rates are rising in B.C., remain steady in Manitoba and are decreasing slightly in Saskatchewan and Alberta. The participation rate is greater than the national average in two Western provinces (Saskatchewan and Manitoba) and below the national average in the other two provinces (Alberta and B.C.). The reasons for these differences appear to be largely institutional; in recent years, both Alberta and B.C. have made large new investments in both colleges and universities. Both provinces, however, have invested relatively more heavily in colleges, which are geographically dispersed and deliver both college programs and university transfer courses.

There is unfortunately no "standard" frontier between secondary and post-secondary education across Canada, and 18 is thus not necessarily the standard age of entry into university. In Quebec, students undertake 11 years of primary and secondary education, followed by two years of college, and then enter university-level studies. In the remaining jurisdictions, students have 12 years of primary and secondary education, followed by entry into a post-secondary institution; however, until 2003, Ontario students usually completed 13 years of primary and secondary education before entering

Figure 2.III.3 — Full-Time University Participation Rate for 18- to 21-Year-Olds by Province From 1989–90 to 2003–04

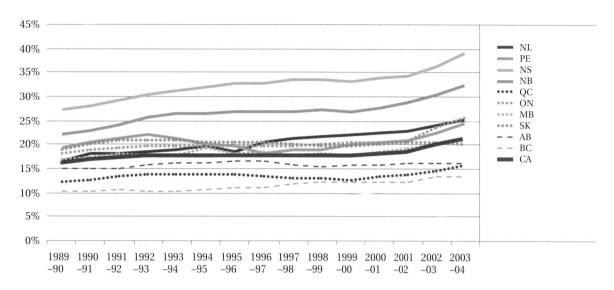

Source: Statistics Canada's University Student Information System and population estimates, AUCC's annual enrolment estimates and authors' calculations.

Figure 2.III.4 — Full-Time University Participation Rate for 19- to 22-Year-Olds (Ontario and Quebec) and 18- to 21-Years-Olds (Rest of Canada) by Province From 1989–90 to 2003–04

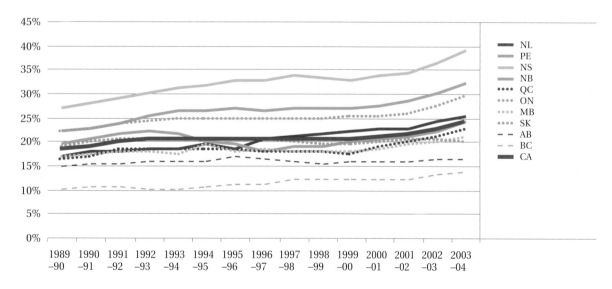

Source: Statistics Canada's University Student Information System and population estimates, AUCC's annual enrolment estimates and authors' calculations.

post-secondary education. As a result, simply reporting the university participation rates for 18- to 21-year-olds puts Quebec (and, until last year, Ontario) at a disadvantage compared to the rest of the country. It therefore makes more sense when examining time-series data to compare the 18- to 21-year-old participation rate of most provinces to the 19- to 22-year-old participation rate of Ontario and Quebec, as in Figure 2.III.4. Examining the data in this fashion not only improves the performance of the two provinces in question considerably, but also increases the national participation rate by three full percentage points (in 2003–04, the participation rate increases from 20.8% to 23.8%).

Trends in participation rates for Ontario and Quebec are intriguingly similar, given their very different tuition and aid policies over the past 15 years. In Ontario, tuition rose and student aid was cut in the 1990s; in Quebec, student aid remained generous and tuition fees were frozen. Yet the results in both provinces were the same in terms of participation rates: growth in the first few years of the 1990s, stability (Ontario) or a slight decline (Quebec) for the remainder of the decade, followed by a surge

at the start of the new decade. The only difference appears to be one of path-dependency; Ontario started out with a higher participation rate and the gap between the two provinces' rates maintained itself exactly over the decade and a half in question.

With respect to the college population, there have been very few changes in participation rates over the past 15 years. This is because neither the population cohort nor the absolute enrolment numbers have changed very much over time. The result is almost a flat-line graph, as shown in Figure 2.III.5. Unfortunately, due to data limitations, no data are available on participation rates for trade-vocational programs. This lacuna may skew the results so that some provinces with extensive college training systems appear to have quite low levels of college enrolment; unfortunately, there is no way at present to overcome this data limitation.

Figure 2.III.5 shows several important facts about college education in Canada and gives particular insight into the situation in Quebec. First, it reveals that Quebec's college population is not only large but also younger than the college population in the rest of the country. Second, while Ontario has a

Figure 2.III.5 — Full-Time College Participation Rate for 18- to 21-Year-Olds by Province From 1989–90 to 2002–03 (Excluding Trade-Vocational Programs)

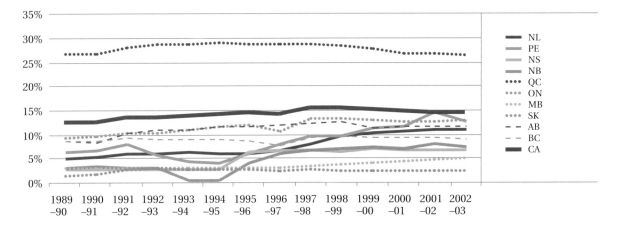

Source: Statistics Canada's Community College Student Information Survey and population estimates, provincial governments' administrative data and authors' calculations.

Note: Poor data collection has resulted in unreliable figures for college enrolment in many Atlantic provinces prior to 1995. Large jumps in provincial totals from these years are likely due to errors or the correction of errors rather than reflective of substantial changes in participation.

Figure 2.III.6 — Full-Time Post-Secondary Participation Rate for 18- to 21-Year-Olds by Province From 1989–90 to 2002–03 (Excluding Trade-Vocational Programs)

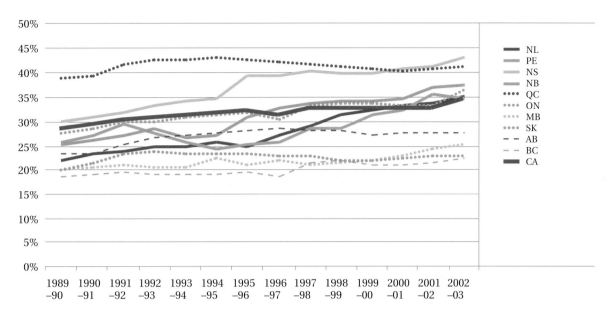

Source: Statistics Canada's University Student Information System, Community College Student Information System, and population estimates; AUCC's annual enrolment estimates, provincial governments' administrative data; and authors' calculations.

college sector whose size is equal to Quebec's, its participation rate is much, much lower. This is due entirely to structural factors in Quebec's CEGEP system, notably the fact that college is a prerequisite for entrance to university for Quebec students. Yet at the same time, it is also true that youth participation rates are decreasing in Quebec and have been for some time. This is not a consequence of a declining youth population, as the figure is a rate rather than an absolute number. Nor is it due to a change in the average age of the Quebec CEGEP population; if anything, the contrary should be true, as CEGEP students have been declining in average age for many years. Instead, this statistic seems to reflect an absolute decline in the rate of attendance, which suggests that educational attainment in Quebec may actually be falling in the long term.

Also noteworthy in Figure 2.III.5 is the fact that several provinces that have weak university partici-pation rates conversely have fairly strong college participation rates. This contrast is most pronounced in Quebec but also noteworthy in Alberta and B.C. as well. On the other hand, provinces with high university participation rates, such as Newfoundland and Labrador, New Brunswick and Nova Scotia, all have relatively feeble college participation rates. Prince Edward Island is the exception, having solid participation rates in both educational sectors.

These inverse relationships suggest that perhaps it is more fruitful to look at participation by combining data from both colleges and universities (i.e., by combining data from Figures 2.III.3 and .5). The results can be seen in Figure 2.III.6.

When looked at from the perspective of total enrolment in both sectors, a slightly different picture arises. Close to 35% of youth nationally are enrolled in some kind of full-time post-secondary program every year. Nova Scotia and Quebec are nearly equal in the percentage of their youth population pursuing post-secondary education (despite having very different tuition fee structures). The three Prairie provinces of Alberta, Saskatchewan and Manitoba have the country's lowest post-secondary participa-tion rates. The good news is that in two provinces— Manitoba and Alberta—the participation rate is increasing; the bad news is that in Saskatchewan it is declining. This is not, unfortunately, simply a case of having an older student population that is not accounted for by the 18- to 21-year-old data. The average age of students in Alberta is indeed slightly higher than the national average, but not nearly enough to make a significant difference to overall attainment rates. This may not bode well for the province's ability to compete in industries that require highly skilled workforces. Alberta may be able to attract educated people from other provinces due to its large population centres, booming economy and low tax rates, but for Manitoba and Saskatchewan the task of creating and keeping a highly educated workforce would seem to be a major challenge for the years ahead.

Comparison of participation rates at an international level is difficult for a number of reasons—different data collection procedures, educational pathways and degree lengths being only the most obvious. In order to circumvent this difficulty, the United Nations Education, Science, and Culture Organization (UNESCO) has come up with a relatively effective—if crude—method of making comparisons across countries. This method of comparison, known as the Gross Enrolment Ratio, takes the sum of all university- or tertiary-level students enrolled at the start of the school year, and expresses this number as a percentage of the mid-year population in the age group covering the five years after the official secondary school leaving age (in the case of Canada, age 20). UNESCO's figures are presented below in Figure 2.III.7.

Figure 2.III.7 — Gross Enrolment Ratios for University-Level Studies in Selected Countries for 2000

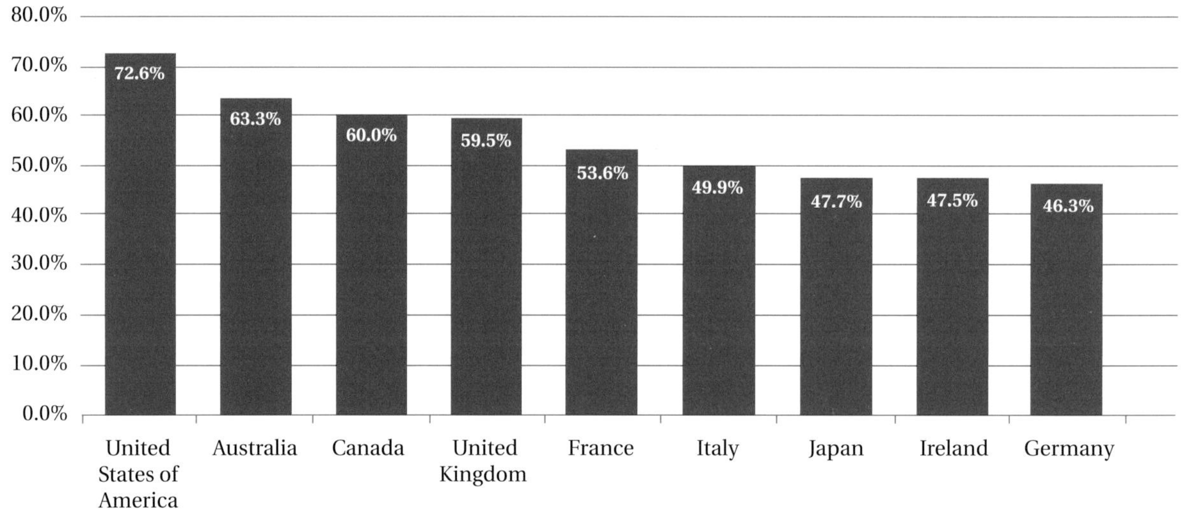

Source: UNESCO's *Global Education Digest.*

IV. Socio-Economic Background

One of the key policy questions in the field of post-secondary education is whether such education is equally "accessible" to all. In other words, do people of different socio-economic backgrounds have the same opportunity to attend post-secondary education? Several recent studies and data sets shed light on this issue.

The most recent data on socio-economic status and post-secondary education participation rates come from the *Post-Secondary Education and Participation Survey (PEPS)*. This survey, conducted for the first time in February and March 2002, surveyed just over 5,000 Canadians aged 18 to 24 across Canada (or 17 to 24 in Quebec, in order to account for that province's different educational system). Although the survey did not ask directly about parental earnings, it did ask about parental occupations, and income figures were derived from these using 2001 census data. *PEPS* results based on family income are therefore best understood as estimates rather than true results.

The *PEPS* data clearly underline the relationship between family income and post-secondary participation. The lower the level of one's family income, the lower one's chances of progressing to post-secondary education. It is not clear from this data source, however, whether or not this participation gap occurs equally across all types of post-secondary education.

The *Survey of Labour and Income Dynamics (SLID)* provides more detailed data on participation. This survey, conducted annually from 1993 to 1998, provides information on the demographic characteristics (e.g., age, sex, marital status, immigrant status, visible minority status, region of birth of parents, household characteristics, economic family characteristics), labour market characteristics, education and income of the general population. The first panel of *SLID* followed a sample of 31,000 Canadians aged 15 and over.

SLID is a longitudinal panel study, meaning that individuals were followed for several years (i.e., between 1993 and 1998). The total number of

Figure 2.IV.1 — Percentage of Canadians Aged 18 to 24 (17 to 24 in Quebec) Who Have Undertaken Any Post-Secondary Studies by Estimated Parental Income (*PEPS* 2002)[a]

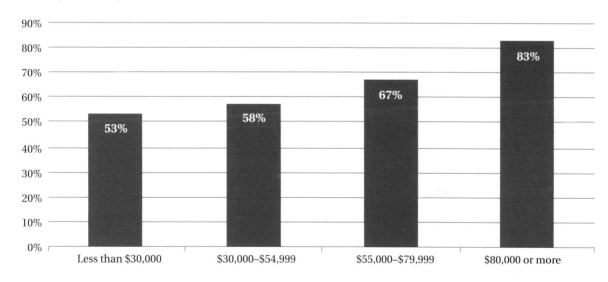

Source: Barr-Telford et al., *Access, Persistence, and Financing*.

Note: [a] Family income is calculated by matching parental occupation with the average pre-tax income for each occupation, as recorded by the 2001 census.

Figure 2.IV.2 — Proportion of Canadians Aged 18 to 21 Accessing Post-Secondary Education by Income Quartile (*SLID* 1998)

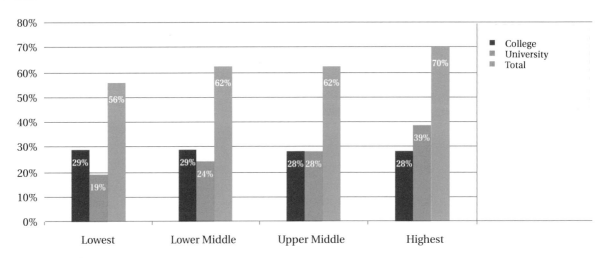

Source: Statistics Canada's *Survey of Labour and Income Dynamics*.

Note: a Lowest quartile = $33,000 or less; lower-middle = $33,000 to $50,000; upper-middle = $50,000 to $67,000; and
highest quartile = $67,000 or more. All figures are based on post-tax household income, including children's earnings.

young people aged 18 to 21 in *SLID* was 1,890. Given the limited number of young people in the survey, all individuals in the survey whose seventeenth birthday occurred between 1993 and 1996 were aggregated to constitute a single group of 18- to 21-year-olds in 1998. This aggregation of cohorts helped overcome problems of variability in the data.

Comparing *SLID* data to the later *PEPS* data to make a cross-period comparison is not very fruitful because the former uses income quartiles to divide the data, while the latter uses income ranges. *SLID* does, however, provide an interesting insight by showing the difference in participation rates for colleges and universities by income quartile.

Among 18- to 21-year-olds in the highest family-income quartile, almost 40% attended university at some point, which made them twice as likely as those from low-income families to have pursued at least some university studies. With respect to college studies, almost 29% of young people from low-income families aged 18 to 21 in *SLID* had attended a community college, CEGEP or trade school.

It is important not to take the *SLID* results too literally. *SLID*'s sample tends to over-report aggregate college attendance compared to aggregate university attendance because of the effect of the upper age cut-off (21) in the province of Quebec. But the overall *distribution* of choices is highly suggestive. Children from low-income families who had pursued any post-secondary education were more likely to have gone to a college than a university, while the reverse was true for children of high-income families. Students from low-income families have a chance of attending college roughly equal to that of high-income youth, but are only half as likely to attend university.

While this situation is of course cause for concern, it is important to note that the general trend in post-secondary enrolment has been one of increasing equity in educational achievement. Using data from the now-discontinued *Survey of Consumer Finances (SCF)* Corak, Lipps and Zhao (2003) provide trend data on enrolment by income bracket from the late 1970s through to the late 1990s. Their data are shown in Figures 2.IV.3 and .4.

Figure 2.IV.3 — College Participation Rates of 18- to 24-Year-Olds by Parental Income Bracket in 2001 Real Dollars (*SCF* 1979–1997)

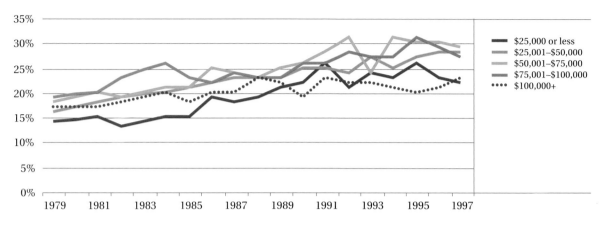

Source: Corak, Lipps and Zhao, *Family Income and Participation in Post-Secondary Education.*

The *SCF* data tell a slightly different story than the *SLID* data about the state of access in the late 1990s. The two data sources concur that there are no major differences in attendance patterns by family income at the college level; the *SCF* implies greater gaps between income brackets than *SLID*, but if anything it suggests a bias *against* upper income groups. At the university level, *SLID* shows a steady increase in participation at all income levels, while *SCF* data suggest that participation rates are quite even

Figure 2.IV.4 — University Participation Rates of 18- to 24-Year-Olds by Parental Income Bracket in 2001 Real Dollars (*SCF* 1979–1997)

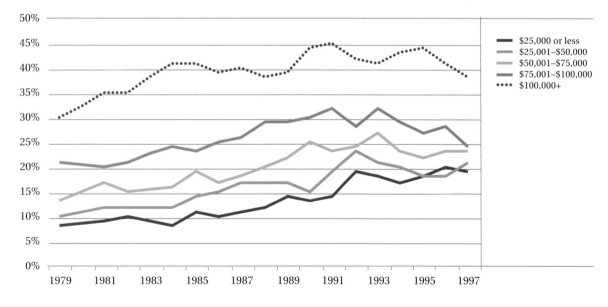

Source: Corak, Lipps and Zhao, *Family Income and Participation in Post-Secondary Education.*

among children of families under $100,000 in family income and only jump significantly once family income surpasses $100,000.

Both Figure 2.IV.3 and .4, however, show a major reduction in educational disparity over the 20-year period under investigation. Most importantly, the participation rate of children from families with family income below $25,000 went from just under 9% for university and 14% for college in 1979 to 20% and 22%, respectively, in 1997. The gradual inclusion of lower-income students in post-secondary education and in the university sector in particular over this period is an important success story in Canadian education.

We know very little about enrolment patterns in individual fields of study. While a few individual institutions (such as the University of Toronto's Law Faculty) have taken to surveying their professional school populations to study their socio-economic background, few national studies have been done with a sufficiently large sample to permit analysis at the faculty or department level. One exception to this is a recent study of the socio-economic origins of first-year medical students by Dhalla et al. (2002), which appeared in the *Journal of the Canadian Medical Association*. Data from this study imply that the pre-tax median family income of Canadian medical students is just over $80,000. No direct comparison to *SLID* data is possible because *SLID* uses post-tax data to determine income, but nevertheless it would appear that this figure is higher than that of university students as a whole.

Overall, there is a consistent pattern: as one moves from college to university as a whole to specific university professional programs, one finds that the student population comes from increasingly higher-income backgrounds. This pattern is repeated when one looks at entrance criteria and tuition fees, which are higher in professional programs than in university generally, which, in turn, is more expensive than college. It is impossible, simply on the basis of the evidence presented in this section, to determine which of the two factors—money or marks—is responsible for the disparity in university participation rates by income group. Such an analysis requires consideration of other factors, which are examined in Chapter 3.

V. Visible Minorities

Until recently, there were few data concerning visible minorities in Canadian post-secondary education. A number of new studies, however, help to clarify the issue considerably.

Nationwide, the 2001 census showed that approximately 16% of the target-age population are visible minorities (the proportion is the same for the entire under-35 population of Canada), with the largest concentrations being in Ontario and B.C. In comparison, the most recent data from the Canadian Undergraduate Survey Consortium (2002) and the Canadian College Student Survey Consortium (2003) show that 14% of university students and 10% of college students identify themselves as visible minorities.

This might seem to indicate a significant under-representation of visible minorities at the post-secondary level. While it is possible that this is the correct interpretation, there are two reasons to avoid jumping to this conclusion. The first is that both the college and university survey consortium's coverage is limited—not all institutions are included in the data (Ontario Colleges are under represented). The second is that surveys of applicants in Ontario, where almost half of the country's visible-minority youth reside, tell a very different story.

For Ontario students, both Acumen Research's 2003 *College Applicant Survey* and 2003 *University Applicant Survey* show that 27% of respondents identified themselves as belonging to a visible-minority group. In comparison, census data show that 22% of the target-age population in Ontario belong to a visible-minority group.

There are basically three ways to reconcile these two sets of contradictory data. First, it is possible that the high numbers in Ontario are offset by low numbers elsewhere, balancing out to produce the national result. This is, however, extremely unlikely, as it implies near-zero participation of visible minorities in colleges outside Ontario. Second, the difference between the higher Ontario applicant

Figure 2.V.1 — Percentage of Post-Secondary Students (Canada) and Applicants (Ontario) Self-Identified as Visible Minority in 2002 and 2003

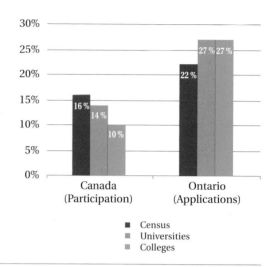

Source: 2001 Census, Canadian Undergraduate Survey Consortium's 2002 *Survey of Undergraduate Students*, Canadian College Student Survey Consortium's 2003 *Canadian College Student Survey* and Acumen Research's 2003 *University Applicant Survey* and *College Applicant Survey*.

numbers and the lower national student numbers could be explained by other barriers to education which prevent visible-minority students from enrolling and/or continuing their studies. This is a plausible explanation for at least part of the discrepancy—Acumen noted that visible-minority applicants are more likely to come from lower-income families, who, as explained in the previous section, are in general less likely to participate in post-secondary education. The third—and most likely—explanation for the difference, however, is simple survey sample bias and normal margins of error.

The 2003 *University Applicant Survey* shows that visible minorities have noticeably higher academic aspirations than non-visible minorities. Visible-minority applicants to universities are approximately 50% more likely than non-visible-minority

Figure 2.V.2 — Educational Aspirations Among Ontario University Applicants by Visible-Minority Status

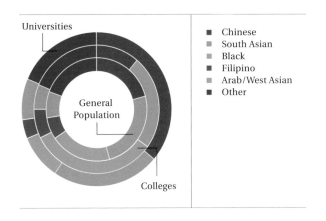

Source: Acumen Research's 2003 *University Applicant Survey.*

applicants to say that they want to gain a medical degree and nearly twice as likely to say that they want to obtain an M.B.A.. In contrast, they are only a little more than half as likely to say that they aspire to a simple Bachelor's degree or teaching credential. Intriguingly, this large difference in aspirations is not matched by a large difference in demonstrated academic potential. The same survey showed that median high school grades of visible-minority university applicants in Ontario are actually slightly lower than those of non-visible-minority university applicants.

The category "visible minority" may, of course, not be the most useful for the purpose of analyzing educational opportunity, covering as it does so many diverse ethnic groups. Generally speaking, surveys of Canadian students do not look at individual ethnicities because the sample sizes required to get valid results at a national level are prohibitively large. The two Ontario applicant studies are therefore unique in Canada in terms of measuring applications by ethnicity.

For the most part, Figure 2.V.3 shows that post-secondary participation patterns for most ethnicities are roughly in line with their share of the population. There are, however, two major exceptions to this

rule: Chinese youth are over-represented among the university applicant population and under-represented among the college population, while the reverse is true among blacks. Another issue of note is that black university applicants are disproportionately (66%) female.

Figure 2.V.3 — Distribution of Ethnicity Among Visible Minorities in Ontario in Universities, Colleges, and the General 18- to 35-Year-Old Population

Source: Source: 2001 Census, Canadian Undergraduate Survey Consortium's 2002 *Survey of Undergraduate Students* and Acumen Research's 2003 *University Applicant Survey* and *College Applicant Survey.*

VI. Students With Disabilities

The standard definition of a "disability" is necessarily somewhat flexible: disability is not a static state, and single descriptions often cannot account for the multitude of circumstances that individuals face. Many Canadian post-secondary institutions define as "disabled" any person who, because of a persistent/permanent physical, sensory, speech/communication, health/medical, psychological/psychiatric, developmental, learning or other disability, experiences difficulties in accessing employment, education or community participation. This definition includes people who identify themselves as having more than one disability.[9]

In the 2001 *Participation and Activity Limitation Survey (PALS),* a national post-census survey of 43,000 people, 12.4% of the Canadian population reported a disability. Not surprisingly, the incidence of disability rises with age, and rates of disability are lower than average in the traditional post-secondary age ranges. For the population aged 15 to 19, the disability rate is 3.5%; for ages 20 to 24, the rate of disability is 4.3%; and for ages 25 to 34, it is 5.2%.[10] The rate for females in the range of 20 to 34 years old is slightly higher than for males.

Few administrative data are available on students with disabilities, in no small part because court interpretations of the Charter of Rights have made it illegal to collect such information. Enrolment information on students with disabilities is therefore largely derived from three surveys. The first major effort to estimate the proportion of the student population having disabilities was the 1991 *Health and Activity Limitation Survey (HALS),* which was a forerunner of the 2001 *PALS. HALS* estimated that there were 112,000 college, CEGEP and university students with disabilities enrolled in post-secondary education in Canada. This represented 7% of total enrolment at the time. The best current surveys of the university and college population are the Canadian Undergraduate Survey Consortium's 2002 *Survey of Undergraduate Students* and the Canadian College Student Survey Consortium's 2003 *Canadian College Student Survey.* These surveys report that 5.4% of university students and 8.1% of college students have a disability, which suggests that across post-secondary education as a whole the figure is between 6% and 7%.

The CUSC and CCSSC data suggest that students with disabilities, on the whole, are somewhat older than students who do not have disabilities, with an average age of approximately 25, which means that the incidence of disabilities among the general student population is 5.2% (based on the *PALS* results described above). The *HALS,* CUSC and CCSSC data therefore suggest that students with disabilities as a whole are slightly *over*-represented in post-secondary institutions. Clearly, this result will not hold true for each type of disability: youth suffering from autism or Down's syndrome are unlikely to be over-represented in post-secondary education.

Due to design limitations on the *Canadian College Student Survey,* we cannot examine the types of disabilities reported among college students. The *Survey of Undergraduate Students,* on the other hand, does permit such an analysis, and the results are shown in Table 2.VI.1.

---

9.   Faba and White 2000, p. 24.

10.   Human Resources and Skills Development Canada 2002. http://www.hrdc-drhc.gc.ca/hrib/sdd-dds/odi/documents/AIPDTR/annex000.shtml.

Table 2.VI.1 — Types of Disabilities Among University Students with Disabilities

Disability	Percentage
Learning	23.9%
Mental health	17.8%
Sight (partial or blind)	10.9%
Other physical disability	10.3%
Hearing	8.8%
Medical condition	8.4%
Mobility	7.4%
Speech	4.5%
Head injury	2.0%
Other	2.0%
Other sight-related	2.0%
Other learning disability	1.3%
Neurological	0.7%

Source: Canadian Undergraduate Survey Consortium's 2002 *Survey of Undergraduate Students.*

Another cautionary note needs to be sounded on the over-representation of students with disabilities. Not only do people differ in the *types* of disabilities experienced but also in their *severity*. One recent paper in the *Canadian Journal of Higher Education* suggests, based on an extensive survey of over 200 university and college disability offices, that only 2.5% (i.e., less than half of all those reporting disabilities in various surveys) of all post-secondary students are registered with their institution to receive disability services.[11] If those requiring institutional services can be deemed to be those with "severe" disabilities, then this suggests that students with "severe" disabilities are in fact under-represented in post-secondary education.

---

11. Fichten et al., "Canadian Post-Secondary Students with Disabilities: Where Are They?"

VII. Aboriginal Students

While it is true that post-secondary participation and attainment rates for Aboriginal youth continue to lag behind those of the rest of the population, it is also true that the number of Aboriginal students studying at the post-secondary level in Canada has increased very significantly over the last 30 years.[12] In fact, Aboriginal participation rates have increased much faster than they have in the population as a whole. Due to a combination of improved funding and increased Aboriginal control of educational institutions, the number of Aboriginal students enrolled each year at Canadian institutions has increased several-fold over the past two decades.

If this success story has gone unreported, it is due in part to the limitations of the data sources from which this information is derived. Aboriginal students are not required to identify themselves as such when they register at an educational institution. Data derived from institutional sources—including data from Statistics Canada—therefore cannot properly establish Aboriginal enrolment patterns. Information on Aboriginal students therefore comes from a variety of smaller surveys and administrative data.

The best available evidence on the number of Aboriginal students comes from the Canadian Undergraduate Survey Consortium's 2002 *Survey of Undergraduate Students* and the Canadian College Student Survey Consortium's 2003 survey. According to these, roughly 3% of the country's undergraduate population is of Aboriginal ancestry (of which just under half are First Nations), while fully 10% of the Canadian college population report being of Aboriginal ancestry (no distinction between Aboriginal and First Nations students is possible for this survey). These figures suggest that there are approximately 24,000 Aboriginal undergraduates and 70,000 Aboriginal college students in Canada.

First Nations Students

The only consistent source of data on this subject—the number of Registered or Status Indians[13] who receive Post-Secondary Student Support Program (PSSSP) funding through Indian and Northern Affairs Canada (INAC)—is unfortunately an incomplete one, as it excludes the large numbers of Métis, Inuit and non-Status Indians studying in Canada, as well as Status Indians who do not use INAC funding in order to pursue post-secondary education.[14] Nevertheless, since Status Indians (i.e., First Nations) make up more than half of the country's Aboriginal population and most appear to use INAC funding, the data can at least provide a starting point for analysis.

The story revealed by these data is remarkable. In the late 1970s, there were approximately 4,100 First Nations students enrolled at Canadian colleges and universities. By 2003, the number was almost 26,000—an increase of nearly 700%. There is one cautionary note, however. The number of students receiving funding leveled off in the the mid-to-late 1990s. One possible reason is that funding levels have remained unchanged, demand has increased and costs have risen. As a result, the various funding programs can either fund fewer students or reduce eligible student awards. Figure 2.VII.1 outlines increases in Status Indian enrolment in Canada over the past two decades.

Setting aside the overall increase in enrolment in Canada during the past 20 years, the surge in enrolment among First Nations students is most probably a cumulative effect of four distinct

---

12. The term "Aboriginal" includes all those described as "First Nations" (a term specifically applied to those persons considered "Status Indians" by the Government of Canada), as well as Inuit, Métis and "non-Status" Indians.

13. INAC defines a Registered Indian or Status Indian as a person registered or entitled to be registered as an Indian according to the *Indian Act*. Approximately half of the Registered Indians in Canada are "treaty Indians" – that is, persons who are affiliated with an Indian First Nation or band which signed a treaty with the Crown. In the 1996 Census, question 21 of the long form identified a Registered Indian as someone who is registered under the *Indian Act*. The question made it clear that this included those who consider themselves "treaty Indians" or "Status Indians," as long as they were also registered under the *Indian Act*, and that it also included those who were registered as a result of the 1985 amendments to the *Indian Act* (often referred to as Bill C-31). The size and composition of the Registered Indian population has changed substantially since the mid-1980s, partly because of the reinstatement of individuals or new registrants following the 1985 amendments to the *Indian Act*. These changes were greater during the 1986–1991 period than during the 1991–1996 period; nevertheless, between 1991 and 1996, about 31,000 individuals were registered as a result of the amendments. This number represented about 5% of the Registered Indian population in 1996 and about 31% of net Aboriginal population growth between 1991 and 1996.

14. These data have some limitations, because the enrolment numbers only include Status Indians who apply for and receive funding through INAC programs. These data also have some gaps with respect to the Northwest Territories and Yukon.

processes. The first of these processes was the shifting of primary and secondary education to First Nations' control in the 1970s. In 1972, the National Indian Brotherhood (now known as the Assembly of First Nations) presented the Government of Canada with a paper entitled *Indian Control of Indian Education*, which laid out First Nations communities' desire to have their children's education guided by their own communities' traditions and values. The following year, First Nations were granted local control of education.[15]

A second factor contributing to the sharp rise in enrolment was the increased federal government funding for students in post-secondary education and the creation of the PSSSP for First Nations students. The program was designed to cover tuition and ancillary fees, as well as living allowances and travel expenses. It is worth noting that funding for this program has not increased in the past decade and as a result groups like the Assembly of First Nations have noted that hundreds, if not thousands, of qualified First Nations students are not getting the necessary funding to pursue post-secondary education.

The third factor is what is known as the "ethnic shift" effect—that is, part of the increase in student numbers is due to a change in the number of people identifying themselves as First Nations. This process was no doubt aided by the expanded definition of "Status Indian" that occurred when the Indian Act was revised in 1986.

Finally, the expansion of Aboriginal studies programs at many Canadian universities and the creation of the Saskatchewan Indian Federated College (now the First Nations University of Canada) in Regina, which is the nation's first Aboriginal-controlled post-secondary institution, have also helped bring about an increase in Aboriginal enrolment.

According to 2003 Status Indian post-secondary education data from INAC, Status Indian students are as likely to study at Canadian universities as at colleges and trade-vocational institutes (there are almost 500 more PSSSP recipients in universities than colleges and trade-vocational institutes). This figure has changed since 1990, when college was the preferred study destination. It is unclear, however, if this is a trend worth monitoring or a statistical anomaly (due to data reporting changes). Figure 2.VII.2 breaks down the types of institutions at which Status Indians study.

The data in Figure 2.VII.2 contradict the earlier observation that Aboriginal/First Nations enrolment (estimates) at the undergraduate level is 24,000 compared to about 70,000 at the college level. There are a number of reasons why PSSSP funding might not follow the enrolment pattern of Aboriginal students as a whole. One is that it is possible that First Nations students are more likely than non-First Nations Aboriginal or students to study at the university level. Another is that a large number of First Nations students attend colleges without the

Figure 2.VII.1 — Recipients of First Nations PSSSP Funding (1980–81 to 2002–03)

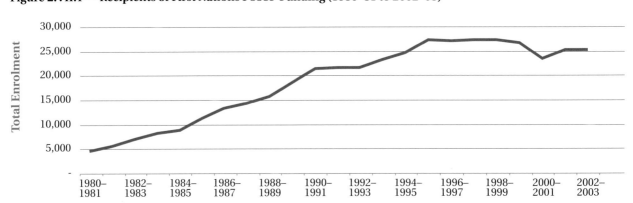

Source: INAC's post-secondary education historical file.

15. INAC 2000, p. 1.

assistance of PSSSP funding, using other financial assistance programs such as the Canada Student Loans Program.

There are some major differences between the fields of study chosen by Status Indians and those chosen by the general student population. INAC data from 2002–03 show that nearly three-quarters of all Status Indian students studying at post-secondary institutions are enrolled in just five areas of study. The top five areas are: general arts and science (17%), social sciences and services (15%), business and commerce (13%), education (13%) and other (unclassified) (12%). In fact, almost 90% of Aboriginal post-secondary students are pursuing one of the ten subjects listed in Table 2.VII.1. The Status Indian population is thus somewhat more likely to be in arts and science or business and commerce and far less likely to be in humanities, natural sciences or mathematics than the general population.

Not surprisingly, the geographical distribution of Status Indians reflects the distribution of First Nations' populations across the country. The institutions with the largest Status Indian populations are all located in Western Canada and Northern Ontario, where Aboriginal population density is the highest. Over 20% of the Status Indians studying in Canada are enrolled at just ten institutions. Figure 2.VII.3 shows the breakdown of the top ten colleges and universities attended by Status Indians.

The personal characteristics of Aboriginal students are also somewhat different from the rest of the student population: according to the CUSC's *Survey of Undergraduate Students*, they are on average both older and more likely to be female. Age, of course, is associated with a number of other important characteristics: Aboriginal students are more likely to be married, have children, or have some kind of disability. Table 2.VII.2 shows the personal profile of Aboriginal and non-Aboriginal university students.

Figure 2.VII.2 — 2001 Status Indian Enrolment Breakdown by Type of Institution[a]

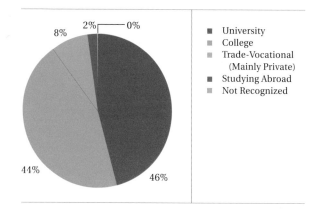

- University
- College
- Trade-Vocational (Mainly Private)
- Studying Abroad
- Not Recognized

Source: INAC's post-secondary education historical file.

Note: [a] Data are based on actual enrolment numbers whenever possible; however, in some instances it is necessary to make regional estimates since not all Indian bands submit full enrolment data regarding educational funds dispersed.

Table 2.VII.1 — Status Indian Post-Secondary Enrolment by Field of Study in 2002–03[a]

Field of Study	Total Number of Students	Proportion of All Students
General arts and sciences	3,563	17%
Social sciences and services	3,270	15%
Business and commerce	2,680	13%
Education	2,672	13%
Other (unclassified)	2,547	12%
Engineering and applied sciences	1,271	6%
Health sciences and related	802	4%
Health professions	627	3%
Fine and applied arts	496	2%
Native studies	490	2%

Source: INAC's post-secondary education historical file.

Figure 2.VII.3 — Top Ten Colleges and Universities Attended by Status Indians in 2002–03

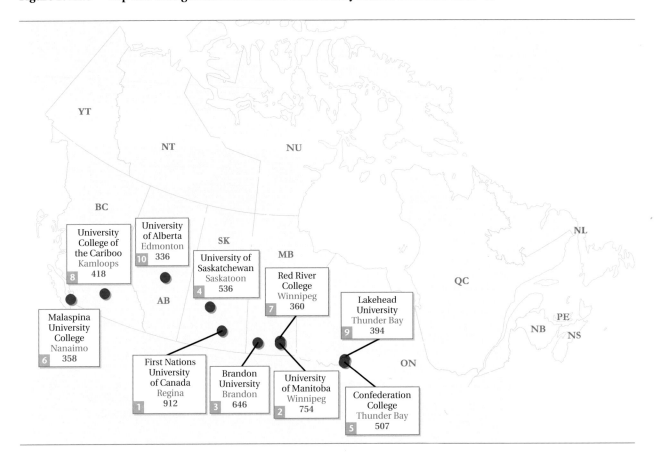

Source: INAC's 2002–03 enrolment database

Note: The total number of enrolled students per institution is calculated by INAC based on responses from Indian bands. If a band does not respond, an INAC regional office supplies estimates in the place of actual numbers. The number listed for each institution is therefore not to be viewed as a precise census but rather as the best available information.

Data on Aboriginal college students tell roughly the same story. The average Aboriginal college student is female and single, and nearly half of all Aboriginal college students have children. As was the case for universities, Aboriginal college students are more likely to be older, married and to have children, when compared to non-Aboriginal students. Also, Aboriginal students are more likely than non-Aboriginal students to be pursuing shorter courses

in college. Table 2.VII.3 shows the personal profile of Aboriginal and non-Aboriginal college students.

Aboriginal Graduates

Aboriginal youth are the fastest growing segment of the Canadian population. They comprise an increasing proportion of the population in a number of regions, including Northern B.C., Northern Ontario,

Table 2.VII.2 — Personal Profile of Aboriginal and Non-Aboriginal University Students

Characteristic	All Students (n=12,695)	Non-Aboriginal Students (n=12,306)	Aboriginal Students (n=389)
Gender			
Male	34.5%	34.7%	28.5%
Female	65.2%	65.0%	71.5%
Age			
18 or less	13.6%	13.7%	10.8%
19	17.4%	17.5%	14.4%
20	15.7%	15.9%	8.7%
21	15.5%	15.6%	11.1%
22	10.7%	10.8%	6.9%
23 or more	26.3%	25.6%	47.8%
Average age	23.19	23.11	25.84
Marital status			
Single	63.3%	64.3%	54.2%
Long-term relationship	27.5%	27.4%	30.8%
Married	8.9%	8.7%	14.7%
Number of Children			
One or more	8.3%	7.6%	29.6%
None	91.7%	92.4%	70.4%
Disability			
Total self-identified	5.4%	5.2%	13.6%

Source: Canadian Undergraduate Survey Consortium's *2002 Survey of Undergraduate Students.*

Manitoba and Saskatchewan. Between 1998 and 2008, the registered Indian population of Saskatchewan is expected to increase by 29% and that of Manitoba by 25.5%.[16] These data imply both challenges and opportunities. As the country faces skilled labour shortages, a declining birthrate and an aging work-force, Aboriginal Canadians will play a pivotal role in the future. In order for this to occur, however, more Aboriginals will need to receive some form of post-secondary training and herein lies the challenge: to encourage and ensure educational opportunities for Aboriginal Canadians. Developing a more highly skilled and educated Aboriginal population is vital for the future economic and social development of entire regions and provinces of Canada.

The good news on this front is that Aboriginal education attainment is on the rise. According to the 2001 Census, more Aboriginal Canadians are completing various levels of education (from secondary school through university) than in the past. The increase does raise an interesting policy question. Given that university and college enrol-ment were basically flat in the 1990s, an increase in educational attainment may mean Aboriginal students are completing programs more than ever before.Figure 2.VII.3 shows the educational attain-ment for Aboriginal Canadians aged 25 to 64 in the 1996 and 2001 Census years.

In addition to the growing number of Aboriginal students pursuing higher education, Aboriginal

16. AUCC, Aboriginal Access to Higher Education. http://www.aucc.ca/_pdf/english/reports/2002/innovation/aboriginal_e.PDF.

Table 2.VII.3 — Personal Profile of Aboriginal and Non-Aboriginal College Students

Characteristic	All Students	Non-Aboriginal Students	Aboriginal Students
Gender			
Male	46.1%	47.4%	36.6%
Female	53.9%	52.6%	63.4%
Age			
19 or less	31.2%	32.5%	21.7%
20–24	39.4%	40.4%	31.6%
25–29	11.8%	11.5%	13.7%
30–39	10.5%	9.2%	20.1%
40 or over	7.2%	6.4%	13.0%
Average age	24.14	23.70	27.46
Marital status			
Married or with a partner in a long-term relationship	28.6%	27.7%	34.7%
Single (including divorced or separated from a spouse)	71.4%	72.3%	65.3%
Number of Children			
One or more	22.0%	28.3%	46.9%
None	78.0%	71.7%	53.1%
Disability			
Total self-identified	5.4%	5.2%	13.6%
Length of program			
Less than 1 year	18.6%	17.0%	31.0%
1 year to 23 months	23.7%	23.3%	26.2%
2 years to 35 months	34.7%	35.4%	29.3%
3 years to 47 months	15.3%	16.1%	9.1%
4 years or more	7.7%	8.2%	4.5%
Type of program			
Access or upgrading program	9.8%	7.4%	27.7%
Career or technical program	67.2%	68.1%	60.4%
University preparation or transfer program	13.7%	14.7%	6.4%
Post-diploma or advanced diploma program	3.3%	3.4%	2.7%
Degree program	5.9%	6.4%	2.8%

Source: Canadian College Student Survey Consortium's 2003 *Canadian College Student Survey.*

Figure 2.VII.4 — Aboriginal Canadian Educational Attainment From Age 25 to 64 in 1996 and 2001

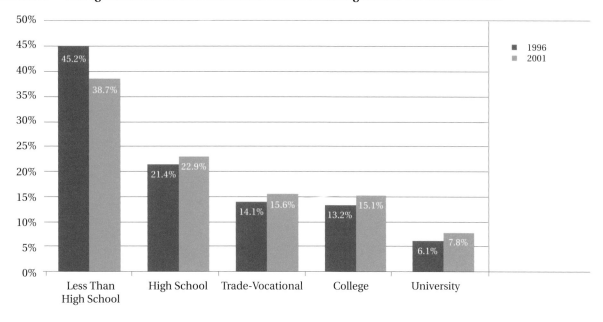

Source: Statistics Canada's 1996 and 2001 Census.

Table 2.VII.4 — Proportion of Canadians Pursuing or Having Pursued Any Post-Secondary Education (1996 and 2001)

Age	Status Indians		Other Aboriginals		Other Canadians	
	1996	2001	1996	2001	1996	2001
15–24	20%	20%	29%	29%	41%	42%
25–44	49%	53%	58%	57%	64%	69%
45–64	37%	45%	47%	48%	50%	56%
65+	10%	14%	20%	20%	20%	32%
Total	37%	40%	47%	45%	51%	55%

Source: Statistics Canada's 1996 and 2001 Census.

Canadians are staying in school for longer periods of time than ever before. In fact, the only educational category to experience a real percentage decline for Aboriginal students was among those not completing high school.

There are some small differences in post-secondary participation within the Aboriginal community.

Status Indian participation has increased since the past Census, while non-Status Indian participation has decreased. Table 2.VII.4 shows that the participation/attainment rates for Aboriginal students who are not Status Indians are still higher than those for Status Indians at all age levels, but lower than those for the population as a whole.

VIII. Students With Dependants

New data from national surveys of college and university students have for the first time made it possible to examine students with dependants in some detail. As far as university students are concerned, 8% of respondents in the 2002 Canadian Undergraduate Survey Consortium's *Survey of Undergraduate Students* reported having children. There was a significant concentration of these students at small, primarily undergraduate institutions; students with dependants were much less common at large, more research-intensive institutions. Specifically, at smaller institutions, students with dependants made up 11% of respondents, while at larger institutions they made up from 6% to 7% of the population. Unsurprisingly, students with dependants are on average considerably older than students without dependants; the average age of university students with dependants is 37.6, compared to 21.7 for students without dependants.

Seventy percent of university students with children have only a single child, and the average number of children per parent is 1.96. University students' children are more or less evenly distributed by age; roughly one-third of these students' children are of preschool age (five or less), while two-thirds are of school age.

On the whole, students with dependants are much more likely to be studying part-time than the rest of the student population. Not surprisingly, this effect varies inversely with the age of the child; as students' children get older, their parents are more likely to study full-time.

The data suggest that approximately 3.3% of the entire undergraduate student body (27,000 students) and about 1.5% of the full-time undergraduate student population (11,000 students) may have childcare needs. One recent publication suggested that there are only about 4,000 daycare spaces available on campuses in Canada, of which perhaps only half are available to students.[17] While one should not conclude on this basis that there is a demand for an extra 25,000 or even 9,000 student daycare spaces on campus, the data do at least strongly suggest that the demand for spaces exceeds the supply.

Among college students, nearly 22% of respondents in the 2003 *Canadian College Student Survey* reported having dependants. Most of these (17%) indicated they had at least one dependant who was a child. Seven percent of respondents said they had an adult dependant, which means that approximately 2% of college students were caring for both children and an adult dependant.

College students' children were likely to be slightly younger than those of university undergraduates—nearly half of all parents had at least one child under the age of six, though it should be noted that college students were far more likely than university students to have children at *all* age levels. Just over 60% of college students with children have a single child, while the average number of children per parent is exactly two.

Female students are more likely than male students to report having dependants. Both the CUSC and CCSSC surveys, as well as the *2001–02 Student Income-Expenditure Survey*, suggest that the ratio of female students with dependants to male students with dependants is approximately 2:1. However, since women form nearly two-thirds of the respondents in all three surveys (partially because of higher female enrolment and partially due to survey response bias), this in fact implies that male and female students are equally likely to have dependants.

Table 2.VIII.1 — Students With Dependants' Registration Status by Age of Children (University Only)

		Dependants Aged 0–5	Dependants Aged 6–11	Dependants Aged 12+
Full-time	88%	44.5%	50%	63.5%
Part-time	12%	55.5%	50%	36.5%

Source: Canadian Undergraduate Survey Consortium's 2002 *Survey of Undergraduate Students.*

17. Junor and Usher, *The Price of Knowledge* (2002).

IX. Students From Rural Areas

Students from rural areas face a number of barriers to post-secondary education that are not faced by urban students. On average, students from rural backgrounds have lower literacy scores than students from urban areas, and face higher educational costs as well, stemming from the cost of transportation and the necessity of living away from home. Both these pressures would lead one to expect that rural students are under-represented in post-secondary education, especially at the university level.

One serious analytical problem in looking at rural and urban students is the difficulty in defining "rurality." It is conceptually simple to define large cities as "urban" and farms as "rural," but there is considerable debate about how to classify the inhabitants of small communities. Different analyses use different measures of rurality, and it is important to understand that studies may not be directly comparable. Even Statistics Canada does not have a single or preferred definition of rurality. For purposes of the Census, however, Statistics Canada defines rurality as any residence located outside a municipality that has an urban core of 10,000 or more people. According to this definition, 20.3% of the Canadian population was "rural" in 2001.

The evidence for poorer academic preparation among rural students comes from data gathered as part of the 2001 Programme for International Student Assessment (PISA) and summarized by Statistics Canada's Fernando Cartwright and Mary Allen in *Understanding the Rural-Urban Reading Gap*. PISA administered tests in reading, math and science to 15-year-olds across Canada and around the world and standardized responses on a scale from 200 to 800. Fifty points on the reading scale is considered to be equivalent to one year of formal schooling.[18]

On average, Cartwright and Allen found students from schools in urban settings in Canada scored about 15 points higher than students from rural areas.[19]

Figure 2.IX.1 — Average Urban and Rural Reading Scores by Province (*PISA* 2000)

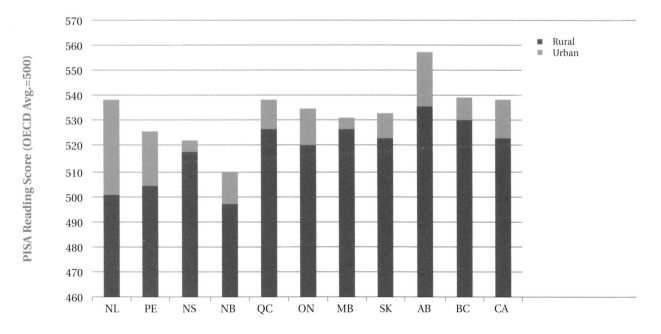

Source: Cartwright and Allen, *Understanding the Urban-Rural Reading Gap.*

18. Wilms, *Ready or Not.*

19. In this study, a "rural" high school is one located in a community with a population of less than 10,000.

Figure 2.IX.2 — Percentage of Canadians Living More Than 80km From Universities and Colleges in 1996 (Using *SLID* Data)

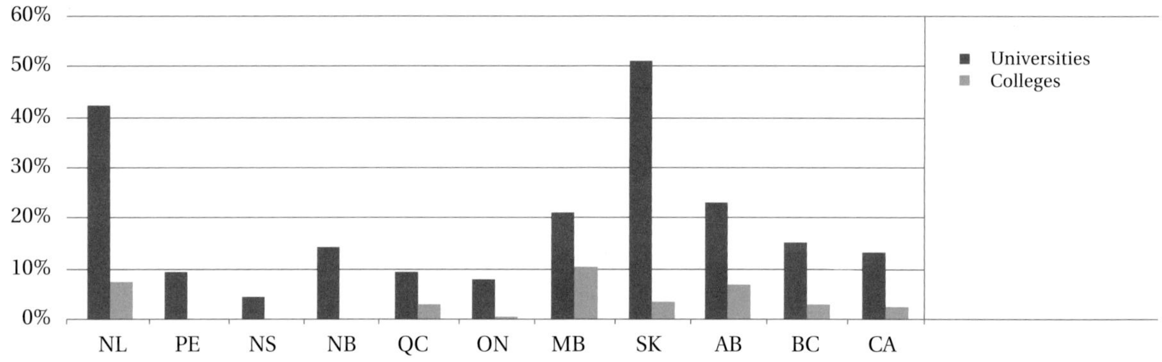

Source: Frenette, *Access to College and University: Does Distance Matter?*

The gap was particularly large in Newfoundland and Labrador, Prince Edward Island and Alberta, and almost non-existent in Manitoba. Smaller but still significant gaps were also found between rural and urban students in math (8 points) and science (11 points). Cartwright and Allen ascribe the difference not to socio-economic differences, which were negligible, but rather to differences in the average level of *adult* educational attainment.

While PISA scores may not be a perfect proxy for university preparedness, currently they are the best standardized measure of academic ability. The Cartwright and Allen results, although not conclusive, certainly suggest that students from rural backgrounds are at a disadvantage in university preparation.

Another way of looking at rurality, at least from the point of view of access to education, is to look not at the size of a community but the "remoteness" of the community as measured by the distance to the nearest post-secondary institution. Despite Canada's enormous size, its dense concentrations of populations mean that only a tiny fraction of the Canadian population lives more than 80km from a post-secondary institution. Just 13% of Canadians live more than 80km from a university and only 2.7% of the population lives more than 80km from a community college.

Figure 2.IX.2 shows that there does appear to be a major distance barrier to attending universities in Newfoundland and Labrador and Saskatchewan and to attending colleges in Manitoba. Across the country as a whole, however, the problem appears to be fairly small. Without minimizing the importance of distance as a barrier to those who face it, this evidence suggests that there are relatively few Canadians for whom distance is really a barrier to post-secondary education.

Another recent Statistics Canada study by Marc Frenette used the *Survey of Labour and Income Dynamics (SLID)* to look at the effect of distance to an institution on post-secondary attendance. This study found that if both a university and a college are "nearby" (defined as within 80km), or if neither were nearby, then youth are relatively equally likely to attend either a college or a university. If, however, a college is appreciably closer than a university (i.e., there is a college within 80km but not a university), then the likelihood of attending a college increased substantially. This effect was noticeable across all income levels, but was particularly strong among children from lower-income families.

The Frenette result is difficult to explain based on the theory that relatively poor academic preparation causes fewer rural students to attend university. This theory would imply that rural students as a whole are less likely to attend university than college, and yet this would appear to be the case only when colleges are appreciably closer than universities. The clear implication is that the higher rates of college attendance over university attendance among these students is the result of student choice rather than institutional selection procedures. Whether the choice is being made for reasons of cost (i.e., universities are too expensive), familiarity (i.e., universities are not well understood—and hence undesirable—because they are not part of the local landscape) or personal/psychological comfort (i.e., going to a university means losing one set of old friends and creating a new set) is not understood.

Complicating matters further is a third data set which suggests that students from rural areas may not be under-represented at all. The Canadian Undergraduate Survey Consortium's 2002 *Survey of Undergraduate Students*, using a sample considerably larger than that of *SLID*, found that students from rural areas (i.e., less than 10,000 inhabitants) are actually *over-represented* among Canadian undergraduates. As shown in Table 2.IX.1, 24.3% of the respondents said they came from a community of 10,000 or fewer people, compared to 20.3% of the Canadian population as a whole. No comparable data are available for community colleges.

Table 2.IX.1 — Distribution of Canadian Undergraduate Students by Size of Home Community in 2002

Size of Community	Number of Students	Percentage	Cumulative Percentage
Lived on a ranch/farm	624	5.1%	5.1%
Less than 5,000	1,404	11.6%	16.7%
5,000 to 9,999	931	7.6%	24.3%
10,000 to 49,999	1,736	14.4%	38.7%
50,000 to 99,999	1,451	11.9%	50.6%
100,000 to 299,999	2,111	17.4%	68.0%
300,000 and over	3,876	32.0%	100.0%
Total	12,133	100.0%	100.0%

Source: Canadian Undergraduate Survey Consortium's 2002 *Survey of Undergraduate Students.*

X. Student Mobility

A central theme of Canadian life is distance. Canada is the world's second-largest territory, and even though most Canadians live in a narrow strip very close to the southern border, we are still spread thinly out across 7,300km from Victoria to St. John's. Many policymakers are concerned about student "mobility" and whether or not increased educational costs have diminished the ability of students to move away from home. Mobility is a fairly indefinite term which has many possible definitions. Traditionally, it has been measured by inter-provincial mobility (which is the only statistic regularly tracked by Statistics Canada), but this is a fairly restrictive definition of mobility. It could equally be measured by the percentage of students who move away from their parents' home or who move more than a certain distance away from their parents' home.

Many policymakers are concerned about student "mobility" and whether or not increased educational costs have diminished the ability of students to move away from home.

At the most basic level of mobility, the Canadian Undergraduate Survey Consortium (2002) and the Canadian College Student Survey Consortium (2003) show that approximately 60% of university students and 47% of college students nationally (54% if Quebec is excluded) live away from their parents. Many of the students who live away from home may, however, still be living in the same city as their parents, so this is a weak indicator of mobility.

Several studies contain data regarding "distance moved in order to study," but they tend to use very different measures. As a result, our knowledge of student mobility is somewhat vague. The *2001–02 Student Income-Expenditure Survey*, for instance, asked students if they had moved in order to attend school, and if so, how far. Unfortunately, as Table 2.X.1 shows, this question was plagued by a high rate of responses indicating movement but not distance.

The Canadian College Student Survey Consortium asked questions regarding whether or not students lived at home and the distance of their permanent home from their educational institution. Combining the two questions, one finds that 24% of respondents who gave valid answers to both questions reported that they both lived away from their parents and had a permanent home that was more than 50km from their educational institution, which is somewhat higher than the Ekos data would suggest.

Inter-Provincial Migration Patterns

Not all students choose to study in their province of residence, for many reasons—a desire to move away from home, a desire to study in a program unavailable in their province of residence, and so forth.

Table 2.X.1 — Distance Moved to Attend Post-Secondary Institution

	University	College	Total
Moved under 20km	1%	1%	1%
Moved 20–70km	3%	1%	3%
Moved 70km or more	20%	8%	16%
Moved, no distance stated	8%	7%	8%
Did not move	67%	82%	71%

Source: Ekos Research's 2001–02 *Student Income-Expenditure Survey*.

The only reliable source of data on inter-provincial student mobility is Statistics Canada, and even this source is plagued with uneven and incomplete reporting from educational institutions. At the college level, several provinces either do not collect or do not report students' province of origin; at the university level, there are significant numbers of students whose province of origin is either not known or not reported. Statistics on student mobility therefore need to be viewed with caution, as they can only approximate, rather than reflect, the real situation. Moreover, due to problems with national enrolment statistics, available data on inter-provincial mobility among students is somewhat out-of-date (the most recent figures are from 1998–99). However, since a historical analysis of mobility trends reveals that the pace of change in inter-provincial mobility patterns is near glacial, we can be reasonably confident that even statistics that are five years old can still provide a reasonably good picture of the present-day situation.

As far as is known, university students are more likely than college students to move to another province in order to pursue post-secondary education. At the university level, just over one in ten students leaves his or her province of origin to study; at the college level, the number is not much more than one in 50. The number for university students has risen somewhat over the past decade, but for most of the past 20 years the number of students studying out of province has remained within a narrow range (8%–10%). The most recent available figures suggest that the number is now 12%, but the rise in this percentage has been accompanied by a rise in the percentage of students whose origin is "unknown" or "unreported," so the increase may be more illusory than real.

Table 2.X.2 describes the in-flow and out-flow of university students for all provinces and the two territories that existed for the entirety of the 1998–99 academic year. The data in this table show that the majority of jurisdictions (i.e., seven of 12) are net "exporters" of students, and only three provinces (Nova Scotia, Quebec and Alberta) "import" more than 1,000 students per year. Apart from Nova Scotia and New Brunswick, the other small provinces are net exporters of students by a considerable margin. There are 60% to 80% more students leaving Manitoba and Saskatchewan rather than coming to study in them; in Prince Edward Island, the out-flow is three times the in-flow, and in Newfoundland and Labrador the ratio is nine to one. Figure 2.X.1 shows the net flow of university students in and out of each province.

Table 2.X.2 — University Enrolment and Student Mobility by Province in 1998–99

Province	Total Number of Students	Total Number of Students Arriving to Study	Total Number of Students Leaving to Study	Net Gain (+) or Loss (-)	Out-of-Province Students as a Percentage of Total Enrolment
NL	15,710	498	4,389	-3,891	3.2%
PE	2,887	552	1,610	-1,058	19.1%
NS	37,241	9,418	4,649	+4,769	25.3%
NB	22,766	5,117	4,596	+521	22.5%
QC	232,278	11,302	8,873	+2,429	4.9%
ON	302,943	17,303	17,072	+230	5.7%
MB	30,735	1,862	2,976	-1,114	6.1%
SK	31,278	2,252	3,758	-1,506	7.2%
AB	73,773	11,327	5,609	+5,718	15.4%
BC	76,750	5,052	9,839	-4,787	6.6%
YT	0	0	450	-450	N/A
NT	0	0	862	-862	N/A

Source: Statistics Canada's University Student Information System.

Figure 2.X.1 — Net Flow of University Students by Province in 1998–99

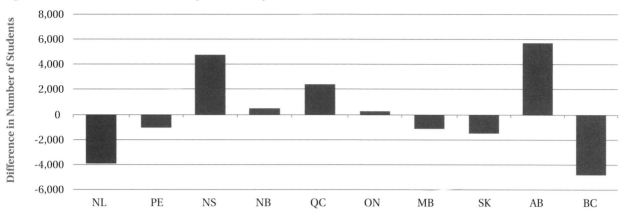

Source: Statistics Canada's University Student Information System.

Table 2.X.3 — Preferred Destinations of Out-of-Province University Students by Jurisdiction in 1998–99

Jurisdiction	Arriving to Study			Leaving to Study		
	1	2	3	1	2	3
NL	ON (168)	NS (116)	AB (50)	NS (2,160)	NB (782)	ON (731)
PE	NB (189)	NS (184)	NL (106)	NS (710)	NB (498)	ON (204)
NS	ON (2,976)	NL (2,160)	NB (2,130)	NB (1,916)	ON (1,283)	QC (522)
NB	NS (1,916)	ON (1,019)	NF (782)	NS (2,130)	QC (1,039)	ON (917)
QC	ON (6,838)	BC (1,461)	NB (1,039)	ON (7,080)	NB (550)	NS (390)
ON	QC (7,080)	BC (3,297)	AB (2,039)	QC (6,838)	NS (2,976)	AB (2,740)
MB	ON (830)	BC (297)	SK (292)	ON (965)	AB (838)	SK (482)
SK	AB (738)	BC (494)	MB (482)	AB (2,209)	ON (640)	BC (314)
AB	BC (3,596)	ON (2,740)	SK (2,209)	ON (2,039)	BC (1,522)	SK (738)
BC	ON (2,123)	AB (1,522)	QC (375)	AB (3,596)	ON (3,297)	QC (1,461)
YT	0	0	0	AB (144)	BC (127)	SK (87)
NT	0	0	0	AB (459)	ON (111)	QC (74)

Source: Statistics Canada's University Student Information System.

Generally speaking, students who leave their province in order to study tend not to travel too far. As Table 2.X.3 shows, in most provinces the major sources of out-of-province students are the neighbouring provinces. Nearly half of all Newfoundland and Labrador students who leave the province go to nearby Nova Scotia, while Ontario attracts 80% of all Quebec university students who leave the province. In all jurisdictions except Yukon, Ontario is one of the three top destinations for students leaving their home

province to study. Newfoundland and Labrador, Prince Edward Island and Manitoba are not among the top three destinations of students from any other province. Alberta is the major destination of students leaving the territories to attend university.

As noted above, data on college student migration patterns suffer from massive under-reporting and gaps, particularly in Western Canada. In the absence of comprehensive data, very little pan-Canadian analysis can be performed. Nevertheless, on the basis of the available data some facts can be ascertained. Virtually all college students from Quebec (99%) and Ontario (98%) come from within the province—in other words, almost no one in either of these provinces goes to another province to pursue college studies. Prince Edward Island, a major exporter of university students, is a major importer of college students; nearly 20% of Holland College's students come from outside Prince Edward Island.

XI. International Mobility

Canada's post-secondary education system is open not just to Canadians but also to students from around the world; at the university level, approximately 2.8% of total enrolment is made up of students from outside the country. Similarly, a large number of Canadian students choose to study outside Canada—primarily, but not exclusively, in the United States. Overall, Canada is a net importer of students, although much more so at the college level than at the university level.

This section examines the available evidence on student "trade" in and out of Canada. Readers should note, however, that most of the data in this section are unchanged from the previous edition of *The Price of Knowledge*. In addition to Statistics Canada's inability to provide up-to-date information on foreign students in Canada, two major foreign agencies—UNESCO and the United States' Institute for International Education—have stopped reporting data in a way that permits an analysis of recent trends in Canadian students abroad. The data in this section are hence somewhat more dated that in the rest of the publication.

International Students in Canada

Since the 1980s, the overall number of international students studying at Canadian post-secondary institutions has increased by almost 35%, primarily through increased enrolment in the college and trade-vocational systems. For most of the 1990s, however, international enrolment actually declined—the exception being the end of the decade, during which an upward spike in international enrolment seems to have occurred. Data from 1999–2000 and preliminary data from 2000–01 seem to indicate that between 1999 and 2001 international enrolment surged by nearly 30%, with the increase more or less evenly split between colleges and undergraduate university programs.

Canada hosts international university students from around the world. In 1995, 40% came from five countries: France, the United States, China, Hong Kong and Malaysia.[20] However, the number of students from Hong Kong has drastically declined over the past decade, largely because of the transfer of Hong Kong to the People's Republic of China in 1997.[21]

Table 2.XI.1 — International Students in Canada by Type of Study From 1990–91 to 2000–01

Year	College/ Trade	University			All Post-Secondary Institutions
		Undergraduate	Graduate	Total University	
1990–91	18,508	20,328	14,859	35,187	53,695
1991–92	17,751	21,748	15,286	37,034	54,785
1992–93	18,509	21,596	15,220	36,816	55,325
1993–94	18,029	20,354	15,097	35,451	53,480
1994–95	15,950	19,141	14,285	33,426	49,376
1995–96	15,884	18,223	13,312	31,435	47,419
1996–97	18,617	18,468	13,214	31,682	50,299
1997–98	17,791	20,026	13,085	33,111	50,902
1998–99	14,661	22,158	13,398	35,556	50,217
1999–00	17,474	26,776	14,595	42,371	58,845
2000–01[a]	20,000	29,077	14,999	44,076	64,076

Source: Canadian Bureau of International Education's *National Report on International Students in Canada 2000–01*.

Note: [a] Estimates are based on the Canadian Bureau of International Education's interpretation of preliminary data from Citizenship and Immigration Canada. The values may vary by +/-15%.

20. AUCC 1999.

21. Kane and Humphries 1999.

Figure 2.XI.1—Top Ten Countries of Origin for International Students in Canada From 1990–91 to 2000–01

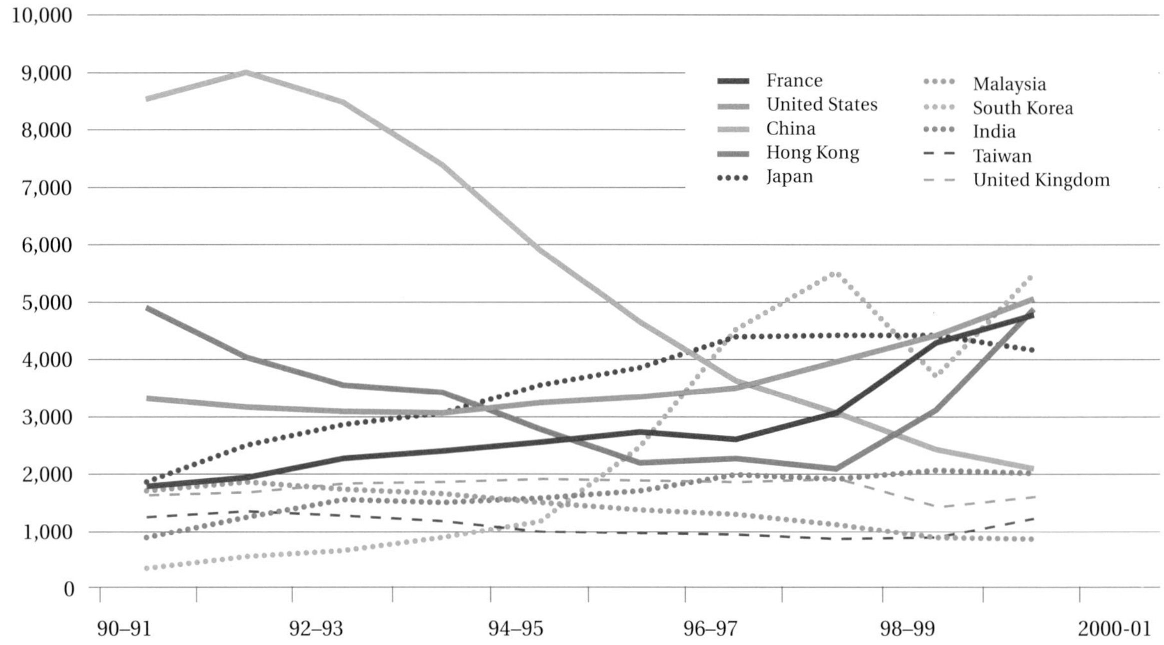

Source: Canadian Bureau of International Education's *National Report on International Students in Canada 1998–99 and 2000–01.*

The number of students from South Korea, on the other hand, has increased remarkably, and in 1999–2000, South Korea became—for the first time since international enrolment data have been collected—the number one provider of international students to the post-secondary education system in Canada. The 5,400 South Korean college and university students in Canada accounted for just under 10% of total international student enrolment. The number of American students, which has always been substantial in Canada, has steadily increased since 1993 and is now above 5,000. Students from China and Taiwan have also been arriving in increasing numbers. Conversely, the number of university exchange students originating from India, Malaysia and the United Kingdom has been decreasing or fluctuating over the past decade. The numbers of students from most other countries has either remained constant or declined during the same period. Figure 2.XI.1 shows trends in the presence of international students from various countries over the 1990s.

A plurality of Canada's international students attended college or university in the province of Ontario in 1998–99. The province has, however, been receiving a declining share of the country's international students for some time. In contrast, international student enrolment in British Columbia and Quebec has increased steadily during the past decade. The increase in B.C. is more or less constant for all levels of education, whereas the increase in Quebec is primarily restricted to undergraduate students. Of particular note in Quebec are French nationals at all universities (these students enjoy generous tuition fee subsidies due to a bilateral agreement between the Government of France and the Government of Quebec) and the significant number of American students, primarily at McGill University.[22] Most other provinces have maintained relatively stable numbers of international students; in 1999, Alberta, Nova Scotia and Saskatchewan had the most international students after Quebec, Ontario and B.C. Table 2.XI.2 shows the levels of international student enrolment at Canadian

22. Canadian Bureau of International Education 2001.

universities by province and level of education in 1998–99 and indicates the proportion of overall enrolment in each province that is accounted for by international students. Figure 2.XI.2 shows the relative changes in international enrolment in Canada by province since 1990.

Table 2.XI.2 — International Students at Canadian Universities by Province and Level of Education in 1998–99[a]

Province	International Undergraduate Students	International Undergraduate Students as a Percentage of All Undergraduates	International Graduate Students	International Graduate Students as a Percentage of All Graduate Students	Total International Students	Total International Students as a Percentage of Total University Enrolment
NL	160	1.4%	275	19.9%	435	3.2%
PE	76	2.8%	15	83.0%	91	2.9%
NS	1,496	5.1%	374	12.7%	1,870	5.7%
NB	674	3.8%	193	14.8%	867	5.4%
QC	7,861	6.7%	5,313	22.7%	13,174	6.3%
ON	6,228	2.6%	3,606	15.0%	9,834	3.8%
MB	707	3.3%	299	14.4%	1,006	3.6%
SK	655	2.8%	456	21.8%	1,111	4.0%
AB	1,519	2.9%	1,013	18.3%	2,532	4.1%
BC	2,782	4.8%	1,854	33.5%	4,636	6.4%
Total	26,776	4.7%	14,595	20.5%	35,556	4.8%

Source: Canadian Bureau of International Education's *National Report on International Students in Canada 2000–01* and Statistics Canada.

Note: [a] While international student data exist for the years since 1998–99, this is the last year for which enrolment data are available on Canadian students. At time of publication, therefore, no comparison figures were possible after 1998–99.

Figure 2.XI.2 — Changes in International University Enrolment in Canada by Province from 1990–91 to 1999–2000

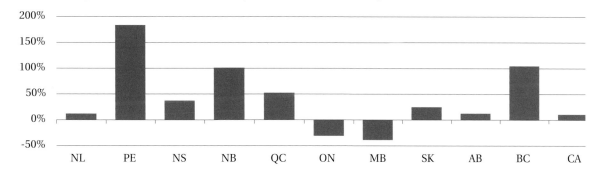

Source: Canadian Bureau of International Education's *National Report on International Students in Canada 1998–99 and 2000–01*.

International students who enrol in universities tend to study at the country's largest institutions. In 1990–91, 14 Canadian universities had at least 1,000 international students, led by the University of Toronto (3,697), McGill University (2,805) and Université de Montréal (2,256). By 1999–2000, only 11 universities had more than 1,000 international students, led by McGill University (4,405), Université de Montréal (3,515) and Université du Québec (2,782). These three universities hosted 10.5%, 8.3%, and 6.6%, respectively, of all international university students in 1999–2000, together accounting for over 25% of international university students in Canada. Table 2.XI.3 shows enrolment levels for international students at the top ten Canadian host universities since 1990–91.

In comparison with other countries, Canada is below average in terms of the percentage of students it receives from other countries, with just 2.8% of all university-level students in 1998 coming from abroad, compared to the OECD average of 5.8%.[23] On the one hand, it should be kept in mind that geography is a factor: many of the countries with high proportions of foreign students are in Europe, where most foreign students are—unlike in Canada—at least from the same continent. Since the creation of the European Union, these students are no longer treated as foreign students and subject to differential fees. On the other hand, a similar geographic barrier has not stopped Australia from becoming a major importer of Asian students. Figure 2.XI.3 shows the percentage of foreign students in selected countries.

Canadians Studying Abroad

Studying abroad can greatly enhance the value of a student's education. A student studying outside his or her country of residence has the opportunity to gain important insights into global issues, acquire new skills and abilities, and perhaps learn a second or third language. The skills acquired while studying abroad then benefit both the individual and society at large.

Table 2.XI.3 — Top Ten Canadian Universities by International Enrolment from 1990–91 to 1999–2000

University	1990–91	1991–92	1992–93	1993–94	1994–95	1995–96	1996–97	1997–98	1998–99	1999–2000
McGill University	2,805	2,792	2,801	3,017	3,478	3,567	3,764	3,867	4,120	4,445
Université de Montréal[a]	2,256	2,352	1,751	1,677	1,628	1,594	1,634	2,227	2,458	3,515
Université du Québec[b]	2,256	2,352	1,751	1,677	1,628	1,594	1,634	2,227	2,458	3,515
University of Toronto	3,697	3,956	3,804	3,421	2,842	2,380	2,158	2,051	2,193	2,582
University of British Columbia	1,586	2,093	2,562	2,045	2,233	2,189	2,184	2,090	2,095	2,165
Université Laval	1,341	1,480	1,576	1,674	1,736	1,528	1,535	1,615	1,702	1,901
York University	1,900	2,058	1,829	1,429	1,047	938	1,067	1,253	1,469	1,748
Concordia University	977	1,032	979	956	962	939	1,014	1,105	1,259	1,483
University of Alberta	1,685	1,590	1,527	1,514	1,308	1,083	1,053	1,088	1,204	1,328
University of Ottawa	890	920	1,030	933	897	883	920	921	1,035	1,185

Source: Canadian Bureau of International Education's *National Report on International Students in Canada 1998–99* and *2000–01*.

Notes: [a] Includes affiliated schools (École Polytechnique and École des Hautes Études Commerciales).

[b] Includes all campuses of the Université du Québec.

23. The difference may in fact be due to data reporting. Canadian foreign enrolment data separate permanent residents and visa students differently than other countries.

Figure 2.XI.3 — Foreign Students as a Percentage of the Overall University Population for Selected Countries in 1998

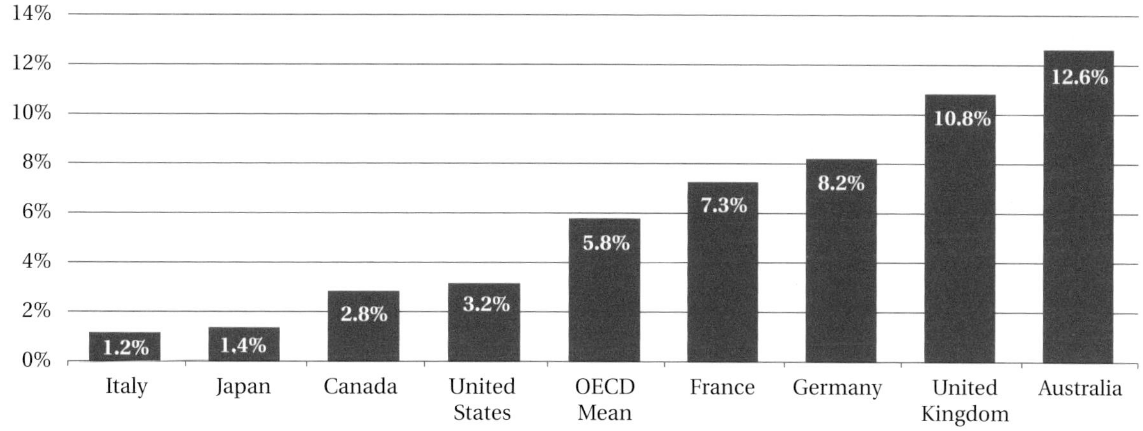

Source: OECD's 2003 *Education at a Glance.*

The number of Canadian students studying abroad has increased by over 50% during the past decade. In 1990–91, there were just under 20,000 Canadians studying abroad, and by the end of the decade that number had increased to just over 30,000. It is unclear how many of these students have left Canada to pursue an entire degree and how many are simply going abroad for a year or a semester, as UNESCO data do not distinguish between the two.

By far the most popular international study destination for Canadian students is the United States— over three-quarters of Canadian students studying abroad are located in the U.S. While the absolute number of Canadian students studying in the U.S. increased during the 1990s, the relative number did not; in 1990, the U.S. accounted for over 80% of Canadians studying abroad. The destination which experienced the greatest relative increase in Canadian students was in fact the United Kingdom, which now hosts over three times as many Canadian students as it did ten years ago. Other popular study destinations for Canadian students are France, Germany, Switzerland and Australia; recent statistical revisions appear to have increased the reported

Table 2.XI.4 — Canadian Students Studying Abroad by Country of Destination From 1990–1991 to 1999–2000

Country	1990–91	1991–92	1992–93	1993–94	1994–95	1995–96	1996–97	1997–98	1998–99	1999–2000
United States	16,443	19,194	20,968	22,665	23,005	24,000	22,984	22,051	22,746	21,4000
United Kingdom	985	1,072	1,242	1,287	1,287	2,900	2,954	2,893	3,342	3,129
France	968	1,040	1,048	1,091	1,091	1,091	1,001	1,091[a]	1,005	976
Germany	399	392	425	425[a]	425[a]	442	437	452	446	424
Switzerland	139	162	167	157	157	150	N/A	150[a]	152	171
Australia	106	121	147	150[a]	175[a]	175[a]	N/A	1,267	1,267	1,267
All other countries	1,330	1,476	1,583	1,672	1,617	N/A	N/A	N/A	N/A	N/A
Total	20,370	23,457	25,580	27,437	28,280	N/A	N/A	N/A	30,255[b]	27,670[b]

Source: UNESCO's *Statistical Yearbook* and UNESCO Institute for Statistics.

Notes: [a] Estimated enrolment numbers.

  [b] Estimates for OECD countries only.

number of Canadians studying Down Under by a factor of ten. Very few Canadians choose to study in non-OECD countries. Table 2.XI.4 shows the number of Canadian students studying abroad since 1989–90 by country of destination.

As indicated earlier, the majority of Canadian students abroad select the U.S. as their study destination. While this might seem natural given the two countries' common border, it should be noted that the "trade" in students is somewhat one-sided: Canadians studying in the U.S. outnumber Americans studying in Canada by a factor of more than four to one. Figure 2.XI.4 shows the location of

Canadian students in the U.S. by state. Perhaps unsurprisingly, five of the top ten states to which Canadian students go are located on the border between the two countries.

The majority of Canadian students study at American universities rather than community colleges. Program availability is likely a major factor for Canadian students who choose to study in American universities. For example, students in Saskatchewan who want to take speech pathology must leave the province, and the closest institute for many is the University of North Dakota in Minot. Similarly, many Ontario students who find them-

Figure 2.XI.4 — Location of Canadian Students in the United States by State in 2000–01 (Top Ten Only)

Source: Institute of International Education's *Locator Report of Canada Foreign Students.*[a]

Note: [a] The Institute's methodology for counting foreign students may be different from that used by UNESCO, which may result in total student numbers being slightly different from those reported in other tables.

selves unable to pursue teacher training within the province choose to do so in New York or Michigan. Another motivation for Canadians to study at American universities is the availability of varsity athletic scholarships. Individuals who excel in various sports such as hockey, golf and volleyball are often recruited by American universities with large athletic scholarships. Figure 2.XI.5 shows the top 15 American institutions where Canadians studied in 2000–01.

By a considerable margin, the American school with the most Canadians is little-known D'Youville College in upstate New York. It offers a graduate program in education that draws a large number of Ontario students who wish to obtain training but are unable to do so within the province. Among the top 15 institutions, ten could be described as internationally renowned research universities, three (D'Youville College, University of Maine at Fort Kent and Minot State University) are small state colleges near the U.S.-Canada border, one (Wayne State University) is a large but not particularly prestigious research university in a bordering state, and the other (Brigham Young University) is a major religious institution.

Figure 2.XI.5 — Location of Canadian Students in the United States by Institution in 2000–01 (Top 15 Only)

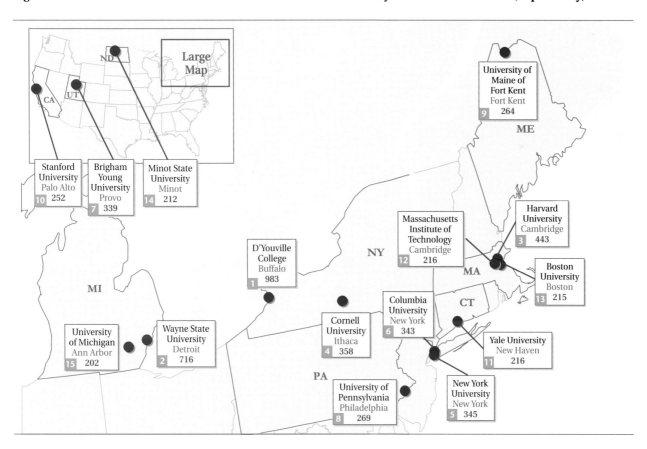

Source: Institute of International Education's *Locator Report of Canada Foreign Students.*

XII. Dropouts, Persistence and Stop-Outs

Accessing post-secondary education is important; persisting through to completion of studies is even more important. There is unfortunately little systematic evidence on persistence collected in Canada, either at the national or provincial level. Even if persistence data were collected, interpreting would be no easy task. When a student leaves an institution before graduation it is sometimes difficult to tell if the student has simply switched to another institution (i.e., "transferred") or has left post-secondary education altogether (i.e., "dropped out"). If the latter, it is impossible to tell, at least at the moment of leaving, whether this departure is in fact a permanent dropout or a more temporary "stop-out."

Dropouts

While reliable data on dropouts are extremely difficult to obtain, two Statistics Canada surveys allow us to measure persistence in an indirect fashion. In a recent report based on the December 2001 follow-up to the *Youth in Transition Survey*, Zeman et al. noted that while 76% of surveyed 22-year-olds had some form of post-secondary education, at the time of the survey only 11% of 22-year-olds (i.e., 14.5% of all those with post-secondary experience) had not

graduated and were not currently pursuing studies.[24] The *YITS* data do not show any variation by province in the proportion of 22-year-olds classified as post-secondary "dropouts" or "leavers."

A second study, by Corak et al., used the *Survey of Consumer Finances*, to track participation rates of 18- to 24-year-olds. In so doing, they captured data not only on participation but also on dropouts, both of which are presented in Figure 2.XII.1. Interestingly, these data seem to show that dropouts have stayed extremely constant over time as a fraction of the youth population, but have declined relative to the fraction of the youth population with post-secondary education. In other words, over time, fewer Canadian students appear to be dropping out of post-secondary education.

Persistence

Another way to look at dropouts and persistence is to look at institutional completion rates. This is not an entirely satisfactory method, for two reasons. First, unlike the system-wide measures noted above, institutional completion rates inevitably overstate dropouts; for instance, a student who leaves one institution and graduates from another is not

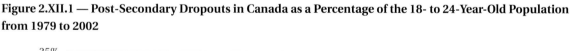

Figure 2.XII.1 — Post-Secondary Dropouts in Canada as a Percentage of the 18- to 24-Year-Old Population from 1979 to 2002

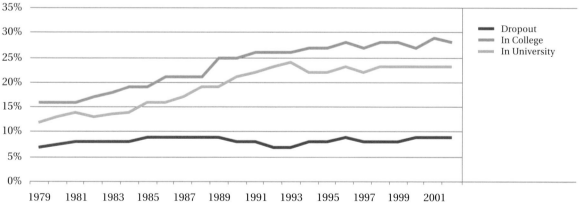

Source: Corak, Lipps and Zhao, *Family Income and Participation.*

24. Zeman, Knighton and Bussiere, *Education and Labour Market Pathways of Young Canadians between Age 20 and 22: An Overview.*

Table 2.XII.1 — Synthetic Completion Rates at Canadian Universities

Institution	Proportion Completing Transition from First Year to Second Year (A)	Proportion of Second-Year Students Completing Within Four Years (B)	Synthetic Completion Rate (A x B)
Memorial University of Newfoudland	83.4%	78.6%	65.6%
University of Prince Edward Island	80.1%	74.3%	59.5%
Dalhousie University	84.7%	85.0%	72.0%
University College of Cape Breton	69.3%	59.6%	41.3%
Acadia University	86.5%	84.1%	72.7%
Mount St. Vincent University	72.8%	68.8%	50.1%
St. Mary's University	91.2%	91.1%	83.1%
St. Francis Xavier University	84.1%	90.3%	75.9%
University of New Brunswick	78.9%	78.6%	62.0%
Université de Moncton	82.4%	60.8%	50.1%
Mount Allison University	82.3%	77.6%	63.9%
St. Thomas University	71.7%	58.0%	41.6%
McGill University	92.6%	92.7%	85.8%
Concordia University	87.9%	77.9%	68.5%
Bishop's University	82.2%	77.7%	63.9%
Université de Montréal	89.4%	91.3%	81.6%
Université de Sherbrooke	91.3%	90.3%	82.4%
Université Laval	95.3%	80.0%	76.2%
University of Toronto	95.0%	91.9%	87.3%
Queen's University	94.5%	92.6%	87.5%
University of Western Ontario	93.3%	91.3%	85.2%
University of Waterloo	92.8%	87.4%	81.1%
Trent University	92.0%	80.8%	74.3%
Brock University	91.4%	78.6%	71.8%
Nipissing University	91.3%	91.2%	83.3%
University of Guelph	91.2%	89.0%	81.2%
Ryerson University	90.0%	80.2%	72.2%
York University	89.9%	82.4%	74.1%
Lakehead University	89.7%	87.0%	78.0%
McMaster University	89.6%	86.7%	77.7%
Wilfrid Laurier University	87.9%	86.9%	76.4%
University of Ottawa	87.6%	87.6%	76.7%
Carleton University	86.6%	77.4%	67.0%
Laurentian University	85.8%	71.7%	61.5%
University of Windsor	78.0%	80.1%	62.5%
University of Manitoba	84.3%	87.4%	73.7%
University of Winnipeg	79.7%	77.9%	62.1%
Brandon University	63.5%	77.6%	49.3%
University of Regina	75.9%	75.6%	57.4%
University of Saskatchewan	80.4%	88.4%	71.1%
University of Alberta	84.3%	74.2%	62.6%
Lethbridge University	73.2%	78.0%	57.1%
University of Calgary	84.3%	78.0%	65.8%
University of British Columbia	90.2%	89.3%	80.5%
Simon Fraser University	85.6%	84.2%	72.1%
University of Northern British Columbia	72.8%	74.9%	54.5%
University of Victoria	85.2%	81.0%	69.0%

Source: *Maclean's* and authors' calculations.

counted as a "completer" in this method of analysis. Some institutional leavers never go back to post-secondary education, but many simply find another institution to attend. Thus, many of the dropouts "caught" by institutional statistics are really just students "churning" in the system—moving from one institution to another.

The second reason that institutional completion rates are not satisfactory is that institutions generally do not make this information available to the public. For the most part, institutions feel that they get a bad rap for the "churning" described above. As a result, for years the only available data on institutional completion rates were from a somewhat obscure statistic provided by institutions to *Maclean's* that captures the proportion of each institution's cohort of second-year students that graduates within four years. Since 2003, however, institutions also provide *Maclean's* with data on the percentage of first-year students who go on to second year. By multiplying these two figures, one can—in theory—arrive at a "synthetic" completion rate that measures the graduation rate of first-year students within five years. The number is "synthetic" because the resulting figure does not measure a true cohort across time; nevertheless, the combination of the two factors is a rough approximation of institutional retention patterns. Synthetic five-year completion rates by university are shown in Table 2.XII.1.

Unsurprisingly, Table 2.XII.1 shows a wide range of institutional retention results. The implicit "synthetic" five-year graduation rate ranges from 87.5% at Queen's University to 41.3% at the University College of Cape Breton. Generally speaking, the institutions with higher retention rates are those that have higher academic entrance standards (i.e., the country's large research universities). This is

not always the case, however: the research-intensive University of Alberta has high entrance standards but a low completion rate, while Nipissing University's 83% completion rate rivals or even surpasses that of some of the country's most prestigious institutions.

Table 2.XII.1, like all completion data, needs to be interpreted with some caution, and not only because of the "synthetic" nature of the cohort being examined. Most notably, it is important not to assume that the "dropout" rate is the inverse of the completion rate, as many of those "non-completers" are simply still in school and taking a longer period of time to graduate. Because completion rates have to be measured at a certain point in time (in this case, five years after the start of the program), institutions where students take longer to complete their studies (e.g., institutions with large proportions of students studying part-time) will appear to be doing worse than institutions where students proceed quickly through their studies, even if, over the long run, the same proportions of students graduate.

Stop-Outs

"Stopping-out"—that is, leaving school for a term or more and then returning to complete a degree—is not all that uncommon. According to data from the Canadian Undergraduate Survey Consortium, 19% of undergraduate students in their graduating year say they have interrupted their studies for one or more terms before returning to complete a degree. If this is true, and if the flow of stop-outs in and out of the system is relatively constant, approximately 27,000 stop-outs, or 19% of graduates (see Chapter 6 section 3), occur every year.

Table 2.XII.2 — Reasons for Interruption of Under-graduate Study Among Graduating Students in 2003

Reason	Proportion of Students (n=11,224)
For employment	6%
To travel	4%
For financial reasons	3%
Due to illness	2%
For other family reasons	2%
Required to withdraw by the university	2%
To have/raise children	2%
Other reasons	5%
Have not interrupted studies	81%

Source: Canadian Undergraduate Survey Consortium—Graduating

Note: Respondents could provide more than one answer, there-fore the second column totals more than 100%.

Table 2.XII.2 looks at reasons for stop-outs among undergraduates. No one factor dominates as an explanation for stop-outs. The most common reason is "employment," followed by "travel" and then "financial reasons." Most students who stop-out for "employment" do not appear to be working for financial reasons (given the option to specify that they had left for financial reasons, a majority chose not to) and are therefore presumably looking to gain labour market experience.

Chapter 3

Barriers to Access and Participation

Chapter 3

Barriers to Access and Participation

I. Introduction

Chapter 2 looked at access in terms of *how many* people go to post-secondary education and *who* goes to post-secondary education. Chapter 3 will consider the barriers to post-secondary education by looking at those who do not go to post-secondary education and why they do not do so. We will also touch on some important policy options available to governments wishing to improve post-secondary education.

This chapter is somewhat different from the others in this book in that it is primarily synthetic analysis rather than presentation of primary data. It begins in Section II by looking at the results of recent survey *data on barriers to post-secondary education.*

Youth who choose not to go on to post-secondary education cite a variety of reasons for their decision, which can be roughly categorized into three major "sets" of barriers. In increasing order of importance, the three kinds of barriers are academic, financial and informational/motivational.

Academic barriers, examined in Section III, are the prime deterrent to post-secondary education for about 10% of youth who do not pursue studies beyond high school. They are a much more important deterrent for students attempting to enter universities (which have selective application procedures) than they are for those attempting to

In increasing order of importance, the three kinds of barriers are academic, financial and informational/motivational.

enter colleges (which do not). Since academic marks are positively correlated to socio-economic background, an increase in selectivity is bound to have a greater negative effect on youth from low-income backgrounds than on those from more affluent backgrounds.

Section IV looks at *financial barriers*, which appear to be the main barrier to entry for one-fifth to one-third of all youth who choose not to pursue post-secondary education. While financial barriers are often considered to be of a single type, there are in fact three different kinds: price constraints (i.e., the price of education is considered too high for the expected return), cash constraints (i.e., the price of education is considered reasonable, but the individual does not have the financial wherewithal to attend) and debt aversion (i.e., the price is reasonable and sufficient funding is available, but the individual is unwilling to borrow). Recently published data suggest that neither debt aversion nor cash constraints are the most important financial barrier. One might therefore conclude that price constraints are the main financial barrier; however, evidence also exists which implies that price constraints are not simply based on tuition *per se* but rather that youth are unwilling to pay the "price" of foregone labour income in order to study.

Section V looks at the largest set of causes of post-secondary non-attendance: *motivational/ informational* barriers. Most surveys show that about half of all youth who do not pursue post-secondary studies say that they are not interested in doing so. These youth appear to come predominantly from lower-income backgrounds. They may be uninterested in higher education in part because of the extremely erroneous information lower-income Canadians appear to have regarding the costs and benefits of post-secondary studies.

The results of the various inquiries into the nature of post-secondary barriers are summarized in Section VI, the chapter's *conclusion*.

II. Survey Data on Barriers to Post-Secondary Education

There is a basic epistemological problem in looking at "barriers" to post-secondary education. How can one *know* what factor or combination of factors was essential in an individual's decision not to attend? The simplest and most direct way to examine this question is simply to ask people about their reasons, as a number of recent Canadian studies have done. This approach, while direct and easily understandable, is certainly open to criticism. In this kind of survey, participants are liable to exaggerate or overemphasize socially desirable answers and minimize or underemphasize socially unacceptable answers. Results will therefore tend to overemphasize external barriers to attendance (e.g., "I didn't go because someone/thing else prevented me from going") and underemphasize internal barriers (e.g., "I didn't go because I wasn't interested"). In addition, individuals are sometimes unaware of the full range of choices facing them and the forces that determine their available opportunities. However, since no other form of data is as easily obtainable, these "self-reports" are in practice the only option available to researchers, and thus form the basis of the analysis in this chapter.

In Canada, three major surveys have asked questions about non-pursuance of post-secondary education: the *School Leavers' Survey/School Leavers' Follow-up Survey (SLS/SLF)*, conducted in 1991 and 1995, respectively; the *Youth in Transition Survey (YITS)*, conducted in 2000; and the *Post-Secondary Education Participation Survey (PEPS)*, conducted in 2002. The *YITS* data are not precisely comparable to the other two because the question about reasons for non-participation was phrased differently, as explained below.

Data on barriers to access from *YITS* are shown in Table 3.II.1. For the purpose of examining barriers to post-secondary education, the key in interpreting *YITS* data is to focus on the third column of Table 3.II.1, which breaks down responses for high school graduates with no post-secondary experience. Fifty-one percent of these students reported a barrier to receiving "as much education as they wanted"—compared to 41% of students actually *enrolled* in post-secondary education and 61% of high-school dropouts. If we consider the obverse, 49% of all high school completers who do not go on to post-secondary studies do not cite *any* barriers at all to obtaining the desired amount of education. This represents the largest category of non-attendees. We can infer that these individuals either do not want to go on to post-secondary studies or they feel that there is no barrier to going at a later date.

Regardless of educational status, financial barriers were the most commonly cited reason for not being able to obtain as much education as desired. Among those respondents who had completed secondary school but were not continuing to post-secondary education, 36% stated that financial barriers were the reason for not being able to get "as much education as they wanted," compared to 28% of post-secondary students and 32% of secondary school dropouts. This certainly indicates that "financial barriers" pose a greater obstacle to secondary school graduates with no post-secondary experience than to post-secondary students, but the difference is not very large. Moreover, the fact that 32% of secondary-school dropouts cite financial barriers suggests that the term "financial barriers" may have as much to do with the challenge of meeting the basic costs of food and shelter and an acceptable standard of living as it does with the cost of tuition.

Finally, *YITS* data indicate that approximately 7% of high school graduates without post-secondary experience perceive their low marks as a barrier to getting "as much education as they want," thus making academic barriers the least important of the three types of barrier.

Table 3.II.1 — Proportion of Young Canadians Who Mentioned Facing Barriers to Achieving Desired Degree of Education by Level of Education and Type of Barrier

Barrier	Educational Status (Proportion of Overall 18- to 20-Year-Old Population)						
	Secondary dropouts (10%)	Secondary continuers (13%)	Secondary graduates, no PSE (23%)	PSE continuers (45%)	PSE graduates (4%)	PSE leavers (5%)	Total
Financial situation	32%	25%	36%	28%	30%	36%	30%
Marks too low	5%	9%	7%	4%	3%	5%	5%
Not interested	7%	5%	4%	5%	3%	5%	15%
Want to stay close to home	<1%	<1%	1%	<1%	<1%	1%	<1%
Takes too long	4%	1%	3%	4%	2%	2%	3%
Want to work	9%	2%	3%	2%	2%	3%	3%
Caring for children	10%	2%	2%	1%	1%	2%	2%
Health	<1%	1%	1%	<1%	<1%	1%	<1%
Not sure what they want to do	<1%	1%	3%	1%	3%	2%	1%
Other	9%	6%	5%	4%	4%	6%	6%
Total (all barriers)[a]	61%	43%	51%	41%	43%	50%	46%

Source: Bowlby and McMullen, *At a Crossroads: First Results for the 18- to 20-Year-Old Cohort of the Youth In Transition Survey.*

Note: [a] Respondents were allowed to give up to three answers. The total number of people reporting at least one barrier will therefore be lower than the sum of individuals citing each individual barrier.

Two surveys held ten years apart, *SLS* and *PEPS*, tell the same general story as *YITS*, but differ with respect to some crucial details. In considering these differences, it is necessary to understand how the question regarding barriers to access was asked in each study. *YITS* asked respondents whether certain barriers would prevent them from getting "as much education as they wanted," while *SLS* and *PEPS* asked about reasons for not pursuing post-secondary education. In other words, *YITS* asked about *potential* barriers at any time in the future; *SLS* and *PEPS* asked about *concrete* barriers in the here and now. In the latter scenario, the proportion of students reporting financial barriers drops substantially, and the number reporting an academic barrier rises. Figure 3.II.1 shows the results of the *SLS* and *PEPS* surveys, which posed identical questions regarding post-secondary non-attendance.

Figure 3.II.1 — Reasons for Not Pursuing Post-Secondary Studies[a]

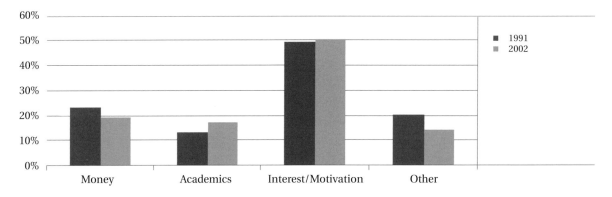

Source: Foley, *Why Stop After High School?*, and Finnie and Laporte, *Student Loans and Access to Post-Secondary Education.*

Reminder: [a] Various categories have been collapsed for ease of analysis. Readers wishing to see the disaggregated survey results may consult the online data tables at www.millenniumscholarships.ca/en/research/factbook.htm.

While *SLS* and *PEPS* generate very similar numbers regarding barriers to education despite the ten-year gap between them, it is worth noting the small decline in the percentage of respondents citing financial barriers and the small rise in those citing academic barriers. This suggests, remarkably, that after a decade in which the average cost of tuition in Canada more than doubled, financial barriers are less important now than they were a decade ago. This result needs to be viewed with some caution, however, as the age groups of the two studies are not identical. *SLS* examined students in the 18- to 20-year-old age bracket; the *PEPS* data presented above examined students in the 17- to 24-year-old age bracket. This distinction is significant, as it is known that reported barriers change as individuals get older. A *PEPS* sample made up of 20- to 24-year-olds would show a lower percentage of non-attendees citing academic barriers as a reason not to attend and a higher proportion citing financial barriers (although this proportion is still lower than it was in the 1991 *SLS*).

In all three surveys roughly half of the respondents gave answers which implied that a lack of interest or motivation was the main reason for not continuing their education. Specifically, in *YITS*, 51% said that they saw no barrier to continuing. In *PEPS*, 49% indicated that they were never interested, preferred working, or would be attending next year.

Roughly half of the respondents gave answers which implied that a lack of interest or motivation was the main reason for not continuing their education.

And in *SLS*, more than 40% reported that they preferred working, wanted time off from studying, were unsure about what to do, or had no interest in post-secondary education. The consistency of these results across time is noteworthy and strongly suggests that the most powerful reason preventing secondary school graduates from attending post-secondary studies is a simple lack of desire or interest.

It is not enough, however, to simply examine aggregate survey response data. Barriers often affect certain categories of young people—usually those considered "low income" or otherwise disadvantaged—more than others. It is therefore necessary to explore how different barriers affect youth of different backgrounds. Table 3.II.2 shows barriers to education by father's education level, which is a strong proxy for socio-economic status (SES).

As Table 3.II.2 shows, neither financial nor academic reasons appears to act disproportionately as a barrier to low-SES students; differences between high- and low-SES students with respect to these two barriers are not statistically significant. It should be borne in mind, however, that even though these factors are distributed fairly evenly across the non-post-secondary population, they still affect far more low-SES youth than high-SES youth, because the former are far more likely than the latter to not pursue post-secondary studies.

Table 3.II.2 — Reasons for Not Pursuing Post-Secondary Education by Father's Education Level for 18- to 20-Year-Old Students

	Less than Secondary	Completed Secondary	College/Trade	University
Financial reasons	22.0%	24.9%	18.7%	25.0%
Academic reasons	6.9%	5.4%	12.1%	6.3%
Interest/motivation reasons	51.2%	46.9%	48.2%	43.2%
Other reasons	20.0%	22.7%	20.9%	25.5%
Total	100.0%	100.0%	100.0%	100.0%

Source: Foley, *Why Stop After High School?*

Table 3.II.3—Reasons for Not Pursuing Post-Secondary Education by Father's Education Level for 20- to 24-Year-Old Students

	Less than Secondary	Completed Secondary	College/Trade	University
Proportion not pursuing PSE	52.0%	39.0%	26.0%	13.0%
Financial reasons	16.4%	15.2%	23.2%	25.8%
Academic reasons	8.7%	8.3%	14.5%	11.1%
Interest/motivation reasons	58.5%	58.2%	37.5%	44.1%
Other reasons	16.5%	18.2%	24.8%	19.1%
Total	100.0%	100.0%	100.0%	100.0%

Source: Finnie and Laporte, *Student Loans and Access to Post-Secondary Education.*

It should also be noted that is not clear whether high- and low-income students are actually facing the same constraints. As seen in Chapters 1 and 2, youth from lower-SES backgrounds are more likely to choose college than university. Since college is both cheaper and less academically selective than universities, it is likely that what these results really show is that high- and low-SES students have equal amounts of difficulty confronting *different* levels of academic and financial barriers.

On the other hand, Table 3.II.2 shows that interest/motivation is correlated with income. In fact, interest/motivation is the *only* type of barrier that affects youth from lower-SES backgrounds proportionately more than youth from higher-income backgrounds. Interest/motivation is therefore not only the most significant barrier to post-secondary education, but also the one most likely to affect lower-SES students. Differences in post-secondary participation rates across SES strata can therefore in some measure be attributed to these basic differences in motivation. This result is consistent with theories of access to post-secondary education that view cultural capital as a determining factor.

The more recent data from *PEPS*, which examine a slightly older sample of students, show a similar result with respect to lack of interest/motivation and academics, but a different result with respect to financial barriers. This data set suggests, counter-intuitively, that financial barriers are cited disproportionately as a barrier by high-SES non-attendees. However, as noted above, there are considerably fewer youth whose parents have post-secondary education who do not attend post-secondary studies themselves, so high-SES non-attendees make up only a small proportion of all those citing financial barriers. Nevertheless, the result is intriguing and undermines the seemingly intuitive link between low-income individuals and financial barriers.

It should be noted that the preceding discussion of barriers assumes that lack of interest/motivation is in fact a barrier. Not everyone would agree—many would say that these people should be excluded from the analysis since the term "barrier" should be reserved for external factors affecting those who have the desire to attend post-secondary education in the first place. Given that roughly half of all non-attendees cite non-interest as a reason for non-attendance, if lack of motivation/interest were discounted, the importance of each of the other barriers would be roughly doubled. Such an approach would be just as valid as the one conducted here; however, given the socio-economic profile of those non-attendees who cite lack of interest as a reason for not attending post-secondary education, this alternate approach would ignore the one barrier that disproportionately affects low-income youth.

III. Academic Barriers

Depending upon which survey is consulted, academic barriers are the prime deterrent to post-secondary education for 7% to 17% of secondary school graduates. This barrier is likely more prevalent at the university level than at the college level, because all universities have selective academic entrance requirements, while the same is not true of colleges. In eight provinces, colleges—a few exceptional programs aside—are effectively open access institutions. In British Columbia and Alberta, this generalization does not hold as colleges are becoming increasingly integrated with the university system and hence are adopting some of their characteristics of institutional selectivity.

Selectivity is a defining feature of universities, and this is what makes the purchase of an education different from the purchase of other goods. With most goods, when there is an excess of demand over supply, prices rise in order to ration supply. Universities, on the other hand, do not ration places on the basis of price, they do so on the basis of academic ability, using secondary school grades as a proxy.

The extent of the problem can be observed partly by simply examining statistics on university admissions. Selectivity has historically been a difficult problem to examine from a methodological point of view, however, because students apply to more than one university (data from the Canadian Undergraduate Survey Consortium's *Survey of First-*

Year Students suggest that, on average, students apply to three universities), and no reliable method has been found to eliminate double-counting of applications to multiple institutions. However, the development of co-ordinated applicant data processing in Ontario, Quebec and British Columbia (which collectively represent over 75% of the Canadian population) allows researchers to examine the question of selectivity with greater accuracy. One recent as-yet-unpublished study by Ken Snowdon of Snowdon & Associates provides some fascinating insights into the nature and severity of academic barriers. Data from this study are presented in Table 3.III.1.

Combining 2001 applicant and admission data from Quebec, Ontario and British Columbia, the Snowdon data show that nearly 13% of all Canadian university applicants are not offered admission based on academic selectivity. This likely understates the problem for two reasons. First, Quebec has an extraordinarily open admissions policy (graduation from CEGEP is technically sufficient for admission), and a more complete national sample would dilute the effect of Quebec's 96% offer rate and bring the average down toward Ontario's level. Second, these data only show the percentage of students admitted to an *institution*; many students are presumably admitted to an institution but denied admission to their preferred program.

Table 3.III.1—Selectivity Indicators Based on 2001 Applications and Admissions Data for British Columbia, Ontario and Quebec[a]

	Applicants	Admission Offers	First-Year Enrolment	Cohort Population (BC–18; ON, QC–19)	Applications as % of Population	Offers as % of Applicants	Enrolment as % of Applicants	Enrolment as % of Population
B.C.	12,878	9,985	7,547	56,460	23%	78%	59%	13%
Ontario	51,750	4,960	49,008	160,228	36%	86%	85%	30%
Quebec	26,097	25,050	20,959	96,197	27%	96%	80%	22%
"Canada"	89,473	84,675	77,514	312,875	31%	87%	80%	25%

Source: Ken Snowdon, *Applicant Data in Canada: Another Perspective on Access.*

Note: [a] More recent data are available and show nearly identical results, but 2001 is used here to avoid any data "noise" from Ontario's double cohort.

Table 3.III.2 — Access to Post-Secondary Education Among 20- to 24-Year-Olds by High School Grades

Secondary School Grades	Total PSE	College/Trade	University
90% or more	89.0%	18.5%	70.5%
80–89%	85.3%	30.4%	54.9%
70–79%	69.6%	44.7%	24.8%
60–69%	47.2%	38.9%	8.3%
50–59%	26.3%	15.4%	10.9%

Source: Finnie and Laporte, *Student Loans and Access to Post-Secondary Education*.

Formal rejection on the basis of academic performance is surely only part of the problem, however. People who apply to university are to a considerable degree self-selecting; many others who might want to go simply never apply because they know (or fear) that they will be rejected. The extent of this problem is largely unmeasurable. However, as noted in Section 1.III, 50% to 60% of secondary students in *all* years of secondary school say they aspire to a university education. Yet according to the data in Table 3.III.1, only 31% appear to actually apply to a university program, which suggests that between one-third and one-half of secondary students with university aspirations do not apply to university after their secondary-school studies. While the precise explanation for this gap is unknown, it would seem likely that self-selection on the basis of academic grades is partly—or even mostly—to blame.

There can be little doubt about the relationship between high school marks and post-secondary participation. Indeed, based on the data shown in Table 3.III.2, the relationship between high school marks and university access appears incontestable. Students with grades of 90% or more are nearly twice as likely as those with grades between 60% and 69% to access post-secondary education in general and over eight times as likely to enter university.

But who, precisely, suffers from these barriers? Are academic barriers "neutral" in the sense that they are equally likely to affect people from all SES backgrounds, or are some groups more likely to face academic barriers than others? Data suggest that there are two sets of academic barriers in Canada—one related to family income and one related to geography.

Low Family Income

Data from the Organization for Economic Co-operation and Development's (OECD) Program for International Student Assessment (PISA), which surveys 15-year-olds in a number of countries around the world, show a significant positive correlation between SES and reading ability in all countries, as shown in Figure 3.III.1 (reading is not a perfect indicator of academic achievement, but it is a reasonable proxy). Canada's correlation between income and achievement is weaker than most (the U.K., the U.S. and Germany are particularly dire on this count, and France also lags behind Canada), but there is still a considerable performance gap between rich and poor. Wilms (2003) notes that 50 points on the PISA test are equivalent to about one year of schooling. This means that the difference in average achievement between 15-year-olds from the top and bottom income quartiles within Canada is equal to a little over one year of schooling.

Other studies also examine the relationship between income and achievement. Ryan and Adams (1999), using data from the *National Longitudinal Survey of Children and Youth*, show that in addition to having significant direct effects that influence performance, higher SES has several indirect effects as well, notably with respect to having more stable family environments and more positive parent-child relationships.

An important—and extremely delicate—question arises at this point: why do students from low-income families frequently do poorly in school? There are two potential explanations:

- Low-income students, on average, receive a poorer education because schools are worse in low-income areas than in high-income areas (the *unequal school environment* theory).

- Low-income students, on average, suffer from a family environment that is unsupportive of education—a by-product of economic insecurity (the *unequal environment theory*, which is closely related to cultural capital theory).

Both of these theories has its proponents and each has data of varying quality to support it.

The unequal school environment theory has a number of very powerful proponents, particularly in the United States, where secondary school financing is tremendously unequal and income groups are more geographically segregated than is the norm in other industrialized countries. Much of the work on school improvement and school effectiveness results from this line of argument. In particular, Adelman (1999) has shown in the U.S. context that a student's secondary school curriculum is the best measure of college preparedness and, in particular, that simply finishing an advanced mathematics course at the secondary level doubles the likelihood of finishing a post-secondary degree. Standardized test scores and grade point averages were found to be much weaker predictors of later academic success. In Canada, Cartwright and Allen (2002) found that "controlling for individual socio-economic background and community conditions, the most important ... school factors [in explaining literacy scores] were disciplinary climate, student behaviour, student-teacher ratios, teacher support, offering of extra-curricular activities, and teacher specialization."

The *unequal environment* theory—in effect, cultural capital theory—also has its proponents. This theory basically argues that, regardless of school curriculum, children from low-income families live

Figure 3.III.1 — PISA Reading Proficiency by Family Socio-Economic Status in Selected Countries

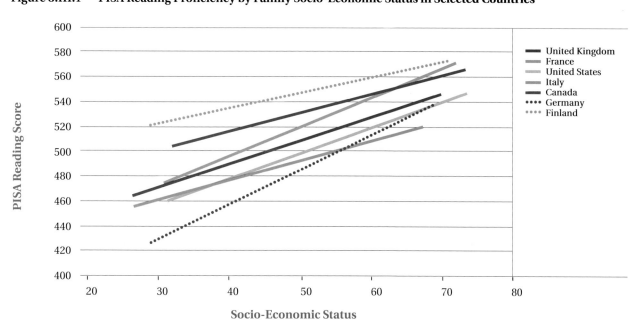

Source: CMEC's 2003 *Pan-Canadian Education Indicators.*

Figure 3.III.2 — PISA Reading Scores and University Admissions Cut-Offs by Province

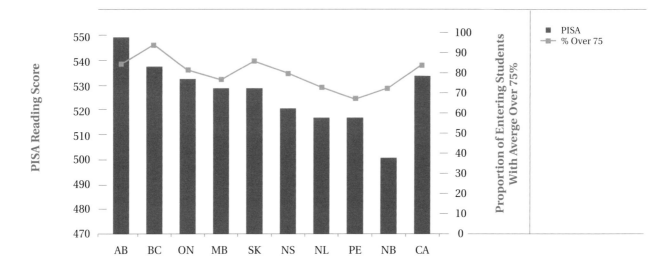

Source: CMEC's 2003 *Pan-Canadian Education Indicators*, 2003 *Maclean's* university rankings and authors' calculations.

Note: [a] More recent data are available and show nearly identical results, but 2001 is used here to avoid any data "noise" from Ontario's double cohort.

in a difficult environment in which to succeed academically. This argument suggests that effects related to *parental environment* (e.g., the likelihood of having books in the house, of being read to at an early age) and *community environment* reinforce the direct effects of low income. Cartwright and Allen (2002) have clearly demonstrated that, in Canada, community environment—in particular, the presence in a community of well-educated adults—has a strong effect on literacy performance (which, of course, influences academic performance and subsequent post-secondary attendance).

Since the relationship between academic achievement and family income or socio-economic status is clear, one would expect there to be a negative relationship between SES and the likelihood of citing "academics" as a barrier to education. Yet tables 3.II.2 and 3.II.3 do not show this; on the contrary, there is no obvious relationship between academic barriers and SES. This paradox can only be explained if students from lower-SES backgrounds are inherently less likely to want to go into a program with high academic standards (i.e., university or university-related college programs). In other words, there is likely a self-selection problem at work here;

youth from low-income backgrounds should cite academics more frequently as a barrier but don't because they have already lowered their aspirations into a less academically-demanding stream.

Geography

Academic barriers to post-secondary education also vary geographically, especially with respect to opportunities at the university level. Simply put, it requires more effort to get into university in some parts of the country than others. Measuring such differences is not always easy, however, particularly because Canada has no nationally accepted marking standard at the secondary level. One way to measure the effect of geographic difference is to look at both average PISA scores (which show the general level of academic achievement in a province) and minimum entrance standards at universities (which in theory show the competitiveness of the entrance standards). These data are displayed in Figure 3.III.2. As in Chapter 1, the percentage of the entering student body with marks over 75% serves as an admittedly imperfect proxy for minimum entrance standards and thus for institutional selectivity.

Holding marks and underlying reading ability constant, universities appear to be considerably more difficult to enter in Western Canada than in the rest of the country, a fact which is presumably related to the relative scarcity of university spots in these two provinces. Alberta and B.C. have both the highest general levels of academic achievement (PISA scores) and the highest entrance requirement standards (percentage of entering population with entering marks above 75%). The three lowest scores in both categories belong to Newfoundland and Labrador, New Brunswick and Prince Edward Island.

Figure 3.III.2 also offers some intriguing insights regarding the relative difficulty of secondary school marking across provinces. Generally speaking, PISA scores and institutional selectivity are positively correlated—that is, in areas where overall academic achievement is high, the grades necessary to get into university are also high, as one would expect. More interesting, however, are those cases where entrances standards are different even though PISA scores are similar. In particular, there seems no obvious explanation as to why entrance requirements are significantly higher in Saskatchewan (PISA score = 529) than in neighbouring Manitoba (PISA score = 529) other than that high schools in Saskatchewan mark more generously. Conversely,

it is difficult to see how universities in New Brunswick (PISA score = 501) can have similar levels of selectivity as those in Newfoundland and Labrador (PISA score = 517) unless good marks are easier to obtain in the former than the latter.

In the preceding discussion, the term "selectivity" has been used as a way to denote the marks required to obtain entrance to a post-secondary institution. While not incorrect, such a definition is incomplete and does not quite do justice to the phenomenon. Selectivity is in part driven by the number of available spaces relative to the demand for spaces. As shown in Chapter 1, the demand for university spaces—as measured by aspirations—is quite high all across the country. Yet as shown in Section 2.VI, there are considerable differences in university participation rates across the country. The fundamental reason for these differences is not demand (which is fairly consistent across the country), but supply (which is not). Because institutions in effect "ration" places by academic ability, a proper analysis of geographic variation in academic barriers therefore needs to take into account not only differences in general academic achievement and minimum entrance standards but also in the supply of university places. All of these factors are presented in Table 3.III.3.

Table 3.III.3—Relative Academic Selectivity Scores by Province

	PISA (a)	% Entering University With Grades Over 75% (b)	Participation Rate (18- to 21-Year-Olds)[a] (c)	Provincial Academic Selectivity Score ([a*b]/c])
AB	550	87.93	15	3,224.10
BC	538	97.79	12	4,384.25
ON	533	85.73	25	1,827.76
MA	529	79.61	18	2,339.65
SK	529	89.62	20	2,370.45
NS	521	83.28	30	1,446.30
NL	517	76.07	22	1,787.65
PE	517	70.36	19	1,914.53
NB	501	75.88	27	1,408.00

Source: CMEC's 2003 *Pan-Canadian Education Indicators*, 2003 *Maclean's* university rankings, Statistics Canada's University Student Information System and authors' calculations.

Note: [a] The participation rate is for 18- to 21-year-olds, except in Ontario, where it is for 19- to 22-year-olds. Nova Scotia's participation rate has been reduced by four points to adjust for the large proportion of out-of-province students.

Curiously, the supply of university places is most plentiful in Eastern Canada, where secondary school achievement (as measured by PISA scores) is lowest, and in shortest supply in Alberta and B.C., where achievement is the highest. This imbalance between potential demand and supply has some serious consequences for access to universities in Alberta and B.C.

Table 3.III.3 introduces a new pan-Canadian measure of academic barriers to university—the provincial selectivity score. An initial "student achievement" score is derived by multiplying two measures of student academic performance (provincial PISA scores and the percentage of students entering university with grades over 75%). Provinces with high overall PISA marks and higher required grades to get into university thus receive a higher score. A "university opportunities" score is then obtained by taking the provincial university participation rate for the relevant age group. The student achievement score is then divided by the opportunities score to generate the provincial selectivity score. A high score indicates more difficulty in obtaining a place, while a low score indicates less difficulty in obtaining a place.

It should be emphasized that a province's selectivity score is not a particularly useful number and should be interpreted with care. Differences in the magnitude of a provincial score are not directly correlated to magnitudes of difficulty in getting into university, because the number is driven to a considerable extent by the size of the system itself. For example, B.C.'s score of 4,384 should not be taken as meaning that it is three times more difficult to obtain a university place in B.C. than it is in New Brunswick or Nova Scotia (1,408 and 1,446, respectively), but it does reflect the fact that there are more than twice as many university places per capita in Nova Scotia and New Brunswick as there are in B.C.

Generally speaking, Table 3.III.3 shows a continuum of difficulty in obtaining university places across the country. At one extreme are New Brunswick and Nova Scotia: these two provinces have the lowest academic barriers to entry into university because they have low student achievement scores and many university places. At the other extreme are B.C. and Alberta, which have both high student achievement and a low number of student places.

IV. Financial Barriers

Although much of the literature on access to tertiary education refers to "financial barriers" as a single phenomenon, a closer inspection reveals that this term covers three quite separate phenomena which, although conceptually distinct, nestle inside one another like Russian dolls. The three phenomena are: *price constraints, cash constraints* and *debt aversion.*

Price constraints affect those who believe that the cost of an educational program is too high relative to the benefit earned. In effect, people affected by price constraints have decided that investment in a course of studies is not likely to yield sufficient lifetime returns (i.e., they don't think it is "worth it"). It is important to note that price constraints are not necessarily solely based on tuition—the "price" of an education includes foregone income as well. As a result, the price of education is much higher for adults with workforce experience than for youth, while males—who tend to do better in the labour market than females—have lower post-secondary participation rates than females. Tuition subsidies and student grants are both examples of programs which reduce price constraints.

For those who believe that a course of tertiary education is a good investment (i.e., those who "pass" the price constraint barrier) there is a second level of financial barrier to be considered: the *cash constraint.* Some of those who wish to attend post-secondary education simply cannot come up with enough money to cover the costs. In principle, this a fairly easy barrier to overcome. The most efficient way to ease cash constraints is through borrowing, which reduces one's future income in order to provide a greater income in the present. Student loan programs are designed to alleviate cash constraints; student grant programs can also alleviate cash constraints, but at a much greater cost to the provider.

Unfortunately, an over-reliance on loans as a policy instrument can lead to the third and final barrier: *debt aversion.* Not all students who are averse to debt are necessarily deterred from entering post-secondary studies; many choose simply to work more than they otherwise would in order to support their studies. However, those who face a cash constraint and cannot overcome this constraint through recourse to the labour market can effectively be deterred from pursuing post-secondary education because of their reluctance to resort to borrowing. There is thus a tension between alleviating the cash constraint barrier and the debt aversion barrier. While the former clearly calls for loans as a solution to the financial barrier, it also creates a new barrier, for which grants (whether given "up-front" or as a form of loan remission) are the only solution.

Both *SLS* and *PEPS* report that the percentage of secondary school graduates citing "financial barriers" as the main reason for not *currently* pursuing post-secondary education is approximately 20%. In *YITS*, 36% of high school graduates not enrolled in post-secondary studies reported that finances are *one* factor blocking them—either now *or in the future*—from getting "as much education as desired." Ideally, it would be possible to determine the extent of each of the three types of financial barriers affecting Canadian students and whether or not these barriers affect people of varying socio-economic backgrounds differently. Unfortunately, few surveys permit either a meaningful disaggregation of the various financial issues or an examination of how the various issues affect students from different socio-economic backgrounds. Both *SLS* and *YITS* asked questions about "financial barriers" to post-secondary education, but respondents were not asked any further details regarding the nature of the barrier(s). Only *PEPS* allows for even a basic disaggregation of data on financial barriers.

Despite these information gaps, there is significant circumstantial evidence regarding the effects of each of the three types of barriers.

> *The three phenomena that make up financial barriers are: price constraints, cash constraints and debt aversion.*

Price Constraints

The evidence to support the notion that price—that is, tuition and foregone income—is a barrier to access is, in an aggregate sense, slim to nonexistent. As has been noted elsewhere (Junor and Usher 2002; Finnie 2003), a relationship cannot be found between provincial tuition rates and provincial participation rates (this is to say that there is neither a negative nor a positive relationship between aggregate enrolment and tuition). Over time, too, aggregate enrolment has increased nationally in tandem with rises in tuition, as seen in Figure 3.IV.1.

The results in Figure 3.IV.1 are not very surprising. Enrolment is fundamentally a function of supply rather than of demand, and to the extent that tuition affects supply, one would expect a positive rather than a negative correlation, assuming that an unmet demand for university education exists. It is perhaps more relevant to consider the relationship between average tuition fees and reported financial barriers, as shown in Figure 3.IV.2.

Figure 3.IV.2 shows that, rather surprisingly, the percentage of high school graduates without post-secondary experience citing "financial barriers" as the reason for not furthering their education has actually dropped four percentage points over the same period that tuition doubled. There are several possible explanations for this result: 1) financial barriers are not primarily related to tuition levels; 2) improvements to student assistance over the past ten years have more than cancelled out the effects of tuition increases; or, 3) financial barriers are not primarily price constraints but instead are either cash constraints or debt aversion.

This analysis approaches the question of price constraints from the perspective of *aggregate* demand. The more important question, however, is *who* is affected by price constraints. Unfortunately, there are no available data that can shed light on this question apart from the general observation, elaborated in Section 3.II, that low-SES youth generally face more barriers than high-SES youth, but financial barriers do not appear to affect proportionately more people from lower-income backgrounds than from higher-income backgrounds. As with academic barriers, this is likely a self-selection phenomenon; youth from low SES backgrounds may be more likely

Figure 3.IV.1 — Tuition and Participation Rates From 1991 to 2003 (in 2003 Real Dollars)

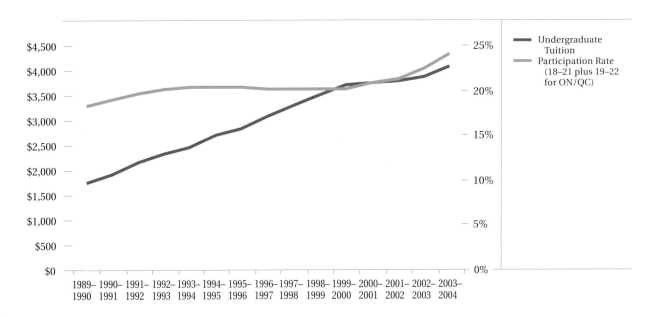

Source: Statistics Canada's University Student Identification System and Annual Tuition and Additional Fees Survey.

Figure 3.IV.2 — Changes in Undergraduate Tuition and Reported Financial Barriers From 1991 to 2003

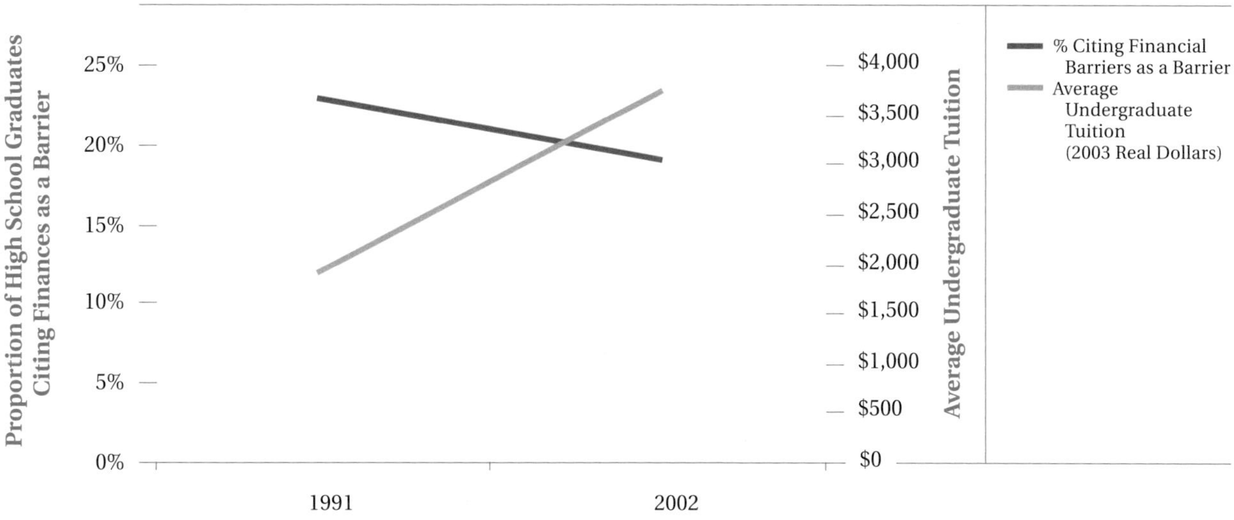

Source: Statistics Canada's Annual Tuition and Additional Fees Survey; Foley, Why Stop After High School?; and Finnie and Laporte, Student Loans and Access to Post-Secondary Education.

to aspire to a college education than a university education, which means that on average they would face lower financial barriers than their higher-SES counterparts.

Cash Constraints

Cash constraints are the most difficult of the three barriers to examine due to the lack of relevant data. While significant efforts have been made recently to examine student income and expenditure patterns, no historical data on student income exist to permit a rigorous analysis of costs and resources. What has been examined in some detail is the relationship between tuition and student loan maxima, which, although not exactly the same, is a closely related issue.

There is no evidence to support the claim that there is a cash constraint because students are simply unable to get loans. In *PEPS*, only 0.1% of high school graduates without post-secondary experience said that their reason for non-attendance was that they could not get a student loan. The more important cash constraint, it would seem, is whether or not a student can get an assistance package of sufficient size to permit him or her to engage in full-time studies.

Hemingway (2003) has looked at the decreasing ability of student loans to meet rising student costs, especially for students from rural areas who must relocate in order to attend post-secondary education. This decrease in the purchasing power of student loans has occurred because, in the nine provinces where the Canada Student Loans Program operates, tuition has risen steadily in recent years while the maximum student loan level has remained constant since 1994. In Quebec, the converse is true: tuition has remained stable but maximum assistance levels have risen with inflation. In both Ontario and Nova Scotia, average tuition now takes up more than half of the value of a student loan, leaving less than $4,500 per year (or less than $600 per month) to cover living expenses. The erosion of the purchasing power of student loans is shown in Figure 3.IV.3.

With respect to cash constraint analysis, Corak *et al* (2003) studied data from the now-abandoned *Survey of Consumer Finances* and noted that the correlation between family income and university attendance dropped dramatically at about the same time that student assistance limits were raised substantially in 1994. On this basis, Corak hypothesizes that an easing of cash constraints (an increase

Figure 3.IV.3—Undergraduate Tuition as a Percentage of the Maximum Student Loan for Single Students without Dependants from 1994 to 2003

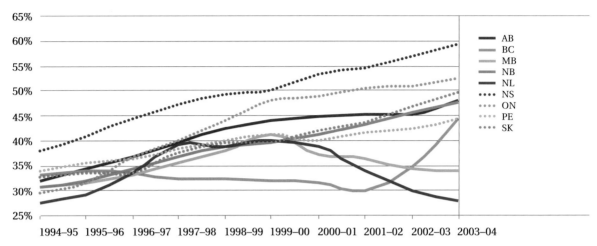

Source: Statistics Canada's Annual Tuition and Additional Fee Survey; author's calculations.

in student loans) reduces barriers to enrolment for youth from low-income families. Corak also notes that university access rates for youth from upper-middle income ($75,000–100,000 per year) families decreased in the mid-1990s. Since these students tend not to have access to student loans, a corollary of this argument is that rises in tuition will compromise access to education for those who have no access to loans. However, because the timing of the reduction in the correlation between family income and university attendance does not correspond

exactly to the timing of the increase in student loans, this hypothesis—while plausible—must still be regarded as unproven.

Debt Aversion

There is an assumption in much of the student financial assistance literature that young people from low-income families are particularly affected by an aversion to debt. Yet this assumption is not actually supported by empirical data. In a 1995 Ekos

Figure 3.IV.4 — Correlation Between Tuition Fees and Post-Secondary Participation From 1984 to 1997

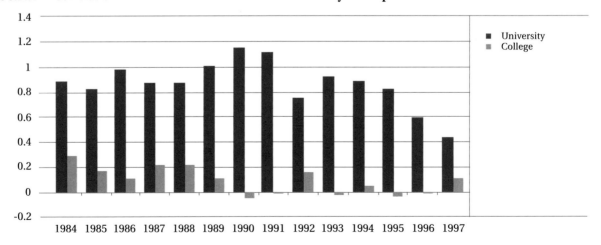

Source: Corak et al, *Family Income and Post-Secondary Participation.*

poll, low-income respondents were slightly *more* likely than respondents from middle- and upper-income groups to answer "yes" to the following question: "If you could, would you borrow money in order to finance studies that would upgrade your skills and lead to higher income?" There are two reasons why this might be the case. First, low-income families have greater difficulties than others obtaining credit and therefore are less likely to refuse credit when it is freely available (as is the case with student loans). Second, a number of studies (Lawrance 1991, Becker and Mulligan 1997, Shapiro 1997, Mayer 1997) examining individuals' "time preferences" (i.e., the premium they will pay for having a good or service in the present rather than in the future) have suggested that individuals' time horizons are shorter as income decreases. In colloquial terms, this means that as income falls, people are more likely to want "one in the hand" rather than "two in the bush" and are thus more concerned with obtaining goods or income in the present than they are with the future trade-offs of their actions. This again suggests that people from low-income backgrounds may be *more* likely to take on debt for educational purposes, not less.

PEPS has produced some interesting evidence on the subject of debt aversion. Finnie and Laporte (2003) have reported that among youth who did not go on to post-secondary studies, 6.6% (about 2% of

Figure 3.IV.6 — Educational Status of Young Canadians Saying They Are Unwilling to Borrow Money for Their Education

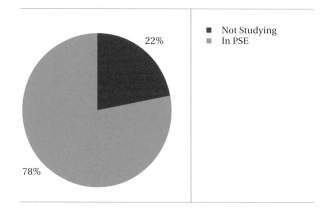

Source: Finnie and Laporte, *Student Loans and Access to Post-Secondary Education.*

all survey respondents) said they did not go because they were not willing to take out a student loan. A far greater percentage of respondents who expressed an aversion to debt actually *did* pursue post-secondary studies (10.1% of these students, or about 7% of all survey respondents, said they were unwilling to take a loan). Among all those expressing an unwillingness to take on debt, those who actually did attend post-secondary education therefore outnumber those who had not attended post-secondary education by factor of 3.5 to 1. These data are displayed in Figures 3.IV.5 and 3.IV.6.

The Finnie-Laporte evidence suggests that debt aversion accounts for approximately one-third of all reported financial barriers, and that 2% of all Canadian youth are deterred from pursuing post-secondary education by debt aversion. Further examination of the *PEPS* data reveals that this group is divided more or less evenly between those who refuse on principle to borrow anything for their education and those who are simply concerned that they would have to borrow too much. This suggests that debt aversion is to a considerable extent a "first dollar" problem and cannot be eliminated without switching to an entirely grant-based system of student assistance.

Figure 3.IV.5 — Percentage of Post-Secondary Students and Non-Attendees Reporting an Unwillingness to Borrow

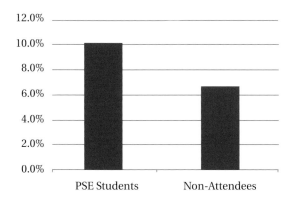

Source: Finnie and Laporte, *Student Loans and Access to Post-Secondary Education.*

V. Motivation/Interest Barriers

As noted in Section 3.II, the most frequently cited reasons why secondary school graduates do not continue to post-secondary education are related to lack of interest or motivation. Unfortunately, existing data cannot address the question of *why* individuals lack interest in post-secondary studies. Is it perhaps because it costs too much (a financial reason in disguise?). Or because they do not enjoy spending time in classrooms (a possible academic barrier in disguise)?

It is therefore not clear how these motivational reasons should be interpreted. After all, if one is not *interested* in post-secondary education, can one really say that there is a barrier to pursuing it? There is a strong and credible case for saying no, or at least for suggesting that some of the people grouped under this barrier are misclassified. It is important to note, however, that given the apparently disproportional effects of interest/motivation on low-income students, removing them from the access equation is essentially the same as saying that even in a world without financial and academic barriers, students from low-income families would be under-represented in post-secondary education.

One set of non-academic, non-financial barriers to education that has consistently been identified in the literature regarding access to education are what might be termed "informational" barriers. Broadly speaking, informational barriers are those for which the "rational" cost-benefit calculation regarding post-secondary education commonly assumed in an orthodox human capital model is distorted by one of three factors:

- *a faulty knowledge or understanding of real post-secondary costs and benefits* (i.e., the individual's expectations about costs and benefits do not reflect reality)

- *differences in what people include in the costs and benefits calculation* (e.g., some people include social costs, such as the psychological price of leaving friends, family, etc., in their calculation of costs)

- *differences in the method of evaluating costs and benefits* (i.e., some people have higher "discount" rates, placing a greater emphasis than economic theory would predict on short-term costs and a lesser emphasis on long-term benefits).

With respect to the first issue, *faulty knowledge or understanding of real post-secondary costs and benefits*, the Canada Millennium Scholarship Foundation has recently produced some significant and troubling data. Public opinion research conducted for the Foundation by Ipsos-Reid in the summer of 2003 shows that the average Canadian overestimates the cost of tuition and significantly underestimates the benefits of a degree. Moreover, the survey found that the extent of the mis-estimation varied inversely with income; that is, low-income Canadians were both more likely to misestimate the cost and the benefits of a university education and to misestimate by a greater degree. In fact, a substantial number of lower-income Canadians appear to believe that university graduates make *less* than high school graduates. The results of this survey are shown in Table 3.V.1.

Table 3.V.1 — Canadians' Perceptions of University Costs and Benefits in 2003

	Average Reported Value	Median Reported Value	"True" Value
Cost of tuition (annual)	$7,774	$4,889	$3,737
Graduates' average annual income	$42,389	$39,967	$61,823

Source: Ipsos-Reid's *Canadians' Attitudes Towards Financing Post-Secondary Education.*

In theory, this reported misestimation has serious implications for access to education. According to human capital theory, people decide to invest in human capital when the benefits of doing so (i.e., the financial returns) outweigh the costs (in this case, tuition plus foregone income). With respect to pursuing post-secondary studies, this human capital equation is usually shown in a diagram such as the one used in Figures 3.V.1, .2 and .3, with the assumption that an individual will choose to go to post-secondary education if the benefits (area A) are greater than the costs (areas B and C).

Figure 3.V.1 shows the human capital equation using the "true" values of university tuition and average university graduates' salaries. In this instance, it is clear that university is a good investment for the average student, with a financial benefit equal to almost 12 times the cost. However, when one enters the data regarding *perceived* costs and benefits, the equation changes considerably. Since Canadians overestimate tuition and underestimate benefits, the perceived lifetime benefits are barely 2.5 times the costs (see Figure 3.V.2). Among low-income Canadians, this figure drops to a mere 1.6 times the cost (see Figure 3.V.3). Spread over a working life of 30 years, this implies an annual return of less than 2% per year, which is hardly a fantastic investment. In short, based on low-income Canadians' own reported views of the costs and benefits of a university education, their lack of interest in university education might be described as completely rational.

While these results are interesting, their applicability may be limited, because the Ipsos-Reid survey from which they are drawn surveyed a random sample of all Canadians rather than a more relevant sample of families with children finishing secondary school. However, as Junor and Usher (2002) have shown, much of the information prospective students receive about post-secondary education comes from family and friends. Hence, if we know that low-income families in general are badly informed about post-secondary education, then it is likely that their children are similarly badly informed, at least in relation to their wealthier peers.

However, as Wolf (2002) points out, not knowing the specifics about educational choices doesn't prevent parents from making choices that are generally rational. The same Ipsos-Reid study also shows that when asked *directly* whether or not university education is a "good investment," over 90% of Canadians reply "yes," with very little variation by income. This suggests that lower-income Canadians understand that university graduates have a certain valuable status within society, even if they do not believe that this status is accompanied by much in the way of monetary rewards. Finally, while there is definite proof both that people misestimate costs and benefits and that misestimation is inversely related to income, there is not yet any direct evidence that this problem is a major deterrent to the pursuit of education, despite the theoretical argument that it is.

There is a considerable amount of literature in the United States on the second informational barrier, *differences in what people include in the costs and benefits calculation*, but little or no data in the Canadian context. The standard human capital model suggests that costs are simply tuition and foregone income. A more nuanced interpretation, ably presented by Rasmussen (2003), suggests that for some there are also psychological costs (e.g., being

Figure 3.V.1 — "True" University Cost-Benefit Analysis

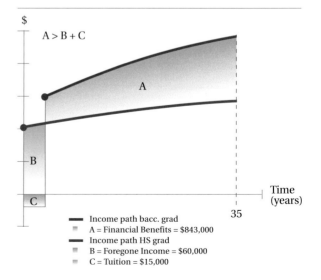

away from family and friends, confronting the unknown), *social costs* (e.g., estrangement from peers and feelings of abandonment in a new campus culture), *cultural costs* (e.g., for minority students attending institutions offering little understanding of their own cultures and attitudes), *physical costs* (e.g., stress incurred when moving to college for the first time) and *spiritual costs* (incurred by exposure to belief systems alien to one's own). In short, when post-secondary education challenges one's personal norms, the "cost" will be higher and therefore a greater deterrent will exist. One may posit that these costs will be higher among "first-generation" students who have not had the benefit of informed parental coaching and advice about post-secondary studies. And since first-generation students tend to be from low-SES families, this conceivably has an important effect on the participation rates of low-income students. While there is virtually no Canadian data on this subject, this type of analysis certainly accords with the educational experiences of Canada's Aboriginal Peoples (see Malataest 2003 for some of the most recent literature on Canadian Aboriginal Peoples and post-secondary education).

Finally, there is the question of how *differences in the method of evaluating costs and benefits* might affect participation, once the "inputs" of cost and

benefit are determined (however discovered and regardless of the accuracy). Manski (1991) in the United States and Andres-Bellamy (1993) in Canada have both cast doubt on the notion that high school students deciding to go to post-secondary studies are in fact "adolescent econometricians," calculating costs and benefits in a "rational" manner, taking into account net present value, and so forth.

Methodologically, this is a very difficult question to examine, and there are very little hard data on this point in either Canada or the U.S. to provide clarification. Research from other fields of social science can be of use, however. As noted in Section 3.IV, some evidence suggests that people with low incomes have different temporal preferences—that is, they have a different investment "horizon"—than people with higher, more stable incomes. While this characteristic should make them less debt averse, and hence more likely to borrow for their education, it should also make them less likely to want to make *any* investment whose return comes only in the long term. Given that post-secondary education—and particularly a university-level degree—is a good that takes a considerable amount of time both to acquire and to show a positive return on investment, this necessarily acts as a deterrent to education for lower-income Canadians.

Figure 3.V.2 — Perceived University Cost-Benefit Analysis for All Canadians

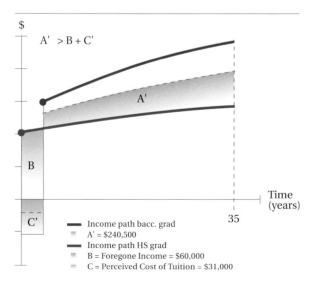

Figure 3.V.3 — Perceived University Cost-Benefit Analysis for Low-Income Canadians

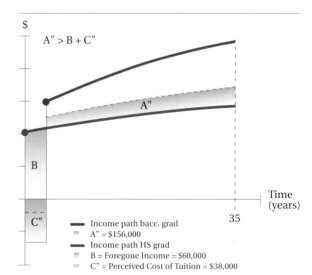

As this short tour of the related literature shows, there is some evidence to show that background characteristics have an effect on the assumptions with which young people approach post-secondary education, and there is a solid theoretical reason to think that these may have an effect on access to post-secondary studies. For the moment, however, that is all there is. Direct evidence to link informational barriers to the problem of access among low-income individuals is virtually non-existent, largely because no major study has tried to explore the issue directly.

Financial Barriers to Particular Programs of Study

Given the rapid increase in fees in professional programs, there has been an understandable concern that higher fees have resulted in access to these programs being increasingly restricted to the children of the country's elite. The only thorough study of this issue to date is Dhalla et. al (2002), which studies the change in the social composition of first-year medical students over the 1990s. Dhalla's results clearly show that, on average, first-year medical students now come from a more privileged background than they did in 1990. However, these same results also show that this trend was true both at medical schools where tuition had increased dramatically and those where it had remained frozen; there was no statistically significant difference between the two. It is therefore difficult to ascribe the increasingly "elite" nature of medical schools to finances. In fact, the pattern of change is more consistent with an explanation based on academic barriers. As demand increased for a limited supply of medical school spaces, academic requirements rose and (for reasons described above in section 3.III) this will usually tend to benefit those from higher-income backgrounds.

VI. Conclusion

In the first three chapters of the book, we have examined how people make decisions about their education, looked at who actually goes to post-secondary education and considered the evidence regarding various barriers to education. What, in sum, can be concluded from this mass of data and analysis about access to education and barriers thereto?

Canada has a very open and accessible system of post-secondary education. Canada's community colleges, in particular, are highly egalitarian institutions. Women and students with disabilities appear to be over-represented among Canadian post-secondary students. The main problems in access appear to occur at the university level and relate mostly to Aboriginal students and students from low-income families, who attend university at much lower rates than more affluent, non-Aboriginal youth.

In this chapter, we have made a number of counter-intuitive observations:

- Despite the fact that access problems primarily affect the poor, the reasons why these youth are systematically under-represented do not appear to be primarily financial in nature.

- Financial barriers, in relative terms, appear to be more of a barrier to high-income non-attendees than low-income non-attendees (nevertheless, in absolute terms there are considerably more of the latter than the former).

- Academic barriers do not appear to be more prevalent among the poor than the rich, even though there is a strong positive relationship between marks and family income.

We have also seen, perhaps less surprisingly, that young people from low-income backgrounds are simply less likely to *want* to pursue post-secondary education for reasons that may have to do with inadequate information but which are, for the moment, unknown. The explanation may simply relate to cultural capital—while most people strive to better

their lives, their horizons are limited by the lifestyle and values they observe as a child. As a result, lower-income youth may simply not see post-secondary education as a choice—not because of the cost, perceived cost, or their academic ability, but simply because it is not part of their worldview.

An extension of this argument may also help to clarify our other counter-intuitive observations; that long before financial issues come into the picture, low-income youth either self-select out of post-secondary education altogether or begin to opt for the version of post-secondary education that is less academically demanding (i.e., non-university-related college programs). This self-selection process, as we saw in Chapter 1, appears to take place primarily based on secondary school marks. If this is true, then perhaps the best way to look at access barriers is not through a prism of family income but one of high school marks (a measure which overlaps considerably—but not entirely—with income). Table 3.VI.1 shows how secondary school achievement affects barriers to post-secondary education.

A key to understanding problems of access to post-secondary education is to understand that there are two very separate systems of post-secondary education in Canada—i.e., universities (which for the purpose of this analysis included university-bound CEGEP-students and university-related programs at Alberta and B.C. colleges) and community colleges—which cater to two very different clienteles. Youth with higher secondary school marks are more likely to come from higher income strata while those with lower marks are more likely to come from lower income strata. The former tend to desire a university education, and the latter tend to desire a college education. These two groups do not compete against each other for access to post-secondary spaces. They are, in effect, in two separate "markets."

The main problems in access appear to occur at the university level and relate mostly to Aboriginal Peoples and students from low-income families, who attend university at much lower rates than more affluent, non-Aboriginal youth.

Table 3.VI.1—Barriers to Education Based on Secondary School Marks

	Youth With High Secondary School Marks	Youth with Low Secondary School Marks
Income bracket	Predominantly above average	Predominantly average or below average
Level of parental education	Predominantly above average	Predominantly near average
Desired education	University (includes university-bound CEGEP programs, and university-stream programs in AB and BC colleges)	College
Level of selectivity faced	High	Low
Cost per year of study	$4,500	$1,600
Number of years of study	4	2
Likelihood of moving away from home	Moderate	Low
Foregone income (@$15K/yr)	$60,000	$30,000

People in these two education markets face two very different sets of barriers. Those with high marks and who want to go to university have higher tuition costs (both in cost per year and length of program), higher overall cost (e.g., they are likelier to have to move to attend their institution of choice), higher foregone income and face greater academic selectivity than low academic achievers who want to go to college. This sounds daunting, but since high academic achievers tend, on average, to come from higher-income families and have access to more financial and cultural capital, they are well equipped to face these barriers.

Those with lower secondary school marks, on the other hand, face lower barriers in terms of cost, distance to institution and academic selectivity. This should mean that they are more successful in reaching their academic goals, but lower average levels of financial resources and cultural capital mean that this is not always true. The reason that the "barrier" levels for high- and low-SES students is not that they are equally capable of overcoming the same barriers, but rather that they are equally capable of overcoming *different* barriers. The relatively surprising results with respect to financial barriers is therefore not because so many low-income students are capable of paying for university; it is because so many low-income students self-select out of the university stream for *non-financial reasons*.

This prism on access provided in Table 3.VI.1 offers insight into most of the basic inequalities in access in Canadian post-secondary education. It also highlights some difficult public policy challenges for people interested in improving access to education for low-income students. From a policy perspective, it is not clear that student assistance or tuition policies alone can do very much to change this basic differences between those with high secondary marks and low secondary marks, and hence these methods are unlikely to change the underlying demand for university education, which is where the real inequality lies.

Financial assistance programs are very good at helping people overcome financial barriers, which are significant at the university level. They are also very good at ensuring that high academic achievers can meet the higher financial burden required to obtain the university education they desire. However, unless more low-income youth become high academic achievers and start to *desire* a university education, the effectiveness of financial policies to favour access to university will be limited. Conversely, if government policies to improve academic achievement among students from lower-income backgrounds prove successful, student financial assistance will *increase* in importance, as universities will have a larger and needier clientele to assist.

Chapter 4

Costs and Resources

Chapter 4

Costs and Resources

I. Introduction

In any discussion about access to education, student finances must obviously be considered. The affordability of a student's education is dependent on both the direct costs (such as tuition, ancillary fees and mandatory supplies) and the indirect costs (living expenses such as housing and childcare). It also depends upon a student's resources, which come primarily from labour income, transfers from parents and family, and various forms of borrowing. This chapter looks at both students' costs and resources, and, while it does not offer any definite conclusions about the affordability of post-secondary education, provides a significant amount of information about student income, expenditures and living conditions.

Figure 4.I.1 — Total Academic Year Expenditures by Type

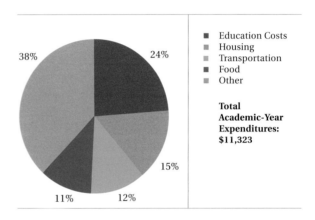

- Education Costs
- Housing
- Transportation
- Food
- Other

Total Academic-Year Expenditures: $11,323

Source: Ekos Research's *Making Ends Meet*.

Student Expenditures

The best examination of student spending patterns to date is Ekos Research's *Making Ends Meet*, which was the first report to use data from the *2001–02 Student Income-Expenditure Survey*, conducted by Ekos on behalf of the Canada Millennium Scholarship Foundation. Figure 4.I.1 shows the average distribution of costs among all students, according to this survey.

Among all students, education costs (i.e., tuition and fees, as well as direct educational costs such as books) comprise 24% of total expenditures. These costs are examined in more detail in Section II (*tuition fees*), Section III (*ancillary fees*), Section IV (*textbook costs*) and Section V (*mandatory supply and equipment costs*). After a brief levelling off at the turn of the decade, tuition fees have once again started rising at a rate considerably faster than the

rate of inflation. This is particularly true of certain professional programs, which in many jurisdictions are now deregulated. In addition, many professional programs have high mandatory supply and equipment costs; the results of a new survey on the costs of mandatory supplies and equipment in select professional programs at universities across the country show that these costs can actually exceed the cost of tuition in some disciplines and/or universities.

Housing costs are dealt with in Section VI. Roughly half of all students live with their parents, and these students incur few, if any, housing costs. For the other half of the student body, housing costs are at least as high as tuition costs. However, housing costs vary enormously across the country by community (although on-campus housing shows less regional variation in rental prices).

Just as housing costs vary substantially between those who live with their parents and those who do not, transportation costs vary substantially between those who have cars and those who do not (over 40% of students interviewed for the *2001–02 Student Income-Expenditure Survey* indicated that they had a car). Data on public and private *transportation costs* are presented in Section VIII.

Other costs include *childcare costs* (Section VII), and miscellaneous costs (Section IX), including food. These other costs make up nearly 40% of all student expenses.

Student Income

Costs are only one side of the affordability equation; it is equally important to examine students' available resources. Figure 4.I.2 shows the aggregate distribution of income among all students, according to the Ekos survey.

By far the most important source of student income is *employment*, which is examined in Section XI of this chapter. In addition to presenting data on employment status, hours worked and income, this

Figure 4.I.2 — Sources of Student Income

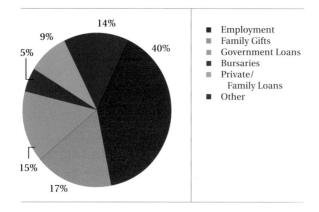

Source: Ekos Research's *Making Ends Meet.*

section also examines the impact of student employment on patterns of study and academic results. New data relating to the distribution of employment income among certain key demographic groups (i.e., Aboriginal students, students with children and students with disabilities) are also presented.

Section X looks at *family contributions*. Although these are roughly as common in terms of incidence as parental contributions, they are, on average, smaller in terms of value. Roughly two-thirds of all family assistance comes from parents; the balance comes in equal proportions from spouses, other family members, or both.

Student assistance programs—both loans and grants—are the subject of Section XII. Contrary to common belief, student income from government loans has been declining sharply over the past seven years. The reasons for this decline will be examined in the section. The average government student assistance grant has decreased in size as well, although the *number of grants* available has more than doubled in the past six years.

In addition to these three primary sources of income, there are a number of *miscellaneous* types of income. Some of these are repayable forms of assistance, such as private bank loans and loans from families. Some are non-repayable forms of income: e.g., scholarships, investment and pension income, and money from special sources such as First Nations band funding and grants for students with disabilities. All of these sources of income are examined in Section XIII.

Finally, it is worth remembering that perception is at least as important as reality in terms of policy development. Section XIV is therefore devoted to *students' perceptions* of their financial situation.

II. Tuition Fees

One of the most discussed and debated subjects in Canadian education is that of rising post-secondary tuition costs. The basic trend in university tuition for full-time students is fairly simple. Nationally, during the 1980s real tuition levels were basically stagnant at about $1,800 (in 2003 real dollars) for both graduate and undergraduate students. In 1990, the situation began to change when the province of Quebec—which had frozen tuition fees since the 1960s—announced a tuition increase of approximately 130% over two years. While Quebec froze its fees again shortly thereafter, tuition in other jurisdictions continued to rise throughout most of the 1990s. Between 1989–90 and 1997–98, undergraduate tuition doubled. Outside Quebec, tuition has continued to rise since then, albeit at a more moderate pace.

Since governments tend to pursue similar tuition policies in both the college and university sectors, the story in the college sector is almost identical to that in the university sector. The only major difference is that Quebec essentially kept its college system free for users throughout the period in question. As a result, the gap between average college and university fees increased in absolute

dollars, although the ratio of annual costs has remained more or less constant at 2 to 1.

The driving force behind tuition growth is not a mystery. At the start of the 1990s, all institutions were heavily reliant on transfers from provincial governments for their operating funds. This left them vulnerable to the cuts in government revenue that occurred as part of a general program of fiscal tightening during the 1990s. Even after government finances improved, increased labour costs and higher student enrolment meant that institutions required increased revenue sources to prevent a decline in the quality of education offered. This search for new revenue sources inevitably included fee-paying students.

Towards the end of the 1990s, the rate of tuition increases in core disciplines began to slow. In real dollars, tuition for core arts and sciences programs did not increase at all between 1998 and 2002. The small increase in average national tuition in the past year is due almost entirely to a major policy shift in British Columbia. Tuition growth in graduate studies and professional programs, however, has continued unabated. Until the mid-1990s, graduate and undergraduate students were paying roughly the same

Figure 4.II.1 — Canadian Tuition Rates From 1989 to 2004 (in 2003 Real Dollars)

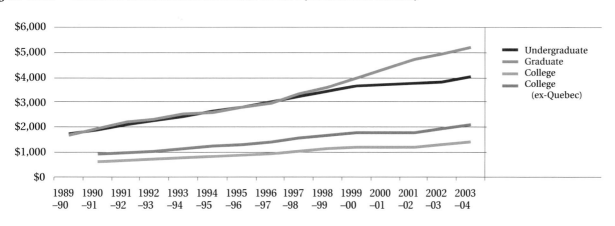

Source: Statistics Canada's Annual Tuition and Additional Fee Survey and the Manitoba Council on Post-Secondary Education.

Figure 4.II.2 — Undergraduate Tuition Rates From 1989–90 to 2003–04 (in 2003 Real Dollars)

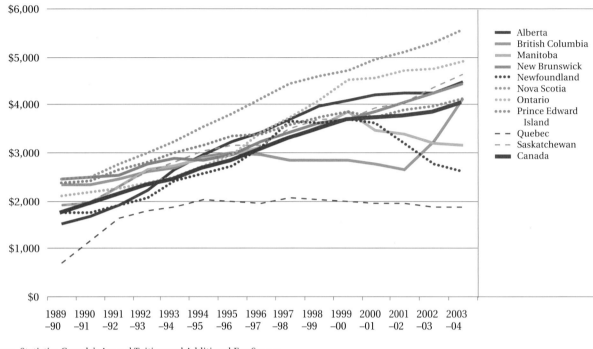

Source: Statistics Canada's Annual Tuition and Additional Fee Survey.

average tuition—but in 2003–04, the national average for undergraduate tuition was $4,025, compared to $5,199 for graduate tuition.[1]

The recent slowing of tuition increases is a result of deliberate government policy. In Quebec, a tuition freeze has been in place for Quebec residents since the start of the 1995–96 academic year. Prince Edward Island, Manitoba, and Newfoundland and Labrador have all in effect had tuition freezes in place for the past five years, and the latter two provinces have also introduced tuition roll-backs of 10% and 25%, respectively. Ontario, which has the country's largest student population and has a major effect on the national average, has limited undergraduate tuition increases to 2% per year since 1999–2000 (and has recently announced a two-year freeze on tuition for 2004–05 and 2005–06). B.C. maintained a seven-year tuition freeze from 1994–95, followed by a 5% roll-back for the 2001–02 academic year; a subsequent change of government resulted in a policy U-turn which caused under-graduate tuition to climb by 56% in two years.

Alberta, Saskatchewan, Nova Scotia and New Brunswick are therefore the only jurisdictions in which annual tuition increases have been both significant and regular over the past five years.

Broadly speaking, the tuition trends observed in the university sector over the past 20 years were also evident at the community college level. However, data on college tuition are not as reliable as data on university tuition, because Statistics Canada does not publish or even collect data on the subject. The best available data on the subject, displayed in Figure 4.II.3, come from a survey conducted by the Manitoba Council on Post-Secondary Education.

Increases in tuition have in some instances been much more dramatic in the college sector than in the university sector. For instance, tuition in Alberta colleges has nearly quadrupled since 1990. In New Brunswick, tuition tripled in the space of four years, from $938 in 1995–96 to $2,645 in 1999–2000.

The annual Manitoba survey of college fees on which Figure 4.II.3 is based (which, in the absence of any Statistics Canada tracking of the subject,

---

1.   "Undergraduate" tuition is the weighted average across all institutions of tuition fees from the faculties of agriculture, architecture, arts, commerce, dentistry, education, engineering, household science, law, medicine, music and science.

Figure 4.II.3 — College Tuition Rates in 1990–1991 and 2003–04 (in Real 2003 Dollars)ᵃ

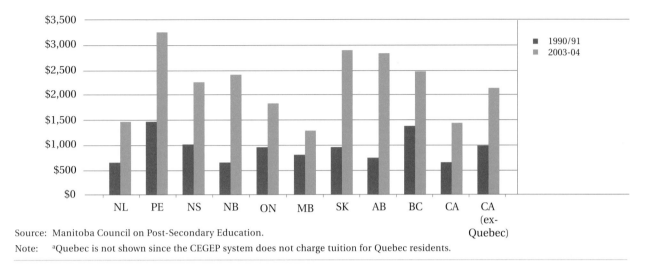

Source: Manitoba Council on Post-Secondary Education.

Note: ᵃQuebec is not shown since the CEGEP system does not charge tuition for Quebec residents.

is the only "national" survey available) records "average" college tuition based on reports from provincial governments. A closer examination of college tuition fees reveals that these "averages" are in fact probably the "mode" (i.e., the most frequently charged) tuition fee. Most institutions offer a selection of courses for which annual tuition is considerably higher than the mode tuition. Unfortunately, no enrolment data are available in order to accurately weight tuition to include both the cheap "mode" courses and the more expensive ones. In other words, Figure 4.II.3 likely understates

college tuition somewhat, but it is impossible to know by how much.

Figures 4.II.1 and .2 showed a major slowing in the rate of tuition increases at the end of the 1990s. While this was true for the main undergraduate programs which account for the vast majority of students, the opposite was true for tuition in professional programs. Tuition fees for these programs are steadily being deregulated across the country (except in Ontario, where fees have recently been re-regulated, although not reduced). While professional and non-direct-entry programs have

Figure 4.II.4 — Tuition Rates for Selected Programs From 1989 to 2004 (in 2003 Real Dollars)

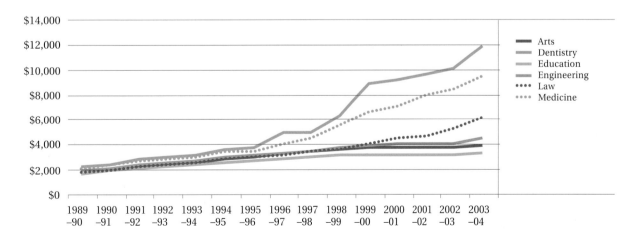

Source: Statistics Canada's Annual Tuition and Additional Fee Survey.

Figure 4.II.5 — Dentistry Tuition Fees From 1989 to 2004 (in 2003 Real Dollars)

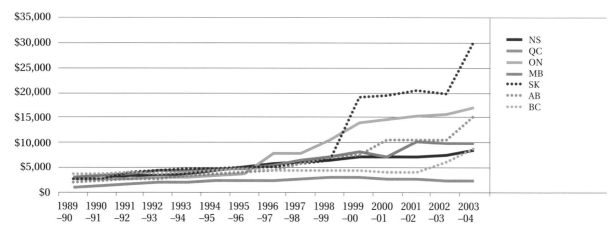

Source: Statistics Canada's Annual Tuition and Additional Fee Survey.

always tended to have higher tuition fees than "core" faculties such as arts, the gap in tuition rates grew enormously during the latter half of the 1990s, particularly for dentistry and medicine. Students in some of these programs are now being asked to pay two or three times the average tuition fees for an undergraduate arts or education student. Figure 4.II.4 shows the changes in tuition rates for selected undergraduate programs.

The national averages for each program or field of study mask substantial variations in fees at the provincial and institutional levels. The national tuition averages for dentistry, medicine and law would be considerably higher were it not for the tuition freezes covering all disciplines in Quebec since the early 1990s.

Figure 4.II.5 shows provincial tuition averages for dentistry. For the last several years there have been strong, steady increases in tuition in Ontario (and, to a lesser extent, Alberta). In contrast to the situation in other undergraduate fields, Nova Scotia has maintained relatively low tuition rates compared to other jurisdictions. Saskatchewan dentistry students' tuition costs tripled in 1998 after a policy change at the University of Saskatchewan. The

University of Saskatchewan recently raised fees again by 50%, to just over $30,000 per year; however, 15 of the 40 student spaces are reserved exclusively for Saskatchewan students, each of whom receive a bursary of $18,000 per year. In net terms, therefore, Saskatchewan has a $30,000 out-of-province fee and a lower in-province fee, and the average *real* rate of tuition is somewhat lower than that portrayed in Figure 4.II.5.

Tuition rises in the faculty of medicine (Figure 4.II.6) have been steadier than those in dentistry—growth, while substantial, is not punctuated by sharp increases in specific years. Growth has been strongest in Ontario, where tuition has tripled in the past six years. Also, B.C. has seen very significant increases since 2001–02, with fees more than doubling in only two years. Alberta, Manitoba, Quebec, and Newfoundland and Labrador have essentially had freezes on medical tuition for the past several years.

Provincial tuition averages for law students do not vary as much as they do for students in medicine and dentistry. Basically, tuition rates for law follow the same pattern as tuition rates for arts programs. Specifically, most provinces are close to the national average, while B.C. and Quebec are significantly

Figure 4.II.6 — Medicine Tuition Fees From 1989 to 2004 (in 2003 Real Dollars)

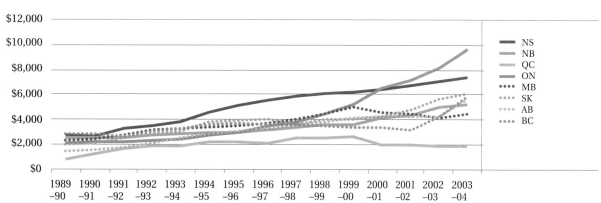

Source: Statistics Canada's Annual Tuition and Additional Fee Survey.

below the average and Nova Scotia and Ontario are significantly higher. As is also the case for medicine, Ontario universities have led the way in tuition increases for law programs. Sharp increases have recently occurred in both Alberta and B.C. Figure 4.II.7 shows the provincial tuition averages for law faculties across the country.

While the average tuition rates for professional programs may seem startling, it is important to keep in mind that their overall impact on access to post-

secondary education is relatively minimal. Students in law, medicine and dentistry together account for less than 3% of all university students in Canada and, moreover, are frequently eligible for very large need-based institutional assistance. Large tuition fee increases in these fields are therefore unlikely to have a major impact on the affordability of post-secondary studies for university students as a whole—but they may have a major impact on the *perception* of affordability.

Figure 4.II.7 — Law Tuition Fees from 1989 to 2004 (in 2003 Real Dollars)

Source: Statistics Canada's Annual Tuition and Additional Fee Survey.

III. Ancillary Fees

Ancillary fees are generally defined as any mandatory and/or universal fee levied by an institution that is not part of the basic tuition charge. These include fees for athletics, health services, student associations, information technology and other fees directly levied by the institution. They do *not* include student fees that are course- or activity-specific (such as lab fees, field trip costs, course supplies and equipment), as these do not meet the "mandatory and/or universal" criterion.

Like tuition, ancillary fees have grown substantially across the country in recent years as institutions try to create new revenue streams in order to meet rising costs. Unlike tuition, however, the student body has some control over the level of certain ancillary fees, since many of them (e.g., student association fees, student health and dental insurance plans, universal bus passes) are initiated by students and help to fund student-run organizations.

Data in this section come from Statistics Canada, which tracks ancillary fees at universities across Canada, and the Canada Millennium Scholarship *Foundation's 2003 College Student Fee Survey*. Due to

As a rule of thumb, ancillary fees are between 10% and 15% of tuition costs at colleges and universities.

the significant variation in the number and types of ancillary fees paid by full-time students at each institution, Statistics Canada only tracks the highest and lowest fees paid by students.

As a rule of thumb, ancillary fees are between 10% and 15% of tuition costs at colleges and universities. Students from low-cost university faculties such as arts or education tend to pay lower fees than their counterparts in professional and graduate programs (e.g., dentistry, medicine). The same appears to be true at Canadian colleges—for instance, students in programs such as digital arts and dental hygiene tend to pay higher fees than students in early childhood education, public relations and so on.

Figure 4.III.1 shows the trends in the average lower and upper range of ancillary fees at Canadian universities. Both the lower and upper range of fees increased by over 90% in the past decade. The majority of these increases, however, have come in the past five years as the content of ancillary fees expands. As noted earlier, the higher value tends to be paid by students in professional and graduate

Figure 4.III.1 — Average University Ancillary Fee Ranges in Canada (in 2003 Real Dollars)

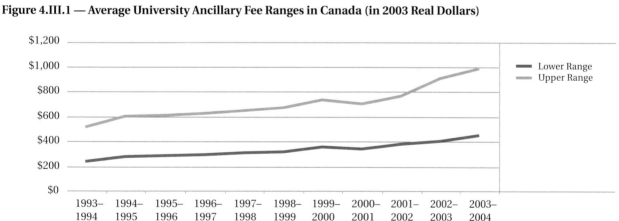

Source: Statistics Canada's Annual Tuition and Additional Fee Survey.

Figure 4.III.2 — College Ancillary Fee Ranges in Canada (in 2003 Real Dollars)

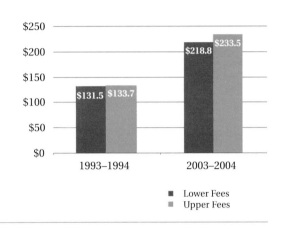

Source: Canada Millennium Scholarship Foundation's *2003 College Fee Survey.*

programs. As such, the trend shown here parallels the overall trend in tuition: charges at professional schools such as dentistry and medicine tend to be increasing much faster than charges in other faculties.

The ancillary fee structure at Canadian colleges is not completely comparable to that of universities, nor is it tracked by Statistics Canada. College

students are required to pay athletic, recreation and student association fees; however, these are often substantially lower than those paid by their university counterparts. There are two main reasons for this difference. First, college ancillary fees are more varied by program and academic stream (e.g., university transfer, upgrading) than those at universities. Second, few college student associations offer their student body services such as health, dental or transit plans—these plans are often expensive, and their absence helps explain the lower fees at colleges.

As is the case for universities, ancillary fees increased over the past decade at Canadian colleges. In real dollars, the lower range of fees increased by 66% and the upper range increased by 75%. Figure 4.III.2 shows the ancillary fee range changes at Canadian colleges during the past decade.

While ancillary fees can vary by province, it is generally true that they represent a significant proportion of all mandatory fees, including tuition. This is definitely the case in Quebec, where a decade-long tuition freeze means that ancillary fees now make up over 26% of the overall mandatory fee at universities. The national average for ancillary

Figure 4.III.3 — University Undergraduate Tuition and Additional Fees by Province in 2003–04

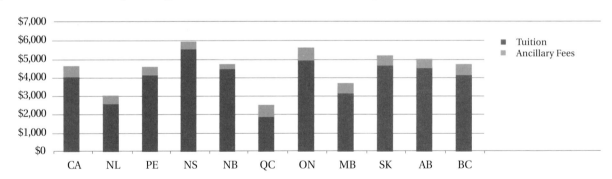

Source: Statistics Canada's Annual Tuition and Additional Fee Survey.

fees is 14% of the cost of tuition. Figure 4.III.3 displays combined university undergraduate tuition and ancillary fees by province.

As shown in Figure 4.III.4, ancillary fees in colleges represent the same percentage of the overall mandatory fee as they do in universities—i.e., 14%. Unfortunately, data limitations on college enrolment do not allow for a proper weighting to be done, and an accurate college provincial fee calculation is therefore not possible. However, in Quebec, the ancillary fee is the *only* mandatory institution fee paid by students.

Canadian universities display significant variation in both the median level and the ranges of their ancillary fees. Students can pay anywhere from $122 to $1,518, depending on their institution and program; even within the same institution, ancillary fee rates can vary by as much as $1,400. At some institutions, ancillary fees represent only a small proportion of tuition fees (e.g., Brandon University and Memorial University), while at others, ancillary fees may amount to over half of tuition (e.g., Concordia University and McGill University).

Figure 4.III.4 — National College Tuition and Additional Fees in 2003–04

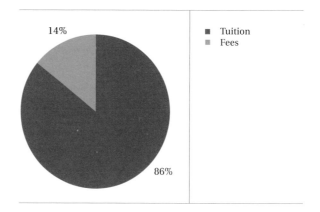

Source: 2003 Council on Post-Secondary Education and the Canada Millennium Scholarship Foundation's *2003 College Fee Survey.*

Unfortunately, data limitations do not allow for a full institutional ancillary fee comparison at the college level. Table 4.III.1 shows the lower and upper ranges for ancillary fees at Canadian universities in 2003–04.

Table 4.III.1 — Lower and Upper Ranges for Ancillary Fees at Canadian Universities in 2003–04

Institution	Lower Range	Higher Range	Fee Midpoint[a]	Tuition Fees (Faculty of Arts)	Ancillary Fees as a % of Tuition
Memorial University of Newfoundland	$416	$484	$450	$2,550	18%
University of Prince Edward Island			$468	$4,110	11%
Acadia University			$356	$7,012	5%
Mount St. Vincent University			$608	$4,850	13%
St. Mary's University	$134	$289	$212	$4,945	4%
Dalhousie University			$478	$5,220	9%
St. Francis Xavier University			$574	$5,310	11%
Université de Moncton			$405	$4,126	10%
University of New Brunswick			$321	$4,510	7%
St. Thomas University			$114	$3,695	3%
Mount Allison University			$187	$5,360	3%
Bishop's University			$763	$1,668	46%
Université Laval	$313	$368	$341	$1,668	20%
McGill University	$1,037	$1,518	$1,278	$1,668	77%
Université de Montréal	$390	$440	$415	$1,668	25%
Université de Sherbrooke	$256	$276	$266	$1,668	16%
Université de Québec	$747	$821	$784	$1,668	47%
Concordia University	$914	$1,049	$982	$1,680	58%
Brock University	$122	$485	$304	$4,184	7%
Carleton University	$518	$603	$561	$4,152	14%
Guelph University			$753	$4,184	18%
Lakehead University			$423	$4,140	10%
Laurentian University	$261	$264	$263	$4,184	6%
McMaster University	$667	$936	$802	$4,133	19%
Nipissing University			$747	$3,950	19%
University of Ottawa	$592	$674	$633	$4,163	15%
Queen's University	$725	$813	$769	$4,193	18%
Ryerson University			$485	$4,262	11%
University of Toronto	$213	$1,479	$846	$4,184	20%
Trent University			$820	$4,184	20%
University of Waterloo			$406	$4,194	10%
University of Western Ontario			$824	$4,140	20%
Wilfred Laurier University	$444	$659	$552	$4,184	13%
University of Windsor	$598	$822	$710	$4,084	17%
York University	$846	$1,018	$932	$4,181	22%
Brandon University			$327	$2,730	12%
University of Manitoba	$317	$881	$599	$2,700	22%
University of Winnipeg			$344	$2,786	12%
University of Regina	$630	$892	$761	$3,890	20%
University of Saskatchewan	$383	$498	$441	$4,356	10%
University of Alberta			$473	$4,309	11%
University of Calgary			$549	$4,380	13%
University of Lethbridge			$846	$3,730	23%
University of British Columbia	$576	$859	$719	$3,459	21%
University of Northern British Columbia			$596	$3,663	16%
Simon Fraser University			$463	$3,711	12%
University of Victoria			$463	$3,635	13%

Source: Statistics Canada's Annual Tuition and Additional Fee Survey.

Note: [a] In many institutions, there exists only one single fee.

IV. Textbooks

In addition to tuition fees and ancillary fees, students are also required to purchase textbooks for their studies. These costs can vary widely from institution to institution and from discipline to discipline, and in most cases depend on the specific combination of classes chosen. Students can also reduce their textbook costs by buying used textbooks (if they are available), sharing textbooks or using versions on reserve at the library. In some cases, professors eschew the use of textbooks in favour of "coursepacks" (bound compilations of articles and/or short monographs).

There is no systematic collection of administrative data on the cost of textbooks. Nor has any survey asked students specifically about the cost of textbook purchases. The best evidence currently available concerning the cost of textbooks is found in a survey conducted by the Canada Millennium Scholarship Foundation in the summer of 2003, which took a "basket of goods" approach to measuring textbook costs.

The textbook study collected information on required textbook costs in over 1,000 courses at Canadian universities. The study covered 18 universities (at least one per province), four faculties (arts, science, engineering and commerce/business administration) and, within each faculty, five departments or programs were chosen.[2] In each department or program at each institution, five one-term courses representing a balance of required and elective courses across all years of undergraduate study were chosen at random. The cost of required textbooks in each of these courses was then determined either by checking the bookstore Web site or through on-site visits to each institution. The result is therefore an average of the costs of required textbooks, and hence a reflection of *expected* expenditure by students, rather than a detailed listing of what students actually spend.

Table 4.IV.1 shows the highlights of the aggregate data from the Foundation's survey. The table makes clear that there is significant variation in the costs of required reading between disciplines. However, most courses of study appear to fall in or near the range of

Table 4.IV.1 — Average Cost of Required Textbooks per One-Term Course in Fall 2003

Discipline	Average Cost per One-Term Course (Number of Courses Surveyed)
Arts/Social Sciences	
Economics	$93.15 (79 courses)
Literature	$90.82 (76 courses)
History	$80.43 (80 courses)
Political science	$70.83 (74 courses)
Sociology	$85.06 (77 courses)
Average Arts/Social Sciences	*$84.16 (386 courses)*
Sciences	
Biology	$97.13 (80 courses)
Chemistry	$108.11 (82 courses)
Computer science	$90.46 (82 courses)
Physical geography	$74.06 (59 courses)
Mathematics	$89.98 (82 courses)
Average Sciences	*$92.99 (385 courses)*
Engineering	
Chemical	$90.15 (56 courses)
Civil	$113.05 (70 courses)
Computer science	$102.87 (45 courses)
Electrical engineering	$109.56 (75 courses)
Mechanical engineering	$97.00 (75 courses)
Average Engineering	*$103.06 (321 courses)*
Commerce/Business	
Finance	$90.99 (59 courses)
"General" business	$94.53 (63 courses)
Human resource management	$79.42 (39 courses)
International business	$84.09 (40 courses)
Marketing	$91.32 (55 courses)
Average Commerce/Business	*$89.09 (256 courses)*

Source: Canada Millennium Scholarship Foundation Textbook Survey 2003

$80 to $90 per course. Engineering texts are considerably higher (mostly over $100) and political science texts are considerably lower ($71). Chemistry textbooks also exceed $100 in cost, but this figure is somewhat inflated by the fact that the survey includes the costs of purchasing molecular model kits.

---

2.   The 18 universities were: British Columbia, Victoria, Alberta, Calgary, Saskatchewan, Manitoba, Toronto, Waterloo, Trent, McMaster, Ottawa, McGill, Laval, Montréal (including Polytechnique and HEC), Moncton, Dalhousie, Prince Edward Island and Memorial.

The survey results displayed in the above table are of course average costs only. Significant variation naturally exists among universities, even within the same discipline. It is not possible to tell on the basis of samples of this size whether or not certain institutions require a more expensive set of textbooks in general or whether the sample is simply too limited to generalize. As a result, this survey does not look at similarities or differences at the institutional level.

It is worth noting, however, that Francophone universities appear to have a very different approach to textbook purchasing than the rest of the country's institutions. The average cost of arts textbooks is $50 per course at the Université de Moncton and Université Laval and $40 per class at the Université de Montréal, compared to the national average of $84.16. In sciences, the Université de Moncton's costs are similar to those of Anglophone universities, but Université Laval's per-course average cost is half the national average and the Université de Montréal's is barely a third. A noticeable but much smaller difference also exists in engineering and commerce departments at Francophone universities. This is a result of Francophone universities requiring students to purchase fewer textbooks on average than their English university counterparts.

V. Supplies and Equipment

In addition to textbooks, another indirect cost students face is of supplies and equipment. Calculating the costs of supplies and equipment in a consistent manner is difficult not only because they can vary so much from class to class (not to mention from institution to institution), but also because they are not necessarily mandatory. Generally, however, these additional costs amount to hundreds of dollars per student.

University students in professional or second-entry university programs in particular often face large additional costs in the form of supplies and equipment that are not optional. The same is true for college students in professional programs (e.g., aviation, graphic design, dental hygiene). Institutions do not include these expenses as part of tuition, yet they are mandatory because it is impossible for students in these programs to complete their studies without them.

The best evidence currently available concerning the cost of supplies and equipment for students in professional or specialty programs is found in a survey conducted by the Canada Millennium Scholarship Foundation in the summer of 2003. A total of 163 university program units at various universities and university colleges across the country were questioned, and 87% of these programs provided the requested data. A total of 159 college program units at various colleges and university colleges across the country were questioned, and almost 91% of these programs provided the requested data.

In the interest of brevity, only those post-secondary programs with substantial associated indirect costs were included. Programs with occasional course-specific fees (such as biology, which sometimes charges fees for field trips) or programs for which a few universities have exceptional costs (e.g., mandatory laptop purchase fees in some management programs) were not included.[3]

Table 4.V.1 — Mandatory Supply and Equipment Cost Ranges in Selected Professional Programs at Canadian Universities in 2003–04

Program	Number of Institutions Offering Program	Number of Respondents	Cost Range for Each Year of Study for Supplies and Equipment
Agriculture[a]	9	6	$0–$435
Architecture	8	7	$0–$4,290
Dentistry[b]	10	10	$0–$24,300
Film studies	18	17	$0–$6,700
Fine arts[c]			
A) Drawing/Painting	23	21	$0–$5,000
B) Photography	12	11	$0–$4,800
C) Sculpture	13	11	$0–$8,000
Forestry	8	7	$0–$4,300
Medicine[b]	16	12	$0–$8,100
Nursing[b]	32	31	$0–$2,000
Pharmacy[a]	8	7	$0–$1,600
Optometry	2	2	$335–$3,400
Veterinary medicine[a]	4	3	$0–$270

Source: 2003 Canada Millennium Scholarship Foundation survey.

Note: [a] The majority of respondents reported no additional cost per year of study.

    [b] Additional costs for medicine, dentistry and nursing students may include mandatory immunizations (some of which are not covered by provincial healthcare plans) and/or CPR course costs. These costs have not been included in the quoted amounts.

    [c] Additional costs for fine arts degrees fluctuate considerably, since expenses are based on the level of concentration (i.e., minor, major, honours) and are assessed by course.

3.   It is worth noting that several professional programs require students to purchase a laptop for their studies. Also, some college programs, such as information technology and graphic design, encourage students to invest in a laptop.

Table 4.V.1 details the subjects and the cost range for mandatory supplies and equipment for various university programs, several of which were identified as having substantial indirect costs associated with the pursuit of a diploma or degree (e.g., costs exceeding $1,000 per year for many students). These fees are all in addition to basic tuition and ancillary fees.

The equipment fees for some of the college and university disciplines shown in Tables 4.V.1 and .2 are quite large and merit further explanation. In many programs (e.g., medicine, massage therapy, dentistry, optometry, architecture), the equipment purchased by students can be used when individuals complete their studies and enter the workforce (dental instruments, stethoscopes, etc.). In that sense, many of these fees could be seen as "investments" rather than "charges." In some health programs (dentistry, dental hygiene and massage therapy), students are required to write professional examinations, and this is included in the final year of study costs. Finally, students in some aviation programs have to pay for flying lessons.

The cost of mandatory supplies and equipment can also vary significantly within a program according to the year of study. Tables 4.V.3 to .8 examine in more detail the additional supply and equipment fees in college, university, and university college programs for which there is a significant variation in these fees by program year.

Table 4.V.2 — Mandatory Supply and Equipment Cost Ranges in Selected Programs at Canadian Colleges in 2003–04

Program	Number of Institutions Offering Program	Number of Respondents	Cost Range for Each Year of Study for Supplies and Equipment
Applied visual arts	41	40	$0–$5,400
Aviation[a]	18	18	$100–$36,000
Drafting	8	8	$0–$1,000
Human services (A–B)			
A) Nursing	31	30	$0–$2,800
B) Massage therapy	8[b]	5	$260–$2,000
Computer technology[c]	35	32	$50–$5,000
Dental hygiene	17	16	$300–$3,820

Source: 2003 Canada Millennium Scholarship Foundation survey.

Note: [a] Some institutions listed flight-training hours in the cost for students.

[b] This number does not include any career colleges that offer massage therapy (e.g., CDI College).

[c] In some programs, studying computer technology requires the purchase of a laptop.

Table 4.V.3 — Mandatory Supply and Equipment Costs by Institution in 2003–04: Architecture

Institution	Additional Fees by Program Year [a,b]				
	First	Second	Third	Fourth	Fifth
Carleton University	$1,000–$1,500	N/R	N/R	N/R	N/A
Dalhousie University	$2,750	$2,400	N/R	N/R	N/A
Université Laval	$4,000	$1,000	$1,000	N/A	N/A
University of Manitoba	$4,220	$3,480	$4,290	N/A	N/A
McGill University	N/R	N/R	N/R	N/R	N/R
Université de Montréal	$0	$0	$0	N/A	N/A
Ryerson University	$2,500	$2,100	$2,000	$2,800	N/A
University of Waterloo	$1,550	$2,200	$2,200	$1,800	$3,800

Source: 2003 Canada Millennium Scholarship Foundation survey.

Note: [a] N/R signifies that the institution chose not to report any fees.

[b] N/A signifies that some of these programs are only three or four years in length.

Table 4.V.4 — Mandatory Supply and Equipment Costs by Institution in 2003–04: Aviation

Institution	Additional Fees by Program Year	
	First	Second
Algonquin College[a]	$26,000	$36,000
Canadore College	$0	$0
Castlegar College	$13,400	$26,000
Centennial College	$200	$200
Confederation College	$345	$0
University College of the Fraser Valley	$4,220	$3,480
Humber College	$960	$960
Medicine Hat College	$0	$0
Mount Royal College	$1,600	$1,600
Northern Alberta Institute of Technology (NAIT)[b]	$2,000	$0
Nova Scotia Community College	$1,500	$1,500
Okanagan University College[c]	$20,000	$19,550
Red Deer College	$275	$0
Red River Community College	$1,200	$1,200
Sault College	$90	$0
Seneca College[d]	$430	$430
Sheridan College	$700	$700
Southern Alberta Institute of Technology	$4,000	$1,000

Source: 2003 Canada Millennium Scholarship Foundation survey.

Note: [a] Algonquin College fees include flying lessons and the purchase of a headset, flight computers and maps.

[b] NAIT requires aviation students to purchase a computer.

[c] Okanagan University College includes all costs associated with the program, including flight training, practice lessons and equipment.

[d] Seneca College's total equipment cost is $860, which has been divided by two to indicate the cost per year for the first two years of the program; however, there are two additional years for which the costs had not yet been approved by the institution at the time of the survey, and which are thus not included here.

Table 4.V.5 — Mandatory Supply and Equipment Costs by Institution in 2003–04: Dentistry

Institution	Additional Fees by Program Year			
	First	Second	Third	Fourth
University of Alberta	$11,070	$8,170	$3,170	$2,920
Dalhousie University	$6,300	$4,500	$1,420	$1,200
Université Laval	$8,300	$3,500	$3,200	$0
University of Manitoba	$9,040	$9,640	$2,150	$1,160
McGill University	$210	$17,320	$8,000	$3,000
Université de Montréal	$7,120	$8,800	$4,080	$540
University of Saskatchewan	$11,000	$7,900	$2,300	$2,500
University of Toronto	$5,950	$5,970	$3,210	$3,780
University of British Columbia[a]	$24,300	$22,200	$21,490	$22,190
University of Western Ontario	$6,670	$6,940	$6,460	$6,010

Source: 2003 Canada Millennium Scholarship Foundation survey.

Note: [a] The University of British Columbia has a clinical lease cost of $17,000 per academic year for each dental student.

Table 4.V.6 — Mandatory Supply and Equipment Costs by Institution in 2003–04: Dental Hygiene

Institution	Additional Fees by Program Year[a,b]	
	First	Second
Algonquin College[c]	$1,500	$2,200
College Boréal	$3,750	$650
Canadore College	$250	$350
CÉGEP de Drummondville	$300	$300
John Abbott College	$830–$1,000	$830–$1,000
Confederation College	$345	$345
Fanshawe College	$3,700	$2,500
George Brown College	$1,600	$3,820
Georgian College[d]	$460	$460
College of New Caledonia	N/R	N/R
Niagara College	$1,000	$1,000
Nova Scotia Community College	N/R	N/R
Red River Community College	$1,125	N/A
Saskatchewan Institute of Applied Science and Technology	$2,970	$1,100
Southern Alberta Institute of Technology	$1,550	$1,550
St. Clair College[c]	$2,000	$2,500
Vancouver Community College[c]	$2,200	$3,500

Source: 2003 Canada Millennium Scholarship Foundation survey.

Note: [a] N/R signifies that the institution reported no fee.

[b] Some colleges did not separate books from supplies and equipment.

[c] Algonquin, St. Clair and Vancouver Community College all include the price of examinations in the last year of the program.

[d] Dental hygiene at Georgian College is a five-semester program and there is a $230 fee per semester.

Table 4.V.7 — Mandatory Supply and Equipment Costs by Institution in 2003–04: Medicine

Institution	Additional Fees by Program Year [a,b]			
	First	Second	Third	Fourth
University of Alberta	$5,390	$3,030	$2,330	$5,260
University of Calgary	N/R	N/R	N/R	N/R
Dalhousie University	$2,000	$0	$0	$0
Université Laval	$100	$0	$0	$0
University of Manitoba	$2,040	$1,840	$0	$500
McGill University	$850	$0	$0	$0
McMaster University	$3,550	$2,180	$8,080	N/A
Memorial University	N/R	N/R	N/R	N/R
Université de Montréal	$2,500	$0	$0	$0
University of Ottawa[c]	$3,740	$0	$0	$0
Queen's University	N/R	N/R	N/R	N/R
University of Saskatchewan	$4,270	$670	$5,020	$11,220
Université de Sherbrooke	N/R	N/R	N/R	N/R
University of Toronto	$600	$500	$500	$500
University of British Columbia	$3,630	$1,060	$1,290	$7,990
University of Western Ontario	$700	$700	$850	$850

Source: 2003 Canada Millennium Scholarship Foundation survey.
Note: [a] N/R signifies that the institution chose not to report any fees.
[b] N/A signifies that the program is only three years in length.
[c] This cost includes the purchase of a laptop.

Table 4.V.8 — Mandatory Supply and Equipment Costs by Institution in 2003–04: Optometry

Institution	Additional Fees by Program Year			
	First	Second	Third	Fourth
Université de Montréal	$3,000	$3,000	$340	$2,500
University of Waterloo	$6,730	$7,510	$2,050	$500

Source: 2003 Canada Millennium Scholarship Foundation survey.

As the preceding tables reveal, mandatory equipment costs vary as much as—if not more than—tuition and ancillary fees across the country. For instance, cumulative equipment costs for dentistry students can vary from about $13,400 at Dalhousie University to over $90,000 at the University of British Columbia. In medicine programs, equipment costs can vary by over $10,000 per student over the course of a degree.

It should be noted that public student assistance programs do not provide nearly enough financial aid to cover the cost of the investment required by students in faculties such as aviation, architecture, dentistry, medicine and optometry. As a result, students in these faculties have almost no choice but to use private student loan schemes to cover their expenses.

VI. Housing

Roughly half of all post-secondary students live away from their parents' place(s) of residence. For these students, housing represents a cost which is at least as significant as the cost of tuition—if not more so.

The most common living arrangement for students is to live with family members: over half of all students in Canadian universities and colleges live with their parents. Most of the remainder of students live in various types of off-campus housing and therefore face the same rental market as other Canadians. A few older students manage to avoid the rental market entirely by owning their own homes; according to data from the Canadian Undergraduate Survey Consortium and the Canadian College Student Survey Consortium, roughly 8% of students—predominantly older ones studying part-time—own their own homes. On-campus housing

is largely (but not exclusively) a university phenomenon and is largely confined to students in the first year or two of studies. Only at a few liberal arts colleges, such as Acadia University and Mount Allison University, is on-campus housing the chosen housing arrangement of the majority of students.

The likelihood of a student living at home diminishes as he or she gets older. The proportion of students living with roommates increases until the age of 22 and declines thereafter. Among students aged 26 or older, two-thirds either live alone or with a spouse. Figure 4.VI.1 breaks down student living arrangements by age.

Results from the *2001–2002 Student Income-Expenditure Survey* show that, on average, students spend $270 per month on housing. Excluding students who live at home (most of whom are living

Table 4.VI.1 — Student Living Arrangements by Region

Living Arrangement	Atlantic	B.C.	Ontario	Prairies	Quebec	Canada
Alone, with dependants	5.4%	4.8%	2.5%	2.1%	2.0%	3.0%
Alone, no dependants	5.4%	7.7%	8.5%	9.7%	12.5%	9.2%
Living with parent(s)	54.2%	49.3%	51.4%	52.2%	50.4%	51.3%
Living with roommates	17.3%	18.8%	20.6%	20.2%	19.6%	19.7%
Living with spouse	14.3%	14.5%	13.9%	12.4%	13.9%	13.7%
Other	3.6%	4.8%	3.2%	3.5%	1.7%	3.2%

Source: Canada Millennium Scholarship Foundation's *2001–02 Student Income-Expenditure Survey.*

Figure 4.VI.1 — Student Living Arrangements by Age

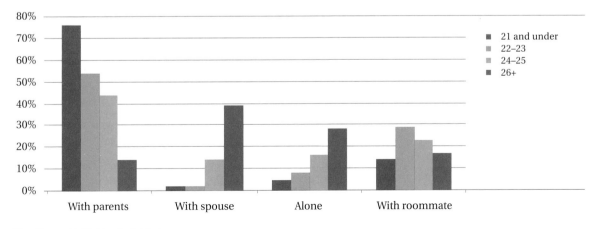

Source: Ekos Research's *Making Ends Meet.*

Figure 4.VI.2 — Cost of Housing by Living Arrangement

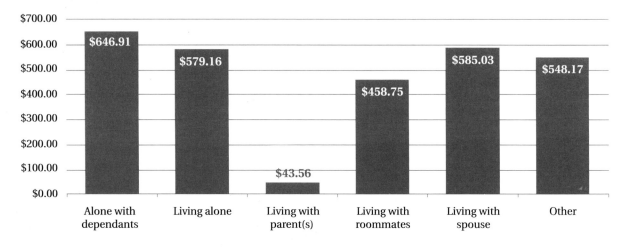

Source: Canada Millennium Scholarship Foundation's *2001–02 Student Income-Expenditure Survey.*

rent-free, although they do, on average, make a contribution of $44 per month to the family coffers), this figure rises to $534 per month. Figure 4.VI.2 shows the cost of housing among students by the type of living arrangement.

The costs of housing also vary tremendously according to the conditions of the local housing market. Students in Ontario face the country's highest rental rates, particularly now that Ottawa has passed Vancouver to become the country's second most expensive rental market. Table 4.VI.2 outlines the cost of a one-bedroom apartment in Canadian cities with multiple post-secondary institutions. While this table serves as a useful "rough guide" to the differences in costs that students face in different cities, individual students will of course have highly variable housing costs, according to the size of apartment they choose to rent, the number of room-mates with whom rent is shared, and so forth.

On-Campus Housing:
Student Residence Costs

Living on campus is a popular option for many students entering post-secondary education for the first time, especially those who are coming to large urban universities from rural or remote areas. On-campus housing provides first-year students

with a sense of community and security, both of which have been demonstrated to have positive effects in terms of student retention.

According to the Canadian Undergraduate Survey Consortium's 2001 *Survey of First-Year Students,* 29% of all first-year students live in on-campus housing, a figure which represents 58% of all first-year students living away from their parents. While the proportion of students who live in residence is relatively high in the first year of studies, the number tends to drop off sharply thereafter as students move off campus.

Most institutions offer a wide variety of housing options to students. These options include dormitory-style housing (each student has a sleeping room but shares the bathroom, kitchen and living room), multiple-room apartments and townhouses (especially common for mature and married students). The price of on-campus housing can vary significantly depending on the type of living arrangement and institution.

Most university residences offer residents a meal plan or a selection of such plans, in addition to room costs. In many cases, purchase of a meal plan is mandatory for students living in residence. Table 4.VI.3 outlines the cost of meal plans at various Canadian post-secondary institutions. The lower and upper ranges reflect the different available meal

Table 4.VI.2 — Rental Rates for One-Bedroom Apartments in Major Canadian Cities in 2003

City	Average Monthly Rent	Cost of Rent for 8 Months
St. John's, NL	$510	$4,080
Charlottetown, PE	$463	$3,704
Halifax, NS	$572	$4,576
Fredericton, NB	$519	$4,152
Moncton, NB	$463	$3,704
Montreal, QC	$505	$4,040
Quebec, QC	$489	$3,912
Sherbrooke, QC	$369	$2,952
Trois-Rivières, QC	$370	$2,960
Guelph, ON	$707	$5,656
Hamilton, ON	$627	$5,016
Kingston, ON	$598	$4,784
Kitchener, ON	$638	$5,104
London, ON	$566	$4,528
North Bay, ON	$499	$3,992
Ottawa, ON	$767	$6,136
Peterborough, ON	$600	$4,800
St. Catharines, ON	$582	$4,656
Sudbury, ON	$513	$4,104
Thunder Bay, ON	$532	$4,256
Toronto, ON	$891	$7,128
Windsor, ON	$637	$5,096
Brandon, MB	$440	$3,520
Winnipeg, MB	$490	$3,920
Regina, SK	$480	$3,840
Saskatoon, SK	$461	$3,688
Calgary, AB	$656	$5,248
Edmonton, AB	$575	$4,600
Lethbridge, AB	$523	$4,184
Prince George, BC	$474	$3,792
Vancouver, BC	$743	$5,944
Victoria, BC	$605	$4,840

Source: Canada Mortgage and Housing Corporation

plan options. It should be noted that these costs are reported on an annual basis, but in most cases the meal plans cover only the eight months of the regular fall and winter terms.

A comparison of Tables 4.VI.2 and .3 shows that there is very little correlation between the cost of off- and on-campus housing in a given metropolitan area. In Ontario, London is one of the cheaper cities in terms of average rental rates—yet the University of Western Ontario's residence fees are among the highest in the country. Montreal's McGill University is an even more extreme example of an expensive residence system in an inexpensive city. But contrary examples can be found, too; Ryerson University, York University and the University of Toronto all have residence options that appear to be considerably cheaper than accommodation in the surrounding community, as does Vancouver's Simon Fraser University. Costs may also vary according to the level of services provided, such as the frequency of cleaning services and the presence of telephone and Internet connections.

Table 4.VI.3 — University Residence and Meal Plan Costs in 2003–04

Institution	Room Only		Meal Plan Only	
	Lower Range	Upper Range	Lower Range	Upper Range
Memorial University of Newfoundland	$1,556	$1,924	$2,484	$2,800
University of Prince Edward Island	$3,142	$3,840	$2,818	$3,208
Acadia University	$3,042	$5,699	$2,415	$2,739
University College of Cape Breton	$2,600	$3,250	$680	$2,530
Dalhousie University			$6,604[a]	$7,839[a]
University of King's College			$6,829[a]	$7,439[a]
Mount St. Vincent University			$5,430[a]	$5,960[a]
Nova Scotia Agricultural College	$3,340	$4,240	$1,840	$1,930
Université Sainte-Anne	$2,491	$3,133	$2,805	$2,915
St. Francis Xavier University	$2,995	$3,740	$2,700	$3,000
St. Mary's University	$3,409	$5,145		
Université de Moncton	$1,682	$4,296	$1,600	$2,276
Mount Allison University	$3,230	$4,000	$2,970	$3,020
University of New Brunswick	$3,350	$5,285	$2,115	$2,360
Université Laval	$1,720	$1,720		
St. Thomas University	$2,800	$4,220	$2,200	$2,650
Bishop's University	$2,800	$4,200	$2,176	$3,240
Concordia University	$2,800	$2,800		
McGill University[b]	$4,356	$7,183	$7,154[a]	$9,544[a]
Université de Montréal	$2,112	$2,256		
École des Hautes Études Commerciales	$1,856	$3,792		
Université de Québec	$1,480	$3,440		
Université de Sherbrooke	$1,328	$2,680	$1,240	$1,760
Brock University	$3,120	$4,320	$2,925	$3,335
University of Guelph	$3,332	$4,600	$2,430	$3,530
Lakehead University	$3,348	$4,631	$2,708	$2,708
Laurentian University	$2,690	$3,295	$500	$2,100
McMaster University	$3,070	$4,395	$1,600	$3,075
Nipissing University	$3,195	$3,630		
University of Ottawa	$3,259	$4,678	$1,625	$2,250
Queen's University	$4,466	$4,466	$3,600	$3,600
Ryerson University	$3,036	$6,069	$1,685	$2,680
University of Toronto	$3,280	$5,344	$1,400	$3,400
Trent University	$3,674	$3,674	$3,157	$3,157
University of Waterloo	$3,828	$4,646	$2,650	$2,650
University of Western Ontario	$4,845	$5,280	$1,300	$2,000
Wilfrid Laurier University	$2,916	$4,975	$2,506	$2,925
University of Windsor	$3,650	$4,337	$998	$3,350
York University	$3,393	$4,794	$1,610	$2,400
Brandon University	$2,143	$3,375	$2,440	$2,440
Canadian Mennonite University	$1,398	$4,128	$2,910	$2,910
University of Manitoba	$4,005	$4,005	$2,750	$2,975
University of Winnipeg	$2,800	$2,800		
University of Regina	$2,818	$3,296		
University of Saskatchewan	$1,470	$2,000	$3,263	$3,263
University of Alberta	$1,840	$3,688	$1,600	$2,200
University of Calgary	$1,580	$5,860	$2,010	$3,240
University of Lethbridge	$1,616	$5,136	$1,820	$2,342
University of British Columbia	$3,138	$3,769	$2,540	$3,223
University of Northern British Columbia	$3,446	$3,977		
Simon Fraser University	$2,230	$3,782		
University of Victoria	$2,160	$2,880	$2,840	$2,840

Source: Statistics Canada's Annual Tuition and Additional Fee Survey (data for Dalhousie University, King's College, Mount St. Vincent University and McGill University were collected independently by the authors).

Note: [a] The price indicated is for both room and board.

[b] Rent at McGill University's room-only residences is for an 11-month lease, rather than the standard 8-month lease.

VII. Childcare Costs

As noted in Section 2.X, approximately 8% of undergraduates and 17% of college students have children. Between a third and a half of these children are too young to attend school, and their parents therefore require some form of childcare. Childcare costs are not a particularly common student expenditure, but they are certainly very significant to those students who have to pay them.

Determining the true cost of childcare for students is not easy. Childcare costs vary considerably according to the childcare facility and the age of the child (i.e., the younger the child, the more expensive the care). To grossly oversimplify a very complex market, the "sticker" price of daycare for most pre-schoolers is in the range of $500 to $700 a month nationally, and more for toddlers under 18 months. This is an enormous expense for students, few of whom earn much more than this amount per month during the school year. However, few students are likely paying the sticker price. Most students benefit from income-based provincial subsidies for childcare. In most of the country, individuals with incomes of less than $15,000 receive maximum daycare subsidies, and those with incomes of up to $30,000 still receive partial subsidies; these figures tend to be somewhat lower in Atlantic Canada.

The *2001–02 Student Income-Expenditure Survey* provides an interesting snapshot of childcare costs. Of the 1,549 original participants in the survey, 170 (10.9%) indicated that they had children. Of those students with dependants who completed the survey for the entire year, 36% said they had no childcare costs, which presumably means their

Approximately 8% of undergraduates and 17% of college students have children. Between a third and a half of these children are too young to attend school, and their parents therefore require some form of childcare.

children were either old enough not to require childcare or their childcare needs are taken care of by other family members. Men with children were more likely than women not to report any childcare costs (45% vs. 30%). With respect to the 64% who reported having childcare costs, these students on average spent $187 per month on childcare, or $1,495 for an eight-month academic year. While this is still a significant amount of money for students, the Ekos figures suggest that average student childcare costs are much lower than the sticker price of childcare would suggest.

The Ekos data also suggest that the student loan maximum allowances for childcare (shown in Table 4.VII.1), which may appear inadequate when compared to the sticker price, in fact are quite adequate to meet the needs of most students. According to the *Student Income-Expenditure Survey*, only 12% of parents with children in care face childcare costs exceeding $400 per month, which in most parts of the country is comfortably covered by student assistance allowances.

The fact that the allowances for assistance are adequate does not mean that no financial barrier exists as a result of childcare costs. As noted elsewhere in this book, student aid maxima may prevent students from getting the money that even government student aid systems say they "need." Nevertheless, the data suggest that the availability and convenience of childcare is probably a more problematic issue than its cost (see Section 2.X for a further discussion of the ratio of daycare spaces to students with dependants).

Table 4.VII.1 — Maximum Student Assistance Allowances for Childcare by Province in 2003–04

Province	NL	PE	NS	NB	QC	ON	MB	SK	AB	BC
Cost per month	$405	$429	$433	$494	$391 (CSL)/ $100 (AFE)	$357	$460	$440	$430	$778

VIII. Transportation

Recent research has shown that student transportation costs make up a considerably larger portion of student expenditures than is commonly assumed. Average transportation costs for students across Canada are $119 per month or 9% of total expenditures. Table 4.VIII.1 shows average transportation expenditures by region, as reported in the *2001–02 Student Income-Expenditure Survey*.

Table 4.VIII.1 — Average Monthly Transportation Expenditures by Region

Region	Average Monthly Expenditures	Proportion of Students Owning Cars
Atlantic	$91	30.6%
Quebec	$113	35.3%
Ontario	$118	32.0%
Prairies	$120	46.7%
British Columbia	$158	48.8%
Canada	$119	38.3%

Source: Canada Millennium Scholarship Foundation's *2001–02 Student Income-Expenditure Survey.*

As can be determined from a brief glance at Table 4.VIII.1, regional expenditures on transportation are related in part to the proportion of students in the region who own their own cars. Roughly four in ten students own their own cars; two-thirds of these individuals purchased or leased the cars themselves, while the remainder received them as a gift from their parents. The proportion of students owning cars is considerably higher in Western Canada than elsewhere in the country. This can largely be explained by the fact that many of the large Western Canadian universities are suburban "commuter" campuses, poorly served by public transportation, and—in the Prairies at least—have exceptionally cold winters, even by Canadian standards. Car ownership has some important

implications for transportation expenditures. On average, students who own cars have monthly average transportation costs of $185; students who do not own cars have monthly transportation costs of $79.

Public Transportation

The cost of monthly public transportation passes varies considerably across the country, from $50 in Brandon to nearly $100 in Toronto (based on prices in March 2004). However, most Canadian municipalities have a reduced monthly transit pass fee for post-secondary students. In addition, student unions at a few universities have negotiated "collective" student transit passes (often called a "UPass" or "university pass") which are in effect bulk purchase arrangements with their local public transportation provider. These student unions hold referenda to get their members to agree to include the cost of a monthly bus pass in their mandatory student fees; if successful, these unions then purchase thousands or even tens of thousands of transit passes at a reduced rate. This arrangement results in significant savings for the students who use public transport; for those who do not it is simply an addition of $100 or so to their annual tuition bill. These arrangements appear to be increasingly popular: the University of New Brunswick, Université de Sherbrooke, University of Alberta and the University of Northern British Columbia are all, at the time of writing, negotiating similar plans with their respective municipalities to begin in 2004–05. Table 4.VIII.2 shows the cost of monthly public transportation passes in major Canadian cities. While the fee to purchase the passes is collected on a per-semester basis along with other tuition and fees, the table expresses the cost of collective transit passes on a monthly basis for ease of comparison.

Table 4.VIII.2 — Cost of Monthly Public Transportation Passes in Major Canadian Cities in 2003–04

City[a]	Regular Transit Pass	Student Transit Pass	Collective Student Transit Pass
St. John's, NL	$58	$50	None
Halifax, NS	$57	$51	$13.75 (St. Mary's only)
Fredericton, NB[b]	N/A[b]	$38	None
Moncton, NB	$46	$36.50	None
Quebec, QC	$59.90	$42.60	None
Sherbrooke, QC	$53	$42	None
Montreal, QC	$59	$31	None
Trois-Rivières, QC	$52	$43	None
Guelph, ON	$55	$55	$11.52
Hamilton, ON	$65	$65	$8.13
Kingston, ON	$60	$46.25	None
Kitchener, ON	$54	$45.33	None
London, ON	$74	$64	$12.29
North Bay, ON	$75	$60	None
Ottawa, ON	$61.95	$50.25	None
Peterborough, ON	$64	$64	$22.23
St. Catharines, ON	$75	$67.5	$15
Sudbury, ON	$66	$63	None
Thunder Bay, ON	$65	$48.75	None
Toronto, ON	$98.75	$87.00	None
Windsor, ON	$72	$50	None
Brandon, MB	$50	$42	None
Winnipeg, MB	$67	$53.90	None
Regina, SK	$52	$45.50	None
Saskatoon, SK	$51	$42	None
Calgary, AB	$65	$65	$12.50
Edmonton, AB	$59	$54	None
Lethbridge, AB	$49	$45.50	None
Prince George, BC	$48	$32	None
Vancouver, BC[c]	$36/$87/$120	$36/$87/$120	$20 (UBC)/ $23 (SFU)
Victoria, BC	$55	$55	$12.75

Source: Educational Policy Institute Survey of Student Public Transportation Costs

Note: [a] Charlottetown is not included because the University of Prince Edward Island is not on a bus route.

[b] Fredericton does not have a general monthly public buss pass.

[c] Vancouver transit charges vary according to the number of geographic zones covered.

Figure 4.IX.2 — Monthly Student Non-Food Consumption Expenditures by Region

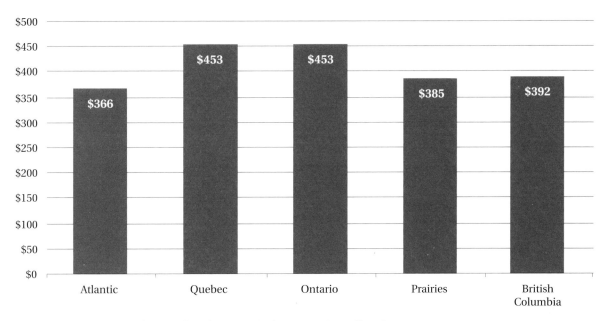

Source: Canada Millennium Scholarship Foundation's *2001–02 Student Income-Expenditure Survey.*

Figure 4.IX.3 – Monthly Student Debt and Investment Expenditures by Region
(Students With Debt and/or Investments Only)

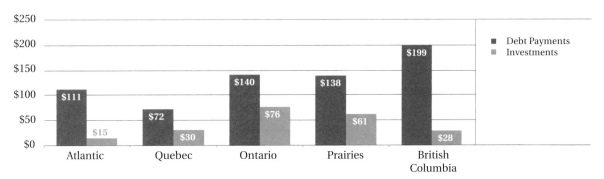

Source: Canada Millennium Scholarship Foundation's *2001–02 Student Income-Expenditure Survey.*

X. Family Contributions

The most common form of financial resource for Canadian students is contributions from family members. The most reliable evidence on this point shows that over 80% of all Canadian students say they receive assistance from a family member at some point during the year. Not all of this money comes from parents; a considerable portion comes from other family members, including spouses. Moreover, many parental contributions are unstable or unpredictable, coming as unexpected or emergency gifts, and a small but significant proportion of parental aid is provided in the form of a loan. This section will look at total family contributions, and then take a more focused look at parental contributions and spousal contributions.

Family Contributions

The most complete survey of student finances in Canada, the *2001–02 Student Income-Expenditure Survey*, shows that four out of five post-secondary students receive money from a family member over the course of a school year. The proportion is higher for younger students just making the transition to post-secondary education (95% among students aged 18 to 19) than for older students. In general, the size of the contribution increases with age, but the

effect is not linear. There are no significant differences in parental support by type of educational institution. Not all assistance from family members comes in the form of a gift; roughly 8% of all family assistance comes in the form of a loan (although presumably these loans are offered on terms that are easier than those for standard loans). Table 4.X.1 shows the incidence and amount of family support.

The Canadian Undergraduate Survey Consortium's *2002 Survey of Undergraduate Students* reports that 54% of undergraduates receive family contributions and that the average contribution is $4,751 per year or approximately $600 per month. For college students, data from the Canadian College Student Survey Consortium's 2003 survey of *Canadian College Student Finances*, while not strictly comparable, show that somewhere between 53% and 70% of college students receive parental assistance.

The CUSC and CCSSC results show considerably lower incidences of parental contributions than those of the *2001–02 Student Income-Expenditure Survey*, which interviewed students on a monthly basis throughout an entire school year. The discrepancy appears to be a product of the way questions were phrased in the various surveys. When the *Student Income-Expenditure Survey* asked students at the start of the year if they expected to

Table 4.X.1 — Incidence and Amount of Family Support

	Incidence of Family Support	Average Annual Amount of Family Support[a]
All Students	81%	$2,683
18- to 19-year-olds	95%	$2,035
20- to 21-year-olds	93%	$2,318
22- to 23-year-olds	83%	$3,045
24- to 25-year-olds	77%	$2,290
26+	60%	$3,484
University students	83%	$2,927
College students	79%	$2,179

Source: Ekos Research's *Making Ends Meet*.

Note: [a] Only those students who receive support are included in this calculation.

Table 4.X.2 — Incidence and Amount of Family Contributions for University Students by Demographic Characteristics

	All Students	Baseline Group[a]	Aboriginal Students	Students With Children	Students With a Disability
Incidence of support	54.4%	57.6%	35.5%	24.6%	53.7%
Average amount of annual support[b]	$4,751	$4,760	$4,766	$3,733	$4,783

Source: Canadian Undergraduate Survey Consortium's 2002 *Survey of Undergraduate Students.*

Note: [a] The "baseline group" here comprises all students other than those with disabilities, with children or of Aboriginal heritage.

   [b] Only those students who receive support are included in this calculation.

receive assistance from their parents over the course of the school year, only 46% said yes. Over the course of the year, an additional 23% of students actually received money from their parents. The discrepancy appears to result mostly from one-time gifts, often received over the December holiday period, and late-year emergency funds. This suggests that surveys which ask questions about contributions on an annual basis are likely to significantly under-report the incidence of parental transfers to students. In addition, those students in the *Student Income-Expenditure Survey* who received parental money but had not reported expecting it at the start of the year on average received considerably less than those who had expected to get parental assistance and in effect "dragged down" the average contribution reported in Table 4.X.1.

The 2002 *Survey of Undergraduate Students* also provides some interesting insight into the different levels of family assistance available to students with different demographic characteristics. Students with

disabilities seem to have the same incidence and amount of family support as the rest of the student population. Aboriginal students are significantly less likely than other students to receive financial support from their families, but those that do receive such assistance receive amounts that are basically identical to those of the student population as a whole. Students with children, on the other hand, are less likely to receive family assistance *and* they receive smaller amounts. Comparable data for college students are not available. Table 4.X.2 shows the incidence and amount of family contributions for university students, by selected demographic characteristics.

Regionally, there are some differences in the amount of money received by students from their families, but these are largely a function of differences in the age composition of the local student body. A more important correlate of family contributions is an individual's living arrangement. Students living with a spouse receive the largest amount of

Table 4.X.3 — Incidence and Amount of Family Support by Living Arrangement

	Incidence of Family Support	Average Annual Amount of Family Support[a]
Living alone with dependants	45%	$2,127
Living alone without dependants	75%	$3,565
Living with parents	88%	$2,021
Living with roommates	78%	$3,431
Living with spouse	69%	$4,660
All students	81%	$2,683

Source: Canada Millennium Scholarship Foundation's 2001–02 *Student Income-Expenditure Survey.*

Note: [a] Only those students who receive support are included in this calculation.

family support by a considerable margin, followed by students living alone and those living with room-mates. Students living at home have the smallest recorded amounts of parental contributions. It should be noted, however, that students in this situation receive substantial contributions by living with their parents (e.g., free rent) that are not recorded by the survey. The amount of family support by living arrangement is shown in Table 4.X.3.

Roughly three-quarters of all family contributions come from parents, with roughly equal portions of the remainder coming from either spouses or other family members (e.g., grandparents). Given that only 10% of students are married, the high share of spousal contributions suggests that spouses, on average, are making a contribution to their partner's income which is, in relative terms, considerably higher than that made by other family members. The shares of total family contributions are shown in Figure 4.X.1.

Parental Contributions

The largest source of family support, by a wide margin, is parental support, which makes up around 60% of all family assistance. Even more so than for family contributions, the incidence of parental support is highly dependent on age, with the likelihood of receiving parental assistance dropping

Figure 4.X.1 — Shares of Family Contributions by Origin

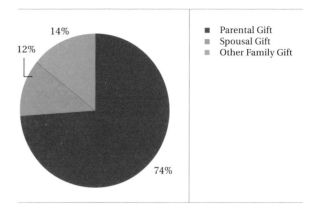

Source: Canada Millennium Scholarship Foundation's 2001–02 *Student Income-Expenditure Survey*

steadily as students get older. The *amount* of parental assistance, however, actually increases somewhat with age. Figure 4.X.2 shows the incidence of and amount of parental contributions by age.

There are significant variations in regional 0 incidences of parental support, but these are largely a function of age. Quebec has much higher levels of parental contributions than other provinces, which appears to be linked to the fact that Quebec's post-secondary population is the country's youngest

Figure 4.X.2 – Incidence and Amount of Parental Contributions by Age

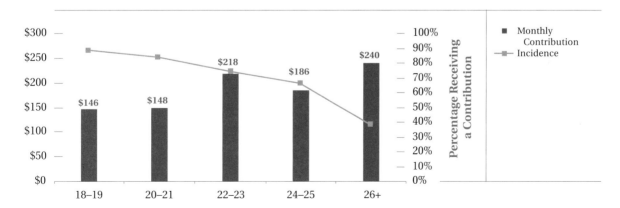

Source: Ekos Research's *Making Ends Meet.*

Table 4.X.4 — Incidence and Amount of Parental Contributions for College Students by Demographic Characteristics

	All Students	Baseline Group[a]	Aboriginal Students	Students With Children	Students With a Disability
$0	54.9%	44.6%	73.2%	85.3%	64.2%
$2,000 or less	30%	35.9%	20.1%	11.0%	25.1%
$2,001 to $7,000	11%	14.2%	4.5%	3.3%	7.1%
$7,001 or more	4.1%	5.3%	2.2%	0.4%	3.6%

Source: David Holmes, Embracing Differences

[a] The "baseline group" here comprises all students other than those with disabilities, with children, or of Aboriginal heritage.

(a substantial part of the college population is under 18 years of age as a result of the province's five-year secondary system).

Some evidence is available on the distribution of parental assistance for selected demographic groups. While no university survey permits a disaggregation of different types of family source, the *Canadian College Student Finances* survey does. It shows a different picture than that for universities shown in Table 4.X.2—for all selected demographic groups, both the incidence of parental support and the amount of parental support fall significantly below the average for the college student population as a whole. Table 4.X.4 shows the incidence and amounts of parental contributions for college students.

Spousal Contributions

Data from the 2001–02 *Student Income-Expenditure Survey* suggest that roughly two-thirds of married or common-law students receive a contribution from their spouse. Of those receiving assistance, the average annual contribution is $4,660. This figure hides a considerable variation within the sample, as the median contribution is just $1,600. Data from spousal contributions are too limited to generate reliable averages by region, age or other characteristic.

XI. Employment Income

Employment is a major source of income for most students.[4] Nearly all students participate in the labour market in the summer, and approximately one-half do so during the academic year as well. Overall, data show that student employment has increased during the 1990s, but not to unprecedented levels. Student employment, like the rest of the labour market, declined at the start of the 1990s and has taken a decade to return to the employment levels of the late 1980s.

Summer Employment

Not all students are able to work during the summer; some, for instance, study for ten or 12 months a year (e.g., students in medical or dentistry programs), making summer employment difficult or impossible to obtain. Aside from these students, the large majority of students find employment during the summer months. Summer employment rates for students aged 18 to 24 in Canada have gone through a series of highs and lows over the past two decades. Throughout the 1980s, according to Statistics Canada's *Labour Force Survey*, student summer

employment rates for individuals aged 18 to 24 began at 69%, slowly decreased until the mid- to late-80s, then rose quickly to reach 70% by 1989. During the recession of the early 1990s, employment rates declined for four consecutive years, with student employment rates finally bottoming out at 62% in 1993. Since then, summer employment rates for 18- to 24-year-olds have been relatively constant (between 65% and 68%).

The national average, however, hides significant variation at the provincial level. Newfoundland and Labrador has consistently had much lower summer employment rates than other provinces; on average, over the past 20 years the Newfoundland and Labrador employment rate has been 15 percentage points lower than the rest of the country. Also, the employment rate in New Brunswick has been consistently about six to eight percentage points below the national average. On the other side of the ledger, employment rates in Saskatchewan, Manitoba and Alberta have been steadily increasing over the past 20 years and are now consistently four to six percentage points higher than the national average. Other provinces tend to stay relatively close to the

Figure 4.XI.1 — Summer Employment Rates for Returning Students Aged 18 to 24 in Canada from 1990 to 2003

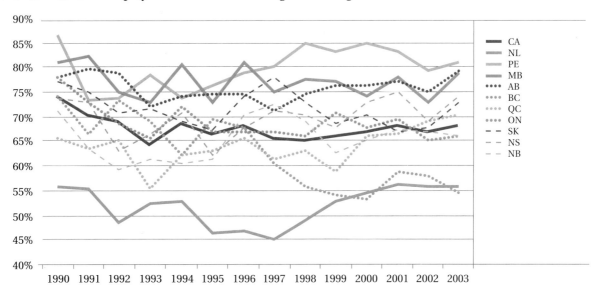

Source: Statistics Canada's *Labour Force Survey*.

4.   The income generated from students is often a necessity and for students accessing student assistance, due to forced savings, it may put them no further ahead.

Table 4.XI.1 — Average Hourly Earnings for Employed Canadian Students (May to August)

Type of Work	1997	1998	1999	2000	2001	2002	2003
Full-time	$8.41	$8.50	$8.81	$9.01	$9.39	$9.53	$9.76
Part-time	$7.28	$7.39	$7.48	$7.59	$7.79	$8.06	$8.16
Total	$7.78	$7.88	$8.05	$8.21	$8.49	$8.69	$8.85

Source: Statistics Canada's *Labour Force Survey V10073.*

national average. Figure 4.XI.1 shows the summer employment rates for returning students aged 18 to 24 in Canada during the past 14 years.

Table 4.XI.1 shows the average hourly wage for students aged 18 to 24 working both full- and part-time during the summer months, as reported by Statistics Canada. Wages have increased steadily over the past five years and, if current trends continue, a full-time summer job in 2004 should have paid (on average) close to $10 an hour and a part-time job almost $8.30 an hour. There is a gender discrepancy in earned wages, as males working full-time earn about fifty cents more per hour than females (the gap does not exist among part-time workers). Considering that the 2004 national (weighted) minimum wage is $7.11, this suggests that

students are generally working in jobs that pay more than the minimum wage. Figure 4.XI.2 shows the minimum wage in each Canadian jurisdiction during the summer months in question for the past decade.

Making Ends Meet sheds additional light on the issue of summer wages. Participants in this survey were asked in September 2001 to report their net summer earnings from May to August 2001. Almost 95% of respondents reported at least some summer employment earnings. The difference between this result and the figure from the *Labour Force Survey* shown in Figure 4.XI.1 is a function of different ways of measuring employment—the *Making Ends Meet* data include all students who worked at any time during the summer, while the *Labour Force Survey* examines only those employed at a certain point in

Figure 4.XI.2 – Minimum Wages by Province From 1995 to 2004 (Summer Only)[a]

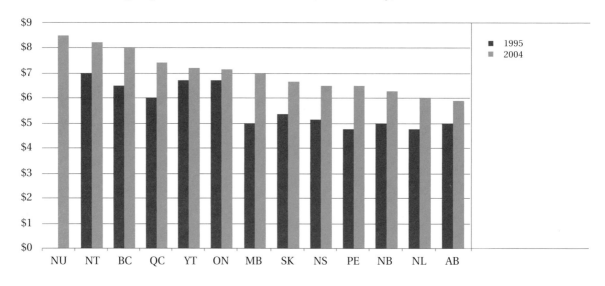

Source: Human Resources and Skills Development Canada's minimum wage databases.

Note: [a] Since August 2001, the B.C. minimum wage is $8.00 per hour (there is, however, a first-job rate of $6.00 per hour that applies to the first 500 hours of employment, or approximately the first six months of a new part-time job).

the summer. Table 4.XI.2 shows the distribution of summer employment income for these students across Canada.

The *Making Ends Meet* data reveal marked differences in summer earnings by age, region and gender. Income rises steadily with age, presumably because the labour market rewards experience. Regionally,

Table 4.XI.2 — Student Summer Income Distribution

Income Level	Distribution
$0	6%
$1–$1,999	12%
$2,000–$3,999	30%
$4,000–$5,999	21%
$6,000+	17%
Don't know/Not reported	14%
Mean (students with income only)	$4,000
Median (students with income only)	$3,200

Source: Ekos Research's *Making Ends Meet*

Table 4.XI.3 — Student Mean Summer Employment Income by Age, Region and Gender

Sociodemographic Characteristic	Mean of All Students	Mean of Students with Summer Earnings Only
Age:		
18-19	$1,900	$2,200
20-21	$2,900	$3,100
22-23	$3,800	$4,200
24-25	$4,100	$4,600
26+	$4,500	$5,600
Region:		
BC	$3,200	$3,800
AB	$4,300	$4,500
SK/MB	$3,600	$3,900
ON	$3,800	$4,300
QC	$3,100	$3,800
Atlantic	$3,100	$3,700
Gender:		
Male	$3,800	$4,300
Female	$3,400	$3,800

Source: Ekos Research's *Making Ends Meet*

students from Alberta enjoy a small summer earnings advantage over the rest of the country; the average student in Alberta reported a summer income of $4,300, compared to a mean of $3,100 for Quebec and Atlantic Canada. Finally, the survey also showed a small difference in the reported average earnings of male and female students. Table 4.XI.3 displays students' mean summer employment income.

Employment While Studying

Employment during the school year forms a major portion of total student income. According to data from the *Labour Force Survey*, roughly half of all Canadian students work over the course of the school year. For most of the 1990s, employment rates among college and university students were roughly equal. At the start of this decade, however, trends in the two student populations started to diverge. Among college students aged 15 to 29, the percentage of students working during their studies has been rising steadily for several years and in the 2002–03 academic year reached an all-time high of 55%. Among university students, the percentage of students employed during the school year has dropped slightly but remains firmly within the narrow range of 44% to 46%, where it has been for the past 15 years. Figure 4.XI.3 breaks down the employment rates for college and university students aged 15 to 29 during the past 25 years.

While *Labour Force Survey* data suggest that roughly 50% of students are employed, they reveal nothing about those students who are "unemployed"—that is, actively searching for work but unable to find any. This is mostly a question of definitions; individuals studying full-time cannot be deemed "unemployed" by Statistics Canada because they are in effect deemed to be "in training." Data from other sources can, however, shed some light on this question.

The *2001–02 Student Income-Expenditure Survey* asked over 1,500 students about their anticipated working arrangements in September 2001 as part of a year-long study. Almost two-thirds (63%) indicated that they expected to be employed throughout the 2001–02 academic year; the proportion was highest

Figure 4.XI.3 — Student Employment Rates During Studies from 1976 to 2003

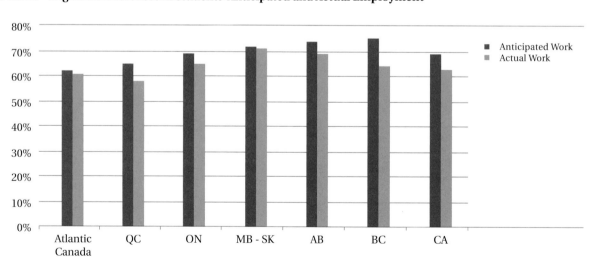

Source: Statistics Canada's *Labour Force Survey*.

in the lowest age groups. These data are over ten percentage points higher than statistics garnered from the *Labour Force Survey* and other surveys—absolute totals are therefore unlikely to be reliable, but differences in reported employment rates of sub-groups are likely to be indicative of differences in the larger student population.

The survey found that gender did not affect the likelihood of anticipating employment during the school year, but region did; students in Western Canada were more likely to anticipate employment during their studies than students in Atlantic or Central Canada. Student perceptions of their employment prospects were more or less

Figure 4.XI.4 – Regional Differences in Students' Anticipated and Actual Employment

Source: Ekos Research's *Making Ends Meet*.

accurate in most parts of the country except for B.C., where students overestimated their employment prospects considerably. Across the country, students were also remarkably accurate in forecasting the number of hours they would work. Figure 4.XI.4 outlines the regional differences for anticipated and actual student employment in Canada.

Making Ends Meet also reported that part-time students are more likely than full-time students to work during the school year by a margin of 86% to 60%. Students in the survey who worked were also less likely to receive government loans and bursaries by a margin of 67% to 57%. While the correlation between work and the absence of student assistance is clear, its cause is not. In particular, it is unclear whether students work because they do not receive loans, or do not receive loans because they work.

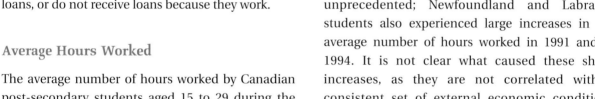

It is unclear whether students work because they do not receive loans, or do not receive loans because they work.

Average Hours Worked

The average number of hours worked by Canadian post-secondary students aged 15 to 29 during the school year has actually declined slightly over the past two decades. College and university students tend to work about the same number of hours and, unsurprisingly, older students tend to work more hours than younger ones. Figure 4.XI.5 outlines the average hours worked by employed college and university students, sorted by age.

There is remarkable consistency in the number of hours worked by students in the "18 to 24" age group. Across provinces and throughout the time period covered, students from this age group worked between 17 and 18 hours a week on average. In the "25 to 29" age group, however, regional differences become more significant. Students in Newfoundland and Labrador, for example, worked over 35 hours a week on average, which is more than five hours above the national average. This number has risen sharply in the last two years, but the rise is not unprecedented; Newfoundland and Labrador students also experienced large increases in the average number of hours worked in 1991 and in 1994. It is not clear what caused these sharp increases, as they are not correlated with a consistent set of external economic conditions (in 1991 and 1994, Newfoundland and Labrador students faced economic slumps and rising tuition,

Figure 4.XI.5 — Average Hours Worked per Week by Employed College and University Students During Studies from 1980 to 2003

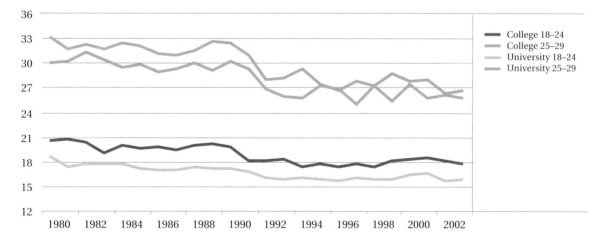

Source: Statistics Canada's *Labour Force Survey A030209R.*

while in 2000–01, the province's economy was growing and tuition was frozen).

Older students in B.C., Alberta and Prince Edward Island have also experienced large fluctuations in the average hours worked during the past decade, none of which are obviously related to changes in overall economic conditions or tuition levels. This may suggest that the number of hours worked by students is not particularly sensitive to broader economic conditions. It is, however, worth noting that, regardless of age, students in Alberta work far more than the national average, which is likely a reflection of the province's strong economy.

Earnings by Traditionally Under-Represented Groups

Employment while in post-secondary education is not for all students. As indicated earlier, some students simply choose not to work or physical limitations prevent them from gaining employment. Both the 2002 Canadian Undergraduate Survey Consortium and 2002 Canadian College Student Survey Consortium surveys asked respondents about their employment status while attending an educational institution. Some data about selected demographic groups in post-secondary education from these sources are shown in Figure 4.XI.6 and Tables 4.XI.4 and .5.

Perhaps unsurprisingly, students with disabilities are less likely than students in the university baseline group to be working off-campus and more likely to be employed on-campus (or doing a hybrid of on- and off-campus work) or not employed at all. Nevertheless, the proportion of these students who are employed is quite remarkable given the extra obstacles that students with disabilities face in the labour market.

Students with dependants are more likely than all other students to be working off-campus. These numbers are not surprising given the additional costs associated with supporting other people while attending post-secondary education. Also, this is consistent with the age data previously discussed with respect to mature students in the labour market.

Finally, Aboriginal students tend to have the least involvement in the labour market and are the most likely to indicate that they are not seeking employment during studies. This is a possible function of the more generous assistance packages received by Status Aboriginal students; however, the data are also consistent with other labour force information that consistently shows lower levels of employment among Aboriginal Peoples compared to non-Aboriginal Peoples.

Students with dependants seem to be doing an incredible job of juggling responsibilities. In addition to academic work (usually part-time) and

Figure 4.XI.6 — Workforce Status Among Selected Demographic Groups

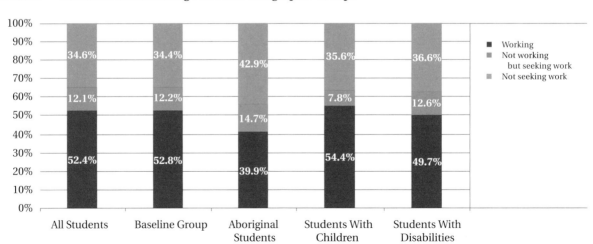

Source: Canadian Undergraduate Survey Consortium's *2002 Survey of Undergraduate Students.*

Table 4.XI.4 — Hours Worked per Week During Studies by University Student Group

Hours Worked	All Students (n=12,578)	Baseline Group (n=10,333)	Aboriginal Students (n=379)	Students With Dependants (n=683)	Students With a Disability (n=986)
10 hours or less	30.2%	32.0%	28.4%	13.7%	28.0%
11 to 20 hours	39.6%	41.9%	34.8%	17.2%	37.0%
21 to 30 hours	14.4%	14.5%	12.9%	13.3%	14.6%
Over 30 hours	14.0%	10.1%	20.0%	52.6%	17.2%
Average number of hours worked	18.3	17.2	19.7	29.7	19.3

Source: Canadian Undergraduate Survey Consortium's *2002 Survey of Undergraduate Students.*

Table 4.XI.5 — Hours Worked per Week During Studies by College Student Group

	All Students (n=6,360)	Baseline Group (n=4,120)	Aboriginal Students (n=746)	Students With Dependants (n=1,374)	Students With a Disability (n=518)
Never or rarely	50.1%	43.6%	63.5%	66.6%	60.0%
Up to 5 hours	8.5%	8.8%	9.9%	7.6%	7.7%
6 to 10 hours	10.9%	11.6%	8.6%	8.4%	10.8%
11 to 20 hours	18.5%	22.4%	10.6%	8.1%	12.5%
More than 20 hours	12.1%	13.7%	7.4%	9.4%	8.9%

Source: Canadian College Student Survey Consortium's *2003 Canadian College Student Finances.*

childcare responsibilities, these students work an average of 30 hours per week. In comparison, Aboriginal students and students with disabilities work an average of 19.7 and 19.3 hours per week, respectively. In all cases, those students from selected demographic groups who work do so for more hours per week than students from the baseline group (17.2 hours per week). Looking at full-time students only, members of the baseline group work an average of 15.4 hours per week, while Aboriginal students work an average of 16.4 hours and students with disabilities 16.3 hours. Full-time students with dependants work an average of nearly 30 hours per week. Table 4.XI.4 shows the hours worked during studies by university student group.

The pattern of employment during school is somewhat different for college students. Among college students, all three of the selected demographic groups are both less likely to work and more likely to work fewer hours than students from the baseline group. Table 4.XI.5 shows the hours worked by college student group.

Factors Influencing a Student's Decision to Work During the Academic Year

The preceding analysis has shown the details of student employment but has not explored students' motivations for working during their studies. Students work for three reasons—two of which are primarily financial. First, students work because their costs exceed their resources. Students' costs (tuition, books, living expenses and so on) have increased significantly in the past decade, and their resources (employment income and student assistance) have not kept pace. The second reason that students work is because their desires exceed their resources. Students want to increase their disposable income and enjoy a comfortable standard of living. As students get older, their living standards evolve. They are no longer willing to share an apartment with two or three roommates and are less likely in general to accept a frugal lifestyle. The third reason—primarily non-financial—that students work is to gain work experience and develop connections and employment networks for the future.

A recent panel survey of students, conducted by Ipsos-Reid for the Canada Millennium Scholarship Foundation, asked respondents why they planned to work during the school year. Respondents were asked to rate their reason for working on a 10-point scale, where 1 indicated that they would be unable to attend post-secondary education without working during the school year and 10 indicated that they were working to increase their standard of living but did not "need" the money to complete their studies.

Not surprisingly, the largest percentage of students indicated that they worked because without the income from work they could not attend school at all. Almost one-third of students responded in the strongest possible way (i.e., a rating of 1) that they worked because they needed to pay the bills. Another 29% (for a total of 60%) gave an answer between

2 and 4, indicating that they agreed more with the statement that they need to work to pay their bills than the statement that they did not really "need" the money. Not all students, however, are working out of necessity. Roughly 29% of working students suggested that they were working primarily because they wanted extra disposable income (i.e., a rating of 6 to 10), and another 11% did not agree strongly with either statement (i.e., a rating of 5).

Similarly, data on working students from the CUSC's *Survey of Undergraduate Students* show that although 53% of students work, only 60% of these (32% of all participants) list in-school income as a "source of money to pay for education." These data correspond to the 60% of people from the Ipsos-Reid student panel who answered 1 to 4 on the scale, indicating that they "needed" the money (rather than simply "wanted" it). Figure 4.XI.7 shows the most important reason why students work during the academic year.

Figure 4.XI.7 — Most Important Reason Why Students Seek Employment During the Academic Year

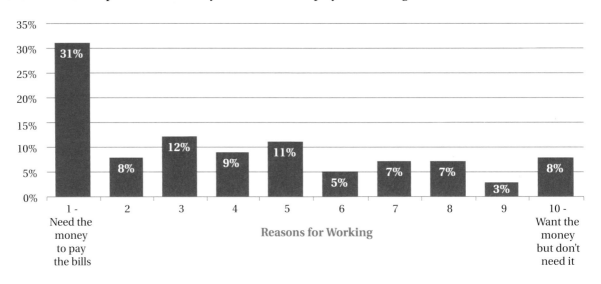

Source: Canada Millennium Scholarship Foundation's 2003 Ipsos-Reid Student Panel

XIa. Student Time Usage

Employment unquestionably serves as an important source of income for students, but some people fear that too much emphasis on work among students is counter-productive, adversely affecting schoolwork and cheapening the "undergraduate experience." Data show, however, that college and undergraduate students make trade-offs between work, school and other activities in very different ways.

It is certainly true that students who work long hours tend to spend less time in class. As Figure 4.XIa.1 shows, undergraduate students who work 20 to 30 hours per week are twice as likely as

Figure 4.XIa.1 — Hours per Week Spent in Class/Lab by Hours of Employment per Week (Undergraduates Only)

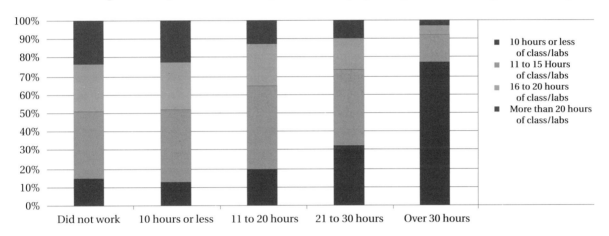

Source: Canadian Undergraduate Survey Consortium's *2002 Survey of Undergraduate Students.*

Figure 4.XIa.2 — Hours per Week Spent in Class/Lab by Hours of Employment per Week (College Students Only)

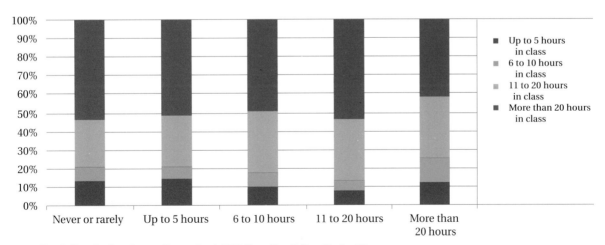

Source: Canadian College Student Survey Consortium's 2003 *Canadian College Student Finances.*

Figure 4.XIa.3 — Weekly Hours Spent Studying Outside of Class by Weekly Hours of Employment (Undergraduates Only)

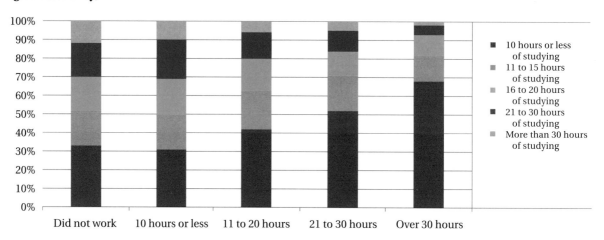

Source: Canadian Undergraduate Survey Consortium's *2002 Survey of Undergraduate Students.*

non-working students to be attending school part-time (defined here as ten or less hours of class and labs per week), while students who work more than 30 hours per week are nearly five times as likely to do so. Similar data for colleges, shown in Figure 4.XIa.2, do not appear to show as much variation in class time by weekly hours of employment.

Of course, class time is only part of the post-secondary academic experience. There is also the issue of study time outside of class. Again, a clear distinction needs to be made between the adjustments that university and college students make in response to increased working hours. Figure 4.XIa.3 shows that, among undergraduate students, there does appear to be a rough inverse correlation between hours worked and time spent studying, at least once the ten-hours-per-week employment threshold has been breached. Figure 4.XIa.4,

Figure 4.XIa.4 — Weekly Hours Spent Studying Outside of Class by Weekly Hours of Employment (College Students Only)

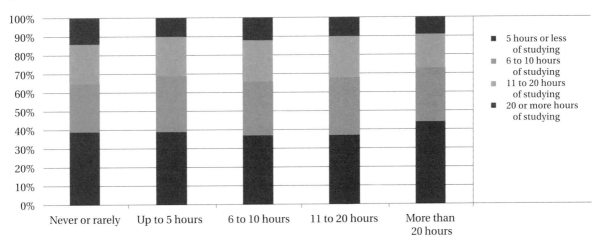

Source: Canadian College Student Survey Consortium's 2003 *Canadian College Student Finances.*

however, shows that at the college level there is very little relationship between hours worked and hours spent studying.

Other major educational aspects of the post-secondary experience include participation in on- or off-campus volunteer activities, participation in social and cultural groups, or other extra-curricular activities. Once again, similar patterns emerge. Among university students, those who work under ten hours per week report more frequent engagement in these activities than those who do not work at all. Engagement decreases slightly with hours of work until the number of weekly hours of work approaches 30, at which point engagement decreases sharply. On the college side, engagement in these activities seems unrelated to weekly hours of work, with students who work 20 hours a week reporting levels of engagement that on average are no different from those reported by students who do not work at all.

XIb. Employment and Academic Performance

Student employment does not appear to have a major impact on grades among Canadian students. As seen in the preceding section, students' primary reaction to having too much work is to cut back on course loads. As a result, students working 30 hours a week or more tend to maintain or even improve upon their grade point average by reducing the number of courses taken but continuing to devote the same amount of time to each course.

As Figure 4.XIb.1 shows, the problem with the notion that work is detrimental to academics is that the relationship between working hours and grades is neither significant nor linear in nature. A plurality of students receives a "B" grade no matter how many hours they work. Students who do not work at all are in the "middle of the pack," academically speaking. Students who work zero to ten hours per week have the best grades of all, but students who work 30 hours or more per week also do reasonably well (although, as seen in Section 4.XIa, they take far fewer courses on average).

The *2001–02 Student Income-Expenditure Survey* produced similar results, as shown in Table 4.XIb.1. The differences in incidence of employment by grade level are modest but significant, while differences in hours worked between grade levels are not significant. There is, however, growing concern in the post-secondary community that students are elongating their studies and this has a direct impact on their indebtedness.

Figure 4.XIb.1 – Distribution of Average Grades by Average Hours of Employment per Week

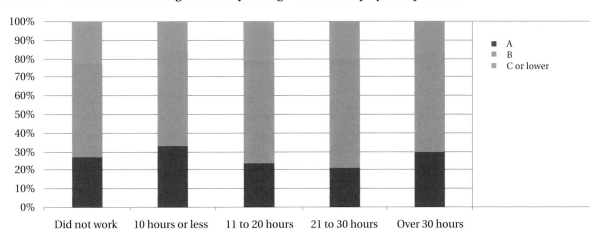

Source: Canadian Undergraduate Survey Consortium's *2002 Survey of Undergraduate Students.*

Table 4.XIb.1 — Student Employment and First-Term Grades for the 2001–02 Academic Year

Grade Average	Proportion Employed	Hours Worked per Week	Monthly Earnings
A	62%	11.8	$504
B	62%	11.5	$469
C	68%	13.5	$438
Total	63%	12.2	$478

Source: Ekos Research's *Making Ends Meet.*

XII. Income From Student Assistance

Government student assistance is used by just under half of all university and college students in any given year. While student assistance is among all students only the third most important source of income (after employment and family contributions), for those students (traditionally low-income) who do borrow, it is usually the largest single source of income.

From an analytical perspective, government student assistance is quite unlike other forms of income. Whereas data on parental contributions, employment and other types of income rely on survey data, data on per-student income from student loans and grants can be obtained directly from administrative student assistance records. Survey research need only be used to determine certain aspects of the distribution of student financial assistance which are not captured by administrative means, such as the differences in student assistance use by particular groups of students (Aboriginal students, students with dependants, etc.).

In much of this chapter, data from Quebec will be displayed seperately from the rest of Canada. This is because of the very different student assistance structure that Quebec has created as a result of opting out of the Canada Student Loans Program.

Loans

The number of student loan recipients rose significantly in Canada in the first half of the 1990s. Some of the largest increases came in 1993 and 1994, when several provincial governments—notably Ontario—abandoned their grant programs in favour of remissible loans. In Quebec, the increases in assistance were even more dramatic; the number of borrowers increased by over 40% between 1990–91 and 1996–97. In the latter half of the 1990s, the number of borrowers declined nationally by nearly 15% from its 1996–97 high of 529,354 to 460,763 in 2002–03, the most recent year for which data are available. More than half of this decline occurred in the province of Quebec, mostly due to the tightening of eligibility criteria. In the rest of Canada (the "Canada Student Loans Program zone"), the decline has been more gradual, and it can largely be attributed to a decline in the number of borrowers from private vocational institutions, which have been the subject of increased regulatory scrutiny since the mid-1990s. Figure 4.XII.1 shows the number of student loan recipients in Canada between 1990–91 and 2002–03.

As the number of borrowers has decreased, so has the amount of borrowing. Since 1996–97, the average

Figure 4.XII.1 — Student Loan Borrowers in Canada From 1990–91 to 2002–03

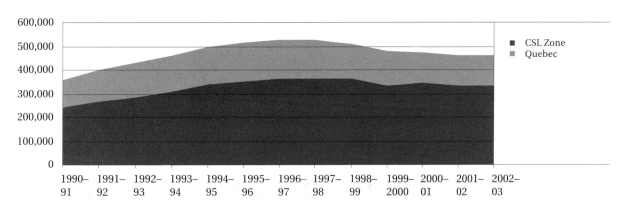

Source: Canada Student Loans Program annual reports and provincial loan program administrative data.

amount borrowed per student, in real dollars, decreased by 22% in Quebec and by 24% in the CSL zone. In 2002–03, the last year for which data are available, average borrowing in Quebec was $2,665 per year and $6,479 in the rest of Canada. Roughly half of the decline can be accounted for by inflation; the remainder is due to the increased availability of grants following the introduction of the Canada Millennium Scholarship Foundation and a reduction in the number of borrowers from private vocational institutions (these institutions tend to have high fees, and hence their students are high borrowers). In 2004, however, both Quebec and the Government of Canada announced increases to their lending limits that will likely reverse this trend to some degree. Figure 4.XII.2 shows the evolution of borrowing patterns in Canada over the past decade.

Grants

Unfortunately, while available administrative data permit an accurate count of the number of grants awarded, there is at present no reliable way to count the number of grant recipients. Ten years ago, this would have been a simple task, as there was only one source of grants in Canada—namely, provincial governments. Since 1995, however, the Government

of Canada has been handing out grants as well. At first, the federal government did this directly through the Canada Student Loans Program's Special Opportunities Grant (renamed the Canada Study Grants in 1998); then it began doing it indirectly through the Canada Millennium Scholarship Foundation, which began life with a $2.5 billion federal endowment in 1998 and distributed its first bursaries on January 4, 2000. As a result, some students now receive grants from two or even three sources each year. The evolution of the number of grants awarded in Canada each year is shown in Figure 4.XII.3.

As Figure 4.XII.3 shows, the number of grants in Canada dropped sharply between 1992 and 1993, when the Government of Ontario switched its grant program to a remissible loan program. The number of grants stayed more or less steady throughout the mid-1990s until 1998, when the Government of Canada created the Canada Study Grant for students with dependants, which increased the number of grants it was distributing by a factor of eight. The following year, the Canada Millennium Scholarship Foundation began its work, and the number of grants increased again. In 2002–03, the number of grants distributed in Canada reached an all-time high of 285,399.

Figure 4.XII.2 – Average Annual Student Loan Borrowing from 1990–91 to 2002–03 (in Real 2003 Dollars)

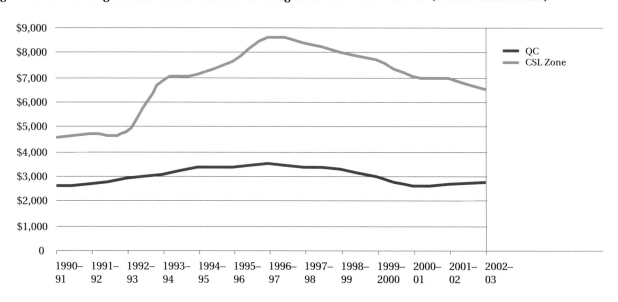

Source: Canada Student Loans Program annual reports and provincial loan program administrative data.

Figure 4.XII.3 — Grants Awarded in Canada From 1990–91 to 2002–03

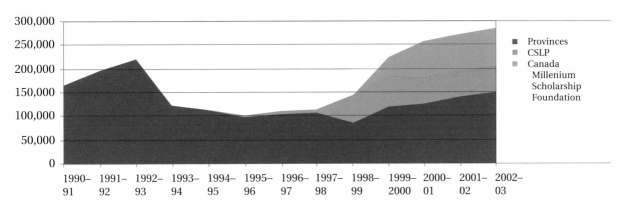

Source: Canada Student Loans Program annual reports, provincial loan program administrative data and the Canada Millennium Scholarship
    Foundation's annual reports.

Figure 4.XII.4 — Average Grant Size by Source From 1990–91 to 2002–03 (in Real 2003 Dollars)

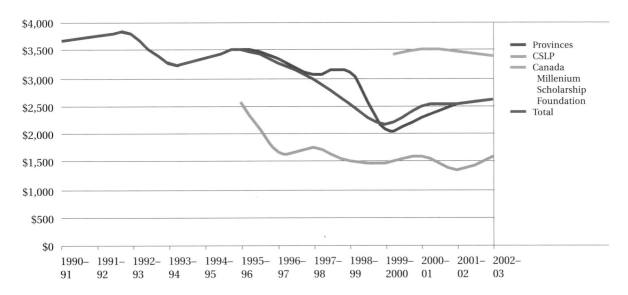

Source: Canada Student Loans Program annual reports, provincial loan program administrative data and the Canada Millennium Scholarship
    Foundation's annual reports.

While an increase in the number of grants is welcome, its effects may be diluted if the average grant size has decreased concomitantly. To some extent, this does seem to have been the case; the average grant nearly halved in size between 1992–93 ($3,737) and 1999–2000 ($2,123). The cause of this decrease was twofold: 1) provincial grants declined in real value, and 2) the many new federal grants were relatively small, which dragged down the average considerably. However, the introduction of the Canada Millennium Scholarship Foundation's bursaries, coupled with an increase in average provincial bursary size, means that the size of the average grant has been climbing again since 2000, and it is now worth $2,577. While it is clear that the average grant size has declined, it should be kept in mind that since far more grants are now awarded, total grant expenditure is considerably higher than it was ten years ago. Data on average grant size in Canada are shown in Figure 4.XII.4.

Figure 4.XII.5 — Number of Loan Remission Payments in Canada From 1990–91 to 2002–03

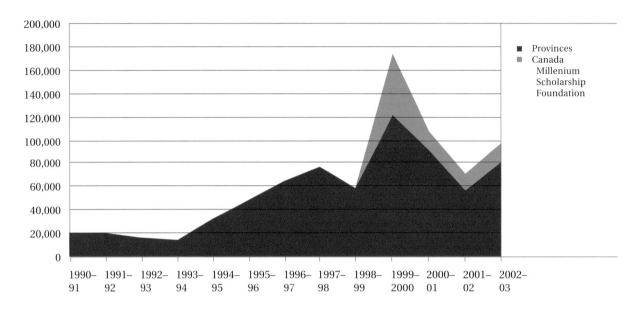

Source: Canada Student Loans Program annual reports, provincial loan program administrative data and the Canada Millennium Scholarship
Foundation's annual reports.

Loan Remission

Loan remission is technically a form of income, as it is a grant paid to a student—or, more accurately, paid to a bank on the student's behalf—to reduce a debt incurred over the course of the previous year or a recently completed course of studies. The only meaningful difference between a grant and loan remission is *when* it is paid. It is important to note, though, that students rarely consider remission as income since it does not put any extra money in students' hands. It is therefore an odd income category—a payment made by governments on a student's behalf which makes students no richer in terms of cash-in-hand.

The Government of Canada has never had a major loan remission program; it has had a debt remission program since 1998, but this has never paid out more than a couple of million dollars a year, and even then payments are made only after students have been out of school for at least 40 months. Remission was developed primarily by provincial governments—notably Ontario, which in

some years has accounted for over 85% of all remission spending in Canada—as a way of compensating for the cancellation of grant programs in the early 1990s. The number of instances of loan remission in Canada increased substantially following Ontario's 1993 switch from grants to remissible loans.

There was also a massive one-year spike in loan remission incidence in 1999–2000, which occurred due to a combination of two factors. The first was a program change in Ontario, which ceased paying remission on a per-degree basis and started paying on an annual basis. The result was a large "double-count" of students, as remission under both the old and new regimes was paid in the same fiscal year. The second was the introduction of the Canada Millennium Scholarship Foundation, which, in its first year, provided roughly half of its bursaries in the form of remission (this proportion has since been reduced to roughly one-sixth). After some fluctuation, the number of students receiving remission is now roughly 100,000. Trends in the number of remission recipients over the past decade are shown in Figure 4.XII.5.

Figure 4.XII.6 — Average Remission Payment by Source From 1990–91 to 2002–03 (in Real 2003 Dollars)

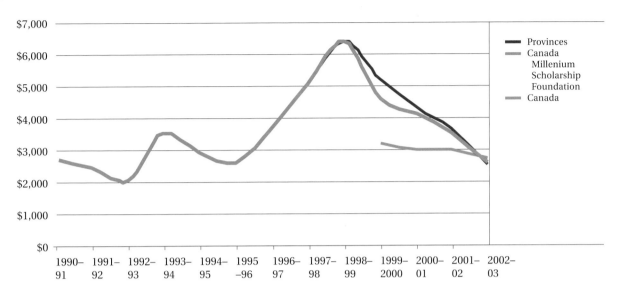

Source: Canada Student Loans Program annual reports, provincial loan program administrative data and the Canada Millennium Scholarship Foundation's annual reports.

The average amount of loan remission grew steadily throughout the 1990s and then fell in the early years of the new decade. The reason for this lies entirely in the aforementioned Ontario policy change; once remission began being paid on an annual—rather than a per-degree—basis, average remission was bound to fall. Students are still receiving roughly the same amount of assistance over the course of a degree, but since the frequency of payment has increased, the annual amount per individual is smaller.

Demographic Differences in Student Assistance

The CUSC *2002 Survey of Undergraduate Students* and the CCSSC *2003 Canadian College Student Finances* each provide certain information about the incidence of student assistance for certain groups that are often deemed "under-represented." It should be noted that since the data below are survey data, the actual amounts of assistance listed are likely to be considerably less accurate than the

Table 4.XII.1 — Incidence and Amount of Student Assistance by Selected Demographic Characteristics (University Students Only)

Source	All Students	Baseline Group	Aboriginal Students	Students With Children	Students With a Disability
Proportion with loan or bursary	31.2%	31.2%	34.4%	30.2%	34.2%
Amount from loan or bursary	$6,217	$6,012	$7,019	$8,935	$5,713

Source: Canadian Undergraduate Survey Consortium's *2002 Survey of Undergraduate Students.*

Note: a The baseline group here refers to all students other than those with disabilities, with children or of Aboriginal heritage.

administrative data based on actual loan records presented in the rest of this section. What is important in the tables below is not so much the absolute incidences or amounts of assistance, but rather the differences between groups.

Among university students, the incidence of student assistance does not appear to vary substantially by demographic characteristic. Students with disabilities and Aboriginal students appear to be marginally more likely to receive student assistance than other students, but the difference is so small as to be within the normal margin of error. Interestingly, students with children are marginally less likely to receive student assistance than other students. This presumably is because students with children are older (and hence have more income of their own) and are likely to have a spouse (and hence have a drastically reduced likelihood of getting assistance because of the spousal contribution rule, as explained in Section 5A.IV). In terms of the size of the assistance package, however, there are significant differences; Aboriginal students and students with children receive assistance packages that are considerably larger than those of other students, while students with disabilities receive packages that are somewhat smaller. Unfortunately, the *Survey of*

Undergraduate Students does not permit any distinction between aid received as a loan and aid received as a grant. Incidences and amounts of student assistance among university students by selected demographic characteristics are shown in Table 4.XII.1.

In contrast to the *Survey of Undergraduate Students*, the *College Student Survey* allows a disaggregation of loan and grant amounts, but only reports the amount of each type of assistance as a few broad ranges. The college data show Aboriginal students, students with children and students with a disability as all being somewhat less likely than the baseline group to have student loans, but conversely somewhat more likely than the baseline group to be receiving grants. Students with children were more likely than other students to have very large (over $7,000 per year) amounts of student loans. Aboriginal college students were much more likely than baseline students to have grants of over $7,000 per year. College students with children were 15 times more likely than baseline students to have grants of this size, and college students with disabilities eight times more likely. Incidences and amounts of student assistance among college students by selected demographic characteristics are shown in Table 4.XII.2.

Table 4.XII.2 — Incidence and Amount of Student Assistance by Selected Demographic Characteristics (College Students Only)

Source	All Students	Baseline Group[a]	Aboriginal Students	Students With Children	Students With a Disability
Government Student Loan					
$0	67.4%	66.5%	78.4%	68.9%	70.4%
$2,000 or less	6.4%	6.7%	5.8%	4.6%	8.9%
$2,001 to $7,000	15.7%	16.9%	8.7%	13.2%	10.8%
$7,001 or more	10.5%	9.9%	7.1%	13.3%	9.9%
Government Student Grant/Bursary					
$0	82.3%	85.7%	72.7%	73.6%	77.8%
$2,000 or less	10.0%	9.3%	10.9%	11.3%	12.5%
$2,001 to $7,000	5.9%	4.6%	8.7%	9.0%	6.7%
$7,001 or more	1.8%	0.4%	7.7%	6.1%	3.0%

Source: David Holmes, *Embracing Differences.*

Note: [a] The baseline group here refers to all students other than those with disabilities, with children or of Aboriginal heritage.

XIII. Miscellaneous Student Income

In addition to the three main sources of student income discussed previously (family, employment and government student assistance), students also have a number of other sources of income. These can basically be sorted into two broad categories: repayable income (i.e., loans from family or private banks) and non-repayable income (income from various government programs, scholarships, child support, etc).

Repayable Assistance

In addition to government student loans, students borrow from two other sources: family members and private banks. In the *2001–02 Student Income-Expenditure Survey*, roughly 32% of all students declared that they had received a loan from a non-government source—a proportion nearly identical to the percentage saying they had taken out a government loan. Students were more or less evenly split between those receiving a loan from a bank and those receiving a loan from a family member. Bank and private loans appear to be an either-or proposition: very few students (4%) said they had received loans from both sources. Statistics Canada's *Post-Secondary Education Participation Survey (PEPS)* found nearly identical results, with

Figure 4.XIII.2 — Average Annual Borrowing by Type of Non-Government Loan

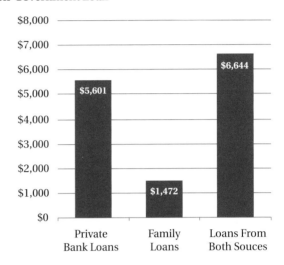

Source: Canada Millennium Scholarship Foundation's *2001–02 Student Income-Expenditure Survey.*

16% of all students reporting family loans and 14% reporting bank loans. Figure 4.XIII.1 shows data on the incidence of non-government loans.

While the incidence of loans from family and banks is roughly equal, the average sum borrowed from each source differs considerably. The *2001–02 Student Income-Expenditure Survey* showed that average bank borrowing was $5,600 per year, while the average family loan was only $1,472. Students with loans from both sources not surprisingly received over $6,600 on average. Other surveys show a similar picture. Statistics Canada's *PEPS* reported means rather than medians, but confirmed the basic pattern: a median of $2,000 for family loans and $5,000 for bank loans. Data on average borrowing by type of non-government loan are presented in Figure 4.XIII.2.

The *2001–02 Student Income-Expenditure Survey* also showed significant regional differences with respect to private borrowing. In most regions of the country, roughly 15% of students said they received private loans; however, in the Maritimes the proportion was 21%, and in Manitoba/Saskatchewan it was 26%. In terms of the amount borrowed,

Figure 4.XIII.1 — Incidence of Non-Government Loans

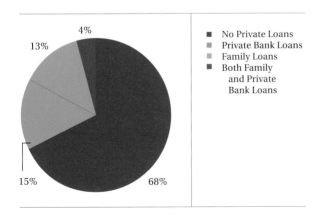

Source: Canada Millennium Scholarship Foundation's *2001–02 Student Income-Expenditure Survey.*

students from Alberta borrowed the most—about 30% higher than the national average. Private borrowing was also linked strongly with age, as shown in Figure 4.XIII.3.

Non-Repayable Income

There are several types of non-repayable income which students receive. The following sections look at scholarships, investment and pension income, and government support programs (other than student assistance programs), respectively.

Scholarships

Information on scholarship income is somewhat scarce. The *2001–02 Student Income-Expenditure Survey* suggests that 23% of students receive some kind of merit-based scholarship each year, which seems quite high, given what is known about the size of the overall merit scholarship sector (see Section 5B.II for further details). The 2002 CUSC *Survey of Undergraduate Students* suggests that roughly 19% of university students receive some sort of "university bursary" in any given year, although it is unclear whether this bursary is merit- or need-based. Aboriginal students and students with children appeared to be much less likely to receive

these bursaries than other students. The 2003 CCSSC *Canadian College Student Finances* survey suggests fewer academic scholarships overall among college students and fewer differences between demographic groups both in terms of the incidence and amount of scholarships. Tables 4.XIII.1 and .2 present data on scholarships for both university and college students.

Investment/Pension Income

The *2001–02 Student Income-Expenditure Survey* suggests that roughly 15% of students receive income from a pension or investment each year, with an average revenue (among those who receive it) of $1,968 per year. This figure appears very high compared to the 2002 CUSC *Survey of Undergraduate Students*, which suggests that only 4.4% of students have investment revenue and 2% have RESP revenue. Respondents in the former survey could conceivably have included some of their own personal savings in this category, which would account for the difference between the two sets of figures.

Unsurprisingly, Aboriginal students and students with children appear to be much less likely than other students to have investment income. Both of these demographic groups, as well as students with

Figure 4.XIII.3 — Private Borrowing by Age

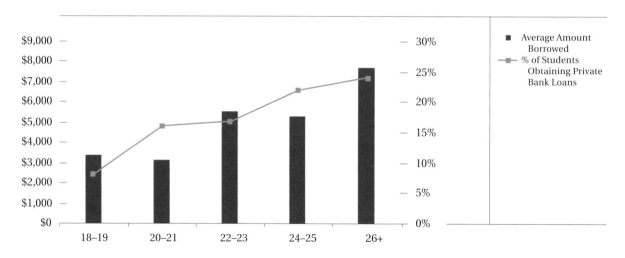

Source: Canada Millennium Scholarship Foundation's *2001–02 Student Income-Expenditure Survey*.

Table 4.XIII.1 — Incidence and Amount of University Bursaries by Selected Demographic Characteristics (University Students Only)

	All Students	Baseline Group[a]	Aboriginal Students	Students With Children	Students With a Disability
Incidence of university bursary	19.1%	20.1%	12.9%	10.0%	20.4%
Average value of university bursary	$1,712	$1,729	$1,697	$1,509	$1,669

Source: David Holmes, *Embracing Differences.*

Note: [a] The baseline group here refers to all students other than those with disabilities, with children or of Aboriginal heritage.

Table 4.XIII.2 — Incidence and Amount of Academic Scholarships by Selected Demographic Characteristics (College Students Only)

	All Students	Baseline Group[a]	Aboriginal Students	Students With Children	Students With a Disability
$0	90.5%	89.6%	91.0%	93.4%	90.7%
$2,000 or less	7.6%	8.6%	6.3%	4.7%	7.5%
$2,001 to $7,000	1.6%	1.7%	1.5%	1.5%	1.2%
$7,001 or more	0.2%	0.1%	1.2%	0.4%	0.6%

Source: David Holmes, *Embracing Differences.*

Note: [a] The baseline group here refers to all students other than those with disabilities, with children or of Aboriginal heritage.

Table 4.XIII.3 — Incidence and Amount of Investment Income and RESPs by Selected Demographic Characteristics (University Students Only)

	All Students	Baseline Group[a]	Aboriginal Students	Students With Children	Students With a Disability
Incidence of investment income (bonds, dividends, interest, etc.)	4.4%	4.5%	1.8%	2.6%	4.6%
Average amount of investment income	$3,030	$3,127	$1,060	$2,594	$1,768
Incidence of RESPs	2.0%	2.2%	0.1%	0.21%	0.4%
Average amount of RESPs	$3,513	$3,440	$7,700	$8,667	$3,330

Source: David Holmes, *Embracing Differences.*

Note: [a] The baseline group here refers to all students other than those with disabilities, with children or of Aboriginal heritage.

disabilities, receive fewer RESPs than other students, although the few who do receive them (less than 1%) receive a fairly substantial amount. Table 4.XIII.3 presents data on RESP and investments among university students.

Government Support Programs Other than Student Assistance

Some college students can receive government support payments for which university students are often ineligible, such as social assistance and employment insurance. Specifically, 12% of college students are recipients of Employment Insurance (EI) benefits, and 4% are recipients of social assistance. Aboriginal students, students with children and students with a disability are all more likely than the "average" student to be recipients of social assistance; students with children are more likely to be EI recipients than other students; and Aboriginal students are somewhat less likely than others to be EI recipients. Data on the incidence and amount of social assistance and employment insurance among college students is presented in Table 4.XIII.4.

In addition to EI and social assistance payments, some students benefit from certain other targeted payments, such as Native band funding and special payments for students with disabilities. Roughly one-quarter of Aboriginal students in Canadian community colleges receive funding from Indian and Northern Affairs Canada, and approximately 15% of college students with disabilities receive dedicated funding for students with disabilities. No comparable data are available for university students. Data on grants for Aboriginal and disabled students are shown in Table 4.XIII.5.

Table 4.XIII.4 — Incidence and Amount of Social Assistance and Employment Insurance Payments by Selected Demographic Characteristics (College Students Only)

Source	All Students	Baseline Group[a]	Aboriginal Students	Students With Children	Students With a Disability
Social/Income Assistance					
$0	96.1%	98.5%	91.4%	90.0%	90.7%
$2,000 or less	2.1%	1.1%	4.6%	3.9%	4.8%
$2,001 to $7,000	0.9%	0.2%	1.6%	2.7%	2.2%
$7,001 or more	1.0%	0.2%	2.3%	3.4%	2.4%
Employment Insurance					
$0	88.4%	89.4%	93.1%	83.2%	88.1%
$2,000 or less	4.0%	3.8%	2.7%	5.0%	3.4%
$2,001 to $7,000	4.2%	4.0%	2.0%	5.7%	2.6%
$7,001 or more	3.4%	2.8%	2.2%	6.1%	3.0%

Source: David Holmes, *Embracing Differences.*

Note: [a] The baseline group here refers to all students other than those with disabilities, with children or of Aboriginal heritage.

Table 4.XIII.5 — Incidence and Amount of Band Funding and Funding for Students With Disabilities by Selected Demographic Characteristics (College Students Only)

Source	All Students	Baseline Group[a]	Aboriginal Students	Students with Children	Students With a Disability
Funding from Indian and Northern Affairs Canada					
$0	96.8%	99.7%	75.1%	92.9%	95.0%
$2,000 or less	1.1%	0.1%	8.4%	2.6%	1.6%
$2,001 to $7,000	1.1%	0.1%	8.2%	1.7%	2.2%
$7,001 or more	1.0%	0%	8.3%	2.8%	1.2%
Government Financial Support for Persons With Disabilities					
$0	97.4%	98.7%	96.2%	96.4%	85.1%
$2,000 or less	1.4%	1.1%	2.4%	1.0%	5.1%
$2,001 to $7,000	0.5%	0.1%	0.5%	1.0%	3.8%
$7,001 or more	0.6%	0.1%	0.8%	1.7%	5.9%

Source: David Holmes, *Embracing Differences.*

Note: [a] The baseline group here refers to all students other than those with disabilities, with children or of Aboriginal heritage.

XIV. Students' Perceptions of Their Finances

Regardless of the "true" or empirical state of students' finances, what matters in terms of access and retention is how students *perceive* their own finances. This section therefore looks at students' views on two key issues: whether or not they have sufficient funding to complete their studies, and their concerns about student debt and repayment thereof.

Concerns About the Amount of Available Funding

In the 2002 *Survey of Undergraduate Students*, 77% of first-year students stated that they were "very" or "somewhat" concerned about having sufficient funds to complete their education. As students get closer to finishing their studies, the level of concern and uncertainty drops—among fourth-year students, only 62% felt significant concern about having enough money to finish their studies.

College students appear to be less concerned about this issue than university students. Among these students, only 46% said they were "very" or "moderately" concerned about having enough funding. Another 21%, however, said they were "mildly" concerned about the amount of funds required to complete their education (this response was not available to students in the university survey). If this figure is included, then the proportion of concerned college students rises to 67%, which is much closer to the result for university students.

In general, Aboriginal students and students with disabilities were more likely than other students to say they were concerned about having enough money to complete their courses. College students with dependants were more likely than others to report concern, while those at the university level with dependants were slightly less likely to report concern. All of these deviations from the norm are quite small, however. Table 4.XIV.1 shows the differences in concern about having sufficient funds to complete one's education.

Concern About Debt

In the summer of 2003, Ipsos-Reid, on behalf of the Canada Millennium Scholarship Foundation, recruited 1,500 students from its ongoing online survey panel to answer a number of questions around student finance. Among the questions were five questions asking students how they felt about debt, borrowing and their own budgeting habits. The results of this survey are shown in Table 4.XIV.2.

Table 4.XIV.1 — Students Indicating Concern About Having Sufficient Funds to Complete Their Education

Source	All Students	Baseline Group	Aboriginal Students	Students With Children	Students With a Disability
College	66.5%	65.0%	67.9%	70.2%	66.4%
University	71.1%	72.3%	73.8%	64.7%	75.8%

Source: Canadian Undergraduate Survey Consortium's *2002 Survey of Undergraduates* and Canada College Student Survey Consortium's 2003 *Canadian College Student Finances.*

Note: a The baseline group here refers to all students other than those with disabilities, with children or of Aboriginal heritage.

The results of the Ipsos-Reid panel show that most students are concerned about the level of debt they are incurring as a result of their studies and most claim that they try to avoid incurring debt whenever possible. Specifically, 78% say they are concerned about the amount of debt they have (a figure that seems rather elevated, given that most studies show that fewer than 60% of all students borrow during their studies); 89% say they try to avoid debt whenever possible; and 72% say they prefer to work more in order to avoid debt.

There exists a significant minority of students—including some of these nominally debt-avoiding students—who take something of a contradictory stance: they report both that they could reduce some of their costs (44%) and that, given the opportunity, they would borrow more money (47%). These results suggest that many students are torn between two competing desires: to have more money in their pockets (by borrowing more) and to spend less in the present (to minimize their debt).

Additional information about views on debt is available from the 2003 *Canadian College Student Finances Survey* (however, no comparable information is available for university students). The survey asked students whether or not they were concerned about the amount of debt they thought they would incur and about their ability to repay their debts within a reasonable time frame. Among all college students, 61.9% expressed some level of concern about total debt, and 55.4% expressed some level of concern about the time required to repay their debts. Since these figures are more or less equal to the percentages of students with debt, this is perhaps not a particularly useful indicator; it simply implies that people with debt are concerned about it. In keeping with overall borrowing patterns, Aboriginal students are much less likely than other students to express concern about debt, while students with children tend to express more concern. Students with disabilities have views that are more or less indistinguishable from the general student population. Table 4.XIV.3 shows college students' levels of concern about debt.

Not surprisingly, students' levels of concern about debt are correlated with the amount of debt they expect to have by the time they graduate. The relationship between the expected final debt level and views on debt is shown in Figure 4.XIV.1.

> *Most students are concerned about the level of debt they are incurring as a result of their studies and most claim that they try to avoid incurring debt whenever possible.*

Table 4.XIV.2 — Students' Perceptions of Their Financial Situation

Statement	Strongly Agree	Somewhat Agree	Somewhat Disagree	Strongly Disagree
I am concerned about the amount of debt I will have when I finish school	50%	28%	9%	13%
I wish I could borrow more during the school year	18%	29%	29%	23%
I try to avoid incurring debt whenever possible	62%	27%	9%	2%
I would rather work to pay for my education now than pay for it later	39%	33%	20%	7%
There are many ways I can reduce my educational costs if I just make a few sacrifices	14%	31%	32%	22%

Source: Canada Millennium Scholarship Foundation's 2003 Ipsos-Reid Student Panel.

Table 4.XIV.3 — Levels of Concern About Debt (College Students Only)

	All Students	Baseline Group[a]	Aboriginal Students	Students With Children	Students With a Disability
Concern About the Amount of Debt Expected at Time of Graduation					
Very concerned	26.3%	25.5%	20.7%	29.6%	28.6%
Moderately concerned	17.8%	17.8%	15.2%	18.1%	16.1%
Mildly concerned	17.9%	19.2%	15.3%	15.7%	13.8%
Not at all concerned	34.5%	35.4%	40.5%	29.9%	35.0%
Don't know	3.6%	2.1%	8.3%	6.7%	6.4%
Concern About Ability to Repay Student Debt Within a Reasonable Time Frame					
Very concerned	22.3%	21.0%	18.5%	26.2%	26.3%
Moderately concerned	16.6%	17.1%	11.3%	16.3%	15.8%
Mildly concerned	16.4%	17.9%	12.8%	13.7%	10.7%
Not at all concerned	41.5%	42.1%	48.5%	38.6%	41.8%
Don't know	3.1%	1.9%	8.9%	5.2%	5.4%

Source: David Holmes, *Embracing Differences.*

Note: [a] The baseline group here refers to all students other than those with disabilities, with children or of Aboriginal heritage.

Figure 4.XIV.1 – Concern About Debt by Level of Anticipated Debt (College Students Only)

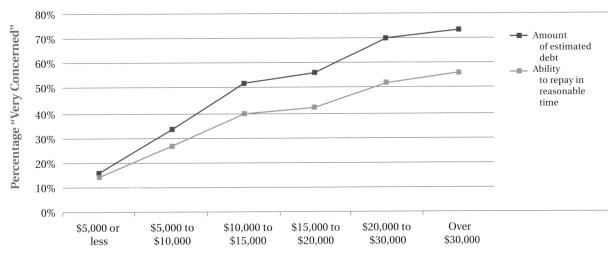

Source: Canada College Student Survey Consortium's 2003 *Canadian College Student Fianances.*

Chapter 5A

Student Aid in Canada

Chapter 5A

Student Aid in Canada

I. Introduction—How Student Assistance Works

To say that Canada does not have a single student aid system is to state the obvious. But it would not be true to claim that the country has 13 separate student aid systems—the system is both more and less complicated than that.

Canada has one national legislative framework (the *Canada Student Financial Assistance Act*) underpinning student assistance in the ten jurisdictions where the Canada Student Loans Program operates and the three where it does not. It has two national loan programs (one for full-time students and one for part-time students). It has three quite separate methods of providing assistance to students (need-based, income based and universal grants). It has five national grant programs, seven provincial/territorial grant programs, nine provincial/territorial loan remission programs, 12 provincial/territorial loan programs, 13 provincial/territorial student assistance programs, 15 major providers of public student assistance, over 40 different student assistance limits (depending on a student's province, marital status, dependants and level of study), more than 100 different loan/grant combinations within these aid limits and hundreds of thousands of possible aid configurations once assessed need is taken into account.

This litany sounds daunting and complex, and to an extent it is. Certainly, the system precludes any easy generalization. One should not, however, be too preoccupied with small differences. Fundamentally, most of the country's student assistance programs follow a single paradigm; while differences exist between provinces, they are less significant than one might expect.

Despite their differences, Canada's many student aid programs are, on a fundamental level, almost identical.

This chapter explains and compares the various provincial and territorial systems of student aid available in Canada. It looks at the policy differences between jurisdictions in all aspects of the aid system, and it does so by following the "life cycle" of the loan, from eligibility to borrowing to repayment, from the point of view of the individual student. At the same time, it will demonstrate that, despite their differences, Canada's many student aid programs are, on a fundamental level, almost identical. Small policy differences among provinces, combined with differing interactions between the three sets of programs (federal government, provincial and territorial governments and the Canada Millennium Scholarship Foundation) and discrepancies in the fiscal capacity of provinces and territories to provide appropriate assistance, conspire to make student aid look vastly more complex than it actually is. In this sense, it is a perfect microcosm of Canadian social policy.

Before embarking on a detailed analysis of the different programs, it is worth taking a step back to look at how the system works as a whole. There are three basic paradigms for student assistance in Canada. What is typically considered to be "the" student aid system in fact represents just one of these paradigms. In this main paradigm—which accounts for 98% or more of the total assistance provided in Canada—aid is given to full-time students on the basis of financial need. There are two other paradigms, however: one for part-time students (in which aid is awarded on the basis of income rather than need) and another which is primarily for Northern residents (in which all students are awarded aid regardless of income or need). While most of this chapter is devoted to the programs that make up the main paradigm, some attention will also be devoted to other paradigms of student financial assistance.

Within the main student aid paradigm, there are three interlocking sets of programs: the Canada Student Loans system, the provincial student assistance systems and the Canada Millennium Scholarship Foundation. Even in Quebec, the Northwest Territories and Nunavut, which have chosen to opt out of the Canada Student Loans Program, the federal system still contributes through a system of alternative payments which support the provincial or territorial component of the paradigm. However, these two or three systems do not interact with one another consistently across all jurisdictions. This leads to significant variations in the aid available to students in each province and territory, even if the underlying principles of the various programs are quite similar.

The thrust of the "micro-policy" of student aid programs is essentially identical in all provinces and territories, but small differences in policy between jurisdictions can lead to vastly different outcomes. All students make a single application to a provincial or territorial government to obtain access to all three forms of student assistance (or just two in jurisdictions operating outside of the Canada Student Loans Program). At this point their *eligibility* (see Section II of this chapter) for student loans is examined and a *need assessment* (Section III) is then conducted. Very simply, a need assessment involves adding up a student's total resources (including those of parents and spouses, if appropriate) and subtracting them from the student's total costs; the resulting figure is defined as the student's "need." If the number is greater than zero, the student can obtain assistance.

The rules differ in each province, but if need is low then assistance generally comes solely in the form of a loan. As need rises, so too does the likelihood that the student will receive part of his or her assistance in the form of a grant. The Canada Millennium Scholarship Foundation's millennium bursaries are specifically intended for the students with the highest need in each province, thus ensuring that at least some grants are available to high-need students in each jurisdiction. Regardless of a student's calculated need, aid is usually capped at a "maximum," which may differ based on the student's province, the student's level of study, the presence of dependants and physical disability (see Section IV on *available aid*).

Some—but not all—aid is *portable* across the country (Section V). All federal assistance and the Canada Millennium Scholarship Foundation's millennium bursaries are portable, as are most provincial loans. Provincial grants tend to be less portable.

While a student remains enrolled on a full-time basis, all governments pay the cost of interest on the loans (Section VI). Before a student leaves school, some provincial governments provide *debt reduction* (sometimes known as loan remission) on loans if students have taken on exceptionally large loan burdens (Section VII). In some provinces, remission occurs on an annual basis, while in others it occurs at the end of a program (whether it be a degree, a diploma or a certificate), or even on a monthly basis.

At the end of their studies, students must *repay* any student loans they have acquired (Section VIII). Even after the end of their studies, however, there are loan subsidies available in the form of grace periods on interest payments, interest relief and debt reduction.

Finally, Section IX looks at the bottom line of all these rules: the *total aid available to students* in aggregate. It also considers changes in the amount of repayable and non-repayable aid over time.

II. Eligibility

Students must apply and qualify for student assistance in their province or territory of residence. "Province or territory of residence" usually means the province or territory where an individual most recently lived for at least 12 consecutive months *without* attending a post-secondary institution on a full-time basis. However, not all jurisdictions have precisely the same residency requirements—the Northwest Territories in particular uses a different criteria for residency—so it is theoretically possible that a Canadian citizen residing in Canada but moving between jurisdictions may be unable to receive student assistance in any jurisdiction.

Generally speaking, to be eligible for student assistance a student must meet the following criteria:

1. Be a Canadian citizen, permanent resident (this includes landed immigrants) or protected person.

2. Be enrolled in or be qualified to enrol in

   a. at least 60% of a full-time course load (usually 40% if the student has a permanent disability)

   b. a program of at least 12 weeks' duration within a period of 15 consecutive weeks

   c. a designated post-secondary institution.

The "full-time course load" criterion exists to ensure that assistance only goes to those individuals who are studying on a full-time basis and are therefore unable to work on a full-time basis. The Government of Canada also has a loans program for part-time students, but its take-up rate is extremely low. Fewer than 4,000 students across the country make use of it (from a pool of over half-a-million part-time students at colleges and universities).

The "12 weeks" criterion exists to ensure that the program is of sufficient quality/intensiveness to be worthy of public subsidy.

The "designated post-secondary institution" criterion is meant to allow governments some control over where students can use their student loan money. Over 2,000 institutions in Canada are designated as eligible to receive Canada Student Loans; 85% of these are for-profit private training institutions. Designation criteria can vary considerably in stringency from jurisdiction to jurisdiction.

In addition, student aid programs usually have some financial criteria which must be met in order to receive assistance. Students who have previously defaulted on a student loan can be denied further loans, and several programs, including the Canada Student Loans Program, require students to pass a credit check as well. This rule tends to apply only to older students who have established some kind of credit history. The general rule, where it exists, is that that an individual with three "credit events" (i.e., missed payments) of over 90 days on amounts exceeding $1,000 during the previous 36 months will be denied a student loan.

Program Limits, Lifetime Limits and Debt Limits

Governments also limit eligibility by imposing temporal and financial limits on eligibility. For each degree, certificate or diploma they undertake, students can only receive assistance for a finite period of time. There is also a limit on "lifetime eligibility."

The time limit for each credential is usually the "normal duration" of the program, plus one year. In theory, "normal duration" represents one year for a certificate, two years for a college diploma and four years for a university degree. In practice, however, things are less simple: exceptions are routinely made for students in longer programs (e.g., engineering, which usually takes five years) and for students who switch degree programs. The limit on lifetime eligibility, including both borrowing and interest-free status, is 340 "weeks of study," (which in practice means ten academic years). A short extension is permitted for doctoral students (400 weeks), and students with disabilities are allowed a longer timeframe (520 weeks). For part-time students, there is no maximum duration of assistance; however, the outstanding principal of all Canada Student Loans cannot exceed a cumulative maximum of $4,000.

Table 5A.II.1 — Comparison of Student Assistance Eligibility Criteria 2003–04

Program	Citizenship	Provincial Residency	60% (40% for Students With Disabilities)	12 Weeks	Credit Checks
Canada Student Loans Program	√	N/A	√	√	√
BC	√	√	√	√	√
AB	√	√	√	Any length, provided studies are full-time	√
SK	√	√	√	√	√
MB	√	√	√	√	√
ON	√	√	√	√	√
QC	√	√	80%		
NB	√	√	√	√	√
PE	√	√	√	√	√
NS	√	√	√	√	√
NL	√	√	80%	√	√
YT	√	Generally requires two years of residency before eligibility for territorial assistance is granted. A shorter (12-month) waiting period for eligibility is only possible if the individual is under 19 and completes at least one year of secondary school in Yukon.	Semester 1–6:60% Semester 7+: 75%	√	√
NT	√	√	√		
NU	√	√	√	√	
Canada Millennium Scholarship Foundation	√	Varies[a]	Varies[a]	Varies[a]	Varies[a]

Note: [a] The Canada Millennium Scholarship Foundation is legally required to integrate with provincial and territorial programs whenever possible. As a result of a series of negotiated agreements with the provinces and territories, eligibility criteria for the Foundation's millennium bursaries in each province and territory are largely similar to those of the provincial or territorial program in each jurisdiction. Eligibility criteria for millennium bursaries therefore vary slightly from one jurisdiction to another. However, the Foundation also has its own eligibility criteria which differ from those of the provincial and territorial programs—most notably, students must have completed at least 60% of a year of full-time studies in order to be considered for a millennium bursary, and only students at the *undergraduate* level are eligible.

A few jurisdictions also put limits on the total amount of assistance an individual can receive. Sometimes these limits are applied to the total amount of assistance received (e.g., millennium bursaries); sometimes they are applied to the total amount borrowed (e.g., British Columbia, Quebec). These categories sound similar but are actually different—jurisdictions with debt limits will permit total borrowing in excess of the debt limit, provided that the student has already paid back some earlier loans, whereas in the case of a limit on total assistance, the student can never receive additional assistance from a particular source once the limit has been reached.

Table 5A.II.2 compares student assistance program limits across the country.

Table 5A.II.2 — Comparison of Student Assistance Program Limits

Program	Limit per Program	Lifetime Limit	Debt Limit
Canada Student Loans Program	Normal duration plus one year	340 weeks (doctorate = 400; students with disabilities = 520)	None
BC	Normal duration plus one year	As per CSLP	$35,000 (borrowing limit)
AB	Normal duration plus one year	**Undergraduate and private vocational school students:** $40,000 Master's — $50,000 Ph.D. — $60,000 **Professional students:** Pharmacy, optometry, veterinary — $50,000 Dental hygienist — $55,000 MBA, chiropractic — $60,000 Law — $70,000 Dentistry, medicine — $95,000	None
SK	Normal duration plus one year	As per CSLP	None
MB	Normal duration plus one year	As per CSLP	None
ON	Normal duration plus one year	As per CSLP, except no limit for students with disabilities	None
QC	Normal duration plus one trimester (grants) Normal duration plus three trimesters (loans)	22 semesters at university level	**Borrowing limits** Secondary School — $21,000 CEGEP (college) — $15,000 to $25,000, depending on the program Undergraduate — $25,000 to $30,000, depending on program length Master's — $35,000 to $40,000, depending on program length Doctorate — $45,000 Outside Canada — $60,000
NB	Normal duration plus one year	As per CSLP	None
PE	Normal duration plus one year	As per CSLP	None
NS	Normal duration plus one year	As per CSLP	None
NL	Normal duration plus one year	As per CSLP	None
YT	Normal duration plus one year	Five years/Ten semesters/ 15 quarters	None
NT	None	20 semesters	$47,000 (borrowing limit)
NU	Normal duration plus one year	None	$26,600 if in receipt of a Basic Grant (see Table 5A.IV.2) $36,000 if not in receipt of a Basic Grant
Canada Millennium Scholarship Foundation	N/A	32 months	$20,000

III. Need Assessment

In most of Canada, student assistance is not a universal program.[1] It is not even an income-tested program. Rather, it is a need-tested program. The distinction between income-tested and need-tested is crucial: the former simply tests income, while the latter tests both income and costs. In an income-tested program, two people with identical incomes will receive the same benefits. In a need-tested program, like student assistance, two people with identical incomes may receive very different benefits if their respective costs for attending post-secondary education are different. The assessment process for student assistance programs is thus considerably more complicated than the assessment process for other income-support programs.

How Need is Assessed

In Canadian student assistance programs need is assessed according to the following four-step procedure:

1. The student's category is identified.

2. The costs of the student's post-secondary studies are assessed.

3. The student's available resources are determined.

4. The student's need is calculated by subtracting available (or expected) resources from assessed costs.

Step 1. Determining a Student's Category

A student's category determines the types of expenses that are considered, as well as the resources that are taken into account when need is assessed.

Each student falls into one of the following six categories:

1. Single Dependent—living at Home (SDH)

2. Single Dependent—living Away from home (SDA)

3. Single Independent—living at Home (SIH)

4. Single Independent—living Away from home (SIA)

5. Married (M)

6. Single Parent (SP).

Different types of students have different assessed costs. Students living at home are considered to have lower costs than students who are living away from home. Married students are considered to have higher costs than single students. Students with children or other dependants have additional costs, based on the number of dependants in the family.

In addition to affecting the way costs are assessed, the distinction between dependent and independent student is crucial in terms of the student's resources. Independent students only have their own resources assessed. Dependent students have their parents' income assessed as well, which makes obtaining assistance considerably more difficult. Married students, similarly, have their partners' resources taken into account. The various definitions of dependent and independent are shown in Table 5A.III.1.

Table 5A.III.1 — Definition of an Independent Student

Program	A student is independent if he or she is ...
Canada Student Loans Program, plus all provinces/ territories except ON and QC	Married/divorced/widowed, has a dependant, has been in the workforce for two years and/or has been out of secondary school for at least four years.
ON	Married/divorced/widowed, has a dependant, has been in the workforce for two years and/or has been out of secondary school for at least five years. (Note: As of August 2004, Ontario will adopt CSL definition.)
QC	Married/divorced/widowed, has a dependant, is at least 20 weeks pregnant, has been in the workforce for two years, has completed a Bachelor's degree, has been out of full-time studies for seven years and/or has no surviving parents.
NU/NT	Not applicable, all students considered independent.

1. Nunavut and the Northwest Territories are an exception: they provide most student assistance on a universal basis rather than according to assessed need.

Step 2. Assessing Student Costs

In the Canada Student Loans Program's need assessment process, the cost of post-secondary studies includes both education and living costs. A student's education and living costs are assessed for the entire academic year. All of the provinces adopt a similar approach, with some differences in Quebec, Ontario and the Northwest Territories. Table 5A.III.2 lists the educational and monthly allowances for each province sorted by student category.

In addition to these costs, there is a range of costs that can be taken into consideration on an exceptional, case-by-case basis. These include alimony and child support, funeral costs, legal expenses, etc. Provinces usually also have some discretion in making allowances for items like relocation expenses.

Table 5A.III.2 — Assessed Costs During Study Period

Program	Tuition and Fees	Books and Supplies	Living Allowances	Travel	Childcare
Canada Student Loans Program, plus all provinces/ territories except AB, ON and QC	Actual amount payable to the educational institution	Up to a maximum of $3,000	See Table 5A.III.3	If living away from home, up to two trips per year (max. $600 per trip)	Actual cost, up to a monthly ceiling which varies from $400 to $800, depending on the province
AB	As per CSLP	Actual costs as stipulated by the institution	See Table 5A.III.3	As per CSLP	Actual cost, up to $430/ month with receipts; if single parent, up to $75/month without receipts; if married, $0 if spouse is not working.
ON	Actual amount, except for deregulated fee programs in Ontario, for which tuition and compulsory fees are capped at $2250/term for non-co-op programs and $2675/term for co-op programs.	As per CSLP	See Table 5A.III.3	As per CSLP	For married students with 1–2 children, actual costs up to $40/wk per child. With 3+ children, up to $80/wk (for the first two children) and Ontario bursary assistance for additional children. For sole-support parents with 1–2 children, actual costs up to $83/wk per child. For 3+ children, up to $166/wk (for the first two children) and Ontario bursary assistance for additional children.
QC	Actual amount, up to a maximum of $6,000/trimester	Up to a maximum of $375/term, depending on the program	See Table 5A.III.3	$498/year if the student is from one of Quebec's "regions périphiques"	Up to $35/week per child (based on cost of public daycare)
NT/NU	Varies depending on territory and Aboriginal status	Varies depending on territory and Aboriginal status	Varies depending on territory and Aboriginal status	Up to two economy-class return trips per year	Varies

Table 5A.III.3 — Monthly Student Living Allowances for 2003–04

Program	NL	PE	NS	NB	QC (CSLP)[a]	QC (AFE)[b]
Single student away from home	$761	$758	$804	$774	$800	$701
Single parent (without dependants)	$1,019	$980	$1,064	$1,036	$1,018	$950
Married student & spouse (without dependants)	$1,519	$1,515	$1,605	$1,555	$1,454	No special calculation—assumed to be single
Each dependant[c]	$349	$393	$415	$391	$406	$325 for the first child; $300 for each additional child
Single student living at home	$348	$380	$374	$372	$370	$325

Program	ON	MB	SK	AB (CSLP/PSL)	BC	YT	NT & NU
Single student away from home	$937	$824	$777	$821/730	$971	$933	$1,127
Single parent (without dependants)	$1,212	$1,007	$966	$1,018	$1,238	$1,295	$1,476
Married student & spouse (without dependants)	$1,799	$1,591	$1,497	$1,584/1,455	$1,920	$1,877	$2,076
Each dependant[c]	$500	$461	$399	$432/315	$518	$417	$581
Single student living at home	$391	$394	$375	$392/347	$402	$409	$431

Source: *Canada Student Loans Program Policy Manual, Aide Financière aux Etudes Student Financial Assistance Guide* and the Government of Alberta.

Note: [a] This column refers to allowable living expenses for students receiving Canada Student Loans and residing in Quebec.

[b] This column refers to allowable living expenses for students receiving assistance through the Government of Quebec's Aide Financière aux Études (AFE). AFE applies the same living allowance calculation regardless of where a student studies. AFE uses a weekly rather than a monthly allowance for living expenses—in this chart, weeks have been converted to months at a rate of 4.35 weeks per month. Childcare costs are calculated on a yearly basis, and have been converted to months by assuming a school year of eight months. Admissible childcare costs are lower in Quebec because the province provides substantial family assistance *outside* the student assistance system.

[c] The amounts in this row are added to the baseline amount for a single parent without dependants.

Table 5A.III.3 shows the living allowances used in the need assessment process by jurisdiction. The amount of the living allowance varies from one jurisdiction to the next according to the cost of living in each province and territory. Of particular interest in this table is the difference between students who receive assistance from the Canada Student Loans Program and those who receive it through Quebec's Aide Financière aux Études. The Canada Student Loans Program clearly allows higher expenses for students in Quebec than the Quebec government does. It is also clear that Quebec students are at a further disadvantage if they leave the province, because the Quebec program does not recognize different cost structures in different provinces. A single Quebec student at the University of Ottawa is thus assumed by the Aide Financière aux Études to be able to survive on $701 a month; a single student from Ontario is assumed by the federal and provincial programs to require $937 to get by.

Table 5A.III.3 also shows that Alberta has, in effect, two cost assessment systems—one to assess eligibility for Canada Student Loans, and one to assess eligibility for provincial student loans. In all categories, the federal allowance is higher than the provincial one.

Step 3. Determining Student Resources

When calculating a student's total resources, assistance programs may take three kinds of resources into account—student resources, family resources and spousal resources. The "expected" contribution from different sources not only differs depending on the source, it often varies by the type of resource. As a result, there are in effect eight different "tax" rates on student resources, depending on the type and source of income.

Table 5A.III.4 looks specifically at the treatment of student income and assets. The comparison shows that there are some significant differences between provinces in terms of calculating student resources and contributions, most notably with respect to personal savings. Quebec and the Northwest Territories do not consider a student's personal savings when calculating resources, whereas in the rest of Canada students are basically required to deplete their savings accounts before they can

Table 5A.III.4 — Student Resources

Program	Pre-Study Income	Study Period Income	Scholarship Income	Savings	Assets
Canada Student Loans Program, plus all provinces except AB, ON and QC	In practice, about $1,600 to $2,200 if the student lived at home, and $25 to $600 if he or she lived away from home[a]	100% of all income over $50/week of study	100% of scholarship income over $1,800	100% of personal savings	Cars worth over $5,000 are considered assets (the first $5,000 is discounted), as is the portion of non-locked-in RRSP exceeding $2,000 x (number of years out of secondary education), if applicable. 100% of assets are considered as resources
AB	As above for CSL; For PSL, if worked less than 2 months, actual savings. 2 months — $720 3 months — $1,080 4 months — $1,450	100% of all income over $225/week	100% of scholarship income over $1,600	Same as above	As per CSLP
ON	As per CSLP	If no scholarship income, then as per CSLP. If scholarship income, then as per CSLP up to a combined work plus scholarship maximum of $3,500	If no work income, then 100% of scholarship income over $3,500. If work income, then 100% of a combined work plus scholarship income of $3,500	As per CSLP	As per CSLP, except for RRSP exception which is $2,000 x number of years out of secondary school
QC	The student's contribution is based on the previous year's educational status: Secondary — $430 College/CEGEP — $940 University — $1,280[b]	50% of all income over the minimum summer contribution	100% of scholarship income over $5,000	0% of personal savings	Assets are not considered as resources
NT (repayable loans only)	10% of net income for four months prior to start of studies	None	0% Scholarships; 100% bursaries and fellowships	0% of personal savings	Assets are not considered as resources
YT and NU	N/A	N/A	N/A	N/A	N/A

Note: [a] The actual amount is the larger of the following two calculations: 1) a minimum monthly contribution (which varies between provinces) or 2) 80% of all income, minus living expenses (as calculated in Table 5A.III.3 above) and taxes.

[b] This amount is based on the assumption that the student did not work in the summer. It may also be reduced based on the number of courses taken over the summer.

receive any government assistance. Some differences also exist between provinces in the treatment of merit scholarship income and work income. Generally speaking, one can say that Quebec and the Northwest Territories' treatment of student income and assets is significantly more lenient than programs in the rest of the country (especially those provinces whose approach is identical to the Canada Student Loans Program).

Table 5A.III.5 shows the differences in the treatment of parental contributions across the country. Differences between provinces within the Canada Student Loans Program "zone" are largely restricted to differences in the treatment of parental assets. Only Ontario takes a different approach to parental contributions; even so, the difference is minimal, amounting in practice to requiring a couple of hundred additional dollars from families in the lower-middle part of the income scale.

Table 5A.III.5 — Calculation of Parental Contribution

Program	Parental Income Exemption	Parental Contribution Rate	Treatment of Parental Assets
Canada Student Loans Program, plus all provinces except AB, ON and QC	The exemption varies by province, but below a minimum amount of after-tax income for a two-person family (between $28,228 in NB and $33,672 in BC, plus $5,000 per extra family member), no contribution is required	45% of the first $3,000 of after-tax income above the exemption level, 60% of the next $3,000 of after-tax income above the exemption level and 75% of all income above that	At the discretion of each province, but generally assets are not considered as resources and so no contribution from assets is required
AB	Same as above	Same as above	5% of net worth of parental business assets over $250,000
BC	Same as above	Same as above	1% of personal assets (excluding RRSPs, vehicles and principal residence) over $150,000
ON (until August 2004 — subsequently, as per CSLP)	As above for CSL; for PSL, below the after-tax minimum of $30,000 for a two-person family (plus $5,000 per extra family member), no contribution is required	If after-tax income is between $30,000 and $40,000, the contribution is $100 plus 5% of income over $30,000. If after-tax income is above $40,000, then contribution formula is identical to that of the Canada Student Loans Program above	No contribution from assets is required
QC	Below a pre-tax minimum income of $21,885 (if parents are living together) or $19,755 (if parents are living apart), plus an additional $2,105 if both parents work, plus $2,660 for the first child and $2,400 for each additional child, no contribution is required	The contribution is 19% of the first $36,000 of pre-tax income above the exemption level, 29% of the next $10,000 in income, 39% of the next $10,000 in income, and 49% of any income above that	Assets under $90,000 ($250,000 for farmers and fishers) are exempt; parents are required to make a contribution equal to 2% of the value of their assets above this level
NT (repayable loans only)	N/A	No contribution required	None
YT and NU	N/A	N/A	N/A

Figure 5A.III.1 — Expected Parental Contributions in Quebec, Manitoba and Ontario

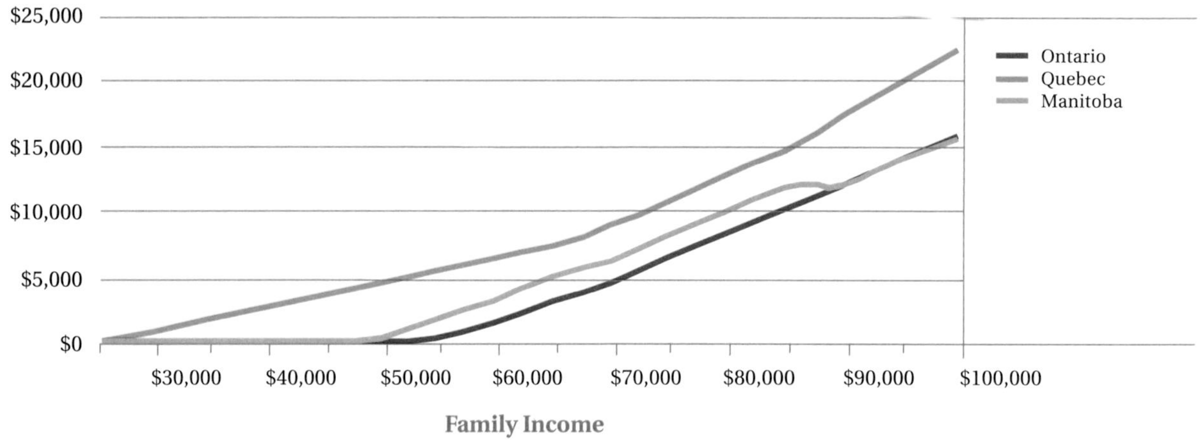

Source: Canada Student Loans Program and Aide Financière aux Études.

Because Quebec's parental contributions are done on a pre-tax rather than a post-tax basis, comparing Quebec's treatment of parental contributions with other programs across the country is somewhat more difficult. Figure 5A.III.1 helps make the comparison clearer. This diagram compares the expected family contribution for three identical families (two parents and two children, only one of whom is enrolled in post-secondary studies) from Quebec, Ontario (a high-cost CSLP province) and Manitoba (a low-cost CSLP province). The difference in required contributions between Ontario and Manitoba is not that surprising, based as they are on different costs of living in the two provinces. The difference between Quebec and Manitoba, two provinces where the cost of living is roughly equal, is more revealing. The threshold at which family contributions are required is much lower in Quebec than in the rest of Canada. Even though the "tax" rate progresses at a higher rate outside Quebec, at any given level of family income, more is required of parents in Quebec than in the rest of the country.

Table 5A.III.6 shows that there are some notable differences in the treatment of spousal income across the country. The minimum income-exemption level is lower in Quebec than in the rest of Canada; on the other hand, the contribution rate progresses more steeply in the Canada Student Loans Program zone than in Quebec, and assets are "taxed" much more severely. Looking back at Table 5A.III.5 reveals that Quebec assesses spousal and parental contributions equally, while in the rest of the country, spouses are required to contribute at much lower levels of income than parents, and their contribution rate progresses more steeply. In fact, in the Canada Student Loans Program zone a married student with no dependants whose spouse earned $25,000 or more would have spousal contributions set so high that he or she would likely be ineligible for loans. A similar student in Quebec would not have any expected spousal contributions and would therefore still receive a substantial amount of assistance. These differences are shown in Figure 5A.III.2.

Table 5A.III.6 — Calculation of Spousal Contribution

Program	Spousal Income Exemption	Spousal Contribution Rate	Treatment of Spousal Assets
Canada Student Loans Program, plus all provinces except AB, ON and QC	Equal to the student's living allowance (see Table 5A.III.3), which in practice amounts to between $11,600 and $14,800 (after tax) per eight-month school year	The highest of the following amounts: 1) a minimum monthly contribution (varies by province between $800 and $1,000/month, minus the monthly living allowance (in practice, about $150), or 2) 80% of all income above the living allowance (see Table 5A.III.3)	Cars worth over $5,000 are considered assets, as are RRSPs worth more than $2,000 x (student's age - 18). 100% of assets are considered as resources.
AB	As above for CSL; For PSL, $200/month	As above for CSL; for PSL, 100% of income above minimum	Same as above
ON	For married students where one partner is a student, 20% of spouse's net income during the study period. Where both spouses are students, 100% of 50% of partner's net income during the study period less an exemption of $50/wk of study	For married students where one partner is a student, the minimum expected contribution is (Ontario minimum wage X average number of weekly work hours X 4.3 less partner's monthly taxes X number of months in the study period). For married students where both spouses are students, there is no expected minimum contribution	Same as above
QC	Below a pre-tax minimum income of $19,755, plus $2,660 for the first child and $2,400 for each additional child, no contribution is required	The contribution is 19% of the first $36,000 of pre-tax income above the exemption level, 29% of the next $10,000 in income, 39% of the next $10,000 in income and 49% of any income above that	Not considered
NT (repayable loans only)	None	10% of net income for four months prior to start of studies	None
YT and NU	N/A	N/A	N/A

Step 4. Calculating Assessed Student Need

This is the simplest part of the need assessment exercise. Assessed need is determined by subtracting the student's total assessed resources from his or her total assessed costs. If the resulting figure is zero or less, then the student is not considered to have "need" and is therefore ineligible for student assistance. If the figure is positive, the student is eligible for assistance. Ideally, the student would be able to receive an amount of assistance equal to his or her assessed need; however, as detailed in Section IV of this chapter, the amount of available aid is finite, therefore the level of assistance received by the student may not always equal his or her assessed need.

The Exception: Part-Time Student Loans

In the much smaller world of part-time student loans, need testing does not exist. Instead, a much simpler family-income test is used in order to determine whether a student is eligible for assistance. Assets, expenditures and so on are not considered.

In addition to being a simpler test, the assessment for part-time students is actually considerably more generous than the need assessment formula for full-time students. An independent full-time student earning $14,000 would be unlikely to receive any assistance under the Canada Student Loans Program. If the same student were to drop one or

Figure 5A.III.2—Expected Spousal Contributions in Quebec, Manitoba and Ontario

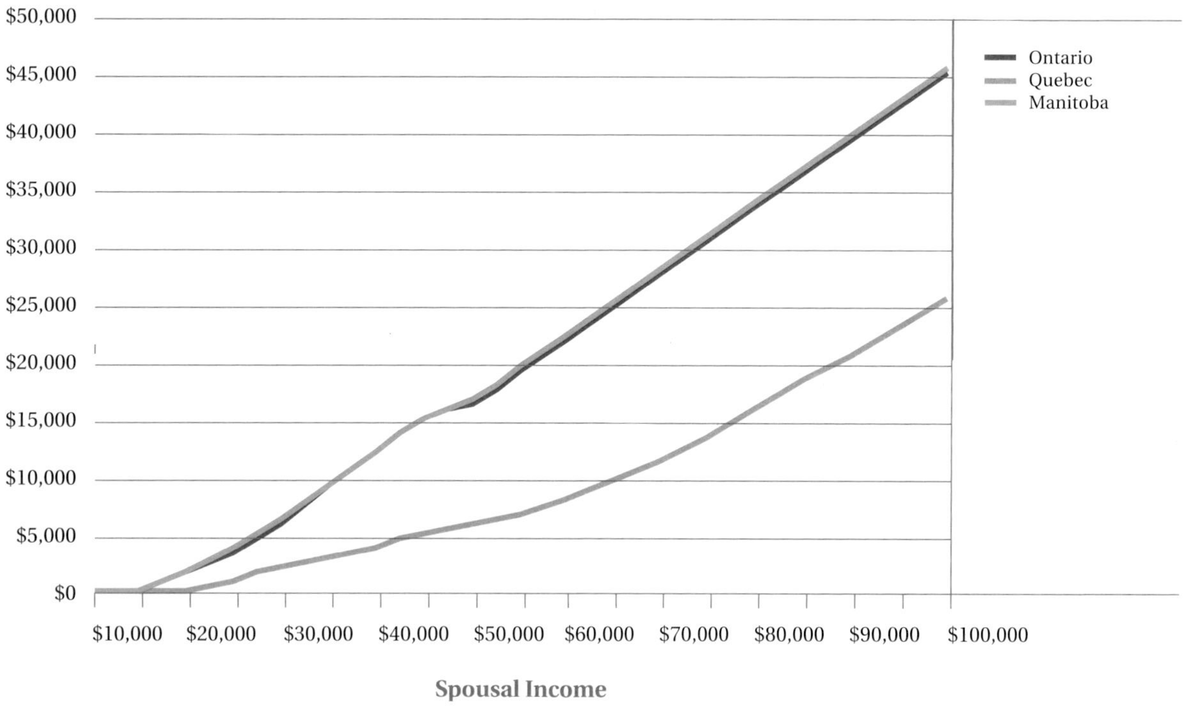

Spousal Income

Source: Canada Student Loans Program and Aide Financière aux Études.

two courses and become a part-time student, he or she would instantly be eligible for $4,000 in loans and $1,200 in grants. The only disadvantage of part-time loans, from a financial point of view, is that the borrower must pay interest on the loan while he or she is still in school (which is not the case for full-time loans).

One might expect that this anomaly would lead some students to drop courses in order to benefit from the less stringent eligibility criteria for assistance; however, evidence shows that the take-up rate on part-time loans and grants is exceedingly low. This suggests that students either do not know about the difference between the two programs or that the financial benefit they would reap by moving to part-time student assistance is outweighed by the accompanying delay in completing their studies.

Table 5A.III.7 — Means Test for Canada Student Loans (for Part-Time Students) and Canada Study Grants (for High-Need Part-Time Students)

Family Size	Maximum Family Income to Qualify for $4,000 Loan	Maximum Family Income to Qualify for $1,200 Grant
1	$26,100	$14,100
2	$34,800	$23,300
3	$43,600	$31,900
4	$50,500	$37,800
5	$56,300	$43,700
6	$62,400	$48,600
7	$68,300	$53,000
8	$72,600	$56,800
9	$75,200	$60,100
10	$78,200	$62,700

IV. Available Aid

Student assistance is available to meet a student's assessed need, as explained in the previous section, up to a pre-determined maximum. This maximum is usually expressed in terms of dollars of assistance per week of study, but can be expressed on an annual basis (as is the case in Quebec and Alberta). Although the Canada Student Loans Program tries to set "equal conditions" across the country by providing aid up to a standard maximum of $165 per week, the actual maximum amount of assistance across the country can vary considerably according to a student's situation and the generosity of the provincial student assistance system.

The Basic Package for Full-Time Students

Single, full-time students (who comprise the vast majority of students in the post-secondary education system) are treated similarly in those provinces which fall within the Canada Student Loans Program zone. Under the "60/40" formula, the Government of Canada provides a student with aid equivalent to 60% of his or her assessed need, up to a maximum of $165 per week. Provincial governments provide the remaining 40%, leading to a loan maximum of $275 per week or $9,350 per year for students in a standard 34-week program. In some provinces, assistance from the Canada Millennium Scholarship Foundation (i.e., millennium bursaries) can be added to student loan maxima; in others, millennium bursaries replace part of the student loan.[2] Table 5A.IV.1 shows the available aid in different provinces across the country.

Figure 5A.IV.1 provides a graphic representation of the aid maxima across the country. Considered in this way, Quebec appears to be considerably more "generous" than other jurisdictions. But these values represent theoretical maxima rather than the amounts which students actually receive. In fact, due to stricter need assessment criteria (see Section III above), lower tuition fees, subsidized daycare, higher family allowances and lower costs of living, students in Quebec tend to have lower need, and thus receive *less* student assistance than students

Figure 5A.IV.1 — Weekly Need-Based Assistance Limits for Single Full-Time Students Without Dependants in 2003–04

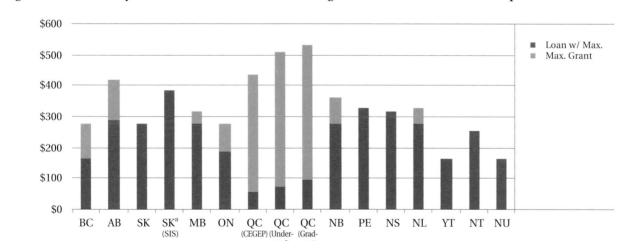

Note: [a] Through its Debt Reduction Program, the Government of Saskatchewan reduces all student loan amounts to a maximum of $200/week of study. See Table 5A.VII.I for a full description.

2.   It is important to note that the Canada's Millenium Scholarship Foundation's Millennium Bursary Program is non-repayable assistance in every Canadian jurisdiction, however, in Manitoba, New Brunswick, Prince Edward Island, Saskatchewan and Nova Scotia the money is paid as loan remission and is not included in the total award to the student. Where millenium bursaries appear as upfront cash grants they are displayed in Tables 5A.IV.1 and .2 and where the bursaries are debt remission they appear in Table 5A.VII.1 dealing with debt reduction.

elsewhere in the country. Similarly, the territories appear to provide less assistance to their students than other jurisdictions, but this is true only insofar as need-based aid is concerned. Most territorial student assistance is provided on a universal basis (as detailed below). When the two types of assistance are combined, the total territorial student assistance maxima are considerably more than those of provincial programs, reflecting the much higher living and transportation costs faced by northern students.

Table 5A.IV.1 — Need-Based Assistance Limits for Single, Full-Time Students With No Dependants in 2003–04 (Based on 34 Weeks of Study)

Province/ Territory	Type of Student	Total Maximum Loan	Total Maximum Grants	Source of Grants	Total Maximum Assistance[a]
BC	Single, no dependants	$275/week	$110/week (weeks 37–136 of post-secondary only)	B.C. Grant, millennium bursary	$275/week
AB	Single, no dependants	$14,300/year ($421/week)	$3,000/semester ($88/week)	Alberta Opportunity Grant (1st or 2nd year), millennium bursary (2nd year onward)	$14,300/year ($421/week)
SK[b]	Single, no dependants	$275/week	$0	N/A	$275/week
	Special Incentive Students[c] (no dependants)	$385/week	$0	N/A	$385/week
MB	Single, no dependants	$275/week	$40/week	Manitoba Study Assistance	$315/week
ON	Single, no dependants	$275/week	$3,000 bursary/year ($88/week)	Millennium bursary	$275/week
QC	Cegep student	$2,005/year[d] ($59/week)	$12,787/year ($376/week)	AFE Bursary, millennium bursary	$14,792/year ($435/week)
	Undergraduate student	$2,460/year[d] ($72/week)	$14,853/year ($437/week)	AFE Bursary, millennium bursary	$17,293/year ($509/week)
	Graduate student	$3,255/year[d] ($96/week)	$14,853/year ($437/week)	AFE Bursary	$18,088/year ($533/week)
NB	Single, no dependants	$275/week	$90/week	New Brunswick Bursary	$365/week
PE	Single, no dependants	$330/week	$0	N/A	$330/week
NS	Single, no dependants	$315/week	$0	N/A	$315/week
NL	Single, no dependants	$275/week	Up to $1,750/year ($51/week)	Millennium bursary	$326/week
YT	Single, no dependants	$165/week	$0 (but see non-need-based aid below)	N/A	$165/week
NT	Single, no dependants	$1,100/month	$0 (but see non-need-based aid)	N/A	$1,100/month ($253/week)
NU	Single, no dependants	$165/week	$0 (but see non-need-based aid)	N/A	$165/week

Note: [a] The values in the "Total Maximum Loan" and "Total Maximum Grants" columns do not necessarily add up to the figure in the final column, "Total Maximum Assistance," because grants sometimes displace loans.

[b] Through its Debt Reduction Program, the Government of Saskatchewan reduces all student loans amount to a maximum of $200/week of study. See Table 5A.VII.I for a full description.

[c] Special Incentive Students include Non-Status Indians, Métis and students residing in northern Saskatchewan.

[d] These totals apply only for students eligible for both loans and grants (students within the normal duration of studies plus one term). If a student is eligible for loans only (students within normal duration of studies plus two or three terms), then the total maximum assistance will be equal to the maximum loan amount.

Non-Need-Based Aid

Some jurisdictions, in addition to (or instead of) need-based aid, also provide non-need-based aid—that is, a flat amount of assistance for all students regardless of income. Table 5A.IV.2 summarizes the different non-need-based programs across the country.

Table 5A.IV.2 — Non-Need-Based Aid Programs in Canada

Province	Name of Program	Type of Student	Amount
PE	Island Student Awards	Third and fourth year at UPEI, second and third year at Holland College and second year at Université Sainte-Anne	$600/year, lifetime maximum of $1,200
YT	Yukon Grant	Any post-secondary student	$1,240/semester plus return airfare to Edmonton or Vancouver
NT	Basic Grant	NT Indigenous Aboriginal Students and all students schooled from grade 1–12 in the NWT	Up to $1,750/semester for tuition and fees, and up to $300/semester for books and supplies and up to two return economy-class return trips/year
	Supplementary Grant	NT Indigenous Aboriginal Students	$300/month if the student is living with his or her parents; minimum $700/month if living alone and it varies after that depending on martial status and dependants
	Remissible Loan (which is remised at a rate of min. $1,000/every four months lived in the NWT if the student graduates and lives in the Northwest Territories after graduation)	NT Indigenous Aboriginal Students and all students schooled from grade 1–12 in the NWT.	$300/month if the student is living with his or her parents; $700/month if living alone or with a working spouse; plus $200/month for the first three dependants and $50/month for each additional dependant
NU	Basic Grant	NU Aboriginals and individuals schooled in NU (one year of grants for every three years of school in NU)	$1,250 plus return airfare to the nearest Arctic college location or the nearest southern "gateway city" (Ottawa, Montreal, Winnipeg or Edmonton)
	Supplementary Grant Primary Loans Secondary Loans	NU Aboriginals	Up to $200 for books plus monthly allowance of between $205 and $1,505, depending on marital status, dependants, etc. (a single independent student with no dependants receives $675/month)
		Students receiving a Basic Grant (see above)	$3,200/year plus $4,000 for the first dependant and $500 for each additional dependant
		Students not receiving a Basic Grant	$4,400/year plus $5,200 for the first dependant and $500 for each additional dependant

Assistance for Students with Dependants

In addition to the aid available in the basic packages, most student aid programs provide students with dependants with extra resources in consideration of their greater level of financial need. The total amount of assistance available for students with dependants, not surprisingly, varies somewhat across the country. Within the Canada Student Loans Program zone there is a standard assistance program known as the Canada Study Grants for Students with Dependants. This program provides an extra $40 per week in grants to students who have either one or two dependants and $60 per week to students with three or more dependants. In addition to this, many provinces set higher assistance limits for students with dependants.

Table 5A.IV.3 — Total Need-Based Assistance Limits for Full-Time Students With One Dependant in 2003–04 (Based on 34 Weeks of Study)

Province	Basic Assistance Limit	Canada Study Grant for Students With Dependants	Additional Provincial/ Territorial Assistance for Students With Dependants	Total Aid Maximum
BC	$275/week	$40/week	Up to $120/week in grants (for the first 170 weeks of post-secondary only) or loans (thereafter)	$435/week
AB	$14,300/year ($421/week)	$40/week	Up to $6,000 in maintenance grants	$21,660/year ($637/week)
SK	$275/week	$40/week	Up to $85/week in grants	$400/week
MB	$315/week	$40/week	None	$355/week
ON	$275/week	$40/week	Up to $185/week in loans (and eligible for remission)	$500/week (also applies to married students)
QC (CEGEP)	$14,792/year ($435/week)	N/A	$3,450 ($112/week)	$18,602/year ($547/week)
QC (undergraduate)	$17,293/year ($509/week)	N/A	$3,450 ($112/week)	$20,743/year ($610/week)
QC (graduate)	$18,088/year ($533/week)	N/A	$3,450 ($112/week)	$21,538/year ($634/week)
NB	$355/week[a]	$40/week	None	$395/week
PE	$330/week	$40/week	None	$370/week
NS	$315/week	$40/week	None	$355/week
NL	$326/week	$40/week	None	$366/week
YT	$165/week	$40/week	None	$205/week
NT	$1,100/month ($253/week)	N/A	None (but see non-need-based aid above)	$1,100/month ($253/week)
NU	$165/week	N/A	None (but see non-need-based aid above)	$165/week

Note: [a] The maximum assistance level from Canada Student Loans, provincial student loans and New Brunswick Bursaries is $10 lower for students with dependants than students without dependants ($355 vs. $365).

V. Portability

In theory, social benefits provided by Canadian governments are portable anywhere in Canada. In practice, it is rarely this simple. In the world of student assistance, the Government of Canada and the Canada Millennium Scholarship Foundation provide fully portable loans and grants. Provinces, on the other hand, tend not to view portability as an unalloyed good, and many have put restrictions on the portability of their assistance, particularly in their grant programs.

Table 5A.V.1 shows the portability of student loans across the country. A check mark indicates full portability of loan assistance within Canada and

throughout the world. Deviations from this norm are noted within the table.

Table 5A.V.2 shows the portability of various grant programs across the country. The same pattern emerges—that is, national programs provide greater portability than provincial ones. Nevertheless, the Government of Canada is not wholly immune from the territorial protectiveness shown by the provinces: it does not allow Canada Millennium Scholarship Foundation bursaries to be granted to students studying outside the country's borders (although semesters abroad as part of exchange programs are permitted).

Table 5A.V.1 — Student Loan Portability in Canada

Jurisdiction	Canada Student Loans	Provincial Student Loans
BC	√	√
AB	√	√
SK	√	√
MB	√	√
ON	Portable to public institutions within Canada, otherwise √	Portable to public institution within Canada. Not portable outside of Canada
QC	Not available	√, except for studies in medicine, natural environment technology, nursing (all levels), police technology, recreation leadership training, social service, special care counselling or aircraft piloting
NB	√	√
PE	√	√
NS	√	√
NL	√	√, but some restrictions exist on debt reduction after studies are complete
YT	√	None
NT	Not available	√
NU	Not available	√

Table 5A.V.2 — Student Grant Portability in Canada

Jurisdiction	Canada Study Grants	Canada Millennium Scholarship Foundation Millennium Bursaries	Provincial Grant Programs
BC	√,_	√	Not portable
AB	√,_	√	√, _, except Alberta Opportunities Bursary which is not portable
SK	√,_	√	√, _
MB	√,_	√	√, _
ON	√,_	√	Ontario bursary funding not portable except to students with disabilities
QC	Not available	√	Within Canada, grants are portable only to public institutions. Outside Canada, grants are portable only if the student is studying in France, pursuing graduate studies or studying in a program which is unavailable within Quebec and which fulfills an imperative economic, social or cultural need of the Quebec collective
NB	√,_	√	None
PE	√,_	√	Island Student Awards are only offered to students studying at UPEI, Holland College and Universite Saite-Anne
NS	√,_	√	None
NL	√,_	√	None
YT	√,_	√	√
NT	Not available	√	√, _
NU	Not available	√	√

Note: √ indicates portability throughout Canada.

_ indicates portability outside Canada.

Portability of assistance can also be restricted by creating pools of student assistance funds available only to students attending particular educational institutions within the province. Ontario, for example, has done this in two ways: 1) by matching private donations for institutional need-based funding, and 2) by requiring institutions to set aside 30% of the value of all tuition-fee income generated by tuition fee increases since 1996 for student assistance. Strictly speaking, these are not "government student assistance programs" because they are managed by non-governmental organizations. Nevertheless, these pools of money—which are worth hundreds of millions of dollars—were created by government dictate and are available exclusively to Ontario students who choose not to leave the province of Ontario.

VI. In-School Interest Subsidy

One of the key features of full-time student loans is that students are not required to pay interest on their loans while they continue to be enrolled in full-time studies. Instead, governments pay the interest on students' behalf. Because these payments never pass through a student's hands, this particular form of assistance is nearly invisible to the recipient. Yet the in-school interest subsidy is one of the largest single expenditures governments make on student assistance. Overall, governments across the country spend approximately $500 million per year on in-school interest subsidies.

Even if they remain largely unaware of it, the in-school interest subsidy is extremely important to students. This can be shown by considering the case of two hypothetical students, both of whom need to borrow $6,000 a year for four years of study, with interest at 9% throughout.

Student 1 does not borrow from government programs, preferring a private lending program. The student therefore has to pay interest on outstanding loans while in school and, upon completion of her studies, must repay the entire amount with no outside assistance. At the end of her studies, this student owes $29,908 (assuming accumulating interest compounding annually). If the loan is paid back over ten years, the total cost of this loan, including interest payments, is $45,463, requiring monthly payments of $378.86.

Student 2 borrows from government student assistance programs. During his four years of study, the federal and provincial governments pay out a combined total of $5,400 in interest payments under the in-school interest subsidy, which in this case is worth 13% of the total value of the loan. Assuming, again, that the loan is paid back over ten years, the total cost of the loan, including interest payments, is $36,483, requiring monthly payments of $304.02.

In short, the in-school interest subsidy may be invisible to the student, but it is by no means insignificant.

Table 5A.VI.1 — Hypothetical Demonstration of the Impact of the In-School Interest Subsidy

	Student 1	Student 2
Amount borrowed	$24,000.00	$24,000.00
In-school interest subsidy (9%)	None	$5,400.00
Amount owed	$29,908.00	$24,000.00
Cost of loan over ten years	$45,463.00	$36,483.00
Monthly payments	$378.86	$304.02

Source: Student Aid Policy Manuals and Authors' calculations.

VII. Debt Reduction

In most provinces, students with significant amounts of debt at the end of a period of study are eligible for some form of debt reduction. Debt reduction, sometimes referred to as loan remission, differs from more traditional student grants only because a student receives it at the end of a period of study rather than the start. With the exception of Alberta and Quebec, provinces that provide "upfront" grants do not have debt reduction measures, and vice versa. Debt reduction amounts are not paid to students—they are paid to the financial institution that holds the student's loan on the student's behalf.

Canada is the only country that uses debt reduction as a major means of providing student aid. The perceived advantage of debt reduction schemes over grants is that by applying them at the end of studies, governments can ensure that valuable funds are not awarded to students who drop out before the end of a year.

Canada is the only country that uses debt reduction as a major means of providing student aid.

In some provinces (Saskatchewan, Manitoba and the four Atlantic provinces), the Canada Millennium Scholarship Foundation's millennium bursaries are awarded either wholly or partly as a form of debt reduction. The eligibility criteria for millennium bursaries in these provinces do not differ significantly from provinces where these awards are given as grants; only the timing of the award is different.

Provincial debt reduction schemes can vary considerably among jurisdictions. Some programs distribute money to students automatically, while others require a student to apply for the program. Some are awarded on an annual basis, while others are only applied at the end of a program of studies.

Table 5A.VII.1 shows the considerable diversity in debt reduction programs across Canada. Notably, unlike upfront grants, provincial loan remission programs are for the most part fully portable. The only exception is Newfoundland and Labrador, where loan remission is restricted to those students who attended a program at a Newfoundland and Labrador institution. Nearly half of all student loan recipients in Newfoundland and Labrador who attend programs long enough to be eligible for loan remission do so outside the province (primarily in Nova Scotia); as a result, this is a fairly serious portability restriction.

There is also an interesting new trend in Canadian student assistance: provincial debt reduction initiatives designed to either recruit or retain post-secondary graduates. These include specific loan forgiveness programs for jobs that are difficult to fill or are in fields with urgent labour market demands (e.g., B.C. has a special loan remission program for nursing and medicine students, Saskatchewan also has targeted bursaries for health professionals) or do not pay well (e.g., childcare, Newfoundland's Early Childhood Education Grants for students studying and obtaining full-time employment in this field who remain in the province). To be eligible, students must be enrolled in an approved two-year program and must have borrowed for at least half the length of the program. The grant covers provincial loan debt incurred while in the ECE program. Such programs, often used in the United States, have frequently been suggested as a way to alleviate chronic labour shortages in specific fields. No study, however, has ever actually demonstrated the effectiveness of these programs (see Kirshtein, 2004).

Table 5A.VII.1 — Debt Reduction Programs Across Canada

Jurisdiction	Program	Description	Automatic
BC	None	N/A	N/A
AB	Alberta Student Loan Relief Benefit	Available to first-time, first-year post-secondary students who have been issued more than $2,500/semester in combined federal and provincial loans and have completed a year of studies. The amount of loan relief is equal to the total value of federal and provincial loans minus $2,500/semester of study (normally, $5,000). It is normally paid as a grant at the start of the second semester of first year and replaces PSL.	Yes
	Loan Relief Program Completion Payment	Available to graduating students who have been issued more than $2,500/semester in combined federal and provincial loans. The amount of loan relief is equal to the total value of federal and provincial loans minus $5,000/year of study. It is paid upon completion of studies and applied against provincial loans.	No
SK	Saskatchewan Student Bursary	Available to all students with loan assistance exceeding $200/week of study for the first 170 weeks of post-secondary study.	Yes
	Remission (Special Incentive Students[3] only)	Available to Special Incentive Students whose total student loan assistance exceeds $105/week of study. Remission is available on the amount between $105 and $180 per week of study, and is only applied to the student's first 60 weeks of post-secondary study. Successful completion of 60% of a full course load is required.	No
	Millennium bursary	Available to undergraduate students who meet minimal merit criteria and are among those with the highest need. The award size varies between $2,000 and $4,000, depending on need.	Yes
	Saskatchewan Study Grant	Available to students with dependant children with loan assistance exceeding $275/week of study	Yes
MB	Manitoba Bursary	Given to students who do not receive a Canada Millennium Scholarship Foundation millennium bursary and who have loans exceeding $6,000. The award reduces outstanding loans to a maximum of $6,000/year.	Yes
	Millennium bursary	Available to undergraduate students who meet minimal merit criteria and are among those with the highest need. The award size varies between $1,000 and $4,500, depending on need.	Yes
ON	Ontario Student Opportunity Grant	If the student's combined federal and provincial loan exceeds $7,000 for two terms or $10,500 for three terms, a grant will be awarded to reduce debt to those amounts. It is paid at the end of each year and applied against provincial loans.	Yes
QC	Remission	Available to students who have completed studies within a normal period of time and who have received a bursary during each year of study. The amount of remission is 15% of the outstanding loan.	No

3.   This category includes Non-Status Indians, Métis and students residing in northern Saskatchewan.

Table 5A.VII.1 — Debt Reduction Programs Across Canada (continued)

Jurisdiction	Program	Description	Automatic
NB	Millennium bursary	Available to undergraduate students who meet minimal merit criteria and are among those with the highest need. The award size varies between $2,000 and $4,000, depending on need.	Yes
NS	Debt Reduction	Available upon successful completion of a program to students who graduate with NSL debt (= 50% of borrowers in NS). The program remits 15% of first-year loans, 25% of second-year, 35% of third-year, 45% of fourth-year and 15% of fifth-year. Additional remission can be gained by working in NS for 50 weeks within three years of graduating (25% bonus) or making 12 loan repayments (10% bonus).	No
	Millennium bursary	Available to undergraduate students who meet minimal merit criteria and are among those with the highest need. The award size varies between $2,000 and $3,500, depending on need.	Yes
PE	Debt Reduction Grant	Available to students who complete a year of studies and whose combined federal and provincial loans exceed $6,000. The amount of loan relief is equal to the provincial portion (i.e., 40%)of the student's loan that exceeds $6,000. It is paid following studies upon receipt of proof of graduation.	No
	Millennium bursary	Available to undergraduate students who meet minimal merit criteria and are among those with the highest need. The award size varies between $2,000 and $4,000, depending on need.	Yes
NL	Debt reduction	Available to students who have graduated in a timely manner from a program of study in NL of at least 80 weeks' length. The student's combined federal and provincial debt must exceed $22,016 for programs between 80 and 128 weeks in length or $172/week for programs that exceed 128 weeks. The amount of loan relief is equal to the total value of the student's federal and provincial loans minus the debt minima specified above. It is paid upon completion of studies and applied against provincial loans.	No
	Millennium bursary	Available to undergraduate students who meet minimal merit criteria and are among those with the highest need. The total award size varies between $2,000 and $3,500, depending on need, and 50% comes in the form of loan remission.	Yes
YT	None	N/A	N/A
NT	Remissible loan	Once a student has successfully completed a program of full-time studies, $1,000 will be deducted from his or her outstanding debt for every three months that he or she continues to reside in NT.	No
NU	Primary Loan	Same as NT's remissible loan.	No

VIII. Repayment

The First Six Months

During the first six months after the end of full-time studies, students are not required to make any payments on their student loans. For this reason, this period is often referred to as the "grace period." The grace period reflects the fact that it usually takes some time for recent students to establish themselves in the labour market and start earning enough income to be able to afford regular loan payments. For most provincial and territorial loan programs, this period represents a continuation of the in-school interest subsidy—the government continues to take responsibility for paying the interest on the loan. This is not the case for the Alberta, Ontario, Quebec and Government of Canada programs, however; in these programs, payments are not required during the first six months after graduation, but interest still accumulates, and the student is eventually required to pay it.

Consolidation

At the end of the six-month grace period, students are required to "consolidate" their loans. This term, unfortunately, is somewhat misleading in most of Canada. In theory, consolidation means combining all outstanding loans into one single loan. However, because federal and provincial loan programs operate under different rules with different subsidies, it is usually not possible to consolidate loans from federal and provincial sources into a single loan, although students in Saskatchewan and Ontario have been able to do so from 2001 onwards for loans contracted in 2001 or later; Newfoundland students have been able since April 1, 2004. Moreover, due to changes in loan program operation, even loans from the same source often may not be consolidated. For instance, Canada Student

Table 5A.VIII.1 — Who Pays the Interest on Loans in the Six-Month Grace Period?

Jurisdiction	Canada Student Loans	Provincial/ Territorial Student Loans
BC	Student	Student
AB	Student	Student
SK	Student	Student
MB	Student	Provincial Government[a]
ON	Student	Student
QC	N/A	Student
NB	Student	Provincial Government
PE	Student	Provincial Government
NS	Student	Provincial Government
NL	Student	Provincial Government
YT	Student	N/A
NT	N/A	Territorial Government
NU	N/A	Territorial Government

Note: [a] For those borrowers in repayment who remain in the province after the end of studies, the Government of Manitoba pays the interest for 12 months instead of six.

Loans received since August 2000 under the new "direct lending" program cannot be combined with Canada Student Loans obtained prior to August 2000 under the old "risk premium" system. As a result, students within the Canada Student Loans Program zone who graduate in 2004 and have been in school since 2000 may have up to four separate loans which they must consolidate separately. Students from the Northwest Territories, Nunavut and Quebec, which are outside this zone and have had fewer policy fluctuations with respect to student loans, have only a single loan to repay.

Table 5A.VIII.2 lists the different loans that students in each jurisdiction must consolidate separately.

Table 5A.VIII.2 — Loan Consolidation Groupings and Possible Number of Total Loans

Jurisdiction	Canada Student Loans	Provincial/Territorial Student Loans	Total Possible Number of Loans to Repay
BC	1995–2000; post-2000	1995–2000; post-2000	4
AB	1995–2000; post-2000	1994–2001; post-2001	4
SK	1995–2000; post-2000[a]	1996–2001; post-2001[a]	3
MB	1995–2000; post-2000	1995–2001; post-2001	4
ON	1995–2000; post-2000[a]	Pre-2001; post-2001[a]	3
QC	N/A	Single loan	1
NB	1995–2000; post-2000	1995–2001; post-2001	4
PE	1995–2000; post-2000	1995–2001; post-2001	4
NS	1995–2000; post-2000	1995–2001; post-2001	4
NL	1995–2000; post-2000	1995–2001; post-2001	4
YT	1995–2000; post-2000	None	2
NT	N/A	Single loan	1
NU	N/A	Single loan	1

Note: [a] Provincial and federal loans made after August 2001 to students from Saskatchewan and Ontario may be consolidated into a single loan.

Repayment Conditions

At the time of consolidation, several decisions need to be made by the borrower. The first—within the Canada Student Loans Program zone at least—concerns the interest rate to be paid. Borrowers in this zone are given the choice between paying interest on federal and provincial loans at a floating rate of prime plus 2.5% or a fixed rate of prime plus 5% (this applies only to loans made after 1995; interest rates on pre-1995 loans are set annually by the Government of Canada). The rate is not negotiable in Quebec—it is set biannually by the provincial government at a fixed rate equal to prime plus 0.5%.

The other major decision that must be made at the time of consolidation is the length of the repayment period. The "default" repayment period is ten years, but longer or shorter periods are possible; many provinces have shorter repayment requirements for smaller loans.

Interest Relief

As noted earlier, it can sometimes take a while before a borrower is established in the labour market with sufficient earnings to make regular loan payments. Young workers frequently face low or unstable incomes for long periods of time. Most students manage to establish themselves within six months; others, however, take longer. For this reason, continuation of interest relief beyond the six-month grace period is possible in some cases for unemployed or low-income borrowers.

Most of the country has followed the Government of Canada's lead in establishing a reasonably generous interest relief regime and—unlike many aspects of student loans—the eligibility criteria and benefits for both the federal and provincial/territorial programs are essentially the same.

Table 5A.VIII.3 — Interest Relief Programs Across Canada

	Canada Student Loans Program	Provincial Student Loans Program
Canada Student Loans Program, plus all provinces except QC	For borrowers who meet a low-income test, the government will pay the interest on their student loan for additional six-month periods up to a maximum of 30 months. If financial hardship persists after 30 months, interest relief may be extended to 54 months providing the student increases the loan repayment period to 15 years and still qualifies, and if the student completed studies within the past five years.	Same as the Canada Student Loans Program
QC	N/A	For borrowers who meet a low-income test and who are either looking for work or unable to work due to illness, the government will pay the interest on their student loan for a six-month period, after which a debtor may reapply for interest relief for a maximum of 24 months. Interest relief is only available if the borrower completed studies within the past five years.
YT	Same as the Canada Student Loans Program	No loan program
NT	N/A	For borrowers living in The NWT who meet a low-income test. The government will pay the interest on their student loan for a three-month period, after which a debtor may reapply for interest relief for a maximum of 36 months. For borrowers living outside the NWT who meet a low-income test. The government will lower the payment on their student loan for a three-month period, after which a debtor may reapply for interest relief for a maximum of 36 months. The 36-month maximum takes into account both interest relief and loan payment reduction.

Debt Reduction in Repayment

Within the Canada Student Loans Program zone, there is one further form of assistance available once income relief is exhausted. If, at this point, the borrower is still deemed incapable of repaying his or her loans, then he or she may become eligible for "Debt Reduction in Repayment." This program enables the borrower to receive a one-time debt reduction of $10,000 or 50% of the outstanding Canada Student Loan balance (whichever is less). Subsequent second and third reductions are worth up to $5,000 after additional 12 month increments. With the exception of Newfoundland and Labrador, all provinces in the Canada Student Loans Program zone offer identical programs within their own student loan programs. Neither Quebec nor any of the territories offer a program of this nature.

Default and Bankruptcy

A "default" refers to a situation in which a borrower has missed payment for a certain period of time (three months under the latest Canada Student Loans program rules; 90 days in Quebec). When a loan goes into default, lenders are entitled to take action—including legal recourse and the use of collection agencies—to recover the loan. The situation of a student who defaults on a student loan is similar to that of someone who misses consecutive credit card payments. The longer the borrower delays in making the payment, the more damage the borrower does to his or her own credit rating. Borrowers in default on student loans are also barred from contracting a new student loan and from receiving in-school interest-free status until accrued interest is paid and six consecutive payments are made.

A "bankruptcy" is much more severe. This is a legal process in which a debtor tries to clear existing obligations to all creditors because of an inability to pay. Under federal legislation introduced in 1998, students cannot avoid repaying student loans through bankruptcy for a period of ten years following the completion of their studies. Should a student declare personal bankruptcy, all student loans "survive" the bankruptcy, and the debtor is still required to meet his or her obligations to the lender with respect to this loan. In effect, governments are given status as "preferred creditors" in view of the fact that the loans made by student loan programs are given on extremely generous terms and involve considerable subsidy through interest relief and so forth.

The 2003 Federal Budget has provided some new flexibility with regard to bankrupt borrowers under the Canada Student Loans Program. Students may be eligible for new loans and/or interest-free status until the end of their program of study or three years after the date of the bankruptcy-related event, whichever is earlier. Borrowers who declare bankruptcy after May 2004 may apply for debt management measures such as Interest Relief and Debt Reduction in Repayment.

IX. Total Aid Available to Students

All of the policies and regulations described in the preceding sections are the rules by which governments disburse student assistance. The purpose of this final section is to look at how much aggregate assistance these programs provide to students. It will not cover the cost of these programs to governments, which is the subject of Section 5C.II; nor will it look at assistance on a per-student basis, as this has already been covered in Section 4.XII. The purpose of this section is to show how much total assistance is available to students in the form of loans, grants and remission, and look at changes in the composition of assistance over time.

Student Loans

Figure 5A.IX.1 shows changes in borrowing patterns from 1990–91 to 2002–03. Contrary to much received wisdom in Canada, total student borrowing has declined significantly over the past several years. The increase in student loans in the early 1990s was mostly due to a combination of rising loan limits and policy shifts by provincial governments to favour loans over grants. As a result, student borrowing increased from $1.5 billion in 1990–91 to just over $3.75 billion in 1996–97, before falling again by 33% in real terms to $2.5 billion in 2002–03.

The drop in borrowing since 1996–97 reflects a number of factors, including:

- A decline in the number of borrowers due to tightening of eligibility and contribution criteria (in Quebec and Ontario), tighter restrictions on loans to students at private vocational institutions (in particular in Newfoundland and Labrador and Ontario), and changes to the definition of an "independent student" (in Ontario only).

- A decline in maximum (real) value of loans due to inflation.

- The creation of the Canada Millennium Scholarship Foundation, which spends over $285 million each year to reduce student debt.

The decline in borrowing has been slightly steeper at the provincial level than at the level of the Canada Student Loans Program. Borrowing at the provincial level has dropped 44% from its 1996–97 peak while loans from the Canada Student Loans Program have only dropped by 22%. As a result, the federal share of student loans in Canada has returned to the 60% share it had in the early 1990s, after hitting a mid-1990s low of just under 49%.

Figure 5A.IX.1 — Aggregate Government Student Loans From 1990 to 2003 (in 2003 Dollars)

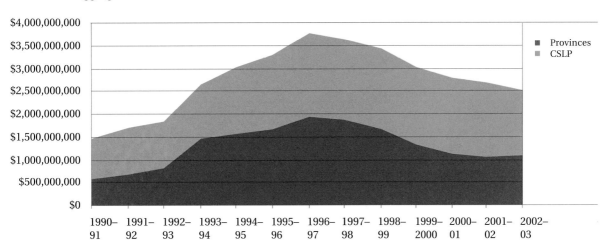

Source: Provincial student assistance programs and Canada Millennium Scholarship Foundation annual reports.

Figure 5A.IX.2 — Aggregate Government Non-Repayable Assistance by Type From 1990 to 2003 (in 2003 Dollars)

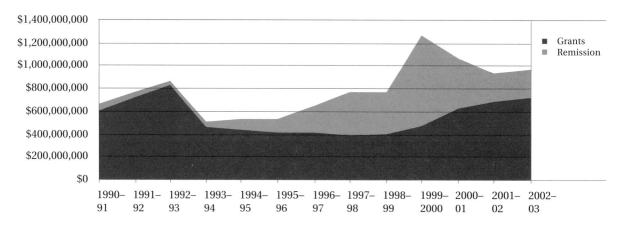

Source: Provincial student assistance programs and Canada Millennium Scholarship Foundation annual reports.

Non-Repayable Assistance

In addition to repayable student loans, Canadian governments also provide two types of non-repayable assistance: grants (money provided at the time of studies) and remission (a grant payable on the student's behalf to a financial institution at the end of a period of studies to reduce an outstanding student loan, as explained in detail in Section 5A.VII). Although Canadian governments cut back on student assistance in the early 1990s, the general trend in non-repayable assistance has been upwards, with annual spending now in the region of $1 billion. Figure 5A.IX.2 shows changes in the level of non-repayable assistance provided over time.

In the early 1990s, provincial governments found that their grant programs' costs were increasing rapidly and had the potential to increase drastically should assistance limits increase (as they did in 1993–94). As most governments were under extreme fiscal pressure at the time, many decided to reduce or eliminate their grant programs at that time. In some cases, these were replaced with loan remission programs. While these remission programs often had similar cost structures to grant programs, payments to students were delayed until the end of the period of studies, by which time the governments' fiscal crisis had usually passed. Most governments eliminated this accounting trick in the

late 1990s and decided either to provide remission on an annual basis or account for it on an accrual basis. The switch from one system to another necessarily involved one year in which booked expenditures were unnaturally high, and the "spike" in student aid in 1999–2000 reflects Ontario's change from one system to another.

As fiscal circumstances improved, governments began to move away from remission programs and back towards grants. Grants comprised 94% of all non-repayable assistance in 1991–92, but declined to only 51% in 1997–98 (and to 38% in the anomalous 1999–2000 year), before rebounding to 75% in 2002–03. This pendulum-swing back towards grants may have already reached its limit, as recent policy announcements in B.C. and Quebec suggest that these two provinces, hitherto largely involved only in grants, will shortly be switching most or all of their non-repayable aid to remission.

Another major change in non-repayable assistance over the last decade is that provincial governments are no longer the sole provider of non-repayable assistance. Until 1995, when it introduced the first Canada Study Grants, the Government of Canada provided no non-repayable aid to students. In the 1998 Federal Budget, however, the Government of Canada created two major new programs: the Canada Millennium Scholarship Foundation (which provides approximately $285 million per year in

Figure 5A.IX.3 — Aggregate Government Non-Repayable Assistance by Source From 1990 to 2003 (in 2003 Dollars)

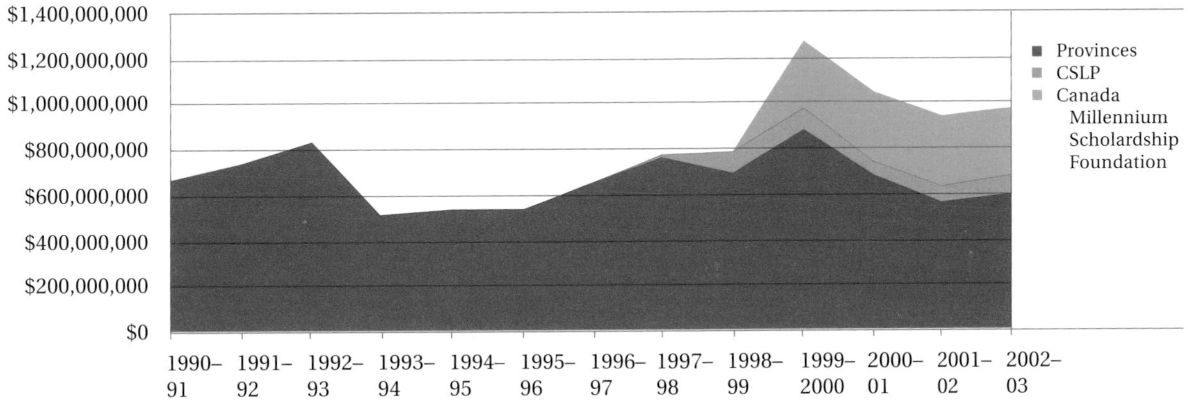

Source: Provincial student assistance programs, Canada Student Loans Program statistical reports and Canada Millennium Scholarship Foundation annual reports.

need-based assistance) and the Canada Study Grants for Students with Dependants (which provides between $50 to $80 million per year in assistance). As a result, provinces are now responsible for only about 60% of all non-repayable assistance in Canada.

Total Assistance

When combining observations regarding repayable and non-repayable assistance, one must take care not to double-count remission assistance. Grants are given *in addition* to loans; remission *replaces* loans and, hence, when counting the total assistance available to students, it is important to keep the two very separate. In Figure 5A.IX.4, which shows the total amount of assistance available to students in Canada, loans that are not remitted are shown as "net loans" and loans which are later remitted are shown as "remission."

The key point in Figure 5.IX.4 is what it reveals about the swinging of the policy "pendulum" in Canadian student aid programs. Assistance—particularly loans—rose in the 1990s and is now beginning to fall. Non-repayable assistance fell from 32% of all assistance in 1990–91 to 14% in 1995–96 and has now risen again to approximately 30%. As noted

earlier, grants once again form the majority of all non-repayable assistance, after remission programs became popular in the mid-1990s. Viewed from the perspective of 2004, the period from 1993 to 1999—which was characterized by an ever-increasing reliance on loans as a policy tool—appears to be a short-term aberration which has now been corrected.

In 2002–03, the most recent year for which data are available, Canadian students received $3.2 billion in loans and grants. This is a drop of 23% from the peak of just under $4.2 billion in 1996–97. More than 100% of this decrease is due to a decrease in loans; non-repayable assistance has actually increased by 47% in the intervening seven years, thanks mostly to the Government of Canada's decision to create the Canada Millennium Scholarship Foundation. Figure 5A.IX.5 shows aggregate need-based assistance by source.

Throughout the 1990s, provincial governments were responsible for approximately 60% of total assistance provided to students. The creation of the Canada Millennium Scholarship Foundation, which began awarding assistance in 1999–2000, neatly reversed the total proportions, so that the Foundation and the Canada Student Loans Program combined now account for 60% of total assistance to students.

Figure 5A.IX.4 — Aggregate Need-Based Assistance by Type From 1990 to 2003 (in 2003 Dollars)

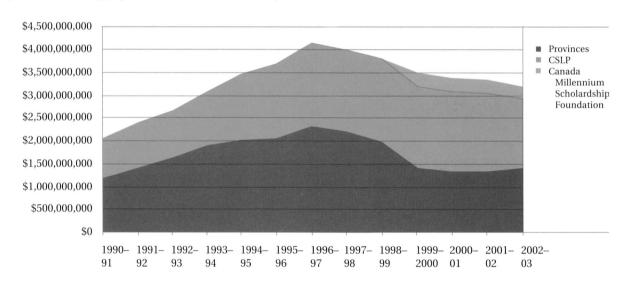

Source: Provincial student assistance programs, Canada Student Loans Program statistical reports and Canada Millennium Scholarship Foundation annual reports.

Figure 5A.IX.5 — Aggregate Need-Based Assistance by Source From 1990 to 2003 (in 2003 Dollars)

Source: Provincial student assistance programs, Canada Student Loans Program statistical reports and Canada Millennium Scholarship Foundation annual reports.

Chapter 5B
Sources of Student Assistance

Chapter 5B

Sources of Student Assistance

I. Introduction

Government student assistance, the subject of Chapter 5A, forms the bulk of student financial aid in Canada. There are, however, several other major sources of assistance that need to be examined to provide a complete picture of student financial aid in Canada. The purpose of this chapter is to give a brief overview of these other sources of funding and how students access them. The cost of these programs will mostly be dealt with in Chapter 5C.

Educational institutions themselves are one of the most important non-governmental sources of student financial aid. New data obtained by the Canada Millennium Scholarship Foundation suggest that Canadian universities (and, to a much lesser extent, colleges) provide undergraduate students with just over $200 million per year in assistance; this sum is more or less evenly divided between need-based assistance and merit-based awards. Collectively, universities are thus the country's third-largest provider of grants after the Government of Quebec and the Canada Millennium Scholarship Foundation. Section II of this chapter provides a detailed examination of *assistance from educational institutions*.

Public aid to students does not come only in the form of student assistance. Governments across the country also spend millions of dollars each year on student employment programs. These programs admittedly are not created solely—or even primarily—to help students financially. Skill development, job experience and the provision of indirect subsidies to non-profit organizations are equally important policy goals for such initiatives. Nevertheless, these programs collectively represent a large source of income for students. The full range of *student employment programs* is described in Section III.

The largest single source of financial assistance for post-secondary education in Canada is tax-based assistance. While the world of taxation and tax breaks may seem far removed from the concerns of students with relatively meagre earnings, there is a large—and growing—number of *tax benefits* which flow to students and their families and now surpasses the size of all Canadian student loan and grant programs combined. Section IV examines the full range of tax deductions, credits and deferrals available to students and shows that, as a consequence, students can earn almost twice as much as non-students before their income becomes taxable.

Section V, *private borrowing and credit cards*, looks at private, unsubsidized educational loans, provided for the most part through the country's chartered banks. Although these loans usually require either a steady income or a parental co-signer (neither of which is required by government student loans), they seem to be providing both a supplement and alternative to government loans. There are limited data on the scale of borrowing from this source, although there is considerable information about the differences in the type of financial products offered by different financial institutions to students. The use of credit cards is also examined in this section.

Section VI is a kind of miscellany, describing the many *other assistance programs* which do not fit into any of the previous sections. These include various programs for Aboriginal students, the increasingly popular Canada Education Savings Grants, the largely unexplored terrain of provincial merit-based assistance programs, and grants from private foundations and other non-government sources.

II. Institutional Assistance

Educational institutions, through the provision of both need- and merit-based awards, are a major funder of student assistance. While the importance of this source of funding has long been recognized, the nature and extent of it have never been particularly well understood. Annual data from the Canadian Association of University Business Officers (CAUBO) and Statistics Canada suggest that institutions spend approximately $500 to $600 million per year on "scholarships, bursaries and prizes." Unfortunately, the CAUBO/StatsCan survey does not break down these data to allow for more detailed analysis. For instance, it does not specify whether this money is distributed on the basis of merit or need or whether it is awarded to graduate or undergraduate students.

The *Survey of Institutional Financial Assistance* conducted by Alex Stephens for the Canada Millennium Scholarship Foundation in the summer and fall of 2001 provides more detailed evidence regarding institutional assistance. The survey asked university and college student assistance officers to provide information about the number and types of awards their institutions provide to students. All universities

and public colleges in Canada were contacted; 41 universities (including all major universities except Memorial University of Newfoundland) and 77 colleges responded.

The results showed that Canadian universities and colleges spend just over $221.6 million per year on student assistance. Need- and merit-based awards each account for about 45% of this total (just over $99 million is spent on each category); the balance comes from institutional work-study funds and "hybrid" awards based on both need and merit (just over $11 million is spent on each category). Figure 5B.II.1 shows the distribution of awards by type.

Perhaps unsurprisingly, the money available for students from institutions is highly concentrated at universities. Specifically, over 95% of institutional funds are awarded by universities. Institutional awards are not available equally at all institutions—over 50% of institutional merit-based awards and 80% of all need-based awards are distributed by Ontario universities. This result would appear to be the outcome of two Government of Ontario policies.

Figure 5B.II.1 — Total Institutional Assistance to Students by Type of Assistance

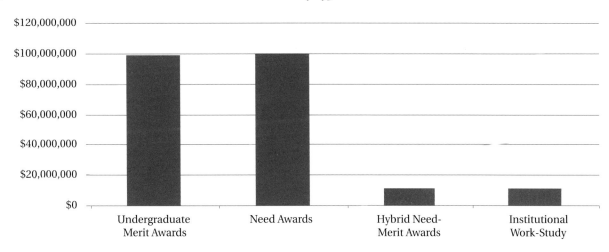

Source: Canada Millennium Scholarship Foundation's *Survey of Institutional Student Financial Assistance* (Forthcoming).

The first of these is a policy requiring institutions to set aside 30% of the value of all income generated by fee increases since 1996–97 for student aid; the second is the government's policy of providing matching funds for all private endowments to institutions earmarked for need-based student assistance. Together, these policies have created very large pools of institutional need-based assistance in Ontario.

The study also found that average award sizes do not vary greatly across the country. Nationally, the average size is just over $1,300 for a merit-based award and just over $1,000 for a need-based award.

These results differ considerably from the CAUBO/StatsCan data, which indicate that institutions spent $542 million on "scholarships, prizes and bursaries" in 2000–01. The discrepancy between the two surveys is likely the result of two factors. First, the CAUBO/StatsCan survey is in effect compulsory and therefore has a higher response rate than the Foundation's survey. Second—and more importantly—the Foundation's survey looked at need-based awards and undergraduate merit awards but did not attempt to measure merit-based assistance for graduate students. Since graduate student merit packages tend to be quite large

(many large institutions have a policy of "fully funding" their Ph.D. students), it is entirely possible that the bulk of the "missing" $300 million is being spent on graduate students.

In addition to financial aid for students, many institutions also provide forms of emergency assistance such as emergency loans and food banks. Data collected from institutions suggest that 17 universities and 22 colleges across Canada have food banks. Approximately a third of these food banks are run by student unions; the remainder are run by educational institutions. Data on the use of food banks are sketchy. Nearly 40% of these organizations were unable to provide any data regarding the size of their budgets or the number of users. The combined budgets of the 24 institutions that were able to provide data totalled $216,685,[1] and overall they served a total of 7,924 clients in 2000–01 (however, there may be multiple counting because some clients could be repeat users).

Another recent study, *Recognizing Excellence? Canada's Merit Scholarships* by Franca Gucciardi of the Canada Millennium Scholarship Foundation, examines institutional merit awards by looking at their selection and tenure criteria. The study reveals that the largest portion of university undergraduate

Figure 5B.II.2 — Institutional Merit Scholarships by Tenure

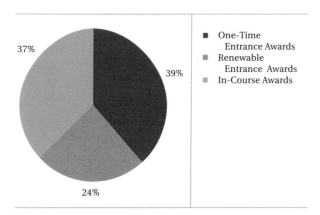

Source: Gucciardi, *Recognizing Excellence? Canada's Merit Scholarships*.

Figure 5B.II.3 — Institutional Merit Scholarships by Type

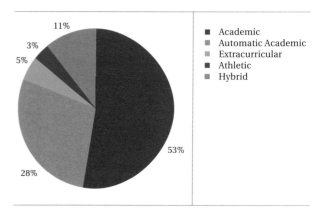

Source: Gucciardi, *Recognizing Excellence? Canada's Merit Scholarships*.

---

1.   This figure does not include the value of any donated foodstuffs.

Figure 5B.II.4 — Value of Athletics Scholarships in Canada by Sport and Gender (2002–03)

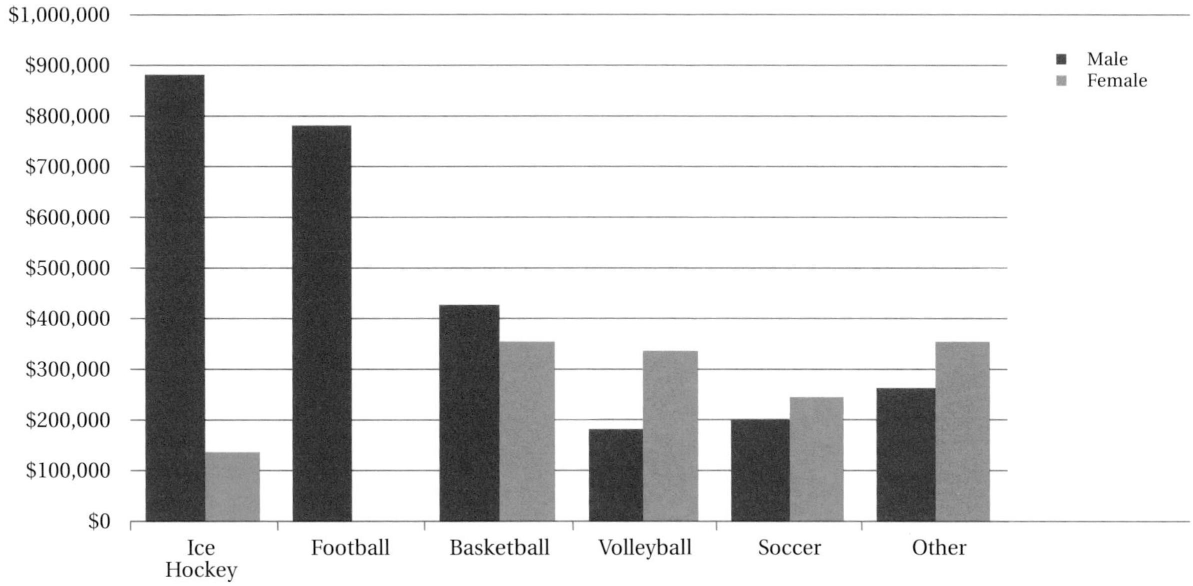

Source: Canadian Interuniversity Sport.

merit scholarship dollars is given in the form of one-time entrance awards which do not provide any assistance to students after their first year of post-secondary education. In fact, assuming that renewable entrance award dollars are split equally among students in different years of study, almost 45% of all scholarship dollars go to first-year students. Figure 5B.II.2 shows the division of institutional merit scholarships by tenure.

The study also found that just over 80% of institutional awards were awarded solely on the basis of marks, either on a competitive basis ("academic") or as automatic awards to students with sufficient grade point averages ("automatic academic"). Of the remaining 19%, well over half was awarded in the form of "hybrid" awards combining both academic merit and financial need, with smaller proportions being distributed as athletic and extracurricular scholarships. Figure 5B.II.3 shows the distribution of institutional merit scholarships by type.

Further analysis is possible in the sub-field of athletic scholarships. Compared to the United States, Canadian athletic scholarships are both

rare and exceedingly small. Athletic scholarship budgets are, however, increasing rapidly. In 2000–01, approximately $2.4 million was disbursed in athletic scholarships; by 2002–03, this had grown to just under $4.2 million. Nationally, the largest providers of athletics scholarships are the University of Alberta ($318,300) and St. Francis Xavier University ($302,433).

Over half of all athletic scholarships are provided by institutions in Western Canada, primarily for hockey, basketball and football. Almost 65% of all athletic scholarships in Canada are awarded to males. This is slightly disproportionate to the overall number of male athletes in the country (males comprise 54% of Canadian Interuniversity Sport-registered athletes). The difference is entirely accounted for by scholarships for hockey and football; in these two sports, males receive 85% and 100% of all scholarships, respectively. In all other sports combined, females receive more than males, both in terms of the number of awards and the value of those awards. Table 5B.II.4 shows the distribution of athletics scholarships by sport and gender.

225

III. Student Employment Programs

In addition to providing direct need-based financial assistance, governments have developed a variety of student employment programs designed to assist students, prospective students and graduates in obtaining employment. The multitude of student employment programs can be divided into the following categories:

* *Mentoring* programs, which provide students with an opportunity to gain exposure to a working environment where they will receive guidance, encouragement and support. These programs are designed to get students thinking about future employment plans.

* *Direct job support* programs, which can either take the form of wage subsidy programs (i.e., governments subsidize a portion of the student's wage for public or private sector organizations) or *job creation* programs (i.e., governments hire directly to create seasonal employment).

* *Job placement* programs often resemble an expanded version of wage subsidy programs, with closer interaction between government departments and organizations. *Counselling* programs are fairly similar, providing students with various government resources, including personal consultations, referrals and job market information.

* *Entrepreneur* programs encourage students to start up small businesses by providing both financial and technical assistance.

There are more than 100 different youth employment programs in Canada. The majority of these programs are targeted to post-secondary students. While most youth employment programs operate throughout the year, some only assist students on a seasonal basis. The programs listed in this section are those targeted only to post-secondary students and/or recent graduates; they therefore do not include programs designed for unemployed or at-risk youth.

Table 5B.III.1 — Newfoundland and Labrador Student Employment Programs

Program Name	Mentoring/ Volunteering	Wage Subsidy/ Job Creation	Job Placement & Counselling	Entrepreneur Program
Conservation Corps of Newfoundland and Labrador (CCNL)	●			
Graduate Employment Program		●		
Linkages		●		
Medical Student Rural Practice Program			●	
Rural Nursing Student Incentive Program			●	
Small Enterprise Co-operative Placement Program			●	
Student Employment Program		●		
Student Social Work Program			●	
Student Work and Service Program		●	●	
Tutoring for Tuition	●	●		
Tutoring/Work Experience Program	●	●	●	
Youth Opportunities Newfoundland and Labrador		●		

Source: Canada Millennium Scholarship Foundation's 2003 student employment survey and the Government of Manitoba's *Inventory of Canada's Youth Employment Programs.*

In Newfoundland and Labrador the majority of student employment programs focus on job creation and provide wage subsidies. There are, however, a few programs designed to attract students to rural and remote areas. Comparatively few projects focus on mentoring or entrepreneurship. In 2003, over 4,900 students benefited from these programs. Table 5B.III.1 shows the various student employment projects in Canada's easternmost province.

In the Maritimes, student employment programs are more or less equally divided between the four types of program categories. Each year, the various programs provide opportunities for over 650 students per year in Prince Edward Island and 675 students per year in Nova Scotia. Comparable data for New Brunswick were unavailable. Table 5B.III.2 shows the breakdown of student employment programs in the Maritimes.

Table 5B.III.2 — Maritime Student Employment Programs

Province	Program Name	Mentoring/ Volunteering	Wage Subsidy/ Job Creation	Job Placement & Counselling	Entrepreneur Program
PE	None			●	
	Health Care Futures				●
	New Entrepreneur Loan Program (Student Component)			●	
	Nursing Student Summer Employment Program		●		
	Student Travel Counsellor		●		
	Jobs for Youth		●		
NS	Career Starts Internship Program	●			
	Co-operative Employment Program		●		
	Nova Scotia Employment Program for Students		●		
	Nova Scotia Youth Conservation Corps (NSYCC)		●		
	Student Loan Employment Program		●		
	Youth Entrepreneurship Scholarships (YES)				●
NB	Federal/Provincial Youth Services Partnership	●		●	
	New Brunswick Public Service Internship Program	●			
	Mentoring Program	●			
	Student Employment and Experience Development (SEED)		●		●
	Student Entrepreneurship Program				●
	Workforce Expansion		●		

Source: Canada Millennium Scholarship Foundation's 2003 student employment survey and the Government of Manitoba's *Inventory of Canada's Youth Employment Programs.*

In Central Canada the student employment programs are likewise more or less equally divided between the four types of program categories. In Ontario, the various programs provide opportunities to over 42,000 students and/or graduates. Comparable data for Quebec were unavailable. Table 5B.III.3 shows the breakdown of student employment programs in Central Canada.

Table 5B.III.3 — Central Canada Student Employment Programs

Province	Program Name	Mentoring/ Volunteering	Wage Subsidy/ Job Creation	Job Placement & Counselling	Entrepreneur Program
QC	Chantier Youth Work Projects	●			
	Engagement Jeunesse	●		●	
	French-Language Assistant Quebec-UK/Ireland/Germany/Spain	●		●	
	Internships in International Government Organizations	●		●	
	Interprovincial Summer Employment Exchange Program	●		●	
	Jobs in Private Businesses		●		
	Official Language Monitoring Program			●	
	Strategic Employment Support Program				●
	Summer Jobs and Internships in Government Departments				●
	Youth Information Highway		●		
ON[2]	Ontario Government Summer Student Hiring		●		
	Ontario/Quebec Summer Student Job Exchange Program	●		●	
	Ontario Internship Program			●	
	Student Venture Loan				●
	Summer Company	●			●
	Summer Jobs Service (SJS)		●		
	Summer Experience Program (SEP) including Ontario Rangers		●	●	
	Young Entrepreneurs Program				●

Source: Canada Millennium Scholarship Foundation's 2003 student employment survey and the Government of Manitoba's *Inventory of Canada's Youth Employment Programs.*

2. Ontario operates two large graduate tax credit programs, which could be included in this section but are better suited to Section IV, dealing with tax expenditures.

In Western Canada the focus of student employment programs tends to be mentoring, wage subsidies and job creation. Manitoba has an abnormally high number of programs, which are quite small and for the most part involve some form of wage subsidy or job creation. Programs in the other three Western provinces are more evenly distributed among the four program types. In Manitoba, these programs provide opportunities for over 2,300 students; in Saskatchewan, they assist over 1,300 students. Comparable figures for Alberta and British Columbia were unavailable. It is unlikely, however, that the Alberta programs provide much in the way of support for current post-secondary students, since the majority of its youth employment programs are targeted at youth at risk. Table 5B.III.4 shows the breakdown for student employment programs in Western Canada.

Table 5B.III.4 — Western Canada Student Employment Programs

Province	Program Name	Mentoring/ Volunteering	Wage Subsidy/ Job Creation	Job Placement & Counselling	Entrepreneur Program
MB	Aboriginal Youth Internship Program		●		
	Business Mentorships	●	●		
	Career Options for Students With Disabilities		●		
	Career Start Program	●	●		
	Manitoba/Quebec Exchange	●			
	Partners for Careers			●	
	STEP Services			●	
	Urban Green Team		●		
	Volunteers in the Public Service	●			
	Young Entrepreneurs				●
	Youth Services Manitoba		●		
SK	Aboriginal Management and Professional Internship Program	●			
	Centennial Student Employment Program		●	●	
	Multi-Party Training Plan	●			
	Spruce Krew		●		
AB	Skills Canada Alberta			●	
	Summer Temporary Employment Program		●		
BC	COOP Education Training Program	●			
	Public Service Internship Program	●	●		
	Youth@BC		●		
	Youth Employment Program (YEP)		●		

Source: Canada Millennium Scholarship Foundation's 2003 student employment survey and the Government of Manitoba's *Inventory of Canada's Youth Employment Programs.*

Table 5B.III.5 — Student Employment Programs in the Territories

Territory	Program Name	Mentoring/ Volunteering	Wage Subsidy/ Job Creation	Job Placement & Counselling	Entrepreneur Program
YT	Student Training and Employment Program (STEP)		●		
	Yukon Youth Conservation Corps (Y2C2)		●		
NT	Northern Graduate Employment Program		●		
	Summer Student Employment Program	●		●	
	Youth Employment Program		●		
NU	Summer Student Employment Program		●		

Source: Canada Millennium Scholarship Foundation's 2003 student employment survey and the Government of Manitoba's *Inventory of Canada's Youth Employment Programs.*

Territorial student employment programs tend to focus on direct assistance through job creation and wage subsidy programs. These programs provide assistance to almost 300 students in Yukon Territory, 500 students in the Northwest Territories and 400 students in Nunavut. Although the absolute number of students assisted may be small, in proportional terms these numbers are substantial, comprising nearly 2% of the entire working-age population. Table 5B.III.5 shows the student employment programs available in the territories.

The Government of Canada has a long history of involvement in student summer employment and creating opportunities for individuals to work in the public service, crown corporations and other federal agencies. It also has a more specific role than provincial governments in assisting Aboriginal students to secure employment. Because the impetus for these programs comes from within each federal government department (unlike the provinces, where all programs tend to be managed by a single ministry), the Government of Canada's list of programs is nothing short of bewildering.

Government of Canada programs are more likely than provincial programs to combine features of different program types (e.g., both mentoring *and* job placement). Over 65,000 students and/or graduates receive opportunities from the Government of Canada each year. Table 5B.III.6 lists national student employment programs funded by the federal government.

Table 5B.III.6 — Government of Canada Student Employment Programs

Program Name	Mentoring/ Volunteering	Wage Subsidy/ Job Creation	Job Placement & Counselling	Entrepreneur Program
Agriculture and Agri-Food Science Horizons	●	●		
Canada's Digital Collections Initiative		●		
Canada Food Inspection Agency Science Horizons	●	●		
Official Language Monitor Program	●			
CIDA International Youth Internship Program				●
Collaborative Research Internships Program (NRC)	●	●		
Community Access Program Youth Employment Project		●		●
Computers for Schools, Technical Work Experience Project	●	●		
DFAIT Youth International Internships				●
First Nations and Inuit Science and Technology Camps	●			
First Nations and Inuit Summer Student Career Placement Program		●		
Innovation and Entrepreneurship Camps	●	●		
International Environmental Youth Corps	●	●		
Internship Program with Innovative Small and Medium Enterprise (NRC)	●	●		
National Information Highway, Science, and Entrepreneurship Camps	●	●		●
NetCorps Canada International				●
Parks Canada Co-operative and Student Employment Program		●	●	
RCMP Summer Student Program	●		●	
SchoolNet Youth Employment Initiative		●		
Science Horizons: Environment Canada Youth Internship Program				●
Science Horizons and Technology Internship Program				●
Science and Technology Internships (two types: DFO and NRC)				●
Student Connections	●			
Student Summer Employment Opportunities (DIAND)		●		
Summer Career Placements (SCP)		●	●	
Summer-Student Connection Program	●			
Technical Work Experience Program, Computers for Schools	●	●		
Web-4-All	●	●		
Young Canada Works (six different programs)	●	●		
Youth Internship Canada (YIC)		●		●
Youth Service Canada	●			

Source: Canada Millennium Scholarship Foundation's 2003 student employment survey and the Government of Manitoba's *Inventory of Canada's Youth Employment Programs.*

IV. Tax Benefits

In addition to raising revenue, the Canadian tax system allows governments to pursue various social policy objectives by encouraging certain types of behaviour via incentives contained within the income tax system. These incentives are known as tax expenditures. Tax expenditures are unlike regular budgetary expenditures because money is not spent directly by governments. Instead, government revenue is simply foregone. In other words, tax expenditures reduce the amount of tax owed. They can take the form of exemptions, deductions, credits or deferrals, all of which are defined as follows:

- *Exemptions* lower the amount of tax payable by making part or all of a certain type of income (e.g., scholarships) non-taxable. As such, they are more valuable to people with higher incomes than people with lower incomes, because tax rates increase as income increases.

- *Deductions* lower the amount of tax payable by reducing total assessed income before tax is calculated. Like exemptions, they are more valuable to people with higher incomes than people with lower incomes.

- *Credits* are applied against the tax owed to reduce the amount of tax payable. They are always worth an amount equal to the lowest marginal tax rate. Therefore, credits were worth 17% until 2001, when the lowest federal tax rate dropped to 16%. In Canada, tax credits are nearly always non-refundable—i.e., if credits remain after the amount of tax owing has been reduced to zero, the balance is not refundable. In certain cases, however, the remaining balance can be "transferred" to a supporting relative or "carried forward" to be applied in a future tax year.

- *Deferrals* occur in programs such as registered savings plans, where any tax payable in relation to that program may be deferred until a later date, thus facilitating the accumulation of savings.

In recent years, past, present and future students have benefited from some significant tax policy changes. This section will examine all the tax benefits available to Canadian post-secondary students, including the pre-study period and benefits after graduation.

Federal Benefits

Tax Deferrals: Registered Education Savings Plans (RESPs)

RESPs are funds to which taxpayers may contribute for the purpose of saving money to cover the costs of a beneficiary's education. The investment return on these funds is not taxable until the funds are withdrawn. Tax on the investment is therefore deferred until the funds are used for their specified purpose. There is a limit to the amount of money that a taxpayer can contribute to an RESP. In 1994 and 1995, a contribution could not exceed $1,500 per beneficiary per year, with an overall lifetime limit of $31,500 per beneficiary. In 1996, the annual limit was increased to $2,000 and the lifetime limit to $42,000. In 1997, the annual limit was increased to $4,000.

Prior to 1997, investment income derived from contributions paid to an RESP could generally only be used to help the designated beneficiary pursue post-secondary education; when withdrawn from the plan, it became taxable income in the beneficiary's hands. If the beneficiary did not attend post-secondary education by the age of 21, then the money reverted to the subscriber and tax was paid on any interest or capital gains. Since 1997, if the designated beneficiary of the RESP is 21 years old and is not engaged in post-secondary study, the subscriber may withdraw the funds from the plan and use them to fill any unused RRSP room he or she may have.

In 1998, the Government of Canada introduced the Canada Education Savings Grant (CESG), which supplements contributions to RESPs with a 20% grant, up to an annual maximum of $400 (see Section 5B.VI for details). The CESG is a cash benefit rather than a tax benefit (and is thus not counted as a tax expenditure), but its introduction added to the cost of the existing tax benefit, as it increased the amount of savings within RESPs.

Tax Exemptions—Scholarship, Fellowship, and Bursary Income

Before 1972, all scholarship, fellowship and bursary income was exempt from income tax. Tax reform legislation in 1972 reduced government tax expenditure in this area by only exempting the first $500 of student income. In the 2000 tax year, this tax exemption was increased to cover the first $3,000 of all scholarship, fellowship and bursary income.

Tax Deductions—Moving Expenses Deduction

Students may deduct from their income any moving expenses incurred when moving to a place of study, provided that they are full-time students and are moving at least 40 kilometres closer to their place of study. Students may also deduct moving expenses incurred in order to move closer to a place of employment, including co-op education and summer jobs. In such cases, moving expenses can only be deducted from income earned in the new location. This deduction is based on the moving expense deduction available to all taxpayers who move at least 40 kilometres closer to a place of employment.

Tax Credits — Tuition Fee Credit

Originally introduced in the 1961 tax year, a 16% tax credit is available for tuition fees paid by students to a recognized educational institution. The credit is available if the total tuition fees paid to the institution exceed $100. The 1997 budget extended the credit to cover all mandatory ancillary fees imposed by post-secondary institutions, except student union fees. All unused portions of this credit may be transferred to a supporting spouse, parent or grandparent, to a maximum of $5,000; since 1997, unused portions may also be carried forward for use in future tax years.

Tax Credits—Education Tax Credit

Students who are enrolled at recognized educational institutions on a full-time basis are entitled to claim a tax credit based on the length and intensiveness of studies. As recently as 1995, this credit was worth a mere $60 per month for full-time students and was unavailable to part-time students. Since 2000, full-time students are awarded a credit of $400 for every month of study, and part-time students are awarded a credit of $120 for every month of study. These credits can be used against either federal or provincial taxes, except in Quebec, where the province has an entirely separate tax collection system (described below), and Prince Edward Island, which, since the decoupling of federal and provincial tax systems, only allows students to claim half the federal credit ($200 per month of full-time study and $60 per month of part-time study).

Table 5B.IV.1 shows the changes in the education tax credit since 1994. In 1994, when the minimum federal tax rate was 17%, eight months of the education amount credit was worth $108.80 in reduced taxes (8 months x $80 x .17). The credit is now worth $512 in reduced taxes. The $400 increase in the value of this credit has offset roughly one third of the national increase in tuition fees over the past seven years.

Table 5B.IV.1 — Education Tax Credit Changes From 1994 to 2001

Year	Value of Education Credit	
	Full-Time (per Month)	Part-Time (per Month)
1994	$80	N/A
1996	$100	N/A
1997	$150	N/A
1998	$200	$60
2000	$400	$120

Source: Canada Customs and Revenue Agency.

Table 5B.IV.2 — Amount and Value of Provincial Tax Credits in 2003

	BC	AB	SK	MB	ON	NB	PE	NS	NF	YK	NT	NU
Amount/Month	$200	$420	$400	$400	$420	$400	$200	$400	$200	$400	$400	$400
Value of Credit	6.05%	10%	11.25%	10.9%	6.05%	9.68%	9.8%	9.77%	10.57%	7.04%	7.2%	4%

Tax Credits—Student Loan Interest

In 1998, the Government of Canada introduced a tax credit on the interest portion of student loan payments made in a given year. This credit, which can be applied to payments under the Canada Student Loans Program and similar provincial programs, may be claimed in the year in which it is earned or in any of the subsequent five years.

Provincial Benefits

All provinces to some extent provide their own versions of tuition and education tax credits. All provinces treat the tuition tax credits in the same manner as the Government of Canada; five provinces also have the same $400 per month credit as the federal government. Three provinces—

British Columbia, Prince Edward Island and Newfoundland and Labrador—declined to match the federal government's $400 per month credit and kept their credits at $200 per month. Two others— Alberta and Ontario—added inflation clauses to their credits, so their credits are now worth more than federal credits ($420 per month in 2003). Table 5B.IV.2 shows the amount of provincial tax credits and the value of tax credits in each province (which is equal to the lowest tax rate in each province).

Quebec

Since the Quebec government collects provincial income tax independently of the federal government, it has its own system of exemptions, deductions, credits and deferrals. However, in most respects the Quebec tax system's benefits match those of

Table 5B.IV.3 — Government of Canada Tax Measures and Their Application in Quebec

Tax Measure	Canada	Quebec
RESP contributions	Tax deferral on interest until student cashes benefit; interest reverts to subscriber if beneficiary does not attend PSE; interest may be transferred to RRSP if subscriber has room.	Tax deferral on interest until student cashes benefit; interest reverts to subscriber if beneficiary does not attend PSE; interest may be transferred to RRSP if subscriber has room.
Scholarship income	First $3,000 exempted	All scholarship income is exempt from tax
Deduction for moving expenses	All moving expenses tax-deductible	All moving expenses tax-deductible
Tuition fees	Credit for tuition and ancillary fees	Credit for tuition fees
Monthly education amount	Credit equal to $400 per month (full-time) or $200 per month (part-time)	None
Student loan interest	Credit equal to interest paid	Credit equal to interest paid

the Government of Canada. Table 5B.IV.3 compares Government of Canada tax measures and Government of Quebec tax measures for students.

It should be noted that tax reform legislation in 1998 allowed Quebec taxpayers to choose between a general personal income tax return and a simplified tax return. The simplified tax return allowed taxpayers to choose to replace the various tax credits and deductions with a flat amount of $2,350 per taxpayer. As a result, many students find it advantageous to forego specific education tax expenditures in favour of claiming the flat amount. In the 2000 tax year, the flat amount was increased to $2,515.

Finally, Quebec has one additional tax measure which is not available elsewhere in Canada. Since 1993, students from a northern village who must pay transportation costs because they live away from home in order to study are provided with financial assistance to help offset the cost and are exempt from paying tax on this assistance.

Saskatchewan

In 2001, the government introduced a tax credit available to all new post-secondary graduates who gain employment in Saskatchewan. This credit is a one-time non-refundable tax credit of $350. It can be claimed by both graduates of Saskatchewan learning institutions and graduates who have come from outside of the province to work. Unused portions of the credit may be carried forward to the next tax year for up to four consecutive years.

Tax Benefits at Work

The best way to examine the effect of the various tax measures is to show how these measures work at the level of the individual full-time student. In this exercise, the effects examined will be limited to those that affect the amount of payable federal tax. Federal tax changes have had an effect on provincial taxes and therefore the amount of payable provincial tax, but these will be excluded in the interests of simplicity.

Without Tax Benefits

In a Canada without tax benefits for post-secondary education, Jane Q. Student earns $10,000 through employment. Jane also has a $3,000 scholarship, which gives her a total income of $13,000.

Employment Income	$10,000.00
Scholarship	$3,000.00
Total Taxable Income	**$13,000.00**
Marginal Tax Rate	x 16%
Federal Tax (before credits)	**$2,080.00**

Jane's federal tax is $2,080.00. This is then reduced by the available tax credits. Because there are no education tax credits in this example, Jane can only access what is known as the "basic personal exemption" of $7,634.00. The next step is to calculate the amount of tax that Jane will pay.

Personal Exemption	$7,634.00
Marginal Tax Rate	x 16%
Total Non-Refundable Tax Credits	**$1,221.44**

Finally, the total value of tax credits can be applied to the total taxable amount to reduce the amount of tax paid.

Federal Tax (before credits)	$2,080.00
Total Non-Refundable Tax Credits	- $1,221.44
Total Federal Tax Payable	**$858.56**

Thus, Jane would have to pay a total of $858.56 in federal taxes.

With Tax Benefits

Jane Q. Student files her taxes for a second time, this time in the real world, with existing Canadian tax benefits.

Employment Income	$10,000.00
Scholarship	$3,000.00
Total Income	**$13,000.00**
Scholarship Exemption	- $3,000.00
Total Taxable Income	**$10,000.00**
Marginal Tax Rate	x 16%
Federal Tax (before credits)	**$1,600.00**

Jane has three main tax credits: the basic personal exemption, tuition and fees (for the purposes of this example, Jane pays the national average for tuition and fees), and the education study credit (for the purposes of this example, Jane attends school for eight months per year).

Personal Exemption	$7,634.00
Tuition and Fees	$3,852.00
Education Amount	$3,200.00
Total	**$14,686.00**
Marginal Tax Rate	x 16%
Total Non-Refundable Tax Credits	**$2,349.76**

The total value of tax credits can now be applied to the total taxable amount to reduce the amount of payable tax.

Federal Tax (before credits)	$1,600.00
Total Non-Refundable Tax Credits	-$2,349.76
Total Federal Tax Payable	**-$749.76**

Not only does Jane not have to pay any taxes, she also receives $749.76 worth of tax credits that can be carried forward to future tax years. In total, therefore, the net effect of the various federal tax exemptions and credits for Jane is $749.76 + $858.56 = $1,608.32. It should be noted that this total would be somewhat higher if provincial credits were included, although the amount would depend on the size of the provincial credits and the province's tax rates.

V. Private Borrowing and Credit Cards

Private Student Loans

Government student loans are not the only financial product available to students. Most major banks also offer lines of credit to students. A line of credit is a type of revolving credit—that is, new funds become available as payments are made on credit already used, which allows one to borrow money as needed, up to a pre-approved maximum. Unlike government student loans, the availability of lines of credit is not based on need. Bank lines of credit can therefore be an attractive option for those who do not qualify for need-tested assistance.

No central statistics are gathered concerning private lines of credit, and banks do not, as a rule, release information concerning borrowers. The best available evidence, which comes from the Canadian Undergraduate Survey Consortium's 2002 *Survey of Undergraduate University Students* and the Canadian College Student Survey Consortium's 2002 survey of *Canadian College Student Finances* suggests that 10% to 20% of all college and university students use private loans as a form of financing, of which approximately a third are simultaneously using public student loans. These studies also suggest that the average amount borrowed annually from these sources is approximately the same as the average amount borrowed from public sources (i.e., the amounts are the same, but incidence is lower). Over the course of a degree, however, private sources are used less than public sources.

To be eligible for a student line of credit, an applicant must provide proof of full- or part-time enrolment at a recognized Canadian university or college. The field of study is generally not considered; however, some financial institutions have special arrangements for students from selected professional programs. The applicant must also be a Canadian citizen or permanent resident (although some financial

One of the benefits of a student line of credit is the ease of quickly accessing funds when they are required; another benefit is that interest is only paid on the amount used.

institutions may grant eligibility to international students who have a Canadian citizen as a co-signer).

Since most students do not have a secure income, a co-signer is often required to guarantee that monthly payments will be made. The co-signer must be: financially independent and able to pay the required interest; of at least the age of majority in the province where the line of credit is set up; and, generally speaking, a Canadian citizen or permanent resident.

Some financial institutions will grant a student line of credit to students without a co-signer, provided that the applicant can prove the financial means by which she or he can make monthly interest payments. In such cases, the applicant must be the age of majority in the province or territory where the line of credit is established and usually must have some previous full-time work experience. The past borrowing and credit histories of both the applicant and the co-signer are checked before a student line of credit is granted.

The financial institution lending the funds sets the loan limit based on the student's financial request, past borrowing history, and current and future ability to repay. While studying, students are only required to make monthly interest payments on the amount of credit used. This is more onerous than repaying government student loans, which, as a rule, do not require students to make payments while they are in school.

Most financial institutions offer a preferential interest rate for students, which is the prime rate plus an added percentage (usually one percentage point). One of the benefits of a student line of credit is the ease of quickly accessing funds when they are required; another benefit is that interest is only paid *on the amount used*. While studying, all Canadian financial institutions allow students to make monthly payments of the interest only.

Upon graduation, there is usually a grace period (typically 12 months, compared to six months for government loans) to allow students to establish themselves in the workforce before requiring them to begin making repayments on the loan principal. At the end of the grace period, the loan switches from a revolving credit line to a regular amortized loan, and monthly payments are required on both the interest and the principal, usually at a higher interest rate than before. The length of the repayment period is negotiated between the bank and the borrower and varies according to the amount borrowed and the borrower's ability to repay. No Canadian bank penalizes for early repayment of the principle. Table 5B.V.1 shows the different student line of credit options available at Canadian banks.

Table 5B.V.1 — Student Line of Credit Options by Financial Institution

	CIBC	Bank of Montreal	National Bank of Canada	Royal Bank	TD Canada Trust	Laurentian Bank	First Nations Bank of Canada[a]	Credit Unions (various)[b]	Scotia Bank
Locations of branches	All provinces	All provinces	BC, AB, SK, MB, ON, QC, NB and NS	All provinces	All provinces	BC, AB, SK, MB, ON and QC	ON, QC and SK	All provinces	All provinces
Co-signer required	Usually	Yes	Yes	Usually	Yes	Yes	Yes	Yes	Yes
Credit history checked	Yes	Yes	Yes	Yes	Yes	Yes	Yes	Yes	Yes
Annual maximum	Flexible—min. $5,000	$6,500	$5,000	Flexible—min. $5,000	$8,000	$5,500	Flexible—min. $5,000	Flexible—$5,000 to $10,000	$6,000
Maximum number of years	N/A	4 years	N/A	N/A	N/A	4 years	N/A	Varies	4 years
Total maximum	$40,000	$26,000	$20,000	Flexible	$32,000	$20,000	$32,000	Flexible	$24,000
Preferential interest rate	Prime + 1% to prime + 2%	Prime + 1%	Prime + 1%	Prime + 1%	Prime + 1%	Prime + 1%	Prime + 1%	Prime + 0.5% to prime +3%	Prime + 1%
Monthly payments while in school	Interest only	Interest only	Interest only	Interest only	Interest only	Interest only	Interest only	Interest only	Interest only
Grace period after graduation	12 months	12 months	12 months	6 months	12 months	12 months	12 months	Up to 12 months	Up to 12 months
Line of credit switches to loan after graduation	Yes	No	Usually	Negotiable	Yes	Yes	Yes	Usually	Yes
Interest rate increases during repayment period	Yes	Yes	Yes	Yes	Yes	Yes	Yes	Usually	Yes

Notes: [a] First Nations Bank of Canada is an affiliate of TD Canada Trust Bank and markets most TD products using the same terms and conditions.

[b] A sample was drawn from six cities: Vancouver, Saskatoon, Winnipeg, Toronto, Montreal and Moncton.

In addition to the programs shown in Table 5B.V.1, several Canadian banks offer improved student line of credit options for individuals in selected professional programs such as medicine, dentistry and Master's of Business Administration. These lines of credit are more advantageous than the normal student line of credit in a number of ways and are offered to students in professional programs because their course of studies has identified them,

as far as banks are concerned, as "preferential customers" and a good credit risk. While details vary among financial institutions, generally speaking these special student lines of credit allow students to borrow more money at lower rates of interest and allow for repayment on a more flexible scale. Table 5B.V.2 outlines the different line of credit options available to students in certain professional programs.

Table 5B.V.2 — Student Line of Credit Programs for Students in Selected Professional Programs by Financial Institution

	CIBC	Bank of Montreal	National Bank of Canada	Royal Bank	TD Canada Trust	First Nations Bank	Scotia Bank
Locations of branches	All provinces	All provinces	BC, AB, SK, MB, ON, QC, NB and NS	All provinces	All provinces	ON, QC and SK	All provinces
Programs	MD, DN, OP and VT	MD, DN, OP, LA, VT, PH and CH	MD, PH, LA, OP, CE, DN and VT	MD, DN, OP, VT, MBA, CH, LA, PH, CE and CA	MD, LA, DN, CA and MBA	MD, LA, DN, CA and MBA	MD, DN, VT, PH, CH, MBA, OP and LA
Annual maximum	$15,000–$25,000	Varies by program	$15,000	Varies by program	$8,000–$15,000	$8,000–$15,000	Varies by program—min. $8,000
Maximum number of years	N/A	N/A	N/A	N/A	N/A	N/A	N/A
Total maximum	$80,000–$125,000	$80,000–$125,000	$60,000	$55,000–$125,000	$12,000–$60,000	$12,000–$60,000	Varies by program—max. $125,000
Preferential interest rate	Prime + 1%	Prime + 0.5%	Prime + 1%	Prime + 1%	Prime + 1%	Prime + 1%	Varies by program
Monthly payments while in school	Interest only	Interest only	Interest only	Interest only	Interest only	Interest only	Interest only
Length of grace period after graduation	6 to 12 months	12 months	12 months	6 months	12 months	12 months	6 to 12 months
Repayment	Maximum 15 years	Varies (maximum 7 years)	Maximum 15 years	Negotiable	Maximum 20 years	Maximum 20 years	Maximum 15 years

Note: Laurentian Bank of Canada offers a student line of credit for "specialized private training." This is somewhat different from the professional program student line of credit. Specifically, the specialized private training student line of credit is for students training in a technical program, vocational program or apprenticeship program offered by CEGEPs or career colleges. The terms and conditions are the same as those for regular student lines of credit, except for the following: the maximum per year is only $1,500, and the preferential interest rate is Prime + 2% rather than Prime + 1%.

Abbreviations: MD = Medicine, DN = Dentistry, VT = Veterinary Science, OP = Optometry, LA = Law, PH = Pharmacy, CH = Chiropractic, CE = Civil Engineering, MBA = Master's of Business Administration.

Credit Cards

Despite increasing concern over students' use of credit cards, the best available data show that student credit card use does not differ substantially from that of the population as a whole. Data on student credit card use come from the *Making Ends Meet* survey conducted by Ekos Research Associates in 2001–02 for the Canada Millennium Scholarship Foundation. Comparative data for the country as a whole were obtained from a national survey conducted in October 2001 by the Canadian Press (CP) and Leger Marketing.

The Ekos Research survey found that nearly two-thirds of Canadian post-secondary students (both at universities and at colleges) possess at least one credit card, and almost 40% report carrying debt on those cards. Table 5B.V.3 breaks down the reported number of credit cards for post-secondary students.

The results from Table 5B.V.3 are very similar to the results for the population as a whole. The CP/Leger Survey on Canadians and credit cards showed that over 75% (n=1,507) of Canadians over 18 had at least one credit card, and over 50% of respondents reported that they had either one or two credit cards.

The Ekos Research survey found a strong correlation between student age and credit card possession. Specifically, credit card ownership and the number of cards possessed increase dramatically with age. Less than 30% of students under 20 years old possess credit cards; however, over 80% of students aged 21 or over possess at least one credit card. Figure 5B.V.1

Table 5B.V.3 — Distribution of Students by Number of Credit Cards Owned

Number of Credit Cards	Distribution
0	35%
1	35%
2	17%
3	5%
4+	5%
Don't know/ No response	3%

Source: Ekos Research's *Making Ends Meet.*

breaks down student credit card possession by students' age.

Data from *Making Ends Meet* show that less than half of students with credit cards carry debt from month to month. Of those who do, the average debt level for students carrying a credit card balance is $1,500; the median is $900. This average student credit card debt level is slightly higher than the average debt level of all credit card holders reported in the CP/Leger Survey ($1,269).

The amount of credit card debt held by a student is directly proportionate to the number of cards he or she holds. The average debt for students with one card is $900; the average rises to $1,600 for students with two credit cards and to over $2,500 for those with three or more.

Figure 5B.V.1 — Number of Credit Cards by Age of Student

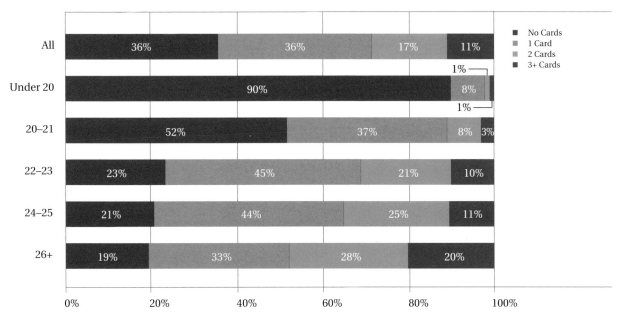

Source: Ekos Research's *Making Ends Meet*.

VI. Other Assistance Programs

In addition to those programs traditionally considered as "student assistance," there are other forms of publicly available funds used by students to pursue post-secondary education that do not fit into the traditional categories of student assistance, tax credits and student employment programs. These programs include the Employment Insurance skills development fund, government and private sector programs for Aboriginal students, government merit scholarships and education savings incentive programs.

Employment Insurance Skills Development Fund

The Government of Canada, in partnership with provincial and territorial governments, provides support to unemployed Canadians seeking to enhance their skills. Funds for these programs are generated through the Employment Insurance skills development fund. Although federally funded, programs are administered by provincial governments in order to ensure that they meet local labour market needs. Each province and territory is given some leeway to tailor the programs to meet their individual requirements.

The Employment Insurance skills development fund provides a level of financial assistance to unemployed individuals who require skill training in order to secure employment. Eligible individuals must first apply and be approved before seeking training and may continue to receive employment insurance while receiving funding. The funding traditionally lasts up to 52 weeks; however, it can be extended for up to three years. These funds are nearly always provided in the form of a grant.

In 2002–03, the Government of Canada invested almost $2 billion in these programs, assisting almost 500,000 unemployed Canadians. However, because the program tends to target short-term training projects offered to individuals, the Employment Insurance skills development fund primarily benefits people wishing to pursue studies at private technical or vocational institutions. It is also common for individuals to enrol in employment or skill seminars run by independent contractors.

As a result of the fund's focus, relatively little of the money makes its way to people who are considered "students" according to traditional Statistics Canada definitions. In the *2003 Canadian College Survey*, almost 10% of respondents indicated using the Employment Insurance skills development fund to help finance their education. This implies that approximately 40,000 college students are using Employment Insurance as a funding source, and that students in diploma or certificate programs at community colleges make up only about 8% of all Employment Insurance skills development fund recipients. On the whole, college students receiving these funds tend to be considerably older and are more likely to have dependants than the average student.

Government Programs for Aboriginal Students

The main program through which the Government of Canada provides support to First Nations students is the Post-Secondary Student Support Program (PSSSP), which provides assistance to First Nations students to help cover the cost of tuition fees, books and travel, as well as providing a living allowance. The PSSSP is valid for all levels of post-secondary education, including community college diploma and certification programs, undergraduate programs and professional degree programs such as medicine and engineering. A smaller program, the University College Entrance Preparation Program (UCEP), provides financial support for individuals seeking to upgrade their academic skills prior to commencing post-secondary education.

The goal of the PSSSP and UCEP is to support the increased participation of Treaty/Status Indians and Inuit students in post-secondary education, thereby improving their employability. Only Status Indians and Inuit living on or off reserve are eligible for these programs. Nationally, almost 100% of combined PSSSP and UCEP funding is delivered directly by First Nations Bands or their administering organizations.[3] Each Band Council defines its own selection criteria and policies. As a result, it is difficult to make general statements about who qualifies for these programs.

Over time, as program funding had remained stable (total program spending was capped in 2001) and demand for funding has increased, program guidelines have become more restrictive—restrictions have been placed on students' eligibility, and daycare and rent subsidies have been removed.[4] The 2003–04 funding allocation for the PSSSP is $304 million. It is estimated that approximately 26,000 students are receiving financial support through the program.

Aboriginal Scholarship Programs

There are hundreds of scholarships, awards, bursaries and fellowships targeting Aboriginal students across the country. These programs, for the most part, are competitive merit-based awards. The Department of Indian and Northern Affairs Canada (INAC) has compiled a fairly comprehensive database of these awards and scholarships, which it publishes on an annual basis. In addition, INAC has made its database of awards for Aboriginal students available on the Internet at http://pse-esd.ainc-inac.gc.ca/abs/. Data posted on the Internet are updated regularly.

According to INAC, there are more than 500 awards for Aboriginal students in Canada, totalling more than $2.5 million annually.[5] The majority of these scholarships are administered by student awards offices at various colleges and universities. Unsurprisingly, institutions that have a high percentage of Aboriginal students (e.g., Cambrian College, Lakehead University, University of Manitoba, First Nations University of Canada, Keyano College and University of Saskatchewan) offer the majority of the awards.

However, the University of Toronto offers over 15 different awards, most of which are worth at least $3,000. The total value of these scholarships is included in the data on institutional scholarships in Section 5B.II.

The National Aboriginal Achievement Foundation is the largest Aboriginal organization to administer Aboriginal scholarships for private corporations. The majority of the Foundation's awards are either targeted to northern residents, students in northern studies or Aboriginal students in traditionally under-represented fields (e.g., law, medicine, journalism). In addition, there are a few corporations—primarily companies dealing with natural resources (e.g., Imperial Oil, Husky Oil, Cogema Resources)—which administer their own scholarships for Aboriginal students.

Government Undergraduate Merit Scholarships

The Government of Canada has a long history of giving merit-based assistance to graduate students, primarily through the three granting councils. It made an exceptional foray into undergraduate merit-based financing with the Canada Scholars Program, which it funded from 1988 to 1995.[6] In 1998, the Government of Canada re-entered the merit award sector by establishing the Canada Millennium Scholarship Foundation. The Foundation began distributing its millennium excellence awards in 2000, granting renewable entrance scholarships based on academic and extracurricular merit to students starting their post-secondary studies. Rather than focusing solely on academic achievement, the program's purpose is to recognize individuals who have shown a commitment to leadership, innovation and the betterment of their communities.[7] In 2003, the Foundation launched a second type of millennium excellence award, known as the national in-course award, to recognize similar qualities among students who have already begun their post-secondary studies.

---

3.   INAC Web site, March 2002: http://www.ainc-inac.gc.ca/ps/edu/ense_e.html.

4.   Malatest and Associates' *Aboriginal Peoples and Post-Secondary Education: What Educators Have Learned*, p. 21.

5.   These figures were obtained from INAC's Web site: http://pse-esd.ainc-inac.gc.ca/abs/index.asp?lang=E.

6.   Founded by the Ministry of Industry, Science, and Technology Canada, the Canada Scholars Program was designed to encourage individuals, especially women, to enter the field of science. The program was eliminated in the 1995 budget and phased out by 1998.

7.   Gucciardi, *Recognizing Excellence?: Canada's Merit Scholarships*.

There are five Canadian jurisdictions that run merit programs with funds of more than $50,000 per year. The most established and elaborate provincial scholarship program is the Alberta Heritage Savings Trust Fund. The Trust Fund was created in 1976, when oil and gas revenues were high and the Alberta government had budget surpluses. The Alberta Heritage Scholarship Fund was created in September 1980 with a $100 million endowment from the Trust Fund. The Alberta Heritage Scholarship Fund distributes approximately 16,000 undergraduate merit scholarships annually.

The newest program is Ontario's Queen Elizabeth II Scholarships. Launched in 2000 and formerly known as the "Aiming for the Top Tuition Scholarships," these are need-merit hybrid scholarships meant to recognize academically strong secondary school students with demonstrated financial need who are going on to post-secondary education. The average value of these scholarships is approximately $2,200.

British Columbia administers four major programs. The District Scholarship Program consists of $1,000 entrance scholarships based on academic merit distributed by individual school districts to over 500 graduating high school students across the province. The Provincial Scholarship Program gives entrance scholarships worth $1,000 or $2,000 based on academic merit to graduating high school students who excel in provincial exams. The Premier's Excellence Award Program distributes 15 entrance scholarships worth $5,000 each on the basis of extracurricular merit. The Passport to Education Program is the largest such program in B.C., providing more than 67,000 entrance scholarships based on academic merit. A high school student in B.C. can receive as many as four of these awards, if he or she is in the top 30% from Grade 9 through 12. They can be redeemed for tuition or other educational expenses, up to a maximum value of $800.

The Yukon Excellence Award is given to students who perform well (80% or better) on Yukon Territorial Examinations. The average value of the award is just over $1,100 per student; it is awarded to over 100 students annually.

The Centennial Merit Scholarship Program in Saskatchewan was created in 2000 to assist students entering post-secondary education with high secondary school marks. In 2002–03, the province invested over $500,000 to assist over 300 students.

Figure 5B.VI.1 — Canadian Government Spending on Merit Scholarships (1990–2003)

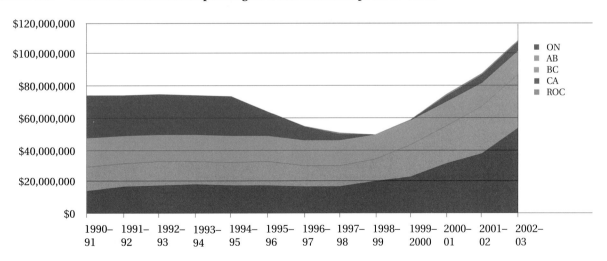

Source: Provincial student assistance programs and Canada Student Loans Program statistical reports.

All told, in 2002–03 the annual commitment to undergraduate merit scholarships from all levels of government was approximately $110 million, of which $95 million came from provincial governments while approximately $15 million came indirectly from the Government of Canada through the Canada Millennium Scholarship Foundation. Figure 5B.VI.1 shows the growth in government merit assistance in the past decade.

The growth in merit scholarships can largely be attributed to two factors in the late 1990s: 1) the creation of the Canada Millennium Scholarship Foundation and its Millennium Excellence Award Program, and 2) the creation of the Queen Elizabeth II Scholarships in Ontario.

Private Merit Scholarships

Scholarship income from corporations or non-profit foundations is an important funding component for select students. There is, however, very little detailed information about this sector; StudentAwards.com undertook the only attempt made at describing this sector in its 2000 National Scholarship Information Project. This project analyzed the scholarship data from StudentAwards.com's own database. While this is the country's largest scholarship database, its comprehensiveness is unknown. According to StudentAwards.com, there are approximately 900 scholarships administered by corporations or non-profit bodies in Canada.

It is easier to examine the "big players" in the scholarship field. There are approximately ten scholarship programs in Canada administered by non-governmental or private organizations with annual commitments of more than $50,000.[8] The biggest is the Canadian Merit Scholarship Foundation Program, with an annual commitment of $1.5 million. This program provides students with a renewable entrance scholarship that recognizes well-rounded students who combine academic promise with character, leadership potential and a commitment to the community.[9]

The Association of Universities and Colleges of Canada (AUCC) and the Canadian Bureau for International Education (CBIE) are the two main administrators of scholarships for private corporations. Most of these programs are actually part of benefits packages offered by companies to their employees and hence should not be counted as merit scholarships per se. One of the biggest corporate programs is the TD Canada Trust Scholarship for Outstanding Community Leadership, which provides 20 renewable and 60 entrance scholarships each year on the basis of general extracurricular merit.

In 2002–03, the total value of the major programs from both non-governmental and private sources was approximately $4.1 million, distributed as less than 1,000 scholarships. It should be noted that this number does not include all actors in the private scholarship sector, but rather only *major* NGO and private scholarship programs, and thus under-represents the size of the sector as a whole.

Canada Education Savings Grants

In 1998, the Government of Canada introduced the Canada Education Savings Grant (CESG), in order to make educational savings via an RESP more financially attractive. The grant is paid directly into a beneficiary's RESP and adds 20% to the first $2,000 in contributions made into an RESP on behalf of an eligible beneficiary each year. The grant can therefore be as much as $400 per year per beneficiary; over 18 years of saving it could amount to a total of $7,200. Table 5B.VI.1 shows the total number of RESP contracts and the value of those contracts.

The introduction of this program seems to have had a major effect on the number of people using RESPs, as the number of RESP contracts is expected

8. These include the Canadian Merit Scholarship Foundation, Garfield Weston Merit Scholarships for Colleges, the Mensa Canada Scholarship Program, the Miller Thompson Foundation Scholarship Program, the Terry Fox Foundation Humanitarian Award, the World Petroleum Congresses, the Foundation for the Advancement of Aboriginal Youth and a few scholarships administered through the Association of Universities and Colleges of Canada including the TD Canada Trust program.

9. Gucciardi, p. 6.

Table 5B.VI.1 — Overview of Registered Education Savings Plans

Year	Number of RESP Contracts	Aggregate Value (in Billions of Dollars)	Average Value of RESP
1998	1,000,000	3.9	$3,900
1999	1,400,000	5.4	$3,857
2000	1,700,000	7.2	$4,236
2001[10]	1,900,000	9.8	$5,157
2002	2,300,000	12.7	$5,521

Source: Canada Education Savings Grant Program

to rise by 130% in the five years following the introduction of the plan. It is impossible to tell, however, if this increase represents a rise in the total number of people saving for their children's education or merely an increase in the use of one particular savings vehicle by people who would have saved for their children's education in any case.

In the 2004 Federal Budget, the Government of Canada introduced measures to enhance the Canada Education Savings Grant for low- and middle-income Canadians. Starting in 2004, a $500 Canada Learning Bond will be provided at birth for children in families that are entitled to the National Child Benefit supplement—generally, families with incomes under $35,000.

Also, the Federal Budget announced that, from 2005, the 20% matching rate would be doubled to 40% for families with incomes of less than $35,000. It also proposes increasing the rate to 30% for families with incomes between $35,000 and $70,000. These enhanced CESG rates will apply to the first $500 contributed in a year to a child's RESP.

---

10. The 2001 and 2002 estimates are based on the actual grant paid, repayment values, and the average rate of Government of Canada marketable bonds over ten years (in 2001, the rate was 5.78%).

Chapter 5C

Government Expenditures on Student Assistance

Chapter 5C

Government Expenditures on Student Assistance

I. Introduction—Government Expenditures on Students

This chapter examines total government expenditures on students, including both expenditures made directly to students in the form of student assistance or tax credits and expenditures on educational institutions.

The most visible form of government expenditure on students is need-based student aid. Canadian governments, as a whole, reduced their commitment to this form of funding in the early 1990s by reducing the number of grants available to students and simultaneously increasing loan limits. Between 1994 and 1998, however, government expenditures on loan and grant programs doubled in real dollars, primarily as a result of major new investments by the Government of Ontario and the Government of Canada. This occurred even though total assistance (i.e., loans and grants) began to decline in 1996, primarily because an increasingly large proportion of assistance was being provided through grants rather than loans (which are cheaper in terms of the cost to governments). In 2000–01, total program expenditures on student assistance in Canada were just over $2 billion. Since then, expenditures have fallen as a result of declining student borrowing. Details about *government expenditures* on *student assistance* are shown in Section II of this chapter.

Government tax expenditures and the Canada Education Savings Grant are the subject of Section III. Little used as a vehicle for funding students as

> *Tax expenditures have in the past few years become more important than student loans and grants as a source of government support for students. Specifically, the Government of Canada has tripled its investment in tax expenditures for post-secondary education since 1996.*

recently as 1996, tax expenditures have in the past few years become more important than student loans and grants as a source of government support for students. Specifically, the Government of Canada has tripled its investment in tax expenditures for post-secondary education since 1996. Provincial government tax expenditures have risen as well, but at a much slower rate. This development has important policy implications, because most tax expenditures—unlike student assistance programs—do not deliver assistance based on a student's level of need. Furthermore, the introduction of the Canada Education Savings Grant has created an additional $360 million per year which is distributed to individuals on the basis of something other than need.

A small but still significant amount of expenditures on students is made via *student employment programs*. Overall, Canadian governments spend about $340 million per year on student employment programs, much of which is used to support seasonal summer employment. These programs and their associated expenditures are reviewed in Section IV.

The largest set of government expenditures on post-secondary education is transfers to educational institutions. In a very real—if often ignored—sense, these transfers are also transfers to students: without them, institutions would need to charge students much higher tuition fees in order to provide quality education. In 2002, Canadian governments

collectively spent approximately $15 billion on edu-
cational institutions, down from $19 billion a decade
earlier. *Government expenditures on post-secondary
institutions* are examined in detail in Section V.

The final section of this chapter combines data
from Sections II through V in order to analyze
aggregate trends in transfers benefiting students.
Since 1995, when the Canada Health and Social
Transfer was introduced, the share of overall post-
secondary expenditures received by individuals
(rather than institutions) has risen substantially.
While this is partially due to increases in need-based
funding, especially grants, it is first and foremost the
result of a massive increase in spending on measures
unrelated to need, such as tax expenditures and the
Canada Education Savings Grants.

III. Tax Expenditures and Canada Education Savings Grants

Tax Expenditures

Over the past decade, government policymakers have increasingly focused on non-need-based means of distributing subsidies for post-secondary education. While matching savings programs have received the lion's share of public attention, these are actually a comparatively minor source of non-need-based expenditures. The main vehicle for spending of this type has been tax expenditures.

Tax credits targeted at post-secondary students have become popular policy tools for the federal government over the past few years. In political terms, tax credits can be defined as "spending" or "tax relief," depending on how the government of the day wishes to portray its record. Due to the transferable nature of these tax credits, they can similarly be heralded either as tax breaks for the young or tax breaks for families. Also, unlike most education-related interventions, the Government of Canada does not need to negotiate with provincial governments in order to implement them.

Modifications to the tax system that benefit students do not receive much attention within the post-secondary community, but these programs nevertheless cost a great deal to implement. Total government tax expenditures for post-secondary students rival total government expenditures on student assistance,[1] and at the federal level the Government of Canada spends considerably more on tax credits than on student assistance. Any examination of government expenditures on student assistance is therefore incomplete without an examination of tax expenditures.

Government of Canada

During the late 1990s, the Government of Canada introduced a series of new tax benefits aimed at students. These included a tax credit for interest payments on student loans, an increase in study credit, increased RESP benefits, increased tax exemptions for scholarships and awards, an expansion of the tuition tax credit to include ancillary fees, a quintupling of the value of the monthly education credit, the introduction of a monthly education credit for part-time students and a change in the rules which allowed students to carry forward any unused tax credits to future tax years. It is easy to overlook the significance of these changes—but when the data are examined, the changes are in fact quite large. Since 1992, the federal government has nearly quadrupled its commitment to post-secondary education tax expenditures. In 2000, for the first time ever, the federal government committed over $1 billion to tax expenditures for Canadian students, and the total is rapidly heading toward $2 billion. Figure 5C.III.1 shows the changes in federal tax expenditures since 1990.

Transferred education and tuition tax credits, which allow students' family members (usually parents) to claim the value of any unused credits against their own taxes, are the largest single student-related tax expenditure. The value of these credits decreased significantly after the tax reform of 1988, which converted all forms of education tax assistance from tax deductions (which benefit the wealthy disproportionately) into credits (which are of equal value regardless of income). Their value then grew rapidly after the 1996 and 1997 budgets, when the tuition tax credit was expanded and the monthly education tax credit rose in value from $60 per month to $200 per month and then, in 2000, to $400 per month. Also, a tax credit for part-time students was introduced in 1998. These measures appear not to have substantially affected the value of the transferred tax credit, presumably because a new provision allows students to carry forward any unused credits to use against future tax liabilities. Since this provision was introduced, students appear to be less likely to transfer unused credits to their parents, preferring instead to keep them for their own future use (nevertheless, in absolute terms, students still transfer far more than they roll over for future years).

1. A tax expenditure is the amount of money it costs the government to provide a tax credit or tax deduction. There is considerable debate about how tax expenditures are calculated, as the method used to calculate their value assumes that everyone who currently benefits from a tax expenditure (in this case, students) would continue with that activity even if the tax support were taken away. Since the data in this book show that aggregate demand for post-secondary education appears to be relatively price-insensitive in Canada, this method of calculating the value of tax credits seems adequate.

At the moment, the fastest-growing tax expenditure is the tax exemption on interest and capital gains on assets held under an RESP, which has quadrupled over the past six years. The rapid growth in this expenditure reflects the phenomenal growth in the program since the introduction of the Canada Education Savings Grant.

Provincial Governments

The Canada Customs and Revenue Agency collects federal and provincial income tax on behalf of every province and territory except Quebec, which collects its own provincial income tax. Combining federal and provincial tax collection efforts saves collection and administration costs and results in only one income tax form to be filled out each year. Income tax in all jurisdictions except Quebec was until recently calculated as a percentage of the federal tax owed. Each province or territory had the power to set its own rate, but this rate was tied to the federal amount.

This meant that any federal tax measures automatically affected provincial and territorial revenue.

A new federal-provincial arrangement has resulted in changes to this system. In the 2000 and 2001 tax years, several provinces changed to the Tax on Income system. Under this system, provincial tax rates are no longer calculated as a percentage of federal tax. Instead, provinces can set their own rates based on federally determined taxable income. This system gives participating jurisdictions greater flexibility in setting tax policy. For example, federal non-refundable tax credits no longer have an effect on provincial revenue unless the province offers the same credit (for the most part, provinces have retained whatever tax credits had previously been in the system, such as education tax credits). Federally imposed deductions and exemptions, which reduce taxable income, will still affect provincial revenues.

The estimated cost to provincial treasuries of tuition and education credits can be calculated by using Revenue Canada statistics on the tuition and

Figure 5C.III.1 — Federal Government Tax Expenditures for Post-Secondary Students Since 1990 (in Millions of 2003 Real Dollars)

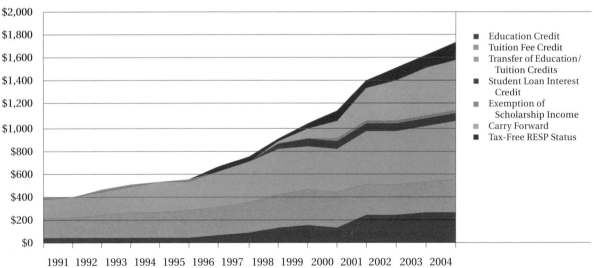

Source: Government of Canada's Department of Finance Tax Expenditures & Evaluations 2002.

Note: These data are drawn from Government of Canada 2002 Expenditures And Evaluations. The 2003 data, however, show a $300 million revision in the carry-forward tax credit over several years. The Department of Finance was unable to provide an explanation for this revision. Given the tremendous growth in enrolment and the value of tuition in Canada, it is the authors' belief that the numbers listed are correct.

Figure 5C.III.2 — Provincial/Territorial Government Tax Expenditures for Post-Secondary Students Since 1990 (in Millions of Real 2003 Dollars)ᵃ

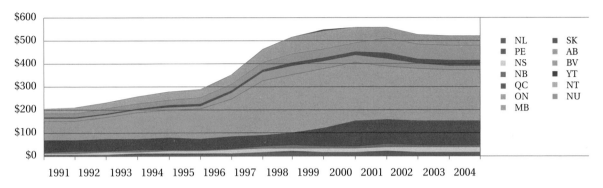

Source: Revenue Canada tax tables and authors' calculations.

Note: ᵃ Data for 2003 and 2004 have been estimated by the authors.

education amounts claimed in each province. The value of provincial tax credits has been decreasing in recent years. This is not because provinces have cut back on the amount of their education credits, but rather because reductions in provincial tax rates have in effect reduced the value of *all* tax credits. Figure 5C.III.2 shows the estimated costs of federal tuition and education credits for provincial and territorial governments.

It should be noted that the data in Figure 5C.III.2, which are based on Revenue Canada tax figures, do not line up perfectly with those from Figure 5C.III.1, which are based on Department of Finance tax expenditure estimates. For reasons that are unclear, but may be related to the way the value of the carry-forward credit is calculated, the amounts of tax credits claimed are lower than the amounts of estimated expenditures. If the Revenue Canada data are correct, then the expenditures shown in Figure 5C.III.1 are too high; conversely, if the Department of Finance data are correct, then the expenditures shown in Figure 5C.III.2 are too low.

In addition to bearing the cost of federal tax credits, several provinces—notably, Quebec, Ontario and Saskatchewan—run tax-based assistance programs of their own.

Quebec
The Government of Quebec administers and collects its taxes independently. Quebec has three main tax expenditures related to post-secondary students: tuition and examination fees, interest on student loans and partial exemption of student income. The partial exemption of student income came into effect in the 2001 budget; early estimates indicate that it costs $7 million per year. Table 5C.III.1 shows Quebec tax expenditures on students in recent years in 2003 dollars.

Ontario
Until 2004, the Government of Ontario offered a graduate transitions tax credit program to assist recently unemployed post-secondary graduates of an Ontario institution in entering the labour force.

Table 5C.III.1 — Estimated Cost of Quebec Tax Expenditures on Students (in Millions of 2003 Real Dollars)

	1994	1995	1996	1997	1998	1999	2000	2001	2002	2003
Tuiton/Examination fees	41	41	42	37	39	54	59	53	51	52
Interest on student loans					7	12	14	14	14	14
Exemption of bursary and award income				74	65	59	51	44	43	43

Source: Government of Quebec.

This program provided a maximum $4,000 tax credit based on 10% of an individual's salary (maximum of 15% for small businesses). The value of this program was estimated at $40 million annually. It was eliminated in the 2004 provincial budget.

Saskatchewan

In 2001, the Government of Saskatchewan introduced a graduate tax credit, available to post-secondary graduates who choose to live in Saskatchewan after graduation. This program will cost approximately $3 million in 2004.

Total Government Tax Expenditures

Calculating total government tax expenditures is relatively simple: it can be done by combining the data presented in Figures 5C.III.1 and .2, as shown in Figure 5C.III.3.

Figure 5C.III.3 shows that total estimated tax expenditures on students for all levels of government in Canada are equal to $2.3 billion in the fiscal year 2004. To put this in perspective, it is roughly equivalent to the total of all government transfers to colleges and universities in Manitoba, Saskatchewan and the four Atlantic provinces *combined*. More importantly, in the last three years, tax-based assistance has grown to the point where it is a larger annual expenditure than need-based loans and grants.

It should be noted that, unlike student assistance programs, almost none of this tax-based assistance is delivered on the basis of need. The education amount and tuition tax credits, which account for over two-thirds of education-related tax expenditures, are need-neutral. Tax sheltered growth for RESPs is technically need-neutral, but since savings are correlated to income (see Section 1.IV), this is in effect

Figure 5C.III.3 — Total Government Tax Expenditures for Post-Secondary Students Since 1990 (in Millions of 2003 Real Dollars)

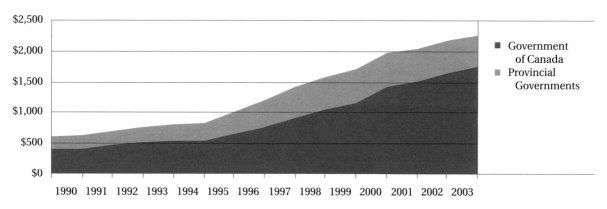

Source: Government of Canada's Department of Finance and Provincial Department of Finance Data.

Figure 5C.III.4 — Canada Education Savings Grant Recipients and Expenditures From 1998 to 2003 (in 2003 Real Dollars)

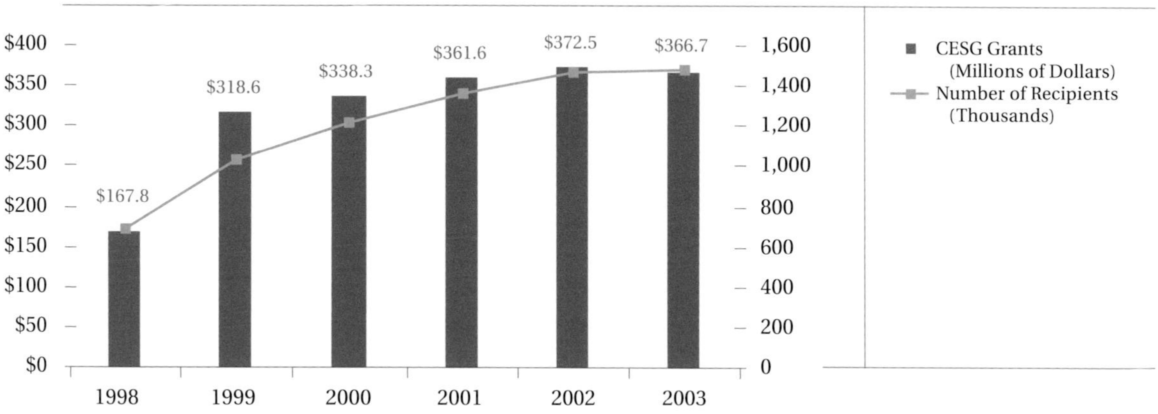

Source: Canada Education Savings Grant program.

a regressive tax expenditure, since it tends to benefit wealthier families. Only the tax credit for income paid on student loans is need-based, and only retrospectively—that is, it assists people who *used to be* in a high need group and, as a consequence of their high level of need, received a student loan.

Canada Education Savings Grants

Since 1971, Canada has had Registered Education Savings Plans, or RESPs, to encourage Canadians to save for their children's education. In 1998, the Government of Canada introduced the Canada Education Savings Grant (CESG), in order to make educational savings via an RESP more financially attractive. The grant is paid directly into a beneficiary's RESP and adds 20% to the first $2,000 in contributions made to an RESP on behalf of an eligible beneficiary each year. This means the grant can be as much as $400 each year per beneficiary, and over 18 years of saving it could amount to a total of $7,200.

The latest data, from the 2002 *Survey of Approaches to Educational Planning*, show that 52% of parents saving for their children's education are using RESPs and hence receiving CESGs as well. The CESG program regularly publishes statistics on the number of beneficiaries and total expenditures. These are presented in Figure 5C.III.4.

Total Non-Need-Based Expenditures

Total spending on non-need-based transfers to individuals has more than tripled in real dollars in the past decade, from $800 million to today's $2.6 billion, 80% of which comes from the Government of Canada. For the most part, this increase has come about through an expansion of federal tax credits. These expenditures are now considerably larger than those on need-based student financial assistance. Trends in spending on non-need-based expenditures are presented in Figure 5C.III.5.

Figure 5C.III.5 — Total Expenditures on Non-Need-Based Transfers to Individuals for Post-Secondary Students Since 1990 (in Millions of 2003 Real Dollars)

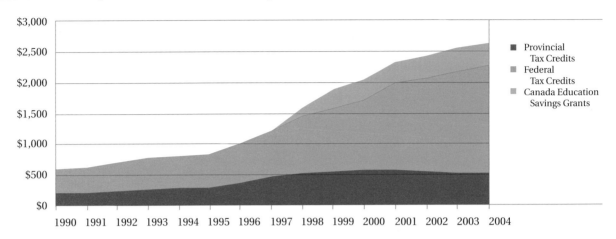

Source: Government of Canada's Department of Finance, Provincial Department of Finance Data and the Canada Education Savings Grant program.

IV. Student Employment Program Expenditures

As noted in Section 5B.III, all Canadian governments operate some kind of youth-oriented employment programs targeting post-secondary students specifically or youth in general. While all employment programs targeted to post-secondary students are youth-focused, the reverse is not necessarily true— many youth programs specifically exclude post-secondary students by targeting youth at risk or unemployed youth. This section only shows the value of those programs that are specific to post-secondary students and graduates or—in a few cases—programs for which all students are eligible, but for which post-secondary students are the main beneficiaries.

Despite the fact that these employment programs are primarily of benefit to students, governments tend not to consider them as student subsidies. This is because governments view student employment programs not only as a transfer of money to students but also as a way of providing non-profit organizations and government departments with cheap seasonal labour. In addition, student employment programs may reinforce government policy initiatives in other areas. For example, a number of overseas internships support Canadian foreign policy initiatives, while closer to home, inter-provincial exchange programs promote Canadian bilingualism and multiculturalism. Private businesses and non-profit organizations also benefit from an injection of educated workers and many, especially NGOs, require government subsidies and grants in order to make these positions available.

The Government of Canada is by far the largest funder of student and youth employment programs in the country; its annual expenditures on such programs exceed $240 million. Federal expenditures on youth employment programs make up about three-quarters of total government expenditures on youth employment programs. The Government of Canada's costs are distributed among 31 different youth employment programs, but about 80% of the total costs can be attributed to just three programs— Youth Internship Canada ($70 million per year),

Figure 5C.IV.1 — 2003 Expenditures on Youth Employment Programs in Canada in Millions of Dollars[a,b]

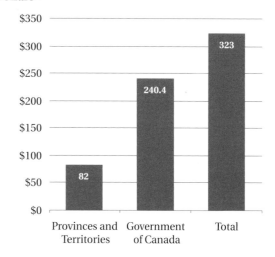

Source: Human Resources and Skills Development Canada and provincial and territorial governments.

Notes: [a] The total costs for the Government of Canada may be slightly higher since three programs (Canada's Digital Collections Program, Parks Canada and Summer-Student Connection Program) did not report program costs.

[b] All provincial expenditures are for 2003, except for Alberta and Quebec, where the most recent available data are from 2001. Also, a handful of provincial programs did not report expenditures.

Youth Service Canada ($40 million per year) and Summer Career Placements ($90 million per year). Figure 5C.IV.1 shows government expenditures on student employment programs in Canada.

Figure 5C.IV.2 shows the reported cost to provincial governments of youth employment programs in 2003. Generally speaking, most provinces with multiple programs have one "main" program and a number of smaller "niche" programs. Saskatchewan, for instance, spends over 90% of its student employment budget on a single program.

In most provinces, direct employment assistance to students takes the form of subsidies to employers. This is not the case in Quebec, where nearly half of all student employment program expenditures is provided through summer jobs and internships in the government itself. In Ontario, nearly twice as much is spent on subsidies to employers as on direct employment through government departments and agencies. In 2003, the Government of Ontario spent over $59 million on student employment programs. Similar numbers for the Government of Quebec were not available.

Manitoba is fairly unusual among provinces, as it distributes its funding fairly evenly through a large number of programs. Conversely, nearly all of Saskatchewan's expenditures are dedicated to its Centennial Student Employment Program. Employment programs in the territories are primarily focused on providing summer student employment.

Figure 5C.IV.2 — 2003 Cost of Student Employment Programs by Province in Millions of Dollars[a,b]

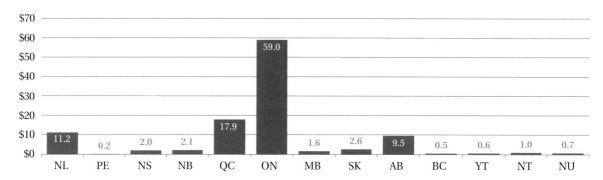

Source: Provincial and territorial governments.

Notes: [a] The total cost for New Brunswick is likely higher than that reported here since the costs for Student Employment and Experience Development were not reported; the cost of this program in 2001 was $6 million. Program costs in Manitoba and Saskatchewan are also slightly under-reported, since four programs in Manitoba (Aboriginal Youth Internship Program, Partners for Careers, STEP Services and Youth Services Manitoba) and two programs in Saskatchewan (Aboriginal Management and Professional Internship Program and Spruce Krew) were not reported. Finally, the following program costs were not reported in British Columbia: COOP Training, Youth Employment Program and Public Service Internships.

[b] All provincial/territorial expenditures are for 2003, except for Alberta and Quebec, where the most recent available data are from 2001.

V. Expenditures on Post-Secondary Institutions

In addition to various forms of direct subsidies provided in the form of student assistance, students also benefit indirectly from a much larger set of subsidies—namely, the subsidies paid directly to post-secondary institutions. Since it is primarily subsidies to institutions that sustain the education system, they could also, in a broader sense, be considered subsidies to students. Without these subsidies, tuition would certainly be much higher than it is at present. During the period of general fiscal restraint in the mid- to late-1990s, transfers to post-secondary institutions in the country as a whole declined.

Data on government expenditures used in this section include spending on operating expenses capital budgets, and sponsored research at colleges, universities and vocational schools, but exclude government spending on student assistance and other expenditures. The exclusion of these two data allows for a more accurate portrayal of government spending on post-secondary institutions. The previous edition of *The Price of Knowledge* included all datasets and was double counting government spending on student assistance since it would have appeared in both Statistics Canada and provincial student aid data. Also, the previous edition did not properly show the actual cuts in post-secondary institutional transfers since the increases in student aid spending would have masked the decline in institutional transfers.

For the most part, the data have come directly from provincial/territorial governments and the Canadian Association of University Business Offices' (CAUBO) annual data release. In some cases, when data were not provided and/or were not available, Statistics Canada's CANSIM II database was used. CANSIM was also used to obtain data about the Government of Canada's expenditures, which,

> *Since it is primarily subsidies to institutions that sustain the education system, they could also, in a broader sense, be considered subsidies to students. Without these subsidies, tuition would certainly be much higher than it is at present.*

because they are split between several departments, cannot easily be collected directly from government sources. In general, however, government sources were preferred over the CANSIM database due to the accuracy of the data. Data provided directly by provinces and territories while in some cases identical to CANSIM data, often come from official government documents with sources. CANSIM data are in effect third-hand information, with a greater potential for human error.

This method of calculating government expenditures is admittedly imperfect. There will undoubtedly be some differences between what government financial reports describe as "spending" and what institutions describe as "income" (as well as what institutions actually spend in a given period of time).[2] Distinctions between different spending categories (i.e., instruction, research, capital) are not always easily made, and none have been attempted here. Unfortunately, existing Canadian data are not good enough at present to attempt a reliable portrayal of trends in these areas. Thus, while changes in overall expenditures are portrayed, changes in the *composition* of spending are not. However, given the recent emphasis on research spending in Canadian universities and the large burst of capital spending in Ontario to accommodate the "double cohort," one might reasonably expect that ostensibly constant spending actually masks real—and perhaps serious—declines in the amount of money being devoted to instruction.

Figure 5C.V.1 shows provincial government transfers in Atlantic Canada. New Brunswick and Prince Edward Island kept their transfers to institutions relatively constant over the period in question. Nova Scotia, on the other hand, showed a pattern of long, steady decline from 1990

---

2.   The Canadian Association of University Business Office also tracks institutional activity. These data were employed in this section for university research expenditures for 2001 and 2002.

Figure 5C.V.I — Government Expenditures on Post-Secondary Institutions in Atlantic Canada (in 2003 Real Dollars)

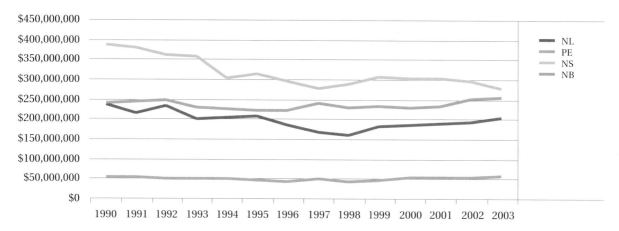

Source: Provincial Department of Education data, Maritime Provincial Higher Education Council, CAUBO 2001 and 2002, provincial budget
documents (supplementary estimates) and Statistics Canada's CANSIM II database (Tables 478-004, 478-005, and 478-007).

to 2000, followed by a period of gentle recovery and consolidation. In Newfoundland and Labrador, the declines were limited to 1994 to 1997, but were never the less still steep. In per-student terms, this decline was likely less severe in Newfoundland and Labrador (where overall population loss created a declining student population for much of the period in question) than in Nova Scotia (where the student population increased over the same period).

Figure 5C.V.2 shows transfers to post-secondary institutions from Ontario and Quebec, Canada's two largest provincial governments. In 1991, both governments spent approximately the same on post-secondary education institutions ($3.8 billion per year), and by 2002, that was no longer true. Though the two provinces decreased transfers in the 1990s, they used very different routes. Quebec's decline in spending was regular and gentle, while Ontario essentially experienced a sharp drop from 1996 onward following the election of a new government with a mandate to reduce public spending. Ontario

also experienced a massive spike in expenditures in 1999, which was largely the result of large-scale construction projects (i.e., Super Build) designed to accommodate the "double cohort" which arrived in Ontario's universities when Grade 13 was eliminated in 2003. Two years later, Ontario expenditures had returned to their pre-1999 level. Also, it is important to note that dramatic decreases in expenditures on trade and vocational institutions likely offset any increase in college and university level.

Since Quebec has fewer citizens and lower per-capita GDP this would signify that in relative terms the province is devoting a greater proportion of its budget expenditures to post-secondary education than Ontario. This is partly because post-secondary education begins two years earlier in Quebec, where secondary school typically ends at the age of 17; in Ontario, until 2003, secondary studies normally ended at the age of 19. The difference in expenditures between the two provinces may also be indicative of different views on the role of the state in

Figure 5C.V.2 — Government Expenditures on Post-Secondary Institutions in Ontario and Quebec (in 2003 Real Dollars)

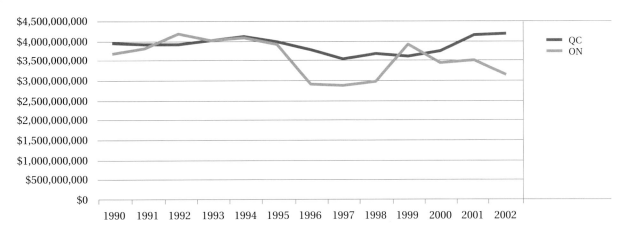

Source: Provincial Department of Education data, CAUBO 2001 and 2002, provincial budget documents (supplementary estimates) and
     Statistics Canada's CANSIM II database (Tables 478-004, 478-005, and 478-007).

Figure 5C.V.3 — Government Expenditures on Post-Secondary Institutions in Western Canada (in 2003 Real Dollars)

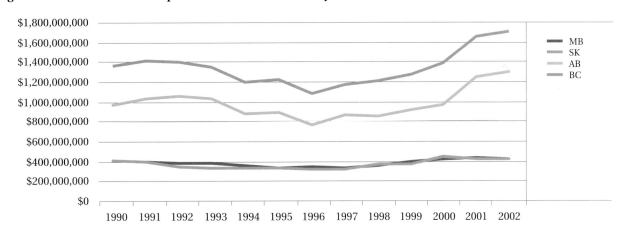

Source: Provincial Department of Learning data, Provincial Department of Advanced Education Data, CAUBO 2001 and 2002, provincial
     budget documents (supplementary estimates) and Statistics Canada's CANSIM II database (Tables 478-004, 478-005, and 478-007).

Figure 5C.V.4 — Government of Canada Expenditures on Post-Secondary Institutions (in 2003 Real Dollars)

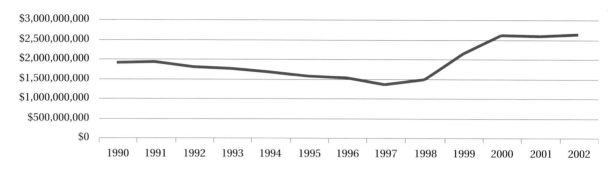

Source: Statistics Canada's CANSIM II database (Tables 478-004, 478-005, and 478-007), CAUBO 2001 and 2002, and Federal
         Expenditure documents.

providing publicly funded services, including post-secondary education. Quebecers, who face higher income taxes than Ontarians, also expect the state to provide additional services. The data provided here also mask one other important development— Quebec has had relatively stable enrolment over time, whereas enrolment has increased in Ontario. On a per-student basis, Quebec is therefore in all likelihood considerably further ahead of Ontario than this graph would suggest.

Western Canada provides interesting examples of provinces' mirroring each other's policies. In Alberta and B.C., expenditures on post-secondary institutions mirrored each other almost exactly. Through peaks and troughs—and despite ideologically opposed governments—the two provinces moved in virtual lock-step throughout the 1990s, albeit with the smaller government (Alberta) trailing the larger one by approximately $300 million per year. Similarly, Manitoba and Saskatchewan had virtually identical spending patterns during the 1990s. Neither province experienced the sharp year-to-year declines or increases that characterized spending in most other provinces; rather, both held spending

more or less constant in real dollars, albeit with slight declines in the mid-1990s and slight rises at the end of the decade. Saskatchewan, however, has seen its spending remain flat in the past few years since peaking in 2000, while Manitoba has experienced a slight increase in expenditures in recent years. Figure 5C.V.3 shows transfers to post-secondary education institutions in the four Western provinces.

The Government of Canada's expenditures on post-secondary institutions are devoted primarily to research funding and retraining programs linked with the Employment Insurance Program. In fact, according to Statistics Canada, well over two-thirds of federal spending on post-secondary institutions comes in the form of research funding to universities. In general, federal expenditures on post-secondary institutions declined throughout the 1990s, however, there has been an increase of over $1 billion in the past five years. It is important to note that any declines in retraining expenditures dwarfed increases in spending on research granting councils. Also, these statistics do not include the Government of Canada's large one-time transfers to foundations

Figure 5C.V.5 — Total Government Expenditures on Post-Secondary Institutions (in 2003 Real Dollars)

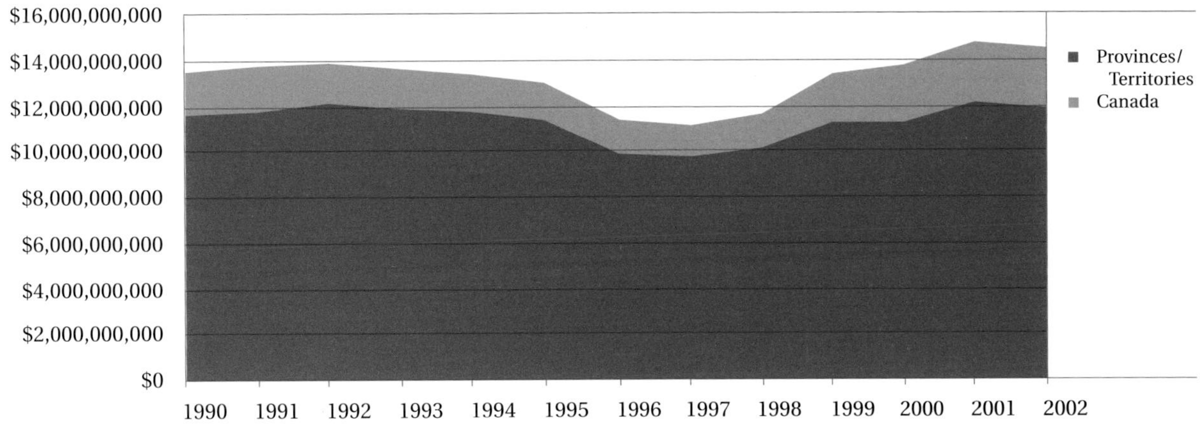

Source: Provincial/Territorial Department of Education data, Provincial/Territorial Department of Learning Data, Provincial/Territorial Department of Advanced Education Data, Federal Expenditure documents, CAUBO 2001 and 2002, provincial/territorial budget documents (supplementary estimates) and Statistics Canada's CANSIM II database (Tables 478-004, 478-005, and 478-007).

related to post-secondary education, including more than $1 billion given to the Canada Foundation for Innovation in 1997, 1999 and 2000 and $2.5 billion given to the Canada Millennium Scholarship Foundation in 1998. Figure 5C.V.4 shows Government of Canada transfers to post-secondary education institutions.

Figure 5C.V.5 shows the total picture with respect to government transfers to institutions. Overall, spending on institutions appears to be at an all-time high (just over $14.5 billion in 2002) after experiencing sharp declines in the mid-to-late 1990s. The declines in transfers to institutions in the 1990s had many consequences, not least of which was sharp increases in tuition fees in all provinces except Quebec.

VI. Aggregate Post-Secondary Expenditures

The preceding sections examined various compo-
nents of spending on post-secondary education in
Canada. The purpose of this section is to pull
together data on different types of spending to
provide an overall analysis of government spending
on post-secondary education.

Transfers to Individuals

Transfers to individuals with respect to post-
secondary education include spending on student
financial assistance (i.e., loans, grants and remission),
tax expenditures, Canada Education Savings Grants
and student employment expenditures, which are
omitted from this analysis due to the unavailability of
time-series data. Over the past decade, total government transfers to individuals have roughly doubled
in real dollars from approximately $2 billion per year
to $4 billion per year. Over half of this increase can be
attributed to an increase in the availability of tax
credits or other tax-based expenditures. Roughly
one-third is due to increases in spending on student
financial assistance, and the balance is accounted for

by Canada Education Savings Grants. Figure 5C.VI.1
tracks the evolution of total government transfers to
individuals with respect to post-secondary education
by type.

Turning to an examination of funds by source,
one finds that nearly all of the increase in transfers to
individuals is due to changes at the federal level. In
real dollars, provincial expenditures on transfers to
individuals (that is, tax expenditures and student
assistance expenditures combined) in 2002 were
virtually unchanged from the corresponding figure
in 1992. The Government of Canada, on the other
hand, increased its expenditures in this area by
almost exactly $2 billion during the same period.
Figure 5C.VI.2 shows the changes in federal and
provincial spending on transfers to individuals
with respect to post-secondary education between
1990 and 2002.

Some previous studies (Junor and Usher 2002;
Usher 2004b) have also divided transfers to individuals on a "need" and "non-need" (or "universal")
basis. The distinction between the two is not based
on whether or not the recipient of the money

**Figure 5C.VI.1 — Government Transfers to Individuals With Respect to Post-Secondary Education by Type From
1990 to 2002 (in 2003 Real Dollars)**

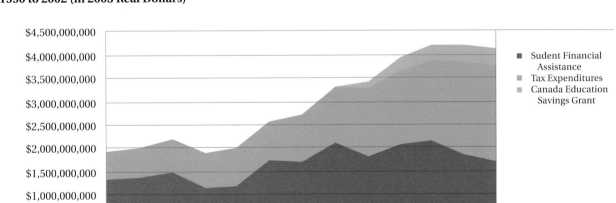

Source: Provincial/Territorial Student Aid offices, Government of Canada's Department of Finance and Provincial Department of Finance
    data, Canada Millennium Scholarship Foundation annual reports and the Canada Education Savings Grant program.

Figure 5C.VI.2 — Government Transfers to Individuals With Respect to Post-Secondary Education by Source From 1990 to 2002 (in 2003 Real Dollars)

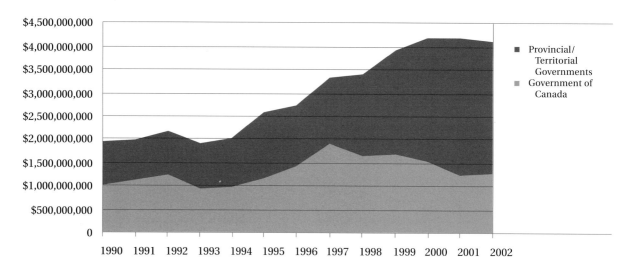

Source: Provincial/Territorial Student Aid offices, Government of Canada's Department of Finance and Provincial/Territorial Department of Finance data, Canada Millennium Scholarship Foundation annual reports and the Canada Education Savings Grant program.

actually "needs" it—rather, the distinction is based on the eligibility criteria. Need-based programs are targeted programs with a means test; non-need programs are universal in the sense that everyone is equally eligible to benefit from them (although in the case of the Canada Education Savings Grant program, not everyone is equally able to benefit because of variation in families' ability to save). Broadly speaking, student loans and grants are "need-based" expenditures, while tax credits and education savings grants are "non-need-based." The exception to this rule is the tax credit for interest paid on a student loan, which is need-based in a retrospective fashion (i.e., anyone can benefit from the credit, provided that at some point in the past they passed a need test and obtained a student loan).

Figure 5C.VI.3 shows the evolution of need- and non-need-based transfers to individuals in Canada. Since the 1997 federal budget (which was the first to contain major new tax expenditures), nearly all expenditure growth in Canada has been on the non-need side. In effect, major increases in need-based spending (such as the Canada Millennium Scholarship Foundation and its millennium bursaries) have been

offset by reductions in other forms of need-based expenditures (such as the cost of loan maintenance—see Section 5C.II). In 2001, for the first time, non-need-based assistance formed a larger part of total transfers to individuals than need-based assistance.

Total Government Transfers With Respect to Post-Secondary Education

A complete examination of government post-secondary spending requires an analysis of spending on institutions as well as individuals. Figure 5C.VI.4 therefore adds data from section 5C.V on institutions into the preceding analysis of transfers to individuals. This chart shows that total government transfers in respect of post-secondary education stayed fairly constant in the first half of the 1990s between $15 and $16 billion. Sharp cutbacks in mid-decade from the governments of Canada, Ontario and Quebec led to a drop in total spending to about $14 billion, even though student aid expenditures were expanding rapidly throughout this period. Since 1999, both expenditures on institutions and expenditures on individuals have been rising

Figure 5C.VI.3 — Need-Based Versus Non-Need-Based ("Universal") Expenditures From 1990 to 2002 (in 2003 Real Dollars)

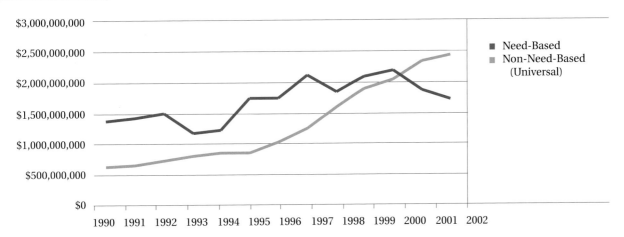

Source: Provincial Student Aid offices, Government of Canada's Department of Finance and Provincial/Territorial Department of Finance data, Canada Millennium Scholarship Foundation annual reports and the Canada Education Savings Grant program.

Figure 5C.VI.4 — Total Government Transfers With Respect to Post-Secondary Education by Type (in 2003 Real Dollars)

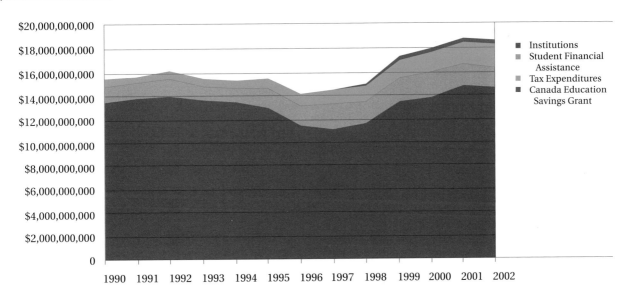

Source: Provincial/Territorial Student Aid offices, Government of Canada's Department of Finance and Provincial Department of Finance data, CANSIM II database (487-004, 487-005 and 487-007), Canadian Association of University Business Offices 2001 and 2002, Government of Canada Part III estimates, Canada Millennium Scholarship Foundation Annual Reports and the Canada Education Savings Grant program.

sharply. As a result, total government expenditures in respect of post-secondary education hit an all-time high in 2001 to $18.9 billion and fell only slightly in 2002.

More dramatic than the increase in total expenditures is the change in the composition of these expenditures. Figure 5C.VI.4 shows clearly the decrease in the proportion of total spending going to institutions and the increasing proportion going to individuals. In the years up to 1994, institutions received about 87% of all transfers in respect of post-secondary education. Following the introduction of the Canada Health and Social Transfer (CHST) and—later in the 1990s—the large increase in tax expenditures for post-secondary education, the balance began to shift so that transfers to institutions now account for only 78% of total expenditures. This is not a paradigmatic shift by any means, but it does represent a general trend toward a form of fiscal federalism where the Government of Canada deals directly with individuals on issues such as education rather than deal with provinces.

Finally, it is important to examine total transfers in respect of post-seconday education in light of other trends. Two very important and commonly used measures are expenditures per student and expenditures as a percentage of Gross Domestic Product (GDP). As enrolments were generally flat across all post-secondary sectors in the 1990s, a slow decline in total expenditures translated into a decline in per-student spending. Per student spending hit its nadir in 1996 at $8,950. A modest rise in 1997 and 1998 were followed by massive increases in 1999 and the years following. These reached a high in 2001 of $11,662/student (an increase of 30% of five years earlier) before falling again, in the face of rapidly rising enrolments, in 2002.

With respect to GDP—which rose substantially during precisely those years when PSE expenditures were falling, the picture is somewhat different. In the late 1990s, Canada recorded some of the highest real growth rates in its post-war history. As a result, flat or falling total expenditures in the 1990s have translated into a major drop in government transfers as a percentage of GDP from a high of 1.80% in 1992 to just 1.35% in 1998. Since then, increases in spending have restored some of this drop, but as of 2002, total government expenditures as a share of GDP are 1.49%, down 17% from a decade earlier. Figure 5C.VI.5 shows comparative measures of post-secondary education transfers from 1990 to 2002.

Figure 5C.VI.5 — Comparative Measures of Post-Secondary Expenditures From 1990 to 2002 (Per-Student Expenditures and Expenditures as a Proportion of GDP)

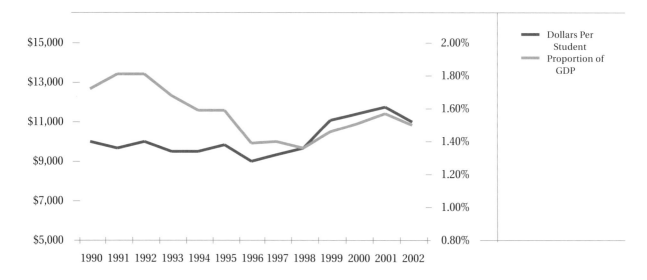

Source: Provincial/Territorial Student Aid offices, Government of Canada's Department of Finance and Provincial Department of Finance data, CANSIM II database (380-002, 487-004, 487-005 and 487-007), Canadian Association of University Business Offices 2001 and 2002, Government of Canada Part III estimates, Canada Millennium Scholarship Foundation Annual Reports and the Canada Education Savings Grant program.

Chapter 6

Student Outcomes

Chapter 6

Student Outcomes

I. Introduction

Thus far, this book has examined students—how young people become students; how many students there are in Canada; what and where they study; how they earn, spend and borrow money; and how governments help students. This is all, however, a means to an end. Students, for the most part, graduate and move on to the labour force. This chapter is about graduates, their lives after graduation and how the legacy of their education affects them later in life.

The first two sections of the chapter look at the act of graduation: how many people manage it and how long it takes them. Specifically, Section II looks at the *time to completion* of university students and concludes that the likelihood of finishing on time increases with the length of program, while *graduation and attainment* rates are examined in Section III.

One of the most noticeable and immediate legacies of graduation—for some at least—is the level of *student debt at graduation*, which is the subject of Section IV. On the basis of the available evidence, the average student debt appears to be just over $20,000 nationally, although there is a significant gap between Quebec and the rest of the country. While this represents a considerable increase since 1990, the evidence suggests that student debt has not been increasing in the past several years and may in fact be decreasing. As mentioned previously, this is a result of frozen loan limits, inflation and the introduction of the Canada Millennium Scholarship Foundation. Section V examines patterns in *student loan repayment* and presents evidence of the effects of increased debt—students are able to pay off much less of their loans than they could even ten years ago.

Increased debt does not, however, appear to have led to an increase in the proportion of students who say they are having difficulty repaying their loans.

Section VI shows that a majority of university and college graduates are now pursuing *further studies* after graduation, although many seem to be taking specific classes to obtain particular job skills rather than engaging in a new course of degree or diploma studies. Students' *transition to the labour force* is the subject of Section VII. Unemployment rates generally decline as level of education rises and length of time in the labour force increases, and new *National Graduate Survey* results show a rebound in graduate employment rates in 2000 after a sub-par showing in the 1995 survey. Clear regional patterns of employment and unemployment rates among recent graduates are also evident.

Section VIII looks at *graduates' earnings*. A graduate's level of education is crucial in determining his or her immediate post-graduation income: on average, university graduates earn substantially more than either college or trade/vocational graduates. There are, however, substantial variations in income depending on the individual's field of study and region. The differences in earnings by field of study are partially responsible for a significant gender gap in earnings as well. Over the longer term, however, the earnings differential between graduates with Bachelor's degrees from different fields of study narrows somewhat.

The final sections of this chapter look at *graduate mobility* (Section IX) and the *benefits of post-secondary education* (Section X)—that is, the financial and non-financial benefits that post-secondary graduates bring to the economy and, in particular, their impact on government revenues and expenditures. Data show that college and university graduates, while making up only 40% of the country's working age population, pay over 60% of the country's personal income taxes and receive less than a third of government transfer payments to individuals. Also, data show a wide variety of positive non-financial outcomes for those with higher levels of education, including better health, lower chances of incarceration and higher rates of volunteerism and civic engagement.

II. Time to Completion

The 2003 Canadian Undergraduate Survey Consortium's (CUSC) *Graduating Students Survey* has a wealth of information regarding the characteristics of graduating students, including the length of time it takes to complete a degree. According to the CUSC, 67% of students in their graduating year completed their entire degree at a single institution. Seventeen percent transferred credits from another university, while another 17%—heavily concentrated in Alberta and B.C.— transferred credits from a college. As mentioned previously, the post-secondary system in Alberta, British Columbia and Quebec allows for a seamless transition from college to university.

Time to completion, as measured from the time a student enrols an institution, depends to a considerable extent on whether or not the student is bringing credits with him or her from another institution. Figure 6.II.1 shows that, as one would expect, the time it takes to receive a degree for university students who transfer credits (from either a college or another university) is shorter than it is for students who complete all their credits at a single institution.

Unfortunately, the CUSC survey is worded in such a way that it is impossible to determine the time elapsed between the start and end of studies for those students who changed institutions over the course of their studies. For the two-thirds of students

Figure 6.II.1 — Time to Completion by Origin of Academic Credits

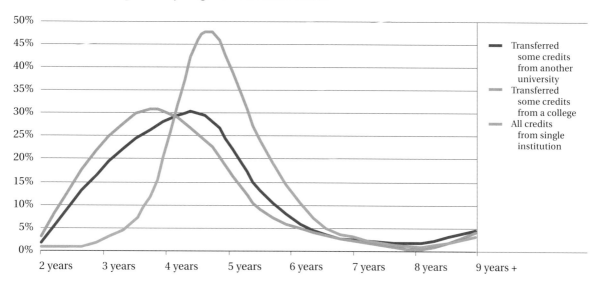

Source: Canadian Undergraduate Survey Consortium's 2003 *Graduating Students Survey*.

Figure 6.II.2 — Time to Completion for Single-Institution University Students by Normal Program Length

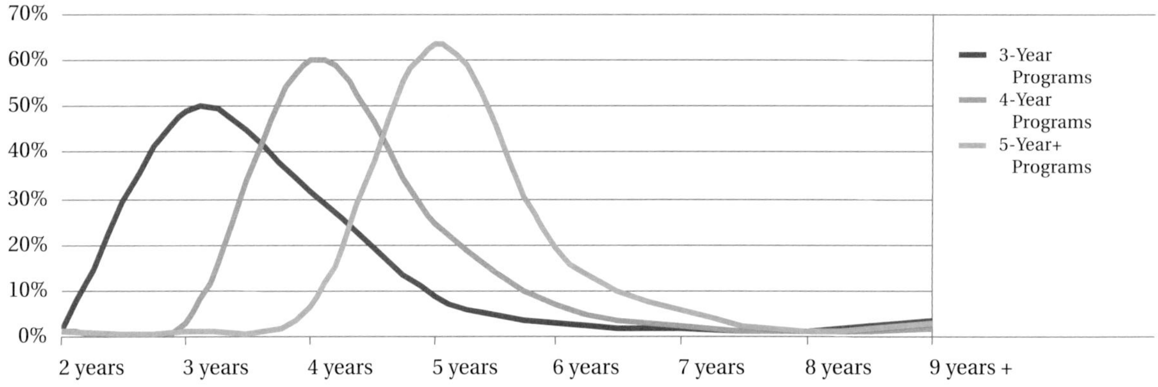

Source: Canadian Undergraduate Survey Consortium's 2003 *Graduating Students Survey.*

who began and ended their undergraduate degrees at the same institution (hereafter called "single-institution students"), however, such an analysis is possible, and the results are shown in Figure 6.II.2.

The CUSC data show that a substantial majority of single-institution students finish their programs "on time" and that in degree programs (i.e., programs of three or more years in length) the proportion of students who graduate on time

increases with the length of the program. There are several possible reasons why this might be the case. One result is that longer programs tend to have more stringent academic entry requirements and thus tend to attract more diligent students than shorter programs. Longer programs also allow students more time to "catch up" if any courses are failed, missed due to illness, or unavailable.

Table 6.II.1 — Length of Program and Average Time to Completion for Single-Institution University Students

Length of Program	Proportion of Students Enrolled	Proportion Completing on Time	Average Time to Completion
Less than 3 years	4.8%	68.3%	2.29 years
3 years	18.4%	50.2%	3.94 years
4 years	67.9%	63.1%	4.56 years
5 or more years	8.9%	71.0%	5.37 years

Source: Canadian Undergraduate Survey Consortium's 2003 *Graduating Students Survey.*

III. Graduation and Attainment Rates

In the absence of a reliable national administrative database that tracks students, it is impossible to know with any certainty what proportion of students who begin post-secondary studies actually graduate in the end. As seen previously (Chapter 2.XII), administrative data are so poor that the best available data yield only a synthetic completion rate—for universities only. Surveys such as Statistics Canada's *Youth in Transition Survey* and the *Post-Secondary Education Participation Survey* are able to give helpful information up to a certain age (22 in the case of YITS; 24 in the case of PEPS), but no survey specifically tracks students all the way to the end of their period of studies.

> *It is impossible to know with any certainty what proportion of students who begin post-secondary studies actually graduate in the end. No survey specifically tracks students all the way to the end of their period of studies.*

In place of graduation rates, it is still possible to track two other important indicators. The first is the total of new graduates each year, and the second is the educational attainment rate of the population as a whole.

Due to ongoing data quality problems at Statistics Canada, data on graduates are not as timely as one might hope; in fact, no data whatsoever are available on the subject since 2000 (or 1999 in the case of college students). The data for the latter half of the 1990s are interesting chiefly for the fact that so little change occurred in this period. University graduation rates stayed constant at approximately 175,000 per year over the period in question, with a slight fall in undergraduate degrees awarded being more or less offset by a small increase in graduate degrees awarded. There was, however, a significant increase in college diplomas awarded in career programs, from 72,000 in 1994–95 to 91,345 in 1997–98. This increase in graduations was considerably larger than the increase in enrolment over the corresponding period, which suggests an improvement in completion rates during this time.

Interestingly, in both sectors the share of females among all graduates was approximately 58% in all years. Compared to their shares of enrolment over the same period, this evidence suggests that females were slightly more likely than males to complete a university program and considerably more likely to complete a college program. Figure 6.III.1 shows data on post-secondary graduates in Canada from 1994–95 to 1999–2000.

Figure 6.III.1 — Post-Secondary Graduates in Canada From 1994–95 to 1999–2000 by Gender and Institution

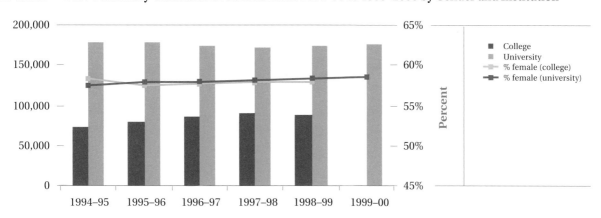

Source: Statistics Canada's *Expanded Student Information Survey* and *Community College Student Information Survey*.

Another way of looking at data on completion is to look at attainment rates. A traditional graduation rate is obtained by looking at a particular cohort of students and determining how many of these students have completed their studies after a given number of years. An attainment rate looks at the issue differently: it represents the proportion of people of a particular age who have completed a given type of studies.

Looking at the 20- to 24-year-old cohort provides a sense of the attainment rates of those who make an immediate transition to post-secondary education. This is not a perfect method of looking at attainment: few 20-year-olds have finished a post-secondary education and many 24-year-olds are still in school. The figure therefore will undoubtedly be lower than the actual attainment rate. Nevertheless, by using a similarly imperfect measurement across the country, it is possible to make comparisons among jurisdictions with respect to attainment.

Figure 6.III.2 shows college and university attainment rates for individuals aged 20 to 24 by jurisdiction. Quebec, by virtue of its CEGEP system (which funnels high school graduates into a two- or three-year college program after just 11 years of primary and secondary school) leads the rest of the country by a considerable distance in terms of attainment. Perhaps more important, however, are some of the subtle differences between provinces. The data show a clear gap between Atlantic Canada and the five provinces to the west of Quebec. In Ontario's case, this can be dismissed as a side effect of having, until the recent elimination of Grade 13, an extra year of secondary school; for the other provinces, the differences in attainment reflect the differences in participation rates seen in Chapter 2. However, while Saskatchewan ranks higher than Alberta and British Columbia on the basis of university participation rates, the reverse is true with respect to university attainment rates. The territories, with no universities of their own, have very few young people with university degrees; however, Yukon is comparable to the provinces in terms of the proportion of young people in the territory who have completed a college education.

Examining attainment rates for the 25- to 44-year-old age cohort—the prime working-age population—shows a rather different picture. In one

Figure 6.III.2 — 2001 College and University Attainment Rates for Individuals Aged 20 to 24 by Jurisdiction

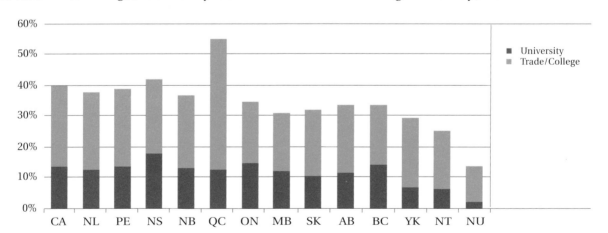

Source: Statistics Canada's 2001 Census.

Figure 6.IV.3 — Incidence of Government Student Loan Debt At Graduation, By Province of Study, Class of 2000

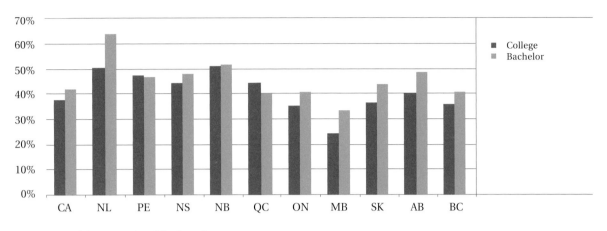

Source: Statistics Canada's 2000 *National Graduate Survey.*

The incidence of student debt does not vary much by type of education, but it does vary substantially by province. In all provinces but Quebec, the incidence of loan borrowing is higher at the Bachelor's level than at the college level, though in most cases the gap is only a couple of percentage points. In the country's three largest provinces—Quebec, Ontario and British Columbia—roughly equal proportions (40%) of university students graduate with debt. Most provinces have slightly higher proportions of graduates with debt; Alberta, Saskatchewan and the three Maritime provinces all have debt incidences of between 43% and 51%. Newfoundland and Labrador, with 64%, has the country's highest

incidence of university graduate debt, while Manitoba's rate of 33% is the country's lowest. In both provinces, geography plays a major role in determining the incidence of debt. Newfoundland's high levels of need (and hence of borrowing) are in large part due to the fact that much of its widely scattered population must leave home in order to pursue post-secondary studies. Conversely, Manitoba, where 80% of the population is concentrated within an hour's drive of one of the province's four universities, has very low need and hence low borrowing. Figure 6.IV.3 shows the incidence of government student loan debt at graduation, by province of study.

Figure 6.IV.4 — Government Student Loan Debt at Graduation by Province in 2000

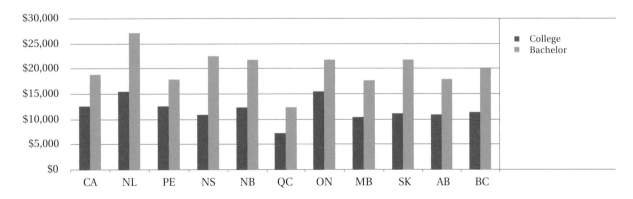

Source: Statistics Canada's 2000 *National Graduate Survey.*

Debt levels are not identical across the country. Not only do family incomes and tuition levels vary across the country, but as noted in Chapter 5A, different provinces also provide very different levels of loans, grants and remission. This results in considerably different debt burdens in different parts of Canada. Government student loan debt at graduation by province is shown in Figure 6.IV.4.

Debt is particularly high in Newfoundland, where family income is considerably lower than in the rest of the country and reliance on government assistance consequently higher. Quebec, with its generous system of grants, has very low levels of student debt compared to the rest of the country. Despite very different tuition regimes, undergraduate debt levels are broadly similar in the other eight provinces, although Manitoba, Alberta and Prince Edward Island are slightly lower than the others. Debt at the college level is effectively the same across the country; the exception is Ontario, where the longer average length of college programs (three years is becoming the standard) is likely the main factor behind the higher average debt level.

Even greater regional disparities exist when it comes to student's graduating with very high levels of debt. For a province to have a lot of students with high debt it must have a high number of students borrowing, reasonably high average need and a system of student assistance that is tilted more towards loans than grants. This is especially true in Newfoundland, where nearly 40% of all university students graduate with over $25,000 in debt, compared to just 13% nationally. Quebec, on the other hand, is just the opposite—virtually no college graduates in that province have $25,000 in debt, while the figure for university graduates is just 2.4%. Other provinces' university graduates are between these two extremes. Figure 6.IV.5, which shows the percentage of graduates with more than $25,000 in debt at graduation by province, demonstrates that high-need, low-grant provinces (e.g., Nova Scotia and New Brunswick) tend to have higher proportions of graduates with debt than either low-need, low-grant provinces (e.g., Manitoba) or high-need, high-grant provinces (e.g., British Columbia and Alberta). College graduates follow roughly the same

Figure 6.IV.5 — Percentage of Graduates With More Than $25,000 in Debt at Graduation, by Province, Class of 2000

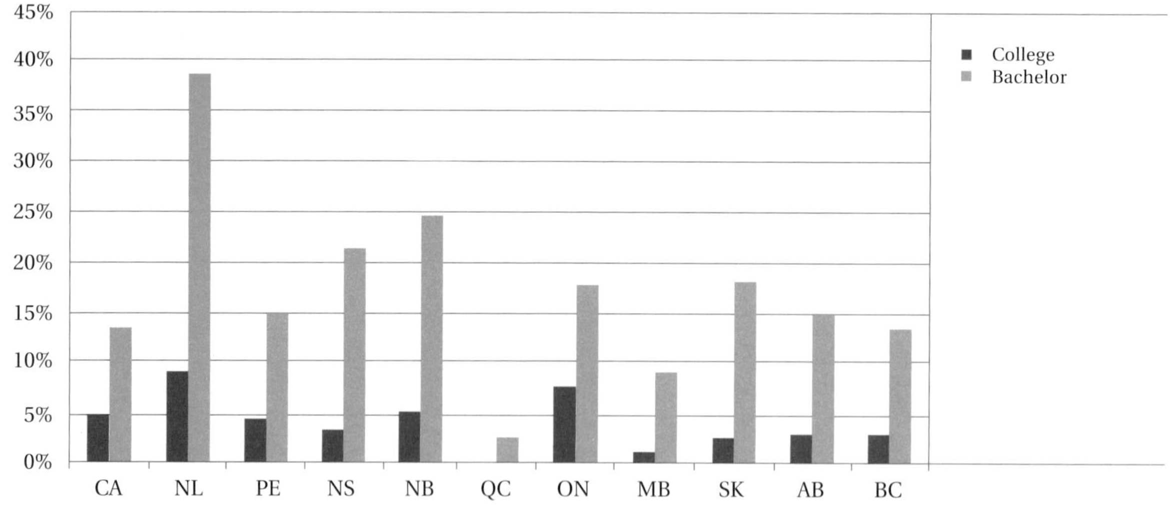

Source: Statistics Canada's 2000 *National Graduate Survey.*

pattern, though the extent of provincial variability is not as great as it is for Bachelor's graduates. Because they are enrolled for much shorter periods of time, college graduates generally are only about one-third as likely to have debt over $25,000 than are Bachelor's graduates.

As noted in Chapter 4.XII and 4.XIII, there are no major differences in terms of the incidence and amount of borrowing among students by demographic characteristics. It is somewhat surprising, therefore, to find that there are some significant differences among demographic groups in terms of debt at graduation. The incidence of student debt among Aboriginal students, students with children

and students with disabilities is only slightly higher than the overall average, however, those who borrow tend to finish with higher average educational debt than other students. One possible explanation for the discrepancy between these results and those in Chapter 4.XII and 4.XIII may lie in the average number of years these students borrow: a longer average borrowing period would result in higher average debt, even if the amount borrowed in any given year is not different from other students. Table 6.IV.1 shows differences in the incidence and amount of student debt by selected demographic characteristics.

Table 6.IV.1 — Incidence and Amount of Debt at Graduation by Selected Demographic Characteristics (University Students Only)

	All Students (n=11,224)		Baseline Group (n=9,745)		Aboriginal Students (n=278)		Students With Children (n=848)		Students With a Disability (n=476)	
	Incidence/Average Debt									
Student loans	41%	$17,569	41%	$16,836	41%	$19,579	45%	$24,430	42%	$19,004
Loans from financial institutions	15%	$10,412	15%	$10,293	12%	$11,253	9%	$11,017	20%	$10,705
Loans from parents/family	19%	$10,686	19%	$10,774	23%	$11,740	16%	$8,755	20%	$9,821
Debt from other sources	6%	$6,131	5%	$5,835	8%	$6,317	10%	$8,555	10%	$5,087
Total average debt	56%	$20,074	55%	$19,485	58%	$21,439	58%	$25,246	58%	$22,023

Source: Canadian Undergraduate Survey Consortium's 2003 *Graduating Students Survey*.

V. Student Loan Repayment

There are regrettably few data regarding the length of time it takes students to repay student loans after graduation. This is because statistical data on graduates tend to end a maximum of five years after graduation. Data can therefore be collected on how much has been repaid in full or in part by the time of the survey, but leave open the question of how long it takes for the remaining debt to be repaid.

It is not uncommon to hear stories of a friend, relative or neighbour declaring bankruptcy due to student debt, or, alternatively, of students taking over ten years to repay their student loans and as a result being unable to afford a house or a new car during that time. While such things undoubtedly happen, it should be borne in mind that these situations may represent the exception rather than the rule. According to the most recent evidence, roughly between one-fifth and one-sixth of all

students who borrow actually repay their loans within two years of graduation. Figure 6.V.1 looks at the borrowing and repayment patterns of the most recent cohorts of post-secondary graduates tracked by Statistics Canada's *National Graduate Survey*.

As seen in the previous section, student debt has risen significantly over the past two decades. As debt has risen, the percentage of total debt repaid within two years of graduation has declined. This decline is constant for all types of education; regardless of the type of degree, the proportion of total loans repaid within two years is less than half of what it was in 1986. Figure 6.V.2 shows the decline in proportions in total debt repaid after two years for the last four cohorts of the *NGS*.

Student loan repayment patterns vary substantially by province. Students in Ontario, in particular, repay very large amounts of their loans in the

Figure 6.V.1 — Debt Repayment Two Years after Graduation (Class of 2000)

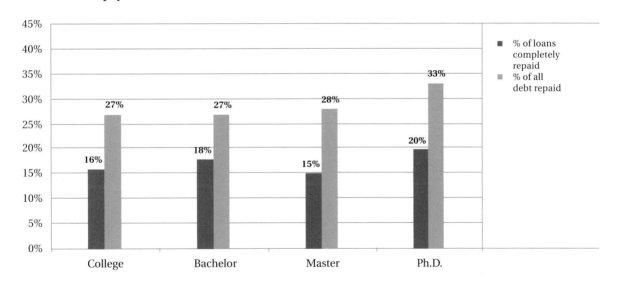

Source: Allan and Vaillancourt, *Class of 2000.*

Figure 6.V.2 — Percentage of Debt Repaid After Two Years by Degree Level and Cohort

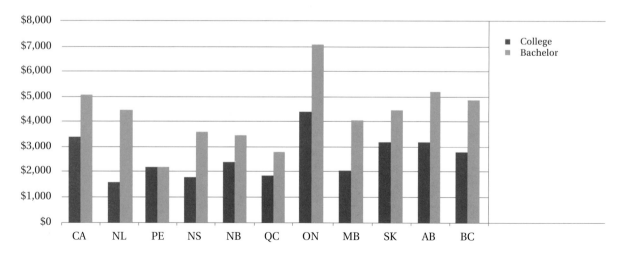

Source: Statistic Canada's 2000 *National Graduate Survey* and Finnie, *Student Loans*.

period just after graduation, while students from Quebec and Prince Edward Island repay very little of their loans. The differences between provinces in repayment patterns are more pronounced at the university level than at the college level. Figure 6.V.3 shows the average amount of government student loan debt repaid within two years of graduation, by level and province of study.

More important than the raw amounts of debt repaid is the percentage of total debt repaid, which can be derived easily by matching repayment figures by level and provinces to similar figures for debt upon graduation found in Section 6.IV. Examining the data in this light provides an altogether clearer picture. The gap between college and Bachelor's graduates in repayment is offset completely by

Figure 6.V.3 — Average Amount of Government Student Loan Debt Repaid Within Two Years of Graduation, by Level and Province of Study, Class of 2000

Source: Statistics Canada's 2000 *National Graduate Survey*.
Note: Data covers only those graduates in the labour force.

Figure 6.V.4 — Average Percentage of Government Student Loan Debt Repaid Within Two Years of Graduation, Class of 2000, by Level and Province of Study

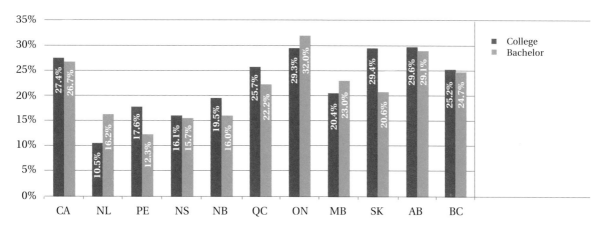

Source: Statistics Canada's 2000 *National Graduate Survey.*
Note: Data covers only those graduates in the labour force.

differences in initial debt; hence, two years after graduation, graduates from both sectors repay almost exactly the same percentage of their debts. At the provincial level, there is a substantial difference in repayment patterns between Ontario and the Western provinces on the one hand and the four Atlantic provinces on the other, with students in the former having the means to repay their debts much more quickly than students from the latter. Quebec forms a kind of intermediate zone between the two groups of provinces; with its students' weak

repayment balanced by their low debt burdens. Figure 6.V.4 shows the average percentage of government student loan debt repaid within two years of graduation by level and province of study.

One mitigating factor in student debt and loan repayment over the past 20 years has been a steady decline in interest rates. Even though student loans now charge a higher premium than they used to (prime plus 2.5% since 1995, as opposed to prime plus 1% prior to that), basic interest rates have declined substantially, as shown in Table 6.V.1.

Table 6.V.1 — Interest Rates on Student Loans by National Graduate Survey Cohort

Graduating Cohort	Prime	Student Loan Interest Premium	Student Loan Interest Rate
1982	15.81%	1.0%	16.81%
1986	10.52%	1.0%	11.52%
1990	14.06%	1.0%	15.06%
1995	8.65%	2.5% (CSL + 8 provinces)/ 1.0% (Ontario, Quebec)	10.15%/9.65%
2000	7.27%	2.5% (CSL + 8 provinces)/ 1.0% (Ontario, Quebec)	9.77%/8.27%
2003	4.50%	2.5% (CSL + 8 provinces)/ 1.0% (Ontario, Quebec)	7.00%/5.50%

Source: Bank of Canada.

Figure 6.V.5 — Average Monthly Student Loan Repayments From 1982 to 2003 (in 2003 Real Dollars)

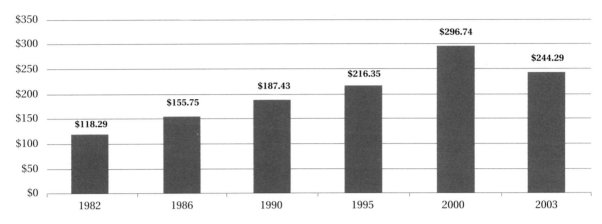

Source: Allan and Vaillancourt, *Class of 2000*; Finnie, *Student Loans*; Bank of Canada; and authors' calculations.

Figure 6.V.6 — Percentage of Graduates Reporting Difficulties in Repayment by Type of Degree

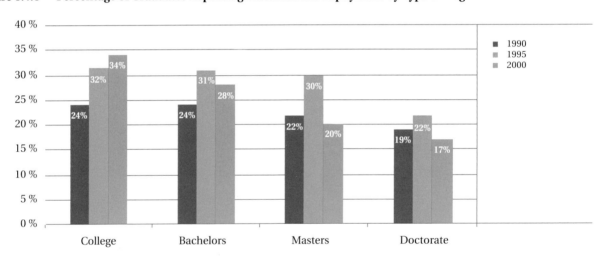

Source: Allan and Vaillancourt, *Class of 2000*; and Finnie, *Student Loans*.

The effect of this declining interest rate has been to slow the increase in the amount of monthly payments borrowers make on their student loans. As a result, actual monthly payments on student debt have only doubled over the past 20 years, despite a three-fold increase in debt over the same period. Figure 6.V.5 shows the changes in average monthly payments in student assistance, based on the average debts shown in Figure 6.IV.1 and the interest rates shown in Table 6.V.1. The figure shows clearly that in periods where debt is stable, changes in interest rates can have a major effect on debt burden. Between 2000 and 2003, when debt was relatively stable, falling interest rates led to an 18% drop in monthly payments.

Another mitigating factor for student debt and loan repayment is the major improvement made to interest relief measures in the Canada Student Loans Program. Whereas ten years ago eligibility was restricted to borrowers who were unemployed, the program has been expanded to the point where single students with "average" debt are not required to make any payments on their student loans until their incomes reach approximately $24,000 per year. While some program changes occurred in 1995, the primary improvement in interest relief occurred after the 1998 federal budget.

Figure 6.V.6 shows the changes over time in the number of college and undergraduate students who have reported having had difficulty in repayment in the two years following graduation. The change, or lack thereof, between the 1995 and the 2000 cohorts is interesting—despite major increases in borrowing, the percentage of students who say they have had repayment problems has stayed relatively constant, increasing only slightly among college students and decreasing slightly among university students. Since overall graduate starting salaries have not dramatically increased and no major changes have been made to student loan flexibility, it seems likely that improved government interest relief programs have played a significant role in minimizing student loan repayment difficulties.

VI. Pursuing Further Studies

The 1990s gave rise to one of the current buzzwords in social policy in Canada—"lifelong learning." This was a direct result of the global transformation of the market and the impact it had on both employees (current and future) and employers. The transition to a knowledge economy means that nobody can afford to rest on educational laurels. One of the ways that individuals can increase their employability is to pursue additional forms of post-secondary education. This section will deal primarily with individuals pursuing a second degree, such as an MBA or Doctor of Dental Medicine (D.D.M).

There are two ways to examine students who have completed their first credentials and are preparing for more learning—1) by examining their desire for more education, and 2) by examining their actual attendance in the following years. The Canadian Undergraduate Survey Consortium's 2003 *Graduating Students Survey* and the Canadian College Student Survey Consortium's 2003 *General Student Survey* asked a series of questions to students on the verge of program completion. The students were asked to identify their scheduled activities one year after graduation and in the future. For the purposes of analysis, these results will serve as graduate educational aspirations or desires.

Students who indicate a desire to pursue further studies may not actually do so for a host of reasons. The aforementioned survey instruments do not track students longitudinally, and as a result one never really knows if or when students actually pursue further studies. Graduating students' actual further post-secondary participation is easier to examine. Statistics Canada's *National Graduate Survey* asks students two and five years after graduation to indicate if they have pursued additional education. These data will here serve as a barometer for graduate's further educational activities.

Graduate Educational Aspirations

Students approaching the end of their program of studies may pursue one of several pathways. Among other things, they may enter the labour market, travel or pursue further studies. The 2003 *Graduating Students Survey* shows that nearly half of respondents indicated that they would be pursuing further studies in the year following graduation. Arts and science graduates were most likely to report plans for more education within the first year after graduation. Students in education, engineering and professional programs were more likely to report that they have no immediate educational plans in their first year after graduating. Table 6.VI.1 shows the future plans of graduating university students.

Table 6.VI.1 — Future Plans of Graduating University Students

Future Plans	All Students (n=11,224)[a]
No immediate educational plans	54%
Plan more education within first year of graduating	44%
Type of Education Desired	
Obtain another Bachelor's degree	10%
Graduate school	22%
Professional school	9%
Technical/vocational school	2%
Community college	2%
Other education	7%
Additional Studies	
Will take additional university courses in future	21%
May take additional university courses in future	26%

Source: Canadian Undergraduate Survey Consortium's 2003 *Graduating Students Survey.*

Note: [a] Respondents could provide more than one answer.

Table 6.VI.2 — College Students' Planned Activities after Graduation

	(n=9,866)ᵃ
Employment	**54%**
Seek employment	48%
Continue working at job	3%
Start own business	3%
Education	**44%**
Pursue a university program	33%
Pursue another college program	11%
Other	**3%**

Source: Canadian College Survey Consortium's 2003 *General Student Survey.*

Note: ᵃ Respondents could provide more than one answer, therefore the figures in this column total more than 100%.

College graduates' future educational plans are similar to those of university graduates. Roughly the same proportion of graduates (44%) reported that they will seek further education. There are some stark differences in where the potential future studies will occur. Only 10% of university graduates seeking further education cited college or vocational studies as a likely destination compared to the vast majority

(75%) of college students seeking further education who plan to study at a university. Table 6.VI.2 shows the plans of college students upon program completion.

The planned educational activities after graduation for college students vary considerably by the type of college program. Most students in access and upgrading or university preparation programs indicated that they will pursue further studies after graduation, while less than 30% of students completing a career or technical degree/diploma indicated that they are likely to pursue further studies. Figure 6.VI.1 shows the difference in future educational aspirations by the type of college program.

Somewhat surprisingly, the number of graduating students who pursued education in the two years following graduation is actually higher than the percentage of graduating students who, at the time they graduated, said they intended to undertake further studies. As Figure 6.VI.2 shows, using data from the 2000 *National Graduate Survey*, the majority of post-secondary graduates (48% of college graduates and 58% of Bachelor's degree graduates) pursued some form of post-secondary education in the first two years after graduation.

Figure 6.VI.1 — Percentage of College Students Who Would Like to Pursue Some Form of Education After Completion of Studies by Type of Program

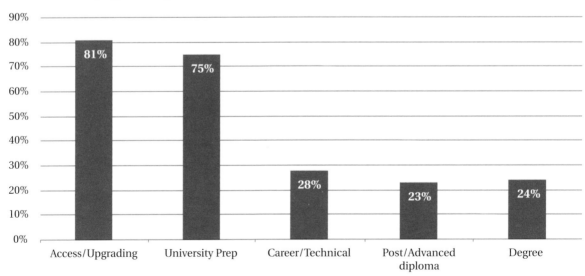

Source: Canadian College Survey Consortium's 2003 *General Student Survey.*

These figures represent an increase over previous surveys, especially at the college level, where the total was fully 50% higher than five years earlier.

Despite the striking increase in further studies, the proportion of graduates who receive additional degrees has stayed constant or even dropped. This suggests either that an increasing proportion of graduates are taking longer to complete a second credential or that they are not pursuing credentials so much as selecting particular courses to enhance their employability. Figure 6.VI.3 shows the percentage of graduates who have received additional qualifications two years after graduation.

Figure 6.VI.2 — Percentage of Students Who Have Pursued Some Form of Education Two Years After Graduation

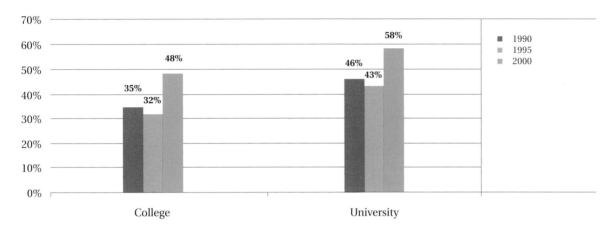

Source: Statistics Canada's 1990, 1995 and 2000 *National Graduate Survey*s.

Figure 6.VI.3 — Percentage of Students Who Have Received Additional Qualifications Two Years After Graduation

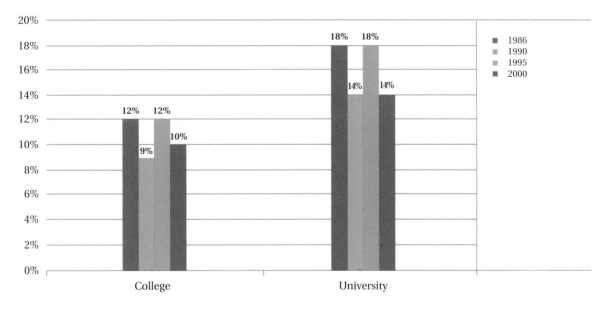

Source: Statistics Canada's 1986, 1990, 1995 and 2000 *National Graduate Survey*s.

Factors Influencing Further Studies

Several factors influence the decision to pursue further post-secondary studies, including the desire to continue one's education, job prospects at the time the decision is being made and personal relationships. One of the most important factors is likely to be the cost and benefit of further education. There are obvious direct expenses, such as tuition, room and board, textbooks and incidental fees; indirect expenses, such as the investment of time and effort and the earnings lost during the period of additional schooling, are, however, often overlooked.

There are a host of socio-demographic and education-related variables that can provide insight into graduates' decisions to pursue further education. In the 2001 edition of *Education Quarterly*, George Butlin examined various factors that may be predictors for participation in further education. Butlin found that, controlling for other factors, the field of study is a key predictor of participation in further post-secondary education. Not surprisingly, Bachelor's degree completers from fields of study associated with specific occupations or professions (e.g., education, commerce, engineering, health sciences) are less likely to participate in further post-secondary education than graduates from humanities and social science programs. Among Butlin's other findings, all else being equal:

- men are more likely than women to participate in Master's and doctoral programs

- graduates whose parents have a university degree are more likely to pursue a first professional, Master's or doctoral degree, compared with graduates whose parents have a high school education

- visible minority status has little impact on the odds of participation in further post-secondary education

- Bachelor's graduates with more than two years of full-time work experience are less likely to pursue further post-secondary education than graduates with no full-time work experience at the time of graduation.[2]

Interestingly, Butlin found that student debt has no obvious deterrent effect on the pursuit of graduate studies. Graduates with less than $15,000 in student loans were just as likely as students with no debt to pursue further post-secondary education. Graduates with more than $15,000 in student debt were actually more likely than students with no debt to pursue further studies, particularly at the professional and graduate levels.

This result is surprising because it is commonly thought that the pressure to repay debt and the danger of increasing the amount of debt by pursuing further education acts as an impediment to further post-secondary education. Since the pursuit of further post-secondary education temporarily postpones repayment of government debt, perhaps the pressure of debt repayment actually acts as an incentive for graduate studies. Students in this situation may take the attitude of "in for a penny, in for a pound"—having invested four or five years of time and a significant amount of money for the first credential, the assumption of additional debt may not be very daunting, given the expected economic return of further studies.

2. Butlin, *Education Quarterly* 7.2 (2001).

VII. Transition to the Labour Force

Making the transition from school to the workforce can often be difficult for students. Students, who generally have little full-time employment experience when they graduate, are particularly susceptible to short-term shifts in the labour market. To a certain extent students can prepare themselves for the labour market by selecting a course of studies likely to result in good employment prospects; however, even this strategy has its limits. The following section presents evidence on graduate employment and unemployment, according to data collected from Statistics Canada's 1986, 1990, 1995 and 2000 NGS and the CUSC's 2003 *Graduating Students Survey*.

Labour Force Preparedness

For the majority of students, entry into the labour force is not a new experience. As indicated earlier, most college and university students work for at least four months of the year (and often more). In preparing to enter the workforce after graduating, students must, however, take the steps necessary to ensure a smooth transition from school to work, such as researching employment prospects, creating a curriculum vitae and establishing employment connections.

According to the 2003 *Graduating Students Survey*, almost 85% of graduating students possess up-to-date curriculum vitae and over 60% of students have already decided on a career field. There was no apparent link, however, between having an up-to-date curriculum vitae and having decided on a career. Students in business programs were among the most likely to have an up-to-date curriculum vitae, despite being no more likely than other students to have decided on a career. Table 6.VII.1 shows employment preparation by discipline for graduating students.

Students graduating from Canadian universities in 2003 were less optimistic about their employment

Table 6.VII.1 — Employment Preparation by Discipline for Graduating Students

Discipline	Decided on a Career	Have an Up-to-Date CV
Education	91%	89%
Professional	83%	89%
Engineering	64%	93%
Overall	61%	84%
Business	57%	91%
Other fields	57%	85%
Arts and humanities	57%	76%
Physical science	54%	82%
Biological science	53%	83%

Source: Canadian Undergraduate Survey Consortium's 2003 *Graduating Students Survey*.

prospects than their 2000 counterparts. The 2000 graduates were probably optimistic due to the economic expansion that occurred throughout the late 1990s. In the 2003 *Graduating Students Survey*, less than 55% of participants thought there would be "some" to "many" jobs in their field of study. In 2000, the corresponding figure was 70%. Figure 6.VII.1 shows university graduates' perception of the job market in Canada.

Expectations of job prospects differ by field of study. Students from engineering and professional programs (dentistry, medicine, etc.) are the most positive about their job prospects, with over half predicting there will be "many" jobs available in their chosen field. Business and education students are the next most likely to see a positive labour market awaiting them upon graduation, while students in arts (humanities and social sciences) and sciences are the most pessimistic about the labour market for their area of study. Figure 6.VII.2 shows perceptions of job prospects by discipline for university students.

Figure 6.VII.1 — University Graduates' Perception of Future Job Prospects

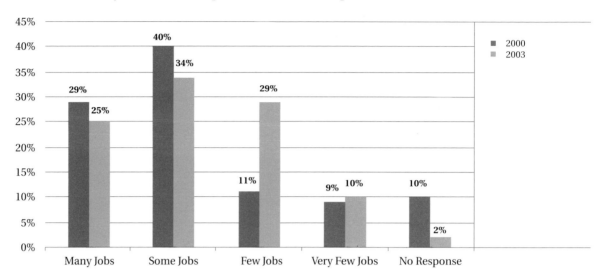

Source: Canadian Undergraduate Survey Consortium's 2000 and 2003 *Graduating Students Survey*.

Note: Totals may be less than 100% due to rounding.

Figure 6.VII.2 — Perceptions of Future Job Prospects by Discipline

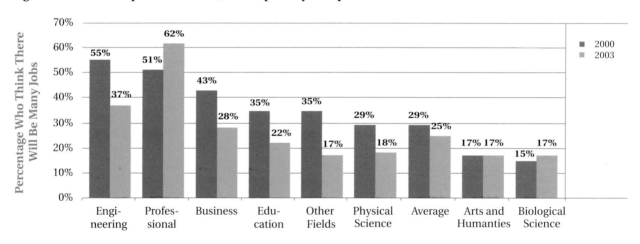

Source: Canadian Undergraduate Survey Consortium's 2000 and 2003 *Graduating Students Survey*.

Figure 6.VII.3 — Percentage of Students Finding Full-Time Employment Within Two Years of Graduation by Level of Education

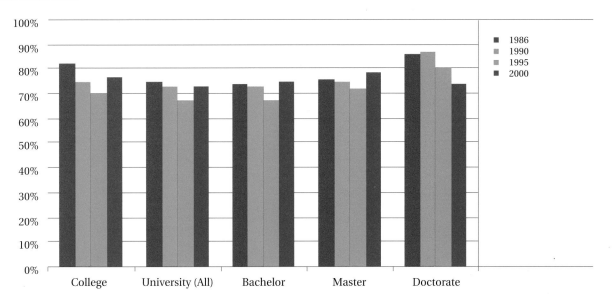

Source: Source: Statistics Canada's 1986, 1990, 1995 and 2000 *National Graduate Surveys*.

Graduate Employment

Except at the doctoral level, the graduating class of 2000 experienced a much smoother transition to the labour market than their counterparts five years earlier, benefiting in part from the expanding Canadian economy of the late 1990s. In general, graduate labour market outcomes differ by the level of education obtained. Students with a Master's degree had the easiest access to full-time employment. In all four survey years, college graduates had greater success than either Bachelor's or Ph.D. graduates in securing full-time employment within two years of graduation, as shown in Figure 6.VII.3.[3]

Tables 6.VII.2 and .3 provide additional data on labour market outcomes for college and university graduates two years after graduation. Overall, there has been little change over time in many of the comparative variables. The percentage of graduates working after two years has stayed fairly constant in all four survey years, although the proportion engaged in full-time work changes considerably with each survey year. Approximately three-quarters of

the college graduating class (77%) and the university graduating class (73%) of 2000 had obtained full-time work two years after graduation—this is an increase from the levels of five years earlier but less than the 1986 levels.

Full-Time Employment by Province

Among university graduates not in school, university graduates from Alberta and Saskatchewan have the highest rates of full-time employment (78%) and those from Newfoundland and Labrador the lowest (72%). Among college graduates, graduates from Prince Edward Island (82%) have the highest rates of employment and those from Newfoundland the lowest (70%). Between 1995 and 2000, full-time employment rates for university graduates increased in all provinces and for college graduates in all provinces except Newfoundland. Figures 6.VII.4, .5, .6 and .7 show college and university graduate employment rates two years after graduation by province.

---

3.   It is important to note that graduates in the former Trade and Vocational category were grouped together with college students in the 2000 *NGS*.

Table 6.VII.2 — Labour Market Outcomes for College Graduates Two Years After Graduation

	1986	1990	1995	2000
Working	89%	86%	85%	88%
Working full-time	82%	75%	70%	77%
Working part-time	8%	10%	14%	10%
Unemployed	7%	9%	9%	7%
Not in the labour force (not working, not looking for work or not available to work)	3%	4%	6%	5%
Labour force participation rate	97%	96%	94%	95%
Unemployment rate	8%	9%	9%	8%

Source: Statistics Canada's 1986, 1990, 1995 and 2000 *National Graduate Surveys.*

Table 6.VII.3 — Labour Market Outcomes for University Graduates Two Years After Graduation

	1986	1990	1995	2000
Working	84%	82%	83%	84%
Working full-time	75%	73%	67%	73%
Working part-time	9%	9%	14%	10%
Unemployed	5%	9%	8%	8%
Not in the labour force (not working, not looking for work or not available to work)	13%	7%	9%	8%
Labour force participation rate	87%	92%	91%	92%
Unemployment rate	5%	10%	9%	8%

Source: Statistics Canada's 1986, 1990, 1995 and 2000 *National Graduate Surveys.*

Figure 6.VII.4 — Percentage of 1986, 1990, 1995 and 2000 College Graduates Working Full-time in Atlantic Canada and Quebec (Two Years After Graduation)

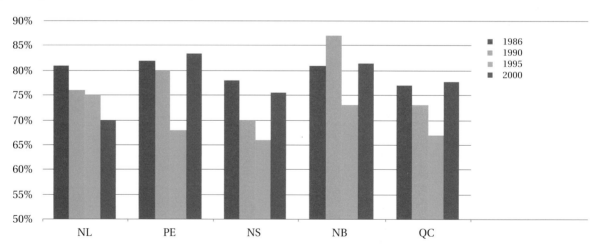

Source: Statistics Canada's 1986, 1990, 1995 and 2000 *National Graduate Surveys.*

Figure 6.VII.5 — Percentage of 1986, 1990, 1995 and 2000 College Graduates Working Full-time in Ontario and Western Canada (Two Years After Graduation)

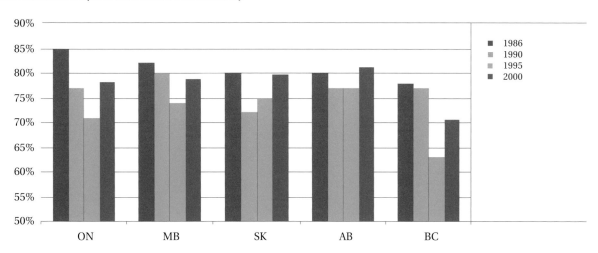

Source: Statistics Canada's 1986, 1990, 1995 and 2000 *National Graduate Surveys*.

Figure 6.VII.6 — Percentage of 1986, 1990, 1995 and 2000 University Graduates Working Full-time in Atlantic Canada and Quebec (Two Years after Graduation)

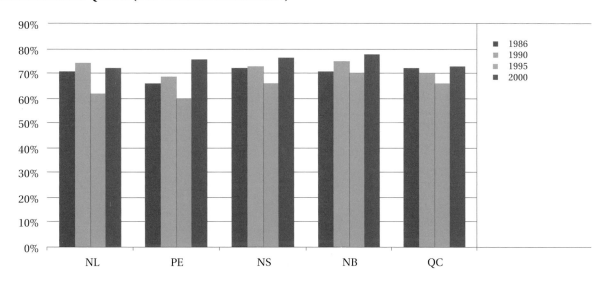

Source: Statistics Canada's 1986, 1990, 1995 and 2000 *National Graduate Surveys*.

Figure 6.VII.7 — Percentage of 1986, 1990, 1995 and 2000 University Graduates Working Full-time in Ontario and Western Canada (Two Years After Graduation)

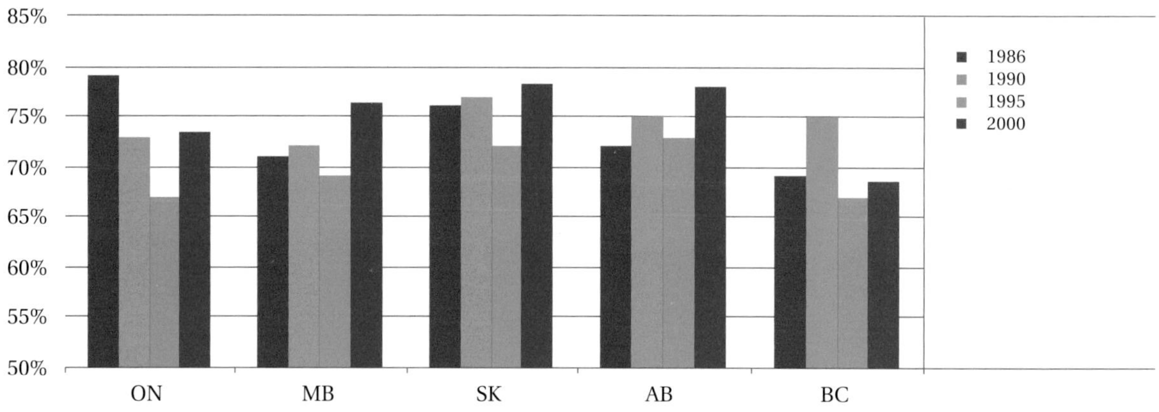

Source: Statistics Canada's 1986, 1990, 1995 and 2000 *National Graduate Surveys.*

Graduate Unemployment

According to data from Statistics Canada, there is a clear relationship between levels of education and levels of unemployment. Simply put, the more post-secondary education a person possesses, the less likely he or she is to be unemployed. The unemployment rate for university graduates is half of that for individuals who completed high school but did not obtain any post-secondary education. This relationship appears to remain constant throughout the economic cycle; it is true both in periods of economic expansion and economic contraction. Throughout the 1990s, the mean annual unemployment rate for individuals possessing a post-secondary degree, diploma or certificate was 9%, with a high of 11.1% in 1993 and a low of 5.6% in 2000. Canadians without a post-secondary credential who had completed some post-secondary

education had a mean unemployment rate of 11.7%, with a high of 13.5% in 1993 and a low of 7.8% in 2001. Finally, those without any post-secondary education at all had a mean unemployment rate of 15.9%, with a high of 18.4% in 1993 and a low of 11.5% in 2000. Figure 6.VII.8 shows the annual unemployment rate for Canadians aged 25 to 29 by level of education from 1990 to 2003.

The *NGS* data on unemployed graduates show that college and university graduates are less likely to be unemployed two years after graduation than trade and vocational graduates. These data have been consistent in all three *NGS* surveys, although the trade and vocational graduate unemployment rate decreased by almost 5% from 1986 to 1995. Figures 6.VII.9, .10, .11 and .12 show the unemployment rates for all post-secondary graduates in Atlantic, Central and Western Canada.

Figure 6.VII.8 — Unemployment Rate for Canadians Aged 20 to 29 From 1990 to 2003 by Level of Education

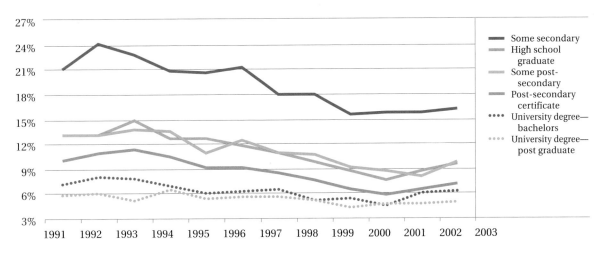

Source: Statistics Canada's *Labour Force Survey*.

Figure 6.VII.9 — College Graduate Unemployment Rates in Atlantic Canada and Quebec Two Years after Graduation

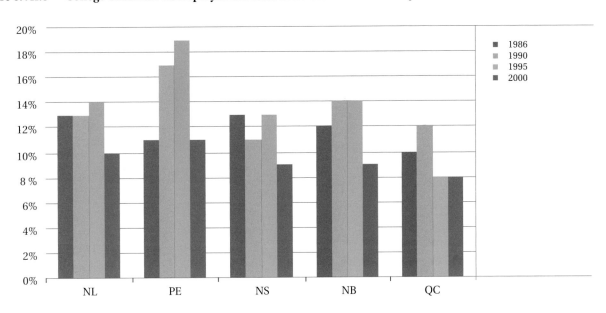

Source: Statistics Canada's 1986, 1990, 1995 and 2000 *National Graduate Surveys*.

Figure 6.VII.10 — Canadian College Graduate Unemployment Rates in Ontario and Western Canada Two Years After Graduation

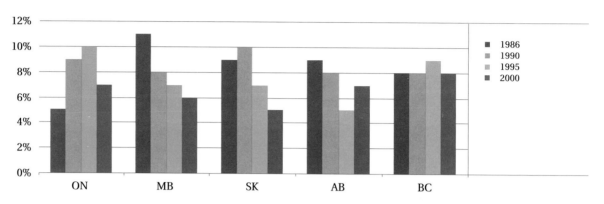

Source: Statistics Canada's 1986, 1990, 1995 and 2000 *National Graduate Surveys*.

Figure 6.VII.11 — University Graduate Unemployment Rates in Atlantic Canada and Quebec Two Years After Graduation

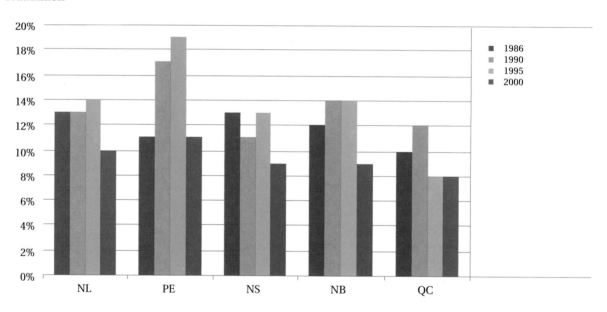

Source: Statistics Canada's 1986, 1990, 1995 and 2000 *National Graduate Surveys*.

Figure 6.VII.12 — University Graduate Unemployment Rates in Ontario and Western Canada Two Years After Graduation

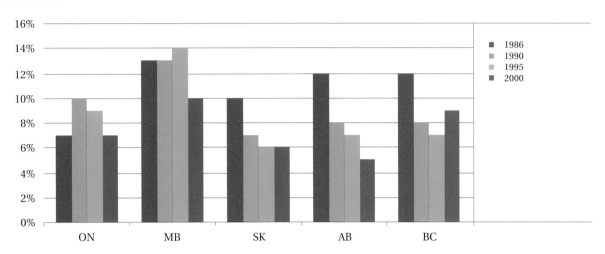

Source: Statistics Canada's 1986, 1990, 1995 and 2000 *National Graduate Surveys*.

VIII. Graduate Earnings

Graduate earnings vary considerably depending on where and what an individual chooses to study. The most important decision appears to be the type of institution at which one chooses to study: university graduates earn significantly more than college graduates.

Graduate earnings at both the university and college levels have been remarkably stable over the past 15 years. Evidence from Statistics Canada's comprehensive *National Graduate Surveys* for the classes of 1986, 1990, 1995 and 2000 shows that current remuneration rates for recent graduates of both colleges and universities are roughly the same as they were in 1986, once inflation is taken into account. Two years after graduation, the classes of 1986, 1990 and 2000 had median earnings of between $39,000 and $40,000 for university graduates and between $30,800 and $31,200 for college graduates. Only the class of 1995—who graduated during the mini-recession of 1995–96—had a noticeably different outcome. Interestingly, however, the recession affected college and university graduates in roughly the same way, thus suggesting that some of the

The most important decision appears to be the type of institution at which one chooses to study: university graduates earn significantly more than college graduates.

common beliefs about the college education advantage in difficult economic times may not be supported by the facts. Figure 6.VIII.1 shows the median graduate earnings by level of education for students two years after graduation for the classes of 1986, 1990, 1995 and 2000.

Individuals with Master's degrees are an exception to the rule of relatively constant returns on education. Unlike Bachelor's degree and doctorate recipients, income levels for recent Master's degree graduates continued to fall despite the economic recovery of the late 1990s. Figure 6.VIII.2 shows median graduate earnings by level of university education two years after graduation.

As in the labour force as a whole, males tend to earn more than females among recent graduates. This tends to be more a result of the concentration of males in high-remuneration subjects (e.g., engineering) than it is of differential rates of pay for equally qualified workers. In the recession of the mid-1990s, women's earnings fell more than those of men; however, by the turn of the decade, recent female university graduates had

Figure 6.VIII.1 — Median Graduate Earnings by Level of Education Two Years After Graduation (in 2002 Real Dollars)

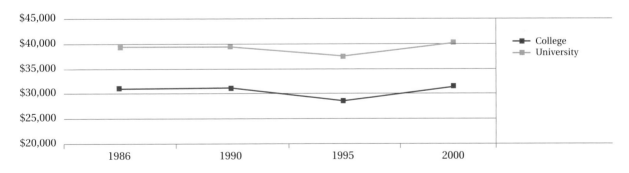

Source: Statistics Canada's 1986, 1990, 1995 and 2000 *National Graduate Surveys.*

Figure 6.VIII.2 — Median Graduate Earnings by Level of University Education Two Years After Graduation (in 2002 Real Dollars)

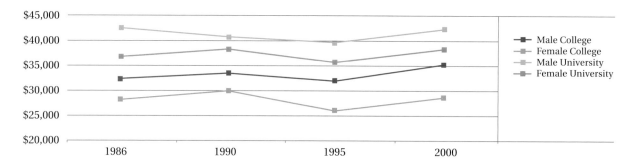

Source: Statistics Canada's 1986, 1990, 1995 and 2000 *National Graduate Surveys*.

made up much of the difference. Figure 6.VIII.3 shows the median graduate earnings by gender and type of education.

No *NGS* data are available for students graduating after 2000 and no single national survey brings together data of this nature on a regular basis. Individual educational institutions do, however, survey their graduates regarding earnings and employment. At the request of the Canada Millennium Scholarship Foundation, Lang Research has twice (in 2002 and 2004) used meta-analysis techniques to try to aggregate a number of these institutional surveys and generate usable information on regional and national labour market conditions for recent graduates.

Lang's findings show that the average starting salary for Canadian university graduates in 2001 was $32,600. By 2003 that number had increased significantly to $41,400. Part of the difference appears to be the result of some methodological changes between the two groups of surveys. The 2003 results are the best available since they are more recent, more universities provided income information and few, if any, adjustments had to be made. Also, the figure for 2003 is considerably closer to the comparable figure in the 2000 *NGS* ($40,000).

The meta-analysis for 2003 shows important differences in the average starting salary of university graduates by region. Graduates of Western

Figure 6.VIII.3 — Median Graduate Earnings by Level of Education and Gender Two Years After Graduation (in 2002 Real Dollars)

Source: Statistics Canada's 1986, 1990, 1995 and 2000 *National Graduate Surveys*.

Figure 6.VIII.4 — Regional Differences in Starting Salary for University Graduates (in 2003 Real Dollars)

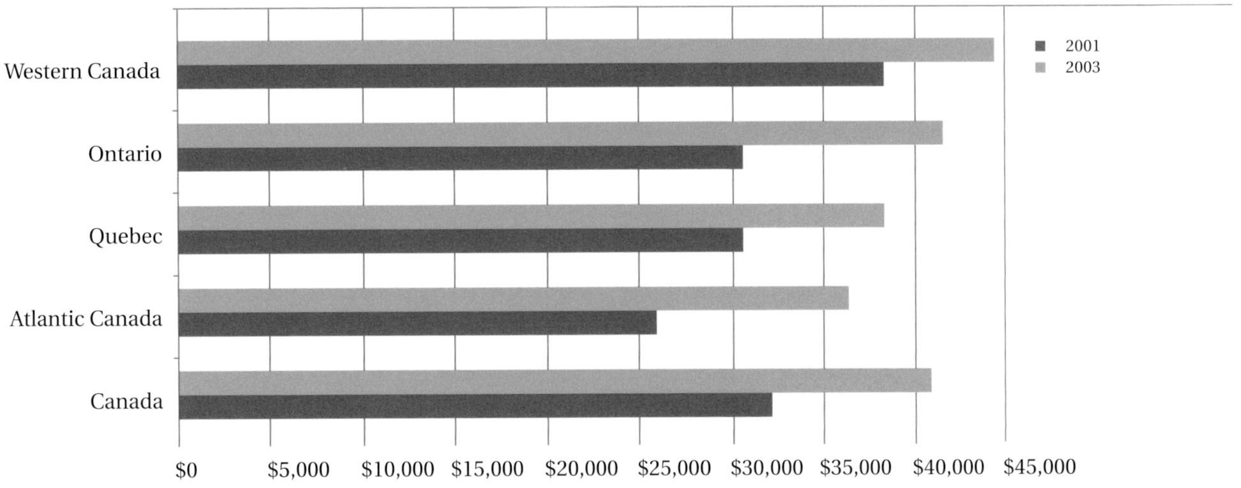

Source: Lang Research's 2002 and 2004 *Meta-Analysis of Post-Secondary Institutional Graduate Surveys.*

Canadian universities earn the highest average starting salary ($45,000), followed by the graduates of universities in Ontario ($42,100) and Quebec ($38,900). Graduates of universities in Atlantic Canada have an average starting salary of $36,800—almost $5,000 below the national average and $9,000 less than the average in Western Canada. This difference in regional results needs to be treated with caution: not only is it possible that some of the regional variation may be due to differences in survey methodology between institutions, but it is worth noting that Atlantic Canada was the region that showed the largest salary growth (nearly 40%) between the 2001 and 2003 survey. Figure 6.VIII.4 shows regional differences in the starting salaries of university graduates for 2001 and 2003.

The average starting salary for college graduates is lower than that for university graduates. In 2003,

the average salary of community college graduates between six months and one year after graduation was $29,200. Due to the timing of the surveys conducted by community colleges (almost all of them are conducted within 12 months of graduation), the income figures can generally be considered starting salaries.

There appears to be some regional variation in the starting salary for college graduates and it closely resembles that of university graduates. Graduates in Western Canada reported the highest salaries, at just over $31,000, followed by Ontario college graduates at $29,400 and graduates of CEGEPs in Quebec at $27,500. Atlantic Canadian college graduates have significant lower starting salaries ($24,800). Figure 6.VIII.5 shows the regional differences for starting salaries of college graduates.

Figure 6.VIII.5 — Regional Differences in Starting Salary for College Graduates (in 2003 Real Dollars)

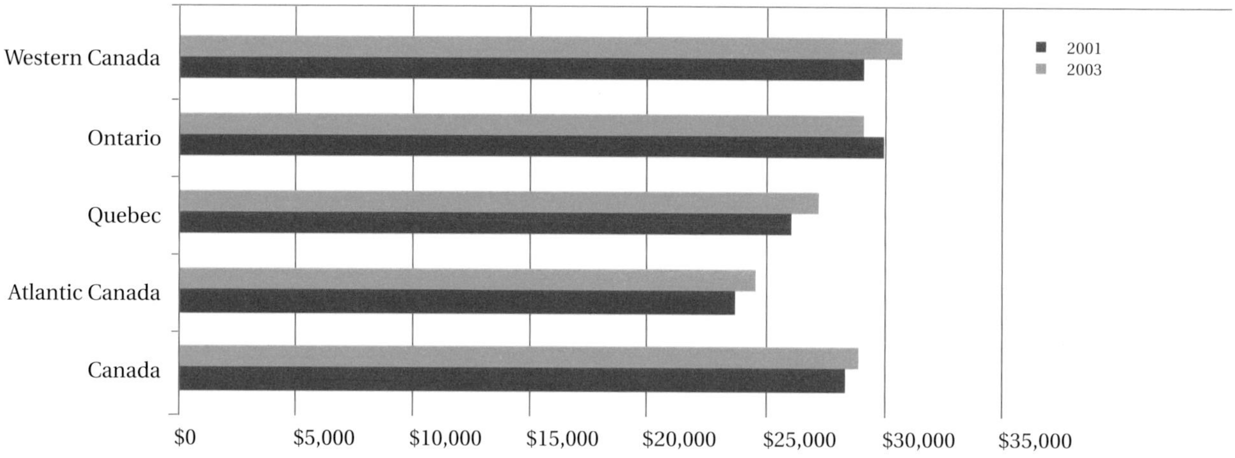

Source: Lang Research's 2002 and 2004 *Meta-Analyses of Graduate Surveys.*

Long-Term Graduate Earnings

Graduate earnings over the long term are difficult to examine because there are no longitudinal surveys in Canada that follow post-secondary graduates for more than five years. Some data on this question are available through the work of Statistics Canada's Andrew Heisz, who examined the financial prospects of B.C. graduates in a paper entitled "Income Prospects of British Columbia University Graduates." Using taxfile data from the years 1982 through 1997, Heisz examined market incomes for graduates from 1974 through 1996. The study found that median incomes from different fields of study tend to converge as graduates age. Graduates from fields of study that have lower median income levels in the years immediately following graduation (e.g., social

science graduates) over time tend to narrow the income gap between themselves and those who start off with relatively high salaries (e.g., education and physical education graduates). Incomes continue to increase for both groups, but they grow faster for graduates who start at the lower end of the scale.

There are also some notable differences in income by gender, as men tend to start at a higher level and have faster growth in all income brackets. There is also a higher degree of income convergence for female graduates. Among female graduates, there is very little variation in income by field of study after 20 years in the workforce. Among male graduates, income gaps narrow but do not converge as closely as they do for females. Figures 6.VIII.6 and .7 show the predicted male and female income trends over a 20-year period.

Figure 6.VIII.6 — Predicted Male Median Income 1 to 20 Years After Graduation (in 2003 Real Dollars)

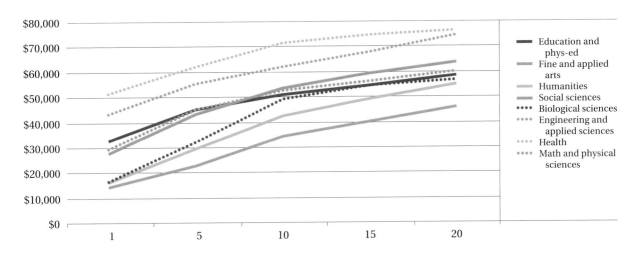

Source: Heisz, "Income Prospects of British Columbia University Graduates."

Figure 6.VIII.7 — Predicted Female Median Income 1 to 20 Years After Graduation (in 2003 Real Dollars)

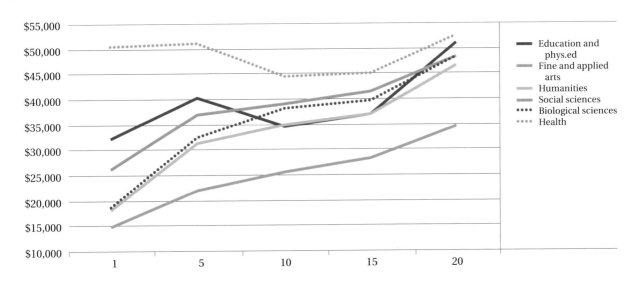

Source: Heisz, "Income Prospects of British Columbia University Graduates."

IX. Graduate Mobility

The migration patterns of post-secondary graduates have been a widely debated subject in the past decade. The primary focus of discussions in newspapers and magazines is on graduates leaving jurisdictions for so-called "greener pastures," a phenomenon often referred to as "brain drain." It is a complex issue that should not be viewed solely through the lens of economics. Graduates appear to change jurisdictions for three main reasons: a) employment opportunities, b) educational opportunities and c) personal relationships.

Different provinces and territories face different issues with respect to migration. In some cases, like Alberta or B.C., the issue is one of intra-provincial mobility—individuals are moving out of rural areas and into larger urban centres. In Newfoundland and Labrador and Saskatchewan, there is a combination of intra-provincial migration from rural to urban areas and inter-provincial migration (i.e., individuals moving out of the jurisdiction).

Nationally, the key issue in the 1990s was the migration of graduates out of the country. This, however, is only half the story. The rarely examined flip side is the number of individuals with post-secondary credentials migrating to Canada. Graduate mobility is a two-way street, and contrary to popular belief, Canada's ostensible brain drain appears to be: a) limited to certain sectors of the economy (such as health and high technology), b) mitigated by immigration from other countries and c) not clearly defined—since the exact number of graduates who leave is unknown, as is the number who return to Canada a few years later.

Intra-Provincial Mobility

Due to the location of most post-secondary institutions in Canada, the majority of students must relocate to larger urban centres to pursue higher studies. This exodus of students from smaller communities raises an important question: where do they settle after their studies? That is, do they return to their homes, or settle elsewhere? Rural depopulation or "out-migration" is an important issue for rural, remote and northern communities struggling to create opportunities to attract or retain individuals.

Out-migration is an issue of particular concern for rural communities in Canada. Many regions are rather fragile with respect to key public services—such as health care and education—and may become weaker as a result of future population

Table 6.IX.1 — Migration Patterns for Canadians by Age and Educational Attainment

Age	Total	Rural	Small- or Medium-Sized Towns	Small- or Medium-Sized Cities	Large Cities
21–25	16.6%	20.9%	19.0%	16.7%	14.8%
26–35	10.3%	10.0%	9.6%	9.7%	10.9%
36–45	5.8%	5.2%	6.4%	5.9%	5.8%
46–55	4.0%	4.8%	4.5%	3.5%	3.6%
56–65	3.7%	4.1%	3.7%	3.2%	3.7%

Highest Level of Schooling	Total	Rural	Small- or Medium-Sized Towns	Small- or Medium-Sized Cities	Large Cities
No university degree	7.0%	7.2%	7.4%	6.9%	7.0%
University degree	9.2%	10.2%	8.9%	8.7%	9.2%

Source: Statistics Canada's 1993 to 2000 *Survey of Labour and Income Dynamics.*

Figure 6.IX.1 — Graduate Origins by Current Location

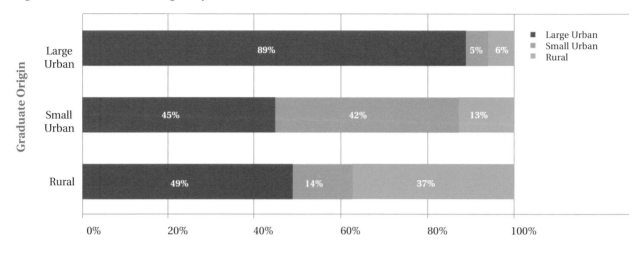

Source: Government of Alberta's *The Class of 2000 Two Years after Graduation.*

declines. Rural out-migration tends to involve young, educated and unattached individuals, creating a heavy reliance on an aging population, which further exacerbates the region's shrinking capacity for economic growth.

Post-secondary graduates often go where career opportunities can be found and this often means relocating to large urban centres. Graduates succumb to the lure of larger markets and often do not return to their original communities. According to Statistics Canada's *Survey of Labour Income and Dynamics (SLID),* university degree holders are more likely to leave rural communities than those without a degree. For example, among rural residents, 10% of those with university degrees leave rural areas each year, compared to 7% of those without such degrees. Table 6.IX.1 shows migration patterns for Canadians by age and educational attainment.

The best available evidence on specific patterns of rural and urban migration among post-secondary graduates comes from *The Class of 2000 Two Years after Graduation* by the Government of Alberta. The data show that almost four in 10 rural graduates relocate back to their original location. Figure 6.IX.1 shows the origins of graduates by current location.

The Government of Alberta survey found some differences by field of study at the university level. Graduates of rural origin who pursued studies in

either engineering or professional programs (law, medicine, etc.) were the least likely to return to their roots. Rural graduates in education, nursing and social work were more likely to return to smaller centres.

Inter-Provincial Mobility

Inter-provincial graduate mobility is a hot topic in many Canadian jurisdictions, especially in Manitoba, Saskatchewan and Atlantic Canada. These regions are not only experiencing intra-provincial mobility among youth (rural depopulation) but are also losing youth to other provinces. Young people are attracted to the opportunities available in Canada's large urban centres. Which often offer greater access to employment and socio-cultural opportunities than their rural counterparts.

According to the 2001 Census, Canada's three largest metropolitan centres—Toronto, Montreal and Vancouver—alone attracted more than 200,000 young adults (aged 15 to 29) between 1996 and 2001. In fact, about one-third of all young people who left non-metropolitan areas during this period moved to one of the three cities. The majority of these migrants had some form of post-secondary education.

The best available evidence on pan-Canadian graduate inter-provincial mobility comes from

Statistics Canada's *National Graduate Survey*. The *NGS* is able to compare graduates' province of study with the province where they are interviewed two and five years after graduation. Also, there are some regionally based studies, such as the Maritime Provinces Higher Education Commission's (MPHEC) *Survey of Maritime Graduates*, which provide supplementary data on the subject.

Graduate inter-provincial mobility in Canada appears to be a phenomenon that is largely confined to university graduates. Very few provinces have difficulty retaining trade, vocational and community college graduates. The exceptions are Newfoundland and Labrador and Prince Edward Island, where there are net out-migration rates of such graduates. Also, Alberta appears to be a magnet for college, trade and vocational graduates as they bring in four graduates for every single graduate lost. Figure 6.IX.2 shows university and college migration for the class of 2000 two years after graduation.

The story is quite different with respect to university graduates: only three Canadian jurisdictions

(Alberta, Ontario and Prince Edward Island) now have a positive graduate migration rate. Figure 6.IX.3 shows the university graduate migration for the classes of 1986, 1990 and 2000.[5]

By far the province with the worst migration rate is Nova Scotia where nearly one-third of university graduates are leaving upon graduation. This is not surprising given the province is also the largest importer of university students in the country. The data show that nearly one in five university graduates are leaving New Brunswick and Saskatchewan within two years of graduation. Also, Manitoba is losing almost 10% of its university graduates within two years. These data are comparable with findings from the MPHEC's Class of 1996 in 2000 and Class of 1999 in 2001, which showed that New Brunswick and Nova Scotia were losing university graduates.

It should be mentioned that this trend has not gone unnoticed by various provinces, and most are taking steps to address it, often by adopting a "two-birds-with-one-stone" approach. That is, some Canadian jurisdictions are using student aid to

Figure 6.IX.2 — University and College Graduate Net Migration for the Class of 2000 Two Years After Graduation[4]

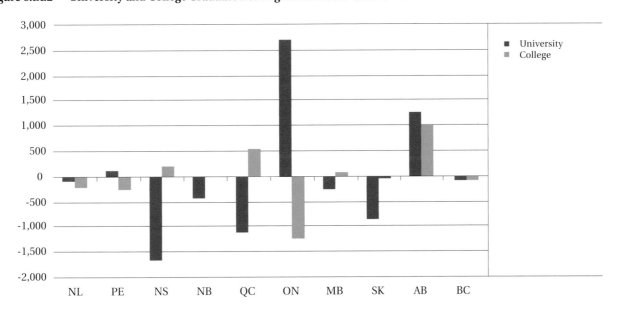

Source: Statistics Canada's *2000 National Graduate Survey*.

4. Trade and Vocational graduate mobility was not available for the class of 2000 due to data problems. The previous trade and vocational data indicated there was little mobility from this group and when combined with college data often resulted in next to no migration for college, trade and vocational graduates.

5. The *National Graduate Survey* class of 1995 was not included in this analysis due to data problems.

Figure 6.IX.3 — University Graduate Migration for the Classes of 1986, 1990 and 2000 Two Years After Graduation[6]

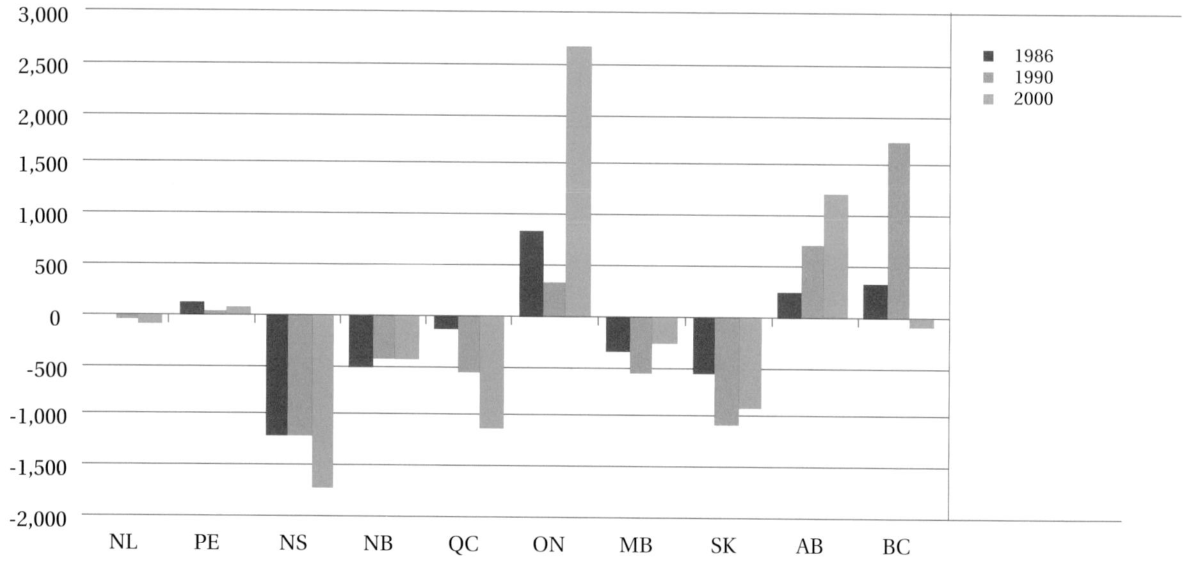

Source: Statistics Canada's *National Graduate Survey*.

address labour market shortages in rural, remote and Northern areas. This form of workplace-contingent aid has grown in popularity in both Canada and the United States in the past decade. Almost all jurisdictions now offer some form of program, primarily targeted at health professionals, such as the following two examples:

- The *Manitoba Medical Student/Resident Financial Assistance Program*, operated by the Government of Manitoba, provides a conditional grant to students and residents studying medicine in Manitoba (as well as students studying medicine in French at the University of Ottawa). Upon completion of their training, all participating physicians are required to work in Manitoba for one year for each grant they receive.

- The *Early Childhood Education Grants* program, offered by the Government of Newfoundland and Labrador, targets early childhood education graduates who obtain full-time employment in this field within the province. To be eligible, students must be enrolled in an approved two-year program and must have borrowed for at least half the length of the program.

Emigrants from Canada (Canadians in the U.S.)

While the migration of Canadian post-secondary graduates to the United States is not a new phenomenon, it received plenty of attention in the 1990s. The so-called "brain drain" became a policy buzzword due to a host of factors: an expanding United States economy (e.g., I.T. sector workers moving across the border), Canadian government fiscal restraint (e.g., health professionals seeking employment), currency issues (the strong United States dollar and relatively weak Canadian loonie), the North American Free Trade Agreement (constraints on obtaining temporary employment in the United States were eased for Canadians), and the opportunity to live in major metropolitan cities like New York and Los Angeles.

Notwithstanding the above factors, the percentage of graduates moving to the United States from Canada is actually quite small. The best available data on the subject come from a report conducted for Human Resources Development Canada by Jeff Frank and Éric Bélair, called *South of the Border: Graduates from the Class of 1995 Who Moved to the United States*. The report draws on *National*

---

6.   The migration rate was calculated by subtracting incoming graduates from departing graduates.

Figure 6.IX.4 — Proportion of Class of 1995 Graduates Who Moved to the United States

Total — 1.5%
Ph.D. — 12%
Master's — 3.2%
Bachelor's — 1.7%
College — 1.4%

Source: Frank and Bélair, *South of the Border.*

Graduate Survey data for the class of 1995 and indicates that just over 4,600 graduates moved to the U.S. between the time of graduation in 1995 and the summer of 1997. This figure represents 1.5% of the roughly 300,000 people who graduated from a Canadian post-secondary institution in 1995.

The distribution of graduates moving to the United States was not equal across all educational credentials. Specifically, the majority of graduates moving to the United States were holders of Master's degrees and doctorates. Figure 6.IX.4 shows the proportion of graduates who moved to the United States by level of study. There are some significant gender differences in these data—the vast majority of Master's and Ph.D. graduates who move are male. Figure 6.IX.5 shows the distribution of graduates who moved to the United States by gender and level of study.

Figure 6.XI.5 — Distribution of Class of 1995 Graduates Who Moved to the United States by Gender and Level of Study

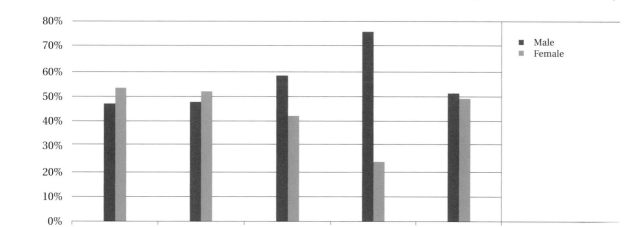

Source: Frank and Bélair, *South of the Border.*

The majority of graduates who moved to the United States were living in Ontario (57%) prior to relocating south of the border, and almost half of all graduates moved into just four states: Texas (16%), California (11%), New York (10%) and Florida (8%).

The reasons for moving to the United States are not always purely economic. Most graduates moved for work-related reasons (57%), but some left for reasons related to education or schooling (23%), and others left for more romantic reasons—to marry or pursue relationships (17%).

While some graduates do move to the United States, it is not clear that their relocation is permanent. Almost one in five graduates had already returned to Canadian soil at the time of the survey (two years after graduating), and an additional 43% stated that they intend to return to Canada. In fact, less than 30% of graduates who had moved to the U.S. indicated that they didn't intend to move back to Canada in the future. Table 6.IX.2 details graduate plans for returning to Canada.

Immigrants to Canada

The migration of educated people is a two-sided issue and the often overlooked side of the equation is the immigration to Canada of trained individuals. While the loss of highly skilled workers to the United States accelerated during the 1990, so too did the influx of highly skilled workers into Canada from the rest of the world. This is particularly true within high-tech industries, where immigrant workers entering Canada outnumbered the outflow to the United States by a wide margin. Indeed, immigrant high-tech workers represented an important part of employment expansion in these industries in the 1990s.

John Zhao, Doug Drew and Scott Murray shed some light on a complex equation in an article appearing in *Education Quarterly* called "Brain Drain and Brain Gain: The Migration of Knowledge Workers from and to Canada." The authors point out that emigrants to the United States are more than twice as likely to hold a university degree as immigrants to Canada. Due to the overall greater

Table 6.IX.2 — Graduates Planning to Return to Canada

Intentions	Percentage
1. 1995 Graduates who were already back in Canada by 1997	18%
2. Plans for the future for those still in the United States	
Return to Canada	43%
Do not intend to return to Canada	29%
Don't know	27%
3. Anticipated time of return[7]	
Within two years	19%
Three to five years	14%
Six years or more	24%
Don't know	43%

Source: Frank and Bélair, *South of the Border.*

number of immigrants, however, there are four times as many university graduates entering Canada from the rest of the world as there are university degree holders of all levels leaving Canada for the United States. The number of Master's and doctoral graduates alone entering Canada from the rest of the world is equal to the number of university graduates at all levels leaving Canada for the United States.

The educational profile of the Canadian working-age population has benefited greatly from the contribution made by immigrants who came to the country in the 1990s. According to the 2001 Census, over 40% of working-age immigrants who arrived in the 1990s were university educated. An additional 13% had a college diploma and 8% a trade certificate. In all, over 60% of all immigrants had qualifications above the secondary school level. This is a substantial increase from the 1970s and 1980s, when less than half of all immigrants had completed some kind of post-secondary training. Figure 6.IX.6 shows the post-secondary credentials of immigrants to Canada in the past three decades.

The educational attainment of immigrants is not necessarily a "feel-good" story in all respects. Educated immigrants to the country face a number of barriers. First, some have credentials that are

---

7.   This applies only to those who indicated they would move back to Canada.

Figure 6.IX.6 — Educational Attainment Levels of Immigrants in the 1970s, 1980s and 1990s

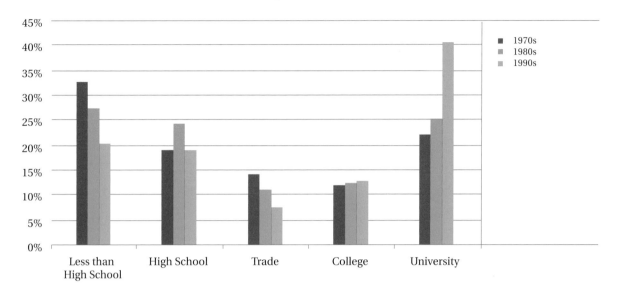

Source: Statistic Canada's 1981, 1991 and 2001 Census.

not recognized by professional associations (such as engineering and health professions). Second, immigrants often face labour market barriers such as language disadvantages, lack of social networks or poor information about the Canadian job market. These factors often result in higher unemployment and underemployment rates among educated immigrants. As a result, higher education levels don't always translate into huge labour market successes for immigrants. Figures 6.IX.7 and .8 show the unemployment and underemployment rates for male and female Canadians, recent immigrants and other immigrants aged 25 to 54 in 1991, 1996 and 2001.[8]

---

8. Immigrants who arrived during the year and a half preceding each census have been excluded.

Figure 6.IX.7 — Unemployment Rates for Canadian-Born Individuals, Recent Immigrants and Other Immigrants by Gender and Census Year

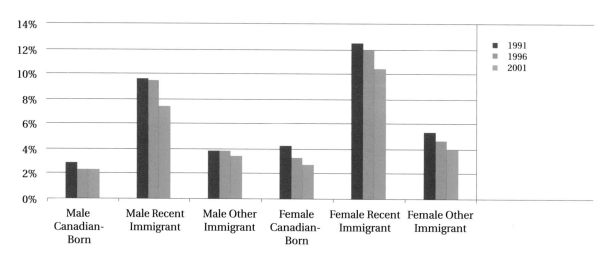

Source: Statistic Canada's 1981, 1991 and 2001 Census.

Figure 6.IX.8 — University Graduates in a Job Requiring at Most Secondary School Level Education for Canadian-Born Individuals, Recent Immigrants and Other Immigrants by Gender and Census Year

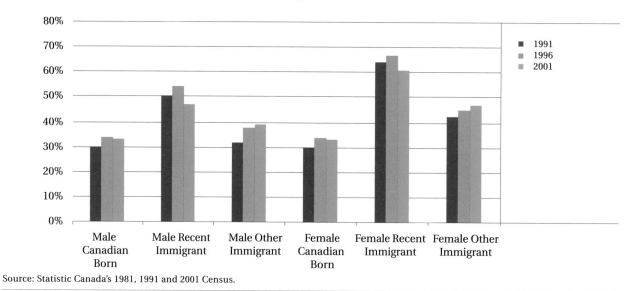

Source: Statistic Canada's 1981, 1991 and 2001 Census.

X. The Benefits of Post-Secondary Education to Individuals and Society

At the heart of the post-secondary funding policy discussion in Canada are two age-old questions: to what extent does the benefit of a post-secondary education accrue to the individual who receives it and to what extent does it benefit society as a whole? And to what extent are the benefits of education financial and to what extent are they non-financial? Earlier sections of this chapter have mostly examined economic returns to the individual; this section will look at the wider benefits of post-secondary education, both to the individual and to society.

The benefits of an educated society are multifaceted and can best be understood by examining the issue from the perspectives of both economists and sociologists. Economists often discuss the obvious individual effects of a post-secondary education—higher incomes, lower unemployment and higher tax rates. Sociologists fill in the other side of the story by analyzing the benefits to society as a whole, such as civic and political participation, healthy and active lifestyles, and lower crime rates.

It is true that there are direct individual financial gains linked to post-secondary education (especially a university degree), but the country as a whole also benefits from an educated populace. A healthier society means lower collective health care costs and longer, more productive lives for everyone. This is just one of the examples that will be examined, showing that not all post-secondary benefits are purely economic, nor can all of them be easily measured. Table 6.X.1 lists the main economic and societal benefits of post-secondary education to both the individual and the country.

The Economic Perspective

The best available evidence indicates that investment in post-secondary education pays substantial returns in the form of increased tax revenues for government treasuries. These revenues allow governments to fund social programs such as health care and education. Post-secondary graduates have

Table 6.X.1 — Post-Secondary Education Benefits for Individuals and Society

	Public Benefits	Individual Benefits
Economic	Increased tax revenues	Higher wages and benefits
	Greater productivity	Employment
	Increased consumption	Higher savings levels
	Increased workforce flexibility	Improved working conditions
	Decreased dependence on government financial support	Personal and professional mobility
Social	Reduced crime rates	Improved health / life expectancy
	Increased charitable giving and volunteering	Improved quality of life for children
	Increased civic engagement	Increased personal status
	Stronger social cohesion / appreciation of diversity	Increased leisure activities and hobbies
	Improved ability to adapt to new and emerging technologies	Better consumer decision making
	Less reliance on health care system	Better ability to cope with stress

Source: Institute for Higher Education Policy, 1998.

322 THE PRICE OF KNOWLEDGE 2004: ACCESS AND STUDENT FINANCE IN CANADA

higher incomes than non-graduates or non-atten-dees and thus pay higher tax rates and require fewer government subsidies.

Statistics Canada's *Survey on Labour and Income Dynamics (SLID)* followed a panel of 15,000 families, regularly surveying the income and labour force status of members of these families over five years. On the basis of these data, it is possible to calculate taxation and dependency statistics by level of education, by examining tax revenues and government transfers to individuals. Figure 6.X.1 shows tax revenues generated by edu-cational attainment.

The impact of post-secondary graduates on the nation's fiscal policy is further highlighted when the relationship between the employed population and government transfers is examined. In 2002, university graduates made up just over 15% of the population, but paid nearly 35% of the nation's income taxes and received just 8% of government transfers. On the other hand, people with less than a high school education, comprising almost 20% of the population, paid only 9% of the

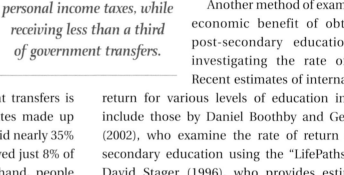

Overall, post-secondary graduates, who make up approximately 40% of the working-age population, pay nearly 65% of the nation's personal income taxes, while receiving less than a third of government transfers.

country's income taxes while receiving almost 40% of government transfers. Figure 6.X.2 shows the breakdown of population, income tax paid and government transfers received by level of education.

Overall, post-secondary graduates, who make up approximately 40% of the working-age population, pay nearly 65% of the nation's personal income taxes, while receiving less than a third of government transfers. It is not an exaggeration to say that the Canadian welfare state as presently constituted would be unable to function without the net tax revenues of post-secondary graduates.

Another method of examining the economic benefit of obtaining a post-secondary education is by investigating the rate of return. Recent estimates of internal rates of return for various levels of education in Canada include those by Daniel Boothby and Geoff Rowe (2002), who examine the rate of return on post-secondary education using the "LifePaths" model; David Stager (1996), who provides estimates of private rates of return by field of study for Ontario university graduates; and François Vaillancourt

Figure 6.X.1 — Tax Revenues by Level of Education

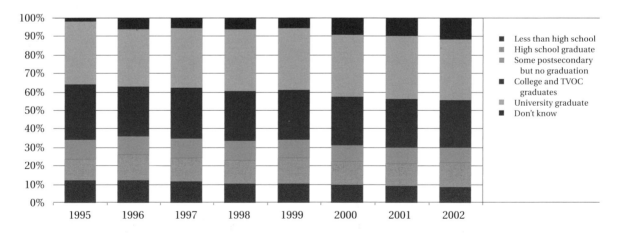

Source: Statistics Canada's 1995 to 2002 *Survey of Income and Labour Dynamics.*

Figure 6.X.2 — Population, Tax Revenues and Government Transfers by Level of Education

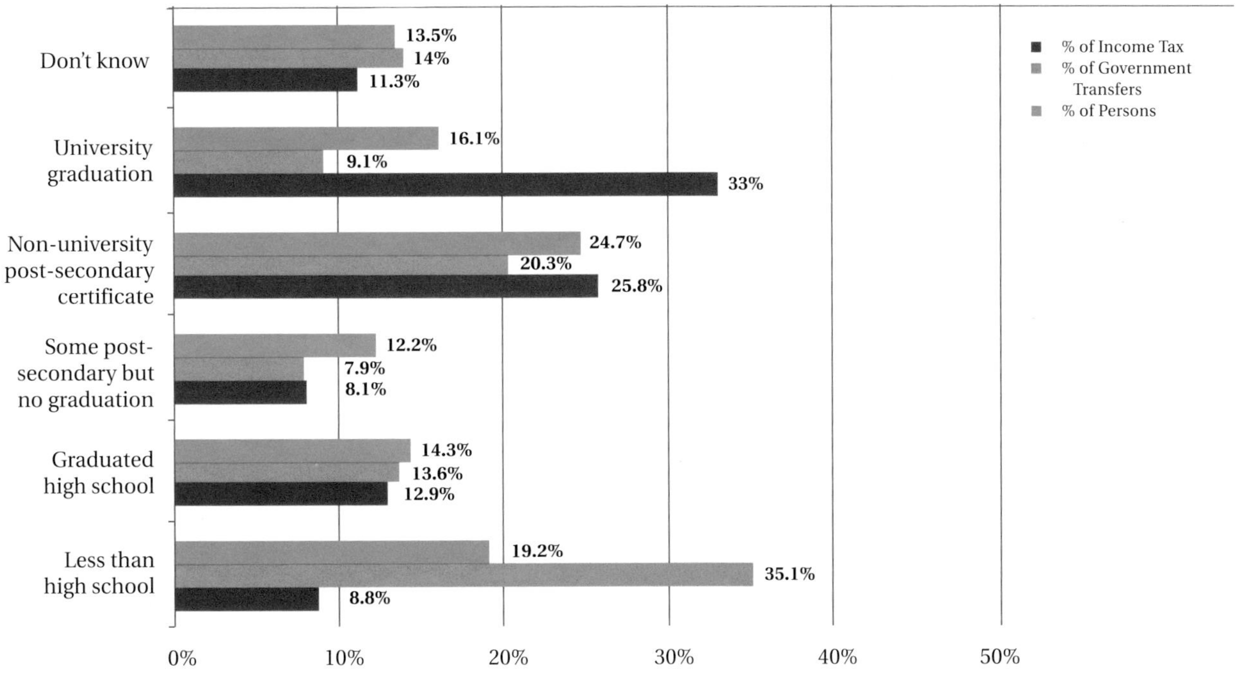

Source: Statistics Canada's 2002 *Survey of Income and Labour Dynamics.*

(1996), who provides estimates of private and public or social rates of return for various levels of education and for Bachelor's and health degrees by field of study in Canada. All of these studies use 1991 Census data on earnings.

The rate of return is usually measured by determining the "internal rate of return" (IRR) associated with an individual's investment in education. The IRR analyzes the lifetime stream of benefits and costs of education to come up with an annual "return" on education similar to that which permits comparison of investments in human capital with other types of investment. There are generally two types of rate of return discussed: the "private rate of return," which accrues to the individual (see Section VIII for further details), and the "total rate of return" which increases the value of the GDP (assuming that an increase in workers' income reflects an increase in the value of the marginal product of labour) relative to the resource cost of education.[9]

Private and total rates of return are good economic predictors of individual and public investment in post-secondary education. Figure 6.X.3 shows the fitted rate of return on a Bachelor's degree in Canada over the past decades.[10]

This graph highlights a number of important points. First, despite a nasty recession and high interest rates in the 1980s, university graduates still enjoyed a fairly good rate of return on their investment. This is likely a result of lower costs of education and lower levels of student borrowing at that time. The importance of the labour market to the rate of return can be seen in the 1990s, when costs substantially increased but the general labour market expanded as well, keeping the rate of return relatively stable. Second, the private return on education is still the best single investment in a market an individual can make. An average private rate of return of 10% annually is considerably higher than the long-run average return on either stocks or

9. Emery, *Total and Private Returns to University Education in Canada.*

10. The fitted rate of return was calculated primarily from Vaillancourt (1995) and Bourdeau, Primeau and Vaillancourt (2002). For more details see *Total and Private Returns to University Education in Canada.*

Figure 6.X.3 — Fitted Rate of Return on Bachelor's Degree in Canada from 1960 to 2000[11]

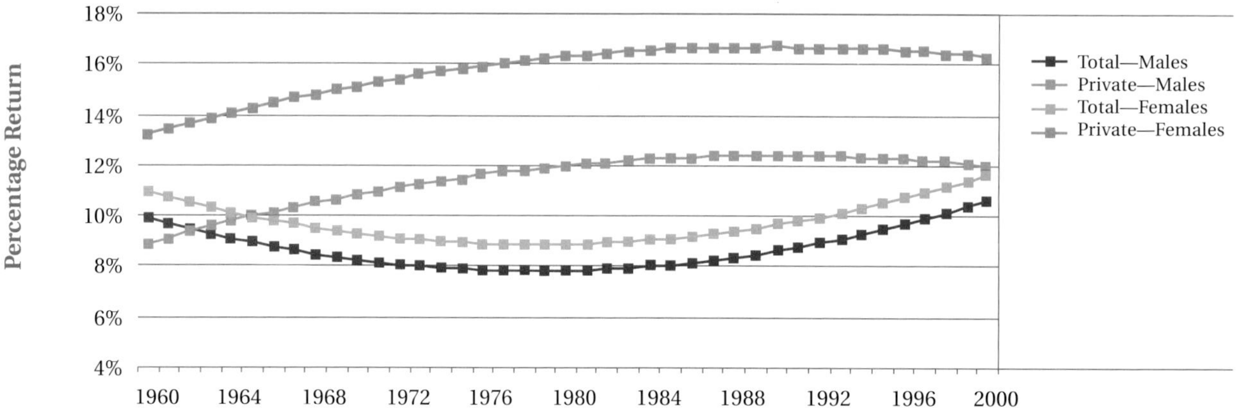

Source: Emery, *Total and Private Returns to University Education in Canada.*

bonds over the same period. Third, the total rate of return—that is, the benefit to society—is, broadly speaking, correlated with tuition fees. As government investment falls and students' share of the total costs rise, the return to the public treasury increases. This occurs since the public rate of return remains constant, however, the initial investment is declining. Conversely, rising tuition will reduce the private rate of return for exactly the same reason.

Table 6.X.1 — College and University Graduate Private Rates of Return in the 1990s

	Rate of Return
College	**15–28%**
Male	15–28%
Female	18–26%
University	**12–20%**
Male	12–17%
Female	16–20%

Source: Boothby and Rowe, *Rate of Return to Education*, and Vaillancourt and Bourdeau-Primeau, *The Returns to University Education in Canada.*

Emery's work focused exclusively on university rates of return and made little mention of college rates of return. The rate of return for college graduates is an important part of the post-secondary equation and can be found in the work of Boothby/Rowe and Vaillancourt. These authors calculated rates of return in the 1990s for college and university graduates. At the community college level, all graduates experienced a positive rate of return. The same, however, was not true for university graduates, only two-thirds of whom had a positive rate of return. The overall rate of return is therefore higher for college students. The university figures are likely influenced by the effect of graduate studies, which, despite bringing higher wages in the short run, tend to have lower private rates of return because of reduced time in the labour force. Table 6.X.1 shows the private rates of return for college and university students in the 1990s.

11. These IRRs are "risk free" rates of return, since they do not incorporate unemployment, mortality, childbearing or health risks that may interrupt a worker's time in the labour force. This is even more significant for female workers, since their working careers are assumed to be uninterrupted from age 23 to 65, which may lead to unrealistically high IRR calculations.

The Sociological Perspective

As mentioned earlier, not all benefits of post-secondary education are purely economic in nature. Other benefits of an educated populace range from stronger social cohesion and appreciation of diversity to less reliance on the health care system. These benefits are often harder to measure than rates of return but are no less important.

Many North American studies have found that an individual's level of education does have an effect on participation in civic and community affairs. Moreover, participation can often build a sense of solidarity, trust and belonging. In the United States, Pascarella and Terenzini (1991) reviewed and reported on several studies that found college graduates tend to take a greater interest in social and political issues and become more involved in the political process. Hyman, Wright and Reed (1975) found the level of education to be consistently and substantially related to being informed about public affairs and elections and to a general interest in politics. These findings held true even when age,

race, religion, socio-economic status and rural origins were controlled. In Canada, work done by André Blais (2000), André Blais, Elisabeth Gidengil, Richard Nadeau and Neil Nevitte (2002) and Pollara Inc. (forthcoming) for the Canada Millennium Scholarship Foundation shows many of the same findings, Canadians' level of education is correlated with civic and political engagement and interest.

Education is also closely linked to charitable giving and volunteering. Sturm (1997) found that many community agencies enjoy voluntary assistance and leadership that draw heavily upon more highly educated groups. Statistics Canada's 1997 and 2000 *National Survey of Giving, Volunteering, and Participating* show that individuals with post-secondary education tend to make charitable donations of larger amounts more often, volunteer greater amounts of their time and participate more actively in civic affairs. Figure 6.X.4 shows the donating rate and average amount donated by level of education in Canada, and Figure 6.X.5 shows the percentage of Canadians aged 15 and older volunteering and average hours volunteered during 2000.

Figure 6.X.4 — Donating Rate and Average Amount Donated by Level of Education in Canada (in 2003 Real Dollars)

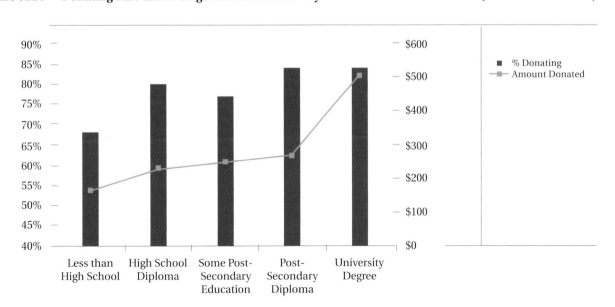

Source: Statistics Canada's 2000 *National Survey of Giving, Volunteering, and Participating.*

Figure 6.X.5 — Percentage of Canadians Aged 15 and Older Volunteering and Average Hours Volunteered per Year by Level of Education

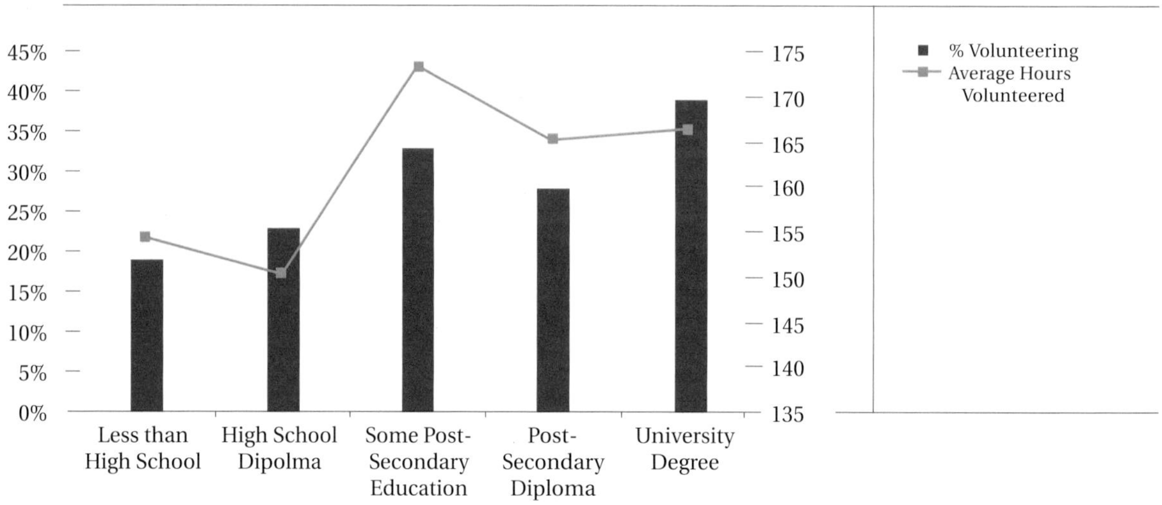

Source: Statistics Canada's 2000 *National Survey of Giving, Volunteering, and Participating.*

There is some evidence of a link between education, crime and incarceration, with greater amounts of time in school being associated with lower levels of criminal activity (OECD 1996 and Ungerleider 1999). Strum (1997) observed education to have an effect on the crime rate when crimes of "profit" are separated from other crimes. That is when other factors are controlled, the relationship of a lack of education to crime can be demonstrated for crimes of profit (e.g., theft) but not for profitless crimes (e.g., sexual assault). Related statistical data show that individuals with a high school education or less comprise only 34% of the population, but make up 75% of the federal prison population and over 70% of the population in provincial jails (Canadian Centre for Justice Statistics 1996 and Ungerleider 1999).

One must, however, be very cautious when considering these findings, as many other variables no doubt influence results. For instance, a possible reason for the low numbers of those with post-secondary education being incarcerated could be a result of the greater probability of such individuals being able to afford proficient legal counsel (due to higher average income levels). In addition, it is almost impossible to conclude whether the same factors that lead individuals to drop out of school, such as an unstable home environment and peer culture, also lead them to engage in criminal activity. Despite data limitations and crude estimates for some of the desired statistics, the results of regression analysis are highly consistent with the proposition that those with lower schooling levels and training, and hence lower potential legal income, have a relatively greater tendency to engage in crimes against property.[12]

Although there are few studies of the allocation of consumer expenditure across different levels of education, there appear to be some statistically

---

12. Erlich, *On the Relation between Education and Crime.*

significant differences in this area. Results of a study by Michael (1975) indicate that the level of formal schooling directly influences consumer behaviour, independent of its effects on income, with education being correlated to spending on a broader category of services. Pascarella and Terenzini (1991) found that, holding income constant, individuals with a college education spend a greater percentage of their income on housing, reading and further education, but a lower percentage on food, clothing, alcohol, tobacco and transportation.

There is some evidence that education has an effect on lifestyle choices, including how individuals spend leisure time. Bowen (1977) indicated that college graduates tend to be less addicted to television than others and more selective in the programs they watch, and are more inclined to read, engage in adult education, attend cultural events and participate in the arts; they are more interested in the pursuit of hobbies and other interests; they are more likely to take part in community and civic affairs; and they are more likely to take vacations.

Education also appears to have a positive impact on an individual's health and well-being. Individuals with higher levels of education tend to enjoy better physical and mental health. Health and Welfare Canada studies (1993) indicate that level of education affects individuals' lifestyle choices related to physical and mental health. On the other hand, D'Arcy (1998) shows that there is a slight difference by level of education with respect to the number of visits to physicians: university-educated people are the most likely to have visited a physician in a calendar year. Since there are no financial impediments to accessing physician services in Canada this would seem to indicate that there are systemic[13] rather than financial barriers in place here.

Individuals who pursue post-secondary education develop analytical, communication and personal skills which prepare them for the "real world."

Also, university educated Canadians are four times as likely to access alternative health care (such as massage therapists and naturopaths) compared to individuals with less than a high school education. This is not surprising given that these services are not traditionally publicly funded and many may be covered under employee health programs.

Health and Welfare Canada (1993) also showed that better-educated people also spend less time in the hospital, are more capable of dealing with physical impairments or limitations, and more often report that they enjoy good health. This is important, since Statistics Canada's 1994 *National Population Health Survey* defined better health as including: being less likely to be overweight; less likely to suffer from chronic high blood pressure or diabetes; more likely to be physically active; less likely to smoke; and more likely to quit smoking. Also, Dr. Joseph Grzywacz et al. in the March 2004 issue of the Journal of Health and Social Behaviour suggest that there is a link between coping with stress and post-secondary education. Although individuals with a post-secondary education in general dealt with more stressful events in their lives (44% of days versus 30% for those who didn't finish high school), post-secondary graduates were less affected by stress and reported on average fewer health complaints.

In conclusion, it is clear that the gains from post-secondary education are not always purely economic. Individuals who pursue post-secondary education develop analytical, communication and personal skills that prepare them for the "real world." These are often referred to as "soft skills," but are as valuable as knowledge of math or science. These invaluable skills are honed in the hallways, classrooms and laboratories of higher learning institutions through relationships between faculty, peers and staff.

---

13. Systemic barriers could include distance to health services, as well as language and cultural barriers.

Tables and Figures

Tables and Figures

Tables

Chapter 1 – Deciding to Go to Post-Secondary

Table 1.III.1 — Secondary Student Educational Expectations by Secondary School Grade — 11
Table 1.III.2 — Secondary School Students' Perceptions of Barriers to Education After High School — 12
Table 1.IV.1 — Parents' Expected Sources of Children's Contributions to Post-Secondary Costs — 23
Table 1.V.1 — Single Most Important Information Source in the Decision to Attend a Specific University — 28

Chapter 2 – A Profile of the Student Body

Table 2.II.1 — Top 20 Canadian Universities by Enrolment in 2001–2002 (Full-Time and Part-Time) — 40
Table 2.II.2 — Largest 20 Canadian Colleges by Enrolment (Including Trade and Vocational) in 1999–2000 — 45
Table 2.VI.1 — Types of Disabilities Among University Students With Disabilities — 60
Table 2.VII.1 — Status Indian Post-Secondary Enrolment by Field of Study in 2002–03 — 63
Table 2.VII.2 — Personal Profile of Aboriginal and Non-Aboriginal University Students — 65
Table 2.VII.3 — Personal Profile of Aboriginal and Non-Aboriginal College Students — 66
Table 2.VII.4 — Proportion of Canadians Pursuing or Having Pursued Any Post-Secondary Education (1996 and 2001) — 67
Table 2.VIII.1 — Students With Dependants' Registration Status by Age of Children (University Only) — 69
Table 2.IX.1 — Distribution of Canadian Undergraduate Students by Size of Home Community in 2002 — 73
Table 2.X.1 — Distance Moved to Attend Post-Secondary Institution — 75
Table 2.X.2 — University Enrolment and Student Mobility by Province in 1998–99 — 76
Table 2.X.3 — Preferred Destinations of Out-of-Province University Students by Jurisdiction in 1998–99 — 77
Table 2.XI.1 — International Students in Canada by Type of Study From 1990–91 to 2000–01 — 79
Table 2.XI.2 — International Students at Canadian Universities by Province and Level of Education in 1998–99 — 81
Table 2.XI.3 — Top Ten Canadian Universities by International Enrolment From 1990–91 to 1999–2000 — 82
Table 2.XI.4 — Canadian Students Studying Abroad by Country of Destination From 1990–1991 to 1999–2000 — 83
Table 2.XII.1 — Synthetic Completion Rates at Canadian Universities — 88
Table 2.XII.2 — Reasons for Interruption of Undergraduate Study Among Graduating Students in 2003 — 90

Chapter 3 – Barriers to Access and Participation

Table 3.II.1 — Proportion of Young Canadians Who Mentioned Facing Barriers to Achieving Desired Degree of Education by Level of Education and Type of Barrier — 94
Table 3.II.2 — Reasons for Not Pursuing Post-Secondary Education by Father's Education Level for 18- to 20-Year-Old Students — 95
Table 3.II.3 — Reasons for Not Pursuing Post-Secondary Education by Father's Education Level for 20- to 24-Year-Old Students — 96
Table 3.III.1 — Selectivity Indicators Based on 2001 Applications and Admissions Data for British Columbia, Ontario, and Quebec — 97
Table 3.III.2 — Access to Post-Secondary Education Among 20- to 24-Year-Olds by High School Grades — 98
Table 3.III.3 — Relative Academic Selectivity Scores by Province — 101
Table 3.V.1 — Canadians' Perceptions of University Costs and Benefits in 2003 — 109
Table 3.VI.1 — Barriers to Education Based on Secondary School Marks — 114

Chapter 4 — Costs and Resources

Table 4.III.1 — Lower and Upper Ranges for Ancillary Fees at Canadian Universities in 2003–04 _____ 126

Table 4.IV.1 — Average Cost of Required Textbooks per One-Term Course in Fall 2003 _____ 127

Table 4.V.1 — Mandatory Supply and Equipment Cost Ranges in Selected Professional Programs at Canadian Universities in 2003–04 _____ 129

Table 4.V.2 — Mandatory Supply and Equipment Cost Ranges in Selected Programs at Canadian Colleges in 2003–04 _____ 130

Table 4.V.3 — Mandatory Supply and Equipment Costs by Institution in 2003–04: Architecture _____ 131

Table 4.V.4 — Mandatory Supply and Equipment Costs by Institution in 2003–04: Aviation _____ 131

Table 4.V.5 — Mandatory Supply and Equipment Costs by Institution in 2003–04: Dentistry _____ 132

Table 4.V.6 — Mandatory Supply and Equipment Costs by Institution in 2003–04: Dental Hygiene _____ 132

Table 4.V.7 — Mandatory Supply and Equipment Costs by Institution in 2003–04: Medicine _____ 133

Table 4.V.8 — Mandatory Supply and Equipment Costs by Institution in 2003–04: Optometry _____ 133

Table 4.VI.1 — Student Living Arrangements by Region _____ 135

Table 4.VI.2 — Rental Rates for One-Bedroom Apartments in Major Canadian Cities in 2003 _____ 137

Table 4.VI.3 — University Residence and Meal Plan Costs in 2003–04 _____ 138

Table 4.VII.1 — Maximum Student Assistance Allowances for Childcare by Province in 2003–04 _____ 139

Table 4.VIII.1 — Average Monthly Transportation Expenditures by Region _____ 141

Table 4.VIII.2 — Cost of Monthly Public Transportation Passes in Major Canadian Cities in 2003–2004 _____ 142

Table 4.VIII.3 — Sample Student Automobile Insurance Costs in Major Canadian Cities (for a 22-Year-Old Driving a 2001 Dodge Neon) _____ 143

Table 4.IX.1 — Selected Monthly Student Expenditures by Living Arrangement _____ 145

Table 4.X.1 — Incidence and Amount of Family Support _____ 149

Table 4.X.2 — Incidence and Amount of Family Contributions for University Students by Demographic Characteristics _____ 150

Table 4.X.3 — Incidence and Amount of Family Support by Living Arrangement _____ 150

Table 4.X.4 — Incidence and Amount of Parental Contributions for College Students by Demographic Characteristics _____ 152

Table 4.XI.1 — Average Hourly Earnings for Employed Canadian Students (May to August) _____ 154

Table 4.XI.2 — Student Summer Income Distribution _____ 155

Table 4.XI.3 — Student Mean Summer Employment Income by Age, Region, and Gender _____ 155

Table 4.XI.4 — Hours Worked per Week During Studies by University Student Group _____ 159

Table 4.XI.5 — Hours Worked per Week During Studies by College Student Group _____ 159

Table 4.XIb.1 — Student Employment and First-Term Grades for the 2001–02 Academic Year _____ 165

Table 4.XII.1 — Incidence and Amount of Student Assistance by Selected Demographic Characteristics (University Students Only) _____ 171

Table 4.XII.2 — Incidence and Amount of Student Assistance by Selected Demographic Characteristics (College Students Only) _____ 172

Table 4.XIII.1 — Incidence and Amount of University Bursaries by Selected Demographic Characteristics (University Students Only) _____ 175

Table 4.XIII.2 — Incidence and Amount of Academic Scholarships by Selected Demographic Characteristics (College Students Only) _____ 175

Table 4.XIII.3 — Incidence and Amount of Investment Income and RESPs by Selected Demographic Characteristics (University Students Only) _____ 175

Table 4.XIII.4 — Incidence and Amount of Social Assistance and Employment Insurance Payments by Selected Demographic Characteristics (College Students Only) _____ 176

Table 4.XIII.5 — Incidence and Amount of Band Funding and Funding for Students With Disabilities by Selected Demographic Characteristics (College Students Only) _____ 176

Table 4.XIV.1 — Students Indicating Concern About Having Sufficient Funds to Complete Their Education _____ 177

Table 4.XIV.2 — Students' Perceptions of Their Financial Situation _____ 178

Table 4.XIV.3 — Levels of Concern About Debt (College Students Only) _____ 179

Chapter 5A — Student Aid in Canada

Table 5A.II.1 — Comparison of Student Assistance Eligibility Criteria 2003–04 — 184

Table 5A.II.2 — Comparison of Student Assistance Program Limits — 185

Table 5A.III.1 — Definition of an Independent Student — 187

Table 5A.III.2 — Assessed Costs During Study Period — 188

Table 5A.III.3 — Monthly Student Living Allowances for 2003–04 — 189

Table 5A.III.4 — Student Resources — 190

Table 5A.III.5 — Calculation of Parental Contribution — 191

Table 5A.III.6 — Calculation of Spousal Contribution — 193

Table 5A.III.7 — Means Test for Canada Student Loans (for Part-Time Students) and Canada Study Grants (for High-Need Part-Time Students) — 194

Table 5A.IV.1 — Need-Based Assistance Limits for Single, Full-Time Students With No Dependants in 2003–04 (Based on 34 Weeks of Study) — 196

Table 5A.IV.2 — Non-Need-Based Aid Programs in Canada — 197

Table 5A.IV.3 — Total Need-Based Assistance Limits for Full-Time Students With One Dependant in 2003–04 (Based on 34 Weeks of Study) — 198

Table 5A.IV.4 — Assistance for Students With Disabilities — 200

Table 5A.IV.5 — Assistance Limits for Part-Time Students — 201

Table 5A.V.1 — Student Loan Portability in Canada — 203

Table 5A.V.2 — Student Grant Portability in Canada — 204

Table 5A.VI.1 — Hypothetical Demonstration of the Impact of the In-School Interest Subsidy — 205

Table 5A.VII.1 — Debt Reduction Programs Across Canada — 208–209

Table 5A.VIII.1 — Who Pays the Interest on Loans in the Six-Month Grace Period? — 211

Table 5A.VIII.2 — Loan Consolidation Groupings and Possible Number of Total Loans — 212

Table 5A.VIII.3 — Interest Relief Programs Across Canada — 213

Chapter 5B — Sources of Student Assistance

Table 5B.III.1 — Newfoundland and Labrador Student Employment Programs — 225

Table 5B.III.2 — Maritime Student Employment Programs — 226

Table 5B.III.3 — Central Canada Student Employment Programs — 227

Table 5B.III.4 — Western Canada Student Employment Programs — 228

Table 5B.III.5 — Student Employment Programs in the Territories — 229

Table 5B.III.6 — Government of Canada Student Employment Programs — 230

Table 5B.IV.1 — Education Tax Credit Changes From 1994 to 2001 — 232

Table 5B.IV.2 — Amount and Value of Provincial Tax Credits in 2003 — 233

Table 5B.IV.3 — Government of Canada Tax Measures and Their Application in Quebec — 233

Table 5B.V.1 — Student Line of Credit Options by Financial Institution — 238

Table 5B.V.2 — Student Line of Credit Programs for Students in Selected Professional Programs by Financial Institution — 239

Table 5B.V.3 — Distribution of Students by Number of Credit Cards Owned — 240

Table 5B.VI.1 — Overview of Registered Education Savings Plans — 247

Chapter 5C — Government Expenditures on Student Assistance

Table 5C.III.1 — Estimated Cost of Quebec Tax Expenditures on Students (in Millions of 2003 Real Dollars) — 258

Chapter 6 – Student Outcomes

Table 6.II.1 — Length of Program and Average Time to Completion for Single-Institution University Students _____ 276

Table 6.IV.1 — Incidence and Amount of Debt at Graduation by Selected Demographic Characteristics
(University Students Only) _____ 285

Table 6.V.1 — Interest Rates on Student Loans by National Graduate Survey Cohort _____ 289

Table 6.VI.1 — Future Plans of Graduating University Students _____ 293

Table 6.VI.2 — College Students' Planned Activities After Graduation _____ 294

Table 6.VII.1 — Employment Preparation by Discipline for Graduating Students _____ 297

Table 6.VII.2 — Labour Market Outcomes for College Graduates Two Years After Graduation _____ 300

Table 6.VII.3 — Labour Market Outcomes for University Graduates Two Years After Graduation _____ 300

Table 6.IX.1 — Migration Patterns for Canadians by Age and Educational Attainment _____ 313

Table 6.IX.2 — Graduates Planning to Return to Canada _____ 318

Table 6.X.1 — Post-Secondary Education Benefits for Individuals and Society _____ 321

Table 6.X.2 — College and University Graduate Private Rates of Return in the 1990s _____ 324

Figures

Chapter 1 – Deciding to Go to Post-Secondary

Figure 1.II.1 — Parental Post-Secondary Education Aspirations by Household Income _____ 5

Figure 1.II.2 — Parental Aspirations by Type of Education _____ 5

Figure 1.II.3 — Parental Aspirations by Highest Education Attained _____ 6

Figure 1.II.4 — Parental Aspirations by Province of Residence and by Type of Education _____ 7

Figure 1.II.5 — Parental Aspirations for Rural and Urban Families _____ 7

Figure 1.II.6 — Parental Aspirations by Gender and Type of Education _____ 8

Figure 1.III.1 — Youth Educational Decision Pathway for 18- to 20-Year-Olds _____ 9

Figure 1.III.2 — Parental Aspirations for Children Expected to Finish High School by Age of Child _____ 10

Figure 1.III.3 — Parents' Perceptions of Barriers Preventing Their Children From Attending University _____ 11

Figure 1.III.4 — Average Age at Which Students Decide to Attend College or University _____ 13

Figure 1.III.5 — Average Age at Which Students Decide to Attend College and University by Gender _____ 14

Figure 1.III.6 — Average Age at Which Students Decide to Attend University by Secondary School Average _____ 15

Figure 1.III.7 — Average Age at Which Students Decide to Attend College by Secondary School Average _____ 15

Figure 1.III.8 — Grade in Which University Applicants Learned About Academic Requirements _____ 16

Figure 1.III.9 — Grade in Which University Applicants Learned about Academic Requirements,
by Academic Achievement _____ 16

Figure 1.III.10 — Educational Aspirations of Secondary School Dropouts _____ 17

Figure 1.IV.1 — Parental Saving Status by Household Income _____ 19

Figure 1.IV.2 — Parental Saving Status by Highest Level of Education _____ 20

Figure 1.IV.3 — Proportion of Parents Who Are Current Savers by Province of Residence _____ 20

Figure 1.IV.4 — Proportion of Parents Who Are Current Savers by Residential Status and Province _____ 21

Figure 1.IV.5 — Parents' Reported Trade-Offs to Save for Children's Education _____ 22

Figure 1.IV.6 — Alternative Financing Strategies Parents Plan to Use to Meet Children's Post-Secondary Costs _____ 22

Figure 1.IV.7 — Parents' Expected Sources of Funding and Children's Actual Sources of Funding for
Post-Secondary Education _____ 23

Figure 1.IV.8 — Parental Activities Prior to Children's Post-Secondary Education _____ 24

Figure 1.V.1 — University Applicant Consideration of College by Grade Average _____ 25

Figure 1.V.2 — Reasons for Choosing University _____ 26

Figure 1.V.3 — Reasons for Applying to College _____ 26

Figure 1.V.4 — Decision to Attend First-Choice Institution Amongst University Applicants _____ 27

Figure 1.V.5 — Top Five Factors in the Selection of College _____ 28

Figure 1.V.6 — Ten Most Influential Recruitment and Marketing Activities for College Applicants _____ 29

Figure 1.V.7 — Average Entering Grades and Proportion of Students With Entering Grades Above 75%
Across Canada From 1994 to 2003 _____ 30

Chapter 2 — A Profile of the Student Body

Figure 2.II.1 — Post-Secondary Enrolment in Canada From 1990–91 to 2003–04 _____ 33

Figure 2.II.2 — Changes in Enrolment by Province (1990–91 = 100%) _____ 34

Figure 2.II.3 — Canadian University Enrolment by Registration Status _____ 35

Figure 2.II.4 — Changes in University Enrolment by Province From 2000–01 to 2003–04 _____ 36

Figure 2.II.5 — Age Distribution of Full-Time University Students in 1980–81, 1989–90, and 1999–2000 _____ 36

Figure 2.II.6 — Mean Age of Full-Time University Students by Province in 1998–99 _____ 37

Figure 2.II.7 — Percentage Change in Part-Time University Enrolment by Age Group From 1988–89 to 1998–99 (1988–89 = 100%) _____ 37

Figure 2.II.8 — Female University Enrolment as a Percentage of Total University Enrolment From 1980–81 to 2000–01 _____ 38

Figure 2.II.9 — University Students by Gender and Province in 2000–01 _____ 39

Figure 2.II.10 — Canadian Full-Time College Enrolment by Type of Program From 1990–91 to 1999–2000 _____ 40

Figure 2.II.11 — Age Distribution of Full-Time College Students in 1990–91, 1994–95, and 1998–99 _____ 41

Figure 2.II.12 — Mean Age of Full-Time College Students by Province in 1998–99 _____ 42

Figure 2.II.13 — Percentage Change in Part-Time College Enrolment by Age Group From 1988–89 to 1998–99 (1988–89 = 100%) _____ 43

Figure 2.II.14 — Female College Enrolment as a Percentage of Total College Enrolment From 1990–91 to 1999–2000 _____ 43

Figure 2.II.15 — Community College Gender Breakdown by Jurisdiction in 1999–2000 _____ 44

Figure 2.III.1 — Youth Cohort Sizes in Canada From 1980 to 1999 _____ 47

Figure 2.III.2 — Changes in the 18- to 25-Year-Old Population by Province From 1980 to 1999 _____ 48

Figure 2.III.3 — Full-Time University Participation Rate for 18- to 21-Year-Olds by Province From 1989–90 to 2003–04 _____ 49

Figure 2.III.4 — Full-Time University Participation Rate for 19- to 22-Year-Olds (Ontario and Quebec) and 18- to 21-Years-Olds (Rest of Canada) by Province From 1989–90 to 2003–04 _____ 49

Figure 2.III.5 — Full-Time College Participation Rate for 18- to 21-Year-Olds by Province From 1989–90 to 2002–03 (Excluding Trade-Vocational Programs) _____ 50

Figure 2.III.6 — Full-Time Post-Secondary Participation Rate for 18- to 21-Year-Olds by Province From 1989–90 to 2002–03 (Excluding Trade-Vocational Programs) _____ 51

Figure 2.III.7 — Gross Enrolment Ratios for University-Level Studies in Selected Countries for 2000 _____ 52

Figure 2.IV.1 — Percentage of Canadians Aged 18 to 24 (17 to 24 in Quebec) Who Have Undertaken Any Post-Secondary Studies by Estimated Parental Income (*PEPS* 2002) _____ 53

Figure 2.IV.2 — Proportion of Canadians Aged 18 to 21 Accessing Post-Secondary Education by Income Quartile (*SLID* 1998) _____ 54

Figure 2.IV.3 — College Participation Rates of 18- to 24-Year-Olds by Parental Income Bracket in 2001 Real Dollars (*SCF* 1979–1997) _____ 55

Figure 2.IV.4 — University Participation Rates of 18- to 24-Year-Olds by Parental Income Bracket in 2001 Real Dollars (*SCF* 1979–1997) _____ 55

Figure 2.V.1 — Post-Secondary Students (Canada) and Applications (Ontario) Self-Identified as Visible Minority in 2002 and 2003 _____ 57

Figure 2.V.2 — Educational Aspirations Among Ontario University Applicants by Visible-Minority Status _____ 58

Figure 2.V.3 — Distribution of Ethnicity Among Visible Minorities in Ontario in Universities, Colleges, and the General 18- to 35-Year-Old Population _____ 58

Figure 2.VII.1 — Recipients of First Nations PSSSP Funding (1980–81 to 2002–03) _____ 62

Figure 2.VII.2 — 2001 Status Indian Enrolment Breakdown by Type of Institution _____ 63

Figure 2.VII.3 — Top Ten Colleges and Universities Attended by Status Indians in 2002–03 ___ 64

Figure 2.VII.4 — Aboriginal Canadian Educational Attainment From Age 25 to 64 in 1996 and 2001 _____ 67

Figure 2.IX.1 — Average Urban and Rural Reading Scores by Province (*PISA* 2000) _____ 71

Figure 2.IX.2 — Percentage of Canadians Living More Than 80km From Universities and Colleges in 1996 (Using *SLID* Data) _____ 72

Figure 2.X.1 — Net Flow of University Students by Province in 1998–99 _____ 77

Figure 2.XI.1 — Top Ten Countries of Origin for International Students in Canada From 1990–91 to 2000–01 _____ 80

Figure 2.XI.2 — Changes in International University Enrolment in Canada by Province From 1990–91 to 1999–2000 _____ 81

Figure 2.XI.3 — Foreign Students as a Percentage of the Overall University Population for Selected Countries in 1998 — 83

Figure 2.XI.4 — Location of Canadian Students in the U.S. by State in 2000–01 (Top Ten Only) — 84

Figure 2.XI.5 — Location of Canadian Students in the U.S. by Institution in 2000–01 (Top 15 Only) — 85

Figure 2.XII.1 — Post-Secondary Drop-Outs in Canada as a Percentage of the 18- to 24-Year-Old Population From 1979 to 2002 — 87

Chapter 3 – Barriers to Access and Participation

Figure 3.II.1 — Reasons for Not Pursuing Post-Secondary Studies — 94

Fig. 3.III.1 — PISA Reading Proficiency by Family Socio-Economic Status in Selected Countries — 99

Figure 3.III.2 — PISA Reading Scores and University Admissions Cut-Offs by Province — 100

Figure 3.IV.1 — Tuition and Participation Rates From 1991 to 2003 (in 2003 Real Dollars) — 104

Figure 3.IV.2 — Changes in Undergraduate Tuition and Reported Financial Barriers From 1991 to 2003 — 105

Figure 3.IV.3 — Undergraduate Tuition as a Percentage of the Maximum Student Loan for Single Students Without Dependants From 1994 to 2003 — 106

Figure 3.IV.4 — Correlation Between Tuition Fees and Post-Secondary Participation From 1984 to 1997 — 106

Figure 3.IV.5 — Percentage of Post-Secondary Students and Non-Attendees Reporting an Unwillingness to Borrow — 107

Figure 3.IV.6 — Educational Status of Young Canadians Saying They Are Unwilling to Borrow Money for Their Education — 107

Figure 3.V.1 — "True" University Cost-Benefit Analysis — 110

Figure 3.V.2 — Perceived University Cost-Benefit Analysis for All Canadians — 111

Figure 3.V.3 — Perceived University Cost-Benefit Analysis for Low-Income Canadians — 111

Chapter 4 – Costs and Resources

Figure 4.I.1 — Total Academic Year Expenditures by Type — 115

Figure 4.I.2 — Sources of Student Income — 116

Figure 4.II.1 — Canadian Tuition Rates From 1989 to 2004 (in 2003 Real Dollars) — 117

Figure 4.II.2 — Undergraduate Tuition Rates From 1989–90 to 2003–04 (in 2003 Real Dollars) — 118

Figure 4.II.3 — College Tuition Rates in 1990–1991 and 2003–04 (in Real 2003 Dollars) — 119

Figure 4.II.4 — Tuition Rates for Selected Programs From 1989 to 2004 (in 2003 Real Dollars) — 119

Figure 4.II.5 — Dentistry Tuition Fees From 1989 to 2004 (in 2003 Real Dollars) — 120

Figure 4.II.6 — Medicine Tuition Fees From 1989 to 2004 (in 2003 Real Dollars) — 121

Figure 4.II.7 — Law Tuition Fees From 1989 to 2004 (in 2003 Real Dollars) — 121

Figure 4.III.1 — Average University Ancillary Fee Ranges in Canada (in 2003 Real Dollars) — 123

Figure 4.III.2 — College Ancillary Fee Ranges in Canada (in 2003 Real Dollars) — 124

Figure 4.III.3 — University Undergraduate Tuition and Additional Fees by Province in 2003–04 — 124

Figure 4.III.4 — National College Tuition and Additional Fees in 2003–04 — 125

Figure 4.VI.1 — Student Living Arrangements by Age — 135

Figure 4.VI.2 — Cost of Housing by Living Arrangement — 136

Figure 4.IX.1 — Monthly Student Food Expenditures by Region — 145

Figure 4.IX.2 — Monthly Student Non-Food Consumption Expenditures by Region — 147

Figure 4.IX.3 — Monthly Student Debt and Investment Expenditures by Region (Students With Debt and/or Investments Only) — 147

Figure 4.X.1 — Shares of Family Contributions by Origin — 151

Figure 4.X.2 — Incidence and Amount of Parental Contributions by Age — 151

Figure 4.XI.1 — Summer Employment Rates for Returning Students Aged 18 to 24 in Canada From 1990 to 2003 — 153

Figure 4.XI.2 — Minimum Wages by Province From 1995 to 2004 (Summer Only) ———————— 154

Figure 4.XI.3 — Student Employment Rates During Studies From 1976 to 2003 ———————— 156

Figure 4.XI.4 — Regional Differences in Students' Anticipated and Actual Employment ———————— 156

Figure 4.XI.5 — Average Hours Worked per Week by Employed College and University Students During
Studies From 1980 to 2003 ———————— 157

Figure 4.XI.6 — Workforce Status Among Selected Demographic Groups ———————— 158

Figure 4.XI.7 — Most Important Reason Why Students Seek Employment During the Academic Year ———————— 160

Figure 4.XIa.1 — Hours per Week Spent in Class/Lab by Hours of Employment per Week
(Undergraduates Only) ———————— 161

Figure 4.XIa.2 — Hours per Week Spent in Class/Lab by Hours of Employment per Week
(College Students Only) ———————— 161

Figure 4.XIa.3 — Weekly Hours Spent Studying Outside of Class by Weekly Hours of Employment
(Undergraduates Only) ———————— 162

Figure 4.XIa.4 — Weekly Hours Spent Studying Outside of Class by Weekly Hours of Employment
(College Students Only) ———————— 163

Figure 4.XIb.1 — Distribution of Average Grades by Average Hours of Employment per Week ———————— 165

Figure 4.XII.1 — Student Loan Borrowers in Canada From 1990–91 to 2002–03 ———————— 167

Figure 4.XII.2 — Average Annual Student Loan Borrowing From 1990–91 to 2002–03 (in Real 2003 Dollars) ———————— 168

Figure 4.XII.3 — Grants Awarded in Canada From 1990–91 to 2002–03 ———————— 169

Figure 4.XII.4 — Average Grant Size by Source From 1990–91 to 2002–03 (in Real 2003 Dollars) ———————— 169

Figure 4.XII.5 — Number of Loan Remission Payments in Canada From 1990–91 to 2002–03 ———————— 170

Figure 4.XII.6 — Average Remission Payment by Source From 1990–91 to 2002–03 (in Real 2003 Dollars) ———————— 171

Figure 4.XIII.1 — Incidence of Non-Government Loans ———————— 173

Figure 4.XIII.2 — Average Annual Borrowing by Type of Non-Government Loan ———————— 173

Figure 4.XIII.3 — Private Borrowing by Age ———————— 174

Figure 4.XIV.1 — Concern About Debt by Level of Anticipated Debt (College Students Only) ———————— 179

Chapter 5A — Student Aid in Canada

Figure 5A.III.1 — Expected Parental Contributions in Quebec, Manitoba, and Ontario ———————— 192

Figure 5A.III.2 — Expected Spousal Contributions in Quebec, Manitoba, and Ontario ———————— 194

Figure 5A.IV.1 — Weekly Need-Based Assistance Limits for Single Full-Time Students Without Dependants
in 2003–04 ———————— 195

Figure 5A.IV.2 — Weekly Need-Based Assistance Limits for Full-Time Students With One Dependant in 2003–04 ———————— 199

Figure 5A.IX.1 — Aggregate Government Student Loans From 1990 to 2003 (in 2003 Dollars) ———————— 215

Figure 5A.IX.2 — Aggregate Government Non-Repayable Assistance by Type From 1990 to 2003
(in 2003 Dollars) ———————— 216

Figure 5A.IX.3 — Aggregate Government Non-Repayable Assistance by Source From 1990 to 2003
(in 2003 Dollars) ———————— 217

Figure 5A.IX.4 — Aggregate Need-Based Assistance by Type From 1990 to 2003 (in 2003 Dollars) ———————— 218

Figure 5A.IX.5 — Aggregate Need-Based Assistance by Source From 1990 to 2003 (in 2003 Dollars) ———————— 218

Chapter 5B — Sources of Student Assistance

Figure 5B.II.1 — Total Institutional Assistance to Students by Type of Assistance ———————— 221

Figure 5B.II.3 — Institutional Merit Scholarships by Tenure ———————— 222

Figure 5B.II.2 — Institutional Merit Scholarships by Type ———————— 222

Figure 5B.II.4 — Value of Athletics Scholarships in Canada by Sport and Gender (2002–03) ———————— 223

Figure 5B.V.1 — Number of Credit Cards by Age of Student ———————— 241

Figure 5B.VI.1 — Canadian Government Spending on Merit Scholarships (1990–2003) ———————— 245

Chapter 5C – Government Expenditures on Student Assistance

Figure 5C.II.1 — Total Expenditures on Student Assistance in Canada From 1990 to 2002 (in 2003 Real Dollars) — 251

Figure 5C.II.2 — Federal and Provincial Shares of Total Assistance Expenditures (in 2003 Real Dollars) — 252

Figure 5C.II.3 — Total Student Assistance Expenditures by Type (in 2003 Real Dollars) — 252

Figure 5C.II.4 — Total Loan Expenditures as a Percentage of Loans Issued — 253

Figure 5C.II.5 — Changes in Government Student Assistance per Client From 1990 to 2002 (in 2003 Real Dollars) — 254

Figure 5C.III.1 — Federal Government Tax Expenditures for Post-Secondary Students Since 1990 (in Millions of 2003 Real Dollars) — 256

Figure 5C.III.2 — Provincial/Territorial Government Tax Expenditures for Post-Secondary Students Since 1990 (in Millions of 2003 Real Dollars) — 257

Figure 5C.III.3 — Total Government Tax Expenditures for Post-Secondary Students Since 1990 (in Millions of 2003 Real Dollars) — 258

Figure 5C.III.4 — Canada Education Savings Grant Recipients and Expenditures From 1998 to 2003 (in 2003 Real Dollars) — 259

Figure 5C.III.5 — Total Expenditures on Non-Need-Based Transfers to Individuals for Post-Secondary Students Since 1990 (in Millions of 2003 Real Dollars) — 260

Figure 5C.IV.1 — 2003 Expenditures on Youth Employment Programs in Canada in Millions of Dollars — 261

Figure 5C.IV.2 — 2003 Cost of Student Employment Programs by Province in Millions of Dollars — 262

Figure 5C.V.I — Government Expenditures on Post-Secondary Institutions in Atlantic Canada (in 2003 Real Dollars) — 264

Figure 5C.V.2 — Government Expenditures on Post-Secondary Institutions in Ontario and Quebec (in 2003 Real Dollars) — 265

Figure 5C.V.3 — Government Expenditures on Post-Secondary Institutions in Western Canada (in 2003 Real Dollars) — 265

Figure 5C.V.4 — Government of Canada Expenditures on Post-Secondary Institutions (in 2003 Real Dollars) — 266

Figure 5C.V.5 — Total Government Expenditures on Post-Secondary Institutions (in 2003 Real Dollars) — 267

Figure 5C.VI.1 — Government Transfers to Individuals With Respect to Post-Secondary Education by Type From 1990 to 2002 (in 2003 Real Dollars) — 269

Figure 5C.VI.2 — Government Transfers to Individuals With Respect to Post-Secondary Education by Source From 1990 to 2002 (in 2003 Real Dollars) — 270

Figure 5C.VI.3 — Need-Based Versus Non-Need-Based ("Universal") Expenditures From 1990 to 2002 (in 2003 Real Dollars) — 271

Figure 5C.VI.4 — Total Government Transfers With Respect to Post-Secondary Education by Type (in 2003 Real Dollars) — 271

Figure 5C.VI.5 — Comparative Measures of Post-Secondary Expenditures From 1990 to 2002 (Per-Student Expenditures and Expenditures as a Proportion of GDP) — 272

Chapter 6 – Student Outcomes

Figure 6.II.1 — Time to Completion by Origin of Academic Credits — 275

Figure 6.II.2 — Time to Completion for Single-Institution University Students by Normal Program Length — 276

Figure 6.III.1 — Post-Secondary Graduates in Canada From 1994–95 to 1999–2000 — 277

Figure 6.III.2 — 2001 College and University Attainment Rates for Individuals Aged 20 to 24 by Jurisdiction — 278

Figure 6.III.3 — 2001 College and University Attainment Rates for Individuals Aged 25 to 44 by Jurisdiction — 279

Figure 6.III.4 — Post-Secondary Attainment Rates by Gender — 280

Figure 6.IV.1 — Incidence and Amount of Student Debt of Bachelor's Degree Graduates From 1982 to 2003 (in 2003 Real Dollars) — 282

Figure 6.IV.2 — Incidence and Amount of Student Debt of College Graduates From 1982 to 2003 (in 2003 Real Dollars) — 282

Figure 6.IV.3 — Incidence of Government Student Loan Debt at Graduation, by Province of Study, Class of 2000 — 283

Figure 6.IV.4 — Government Student Loan Debt at Graduation by Province in 2000 — 283

Figure 6.IV.5 — Percentage of Graduates With More Than $25,000 in Debt at Graduation, by Province, Class of 2000 — 284

Figure 6.V.1 — Debt Repayment Two Years After Graduation (Class of 2000) — 287

Figure 6.V.2 — Percentage of Debt Repaid After Two Years by Degree Level and Cohort ———————— 288

Figure 6.V.3 — Average Amount of Government Student Loan Debt Repaid Within Two Years of Graduation, by Level and Province of Study, Class of 2000 ———————— 288

Figure 6.V.4 — Average Percentage of Government Student Loan Debt Repaid Within Two Years of Graduation, Class of 2000, by Level and Province of Study ———————— 289

Figure 6.V.5 — Average Monthly Student Loan Repayments From 1982 to 2003 (in 2003 Real Dollars) ———————— 290

Figure 6.V.6 — Percentage of Graduates Reporting Difficulties in Repayment by Type of Degree ———————— 290

Figure 6.VI.1 — Percentage of College Students Who Would Like to Pursue Some Form of Education After Completion of Studies by Type of Program ———————— 294

Figure 6.VI.2 — Percentage of Students Who Have Pursued Some Form of Education Two Years After Graduation ———— 295

Figure 6.VI.3 — Percentage of Students Who Have Received Additional Qualifications Two Years After Graduation ———— 295

Figure 6.VII.1 — University Graduates' Perception of Future Job Prospects ———————— 298

Figure 6.VII.2 — Perceptions of Future Job Prospects by Discipline ———————— 298

Figure 6.VII.3 — Percentage of Students Finding Full-Time Employment Within Two Years of Graduation by Level of Education ———————— 299

Figure 6.VII.4 — Percentage of 1986, 1990, 1995, and 2000 College Graduates Working Full-time in Atlantic Canada and Quebec (Two Years After Graduation) ———————— 300

Figure 6.VII.5 — Percentage of 1986, 1990, 1995, and 2000 College Graduates Working Full-time in Ontario and Western Canada (Two Years After Graduation) ———————— 301

Figure 6.VII.6 — Percentage of 1986, 1990, 1995, and 2000 University Graduates Working Full-time in Atlantic Canada and Quebec (Two Years After Graduation) ———————— 301

Figure 6.VII.7 — Percentage of 1986, 1990, 1995, and 2000 University Graduates Working Full-time in Ontario and Western Canada (Two Years After Graduation) ———————— 302

Figure 6.VII.8 — Unemployment Rate for Canadians Aged 20 to 29 From 1990 to 2003 by Level of Education ———— 303

Figure 6.VII.9 — College Graduate Unemployment Rates in Atlantic Canada and Quebec Two Years After Graduation ———————— 303

Figure 6.VII.10 — Canadian College Graduate Unemployment Rates in Ontario and Western Canada Two Years After Graduation ———————— 304

Figure 6.VII.11 — University Graduate Unemployment Rates in Atlantic Canada and Quebec Two Years After Graduation ———————— 304

Figure 6.VII.12 — University Graduate Unemployment Rates in Ontario and Western Canada Two Years After Graduation ———————— 305

Figure 6.VIII.1 — Median Graduate Earnings by Level of Education Two Years After Graduation (in 2003 Real Dollars) ———————— 307

Figure 6.VIII.2 — Median Graduate Earnings by Level of University Education Two Years After Graduation (in 2003 Real Dollars) ———————— 308

Figure 6.VIII.3 — Median Graduate Earnings by Level of Education and Gender Two Years After Graduation (in 2003 Real Dollars) ———————— 308

Figure 6.VIII.4 — Regional Differences in Starting Salary for University Graduates (in 2002 Real Dollars) ———————— 309

Figure 6.VIII.5 — Regional Differences in Starting Salary for College Graduates (in 2002 Real Dollars) ———————— 310

Figure 6.VIII.6 — Predicted Male Median Income 1 to 20 Years After Graduation (in 2002 Real Dollars) ———————— 311

Figure 6.VIII.7 — Predicted Female Median Income 1 to 20 Years After Graduation (in 2003 Real Dollars) ———————— 311

Figure 6.IX.1 — Graduate Origins by Current Location ———————— 314

Figure 6.IX.2 — University and College Graduate Net Migration for the Class of 2000 Two Years After Graduation ———— 315

Figure 6.IX.3 — University Graduate Migration for the Classes of 1986, 1990, and 2000 Two Years After Graduation ———— 316

Figure 6.IX.4 — Proportion of Class of 1995 Graduates Who Moved to the United States ———————— 317

Figure 6.XI.5 — Distribution of Class of 1995 Graduates Who Moved to the United States by Gender and Level of Study ———————— 317

Figure 6.IX.6 — Educational Attainment Levels of Immigrants in the 1970s, 1980s, and 1990s ———————— 319

Figure 6.IX.7 — Unemployment Rates for Canadian-Born Individuals, Recent Immigrants, and Other Immigrants by Gender and Census Year ———————— 320

Figure 6.IX.8 — University Graduates in a Job Requiring at Most Secondary School Level Education for Canadian-Born Individuals, Recent Immigrants, and Other Immigrants by Gender and Census Year ———————— 320

Figure 6.X.1 — Tax Revenues by Level of Education ———————— 322

Figure 6.X.2 — Population, Tax Revenues, and Government Transfers by Level of Education _____ 323

Figure 6.X.3 — Fitted Rate of Return on Bachelor's Degree in Canada From 1960 to 2000 _____ 324

Figure 6.X.4 — Donating Rate and Average Amount Donated by Level of Education in Canada (in 2003
Real Dollars) _____ 325

Figure 6.X.5 — Percentage of Canadians Aged 15 and Older Volunteering and Average Hours Volunteered per
Year by Level of Education _____ 326

Bibliography

Bibliography

Acumen Research. *2003 Ontario College Applicant Survey*. London, Ontario: 2003.

----. *2001 Ontario University Applicant Survey*. London, Ontario: 2001.

----. *2002 Ontario University Applicant Survey*. London, Ontario: 2002

----. *2003 Ontario University Applicant Survey*. London, Ontario: 2003

Adelman, Cliff. *Answers in the Tool Box: Academic Intensity, Attendance Patterns, and Bachelor's Degree Attainment*. Washington, DC: U.S. Department of Education, 1999.

Alberta. Budget estimates 1991–2004.

Allan, Mary and Chantelle Vaillancourt. *Class of 2000: Profile of Postsecondary Graduates and Student Debt*. Ottawa, Ontario: Statistics Canada, 2004.

Andres-Bellamy, Lesley. "Life Trajectories, Action and Negotiating the Transition from High-School" in *Transitions: Schooling and Employment in Canada*. Paul Anisef and Paul Axelrod (eds), Toronto, Ontario: York University Press, 1993.

Association of Universities and Colleges of Canada. *Trends: the Canadian University in Profile*. Ottawa, Ontario: AUCC, 1999.

----. *Aboriginal Access to Higher Education*. Ottawa, Ontario: AUCC, 2004.

Barr-Telford, Lynn et al. *Access, Persistence and Financing: First Results from the Post-Secondary Education and Participation Survey (PEPS)*. Ottawa, Ontario: Statistics Canada, 2003.

Becker, Gary S. and Casey Mulligan. "The endogenous determination of time preference" in *Quarterly Journal of Economics* 112.3 (1997).

Bélair, Éric and Jeff Frank. *South of the Border: Graduates from the Class of 1995 who Moved to the United States*. Ottawa, Ontario: Statistics Canada, 1999.

Boothby, Daniel and Geoff Rowe. *Rate of Return to Education*. Ottawa, Ontario: Human Resources Development Canada, 2002.

Bowen, Howard. *Investment in Learning: The Individual and Social Value of American Higher Education*. San Francisco: Jossey-Bass, 1977

Bowlby, Jeff and Kathryn McMullen. *At a Crossroads: First Results of the 18–20 Cohort of the Youth in Transition Survey*. Ottawa, Ontario: Statistics Canada, 2002.

British Columbia. Budget estimates 1991–2004.

Butlin, George. "Bachelor's Graduates who Pursue Further Postsecondary Education" in *Education Quarterly Review* 7.2 (2001).

Canada. Customs and Revenue Agency Database.

----. Council of Ministers of Education, Canada and Statistics Canada. *Education Indicators in Canada: Report of the Pan Canadian Education Indicators Program 2003*. Toronto, Ontario: Canadian Education Statistical Council, 2003.

----. Health Canada. *Canada's Health Promotion Survey 1990: Technical Report*. Ottawa: Minister of Supply and Services Canada, 1993.

----. Human Resources Development Canada. *Access to Post-Secondary Education and Labour Market Transition of Post-Secondary Students*. Ottawa, Ontario: HRDC, 2001.

----. Human Resources Development Canada. Canada Student Loans Program estimates 1991–2002.

----. Human Resource Development Canada. *Canada Student Loans Program Policy Manual*. Ottawa, Ontario: HRDC, 1998.

----. Human Resources Development Canada. *Canada Student Loans Program: Review of the Government of Canada's Student Assistance Programs, Loan Year 1998–1999*. Ottawa, Ontario: HRDC, 2000.

----. Human Resources Development Canada and Statistics Canada. *At a Crossroads: First Results of the 18 to 20-Year-Old Cohort of the Youth in Transition Survey*. Ottawa, Ontario: HRDC, 2002.

----. Human Resources Development Canada and Statistics Canada. *High School May Not Be Enough: An Analysis of Results from the School Leavers Follow-up Survey 1995*. Ottawa, Ontario: HRDC, 1998.

----. Indian and Northern Affairs Canada. *Aboriginal Post-Secondary Education and Labour Market Outcomes*. Ottawa, Ontario: INAC, 1996.

----. Indian and Northern Affairs Canada. *Information 2000*. Ottawa, Ontario: INAC, 2000.

----. Indian and Northern Affairs Canada. *Research and Analysis Directorate*. Ottawa, Ontario: INAC, 1996.

----. Statistics Canada. *Annual Survey on Tuition and Additional Fees at Canadian Universities*.

----. Statistics Canada. CANSIM II, Table 478-004.

----. Statistics Canada. CANSIM II, Table 478-005.

----. Statistics Canada, CANSIM II, Table 478-007.

---- Statistics Canada. 1997 *National Survey of Giving, Volunteering and Participating*. Ottawa: Minister of Industry, 1998.

----. Statistics Canada. *Community College Student Information Survey*.

----. Statistics Canada. *General Social Survey 1986*. Ottawa, Ontario: Statistics Canada, 1986.

----. Statistics Canada. *General Social Survey 1994*. Ottawa, Ontario: Statistics Canada, 1994.

----. Statistics Canada. *Health and Activity Limitation Survey 1991*. Ottawa, Ontario: Statistics Canada, 1991.

----. Statistics Canada. *International Student Participation in Canadian Education 1993–1995*. Ottawa, Ontario: Statistics Canada, 1998.

----. Statistics Canada. *Labour Force Survey A030209R*.

----. Statistics Canada. *National Graduate Survey 1982.* Ottawa, Ontario: Statistics Canada, 1984.

----. Statistics Canada. *National Graduate Survey 1986.* Ottawa, Ontario: Statistics Canada, 1986

----. Statistics Canada. *National Graduate Survey 1990.* Ottawa, Ontario: Statistics Canada, 1992.

----. Statistics Canada. *National Graduate Survey 1995.* Ottawa, Ontario: Statistics Canada, 1997.

----. Statistics Canada. *National Graduate Survey 2000.* Ottawa, Ontario: Statistics Canada, 2003.

----. Statistics Canada. *National Population Health Survey 1994.* Ottawa: Minister of Industry, 1995.

----. Statistics Canada. *School Leavers Survey.* Ottawa, Ontario: Statistics Canada, 1991.

----. Statistics Canada. *Survey Approaches to Educational Planning 1999.* Ottawa: Statistics Canada, 2000.

----. Statistics Canada. *Survey Approaches to Educational Planning 2002.* Ottawa: Statistics Canada, 2003.

----. Statistics Canada. *Survey of Labour and Income Dynamics 1993–2003.*

----. Statistics Canada. *University Student Information Survey.*

----. Statistics Canada and Canada Mortgage and Housing Corporation. CANSIM 027-0040.

Canada Millennium Scholarship Foundation. *Annual Report 2001.* Montreal, Quebec: Canada Millennium Scholarship Foundation, 2001.

----. *Annual Report 2002.* Montreal, Quebec: Canada Millennium Scholarship Foundation, 2002.

----. *Annual Report 2003.* Montreal, Quebec: Canada Millennium Scholarship Foundation, 2003.

----. *Additional Supplies and Equipment Survey.* Montreal, Quebec: Canada Millennium Scholarship Foundation, unpublished.

----. *2003 College Student Fee Survey.* Montreal, Quebec: Canada Millennium Scholarship Foundation, unpublished.

----. *2003 Textbook Survey.* Montreal, Quebec: Canada Millennium Scholarship Foundation, unpublished.

Canadian Association of University Business Offices. CAUBO databases.

Canadian Centre for Justice Statistics. *A One-Day Snapshot of Inmates in Canada's Adult Correctional Facilities* in Juristat, 1996 Vol. 18 (8).

Canadian Interuniversity Sport. CIS database.

Canadian Undergraduate Survey Consortium. *First-Year University Students Survey.* 2001.

----. *Graduating Students Survey.* 2000.

----. *Graduating Students Survey.* 2003.

----. *Survey of Undergraduate Students.* 2002

Cartwright, Fernando and Mary K. Allen. *Understanding the Urban-Rural Reading Gap.* Ottawa, Ontario: Statistics Canada, 2002.

The Consumer's Guide to Insurance, InsuranceHotline.com, http://www.insurancehotline.com (accessed spring 2004).

COMPAS Research Inc, *Post-Secondary Education: Cultural, Scholastic and Economic Drivers,* Montreal, Quebec: Canada Millennium Scholarship Foundation, forthcoming.

Corak, Miles. et al. *Family Income and Participation in Post-Secondary Education.* Ottawa, Ontario: Statistics Canada, 2003.

D'Arcy, Carl. "Health Status of Canadians." *Health and Canadian Society: Sociological Perspectives 3rd Edition.* David Coburn, Carl D'Arcy and George M. Torrance (eds). Toronto: University of Toronto Press, 1998.

Dhalla, Irfan A. et. al. "Characteristics of first-year students in Canadian Medical Schools" in *Canadian Medical Association Journal* 166.8 (2002).

Educational Policy Institute. *Survey of Student Public Transportation Costs.* Toronto, Ontario: Educational Policy Institute, unpublished.

Ekos Research. *Making Ends Meet: The 2001–02 Student Financial Survey.* Montreal, Quebec: Canada Millennium Scholarship Foundation, 2003.

Erlich, Isaac. "On the Relation Between Education and Crime." Report Prepared for the Carnegie Commission on Higher Education. Berkeley: Carnegie Foundation for the Advancement of Teaching, and the National Bureau of Economic Research, 1975.

Emery, Herb. "Total and Private Returns to University Education in Canada: 1960–2030 and in Comparison to Other Post-Secondary Training". *Higher Education in Canada.* February 2004. Kingston, Ontario: John Deutsch Institute for the Study of Economic Policy, 2004.

Fichten, Catherine S. et al. "Canadian Postsecondary Students With Disabilities: Where Are They?" *Canadian Journal of Higher Education* XXXIII. 3 (2003).

Finnie, Ross and Christine Laporte. "Student Loans and Access to Post-Secondary Education: Preliminary Evidence From the Post-Secondary Education and Participation Survey". *Pathways to Access.* October 2003. Ottawa, Ontario: Canada Millennium Scholarship Foundation, 2003.

Foley, Kelly. *Why Stop After High School? A Descriptive Analysis of the Most Important Reasons that High-School Graduates Do Not Continue to PSE.* Montreal, Quebec: Canada Millennium Scholarship Foundation, 2001.

Foot, David K and Daniel Stoffman. *Boom, Bust and Echo: How to Profit from the Coming Demographic Shift.* Toronto: Macfarlane Walter & Ross, 1997.

Frenette, Marc. *Access to College and University: Does Distance Matter?* Ottawa, Ontario: Statistics Canada, 2003.

Government of British Columbia, British Columbia Insurance Corporation, http://www.icbc.com/ (accessed spring 2004).

Government of Manitoba, Manitoba Public Insurance, http://www.mpi.mb.ca/IRC/vehicle.asp (accessed spring 2004).

Government of Saskatchewan, Saskatchewan Government Insurance Canada,
http://www.sgi.sk.ca/sgi_internet/rates/rate_calc.htm (accessed spring 2004).

Gucciardi, Franca. *Recognizing Excellence? Merit Scholarships in Canada.* Montreal, Quebec: Canada
Millennium Scholarship Foundation, 2004.

Heisz, Andrew. *Income Prospects of British Columbia University Graduates.* Ottawa, Ontario: Statistics
Canada, 2001.

Hemingway, Fred. *Assessing Canada's Student Aid Need Assessment Policies.* Montreal, Quebec: Canada
Millennium Scholarship Foundation, 2003.

Holmes, David. *Embracing Differences.* Montreal, Quebec: Canada Millennium Scholarship Foundation,
forthcoming.

Hyman, Herbert, Charles Wright and John Reed. *The Enduring Effects of Education.* Chicago: University of
Chicago Press, 1975.

Institute for Higher Education Policy. "Reaping the Benefits: Defining the Public and Private Value of Going to
College." Washington: 1998.

Institute of International Education. "Locator Report of Canada Foreign Students" *Open Doors 1999–2000
Statistical Summary.* New York, NY: IIE, 2000.

Ipsos-Reid. *Canadians' Attitudes Towards Financing Post-Secondary Education.* Montreal, Quebec: Canada
Millennium Scholarship Foundation, 2004.

Ipsos-Reid. *2003 Student Finance Panel Study.* Montreal, Quebec: Canada Millennium Scholarship
Foundation, unpublished.

Johnson, Ann Dowsett, ed. *The Maclean's Guide to Canadian Universities 1998.* Toronto, Ontario: Rogers
Media, 1998.

----. *The Maclean's Guide to Canadian Universities 1999.* Toronto, Ontario: Rogers Media, 1999.

----. *The Maclean's Guide to Canadian Universities 2000.* Toronto, Ontario: Rogers Media, 2000.

----. *The Maclean's Guide to Canadian Universities and Colleges 2001.* Toronto, Ontario: Rogers Media, 2001.

----. *The Maclean's Guide to Canadian Universities 2002.* Toronto, Ontario: Rogers Media, 2002.

----. *The Maclean's Guide to Canadian Universities 2003.* Toronto, Ontario: Rogers Media, 2003.

----. *The Maclean's Guide to Canadian Universities 2004.* Toronto, Ontario: Rogers Media, 2004.

Junor, Sean and Alex Usher *The Price of Knowledge: Access and Student Finance in Canada.* Montreal, Quebec:
Canada Millennium Scholarship Foundation, 2002.

Kane, Murray and Kim Bartlett. *The National Report on International Students in Canada 2000/01.* Ottawa,
Ontario: Canadian Bureau for International Education, 2002.

Kane, Murray and Jennifer Humphries. *The National Report of International Students in Canada 1998/99.*
Ottawa, Ontario: Canadian Bureau for International Education, 1999.

Kirshtein, Rita J. et. al. *Workforce Contingent Financial Aid: How States Link Financial Aid to Employment.* Indianapolis, Indiana: Lumina Foundation for Education, 2004.

Lang Research. *Report on the Meta-Analysis of Post-Secondary Institutional Graduate Surveys.* Montreal, Quebec: Canada Millennium Scholarship Foundation, 2002.

----. *Meta-Analysis of Post-Secondary Institutional Graduate Surveys 2004.* Forthcoming.

Lawrance, Emily C. "Poverty and the Rate of Time Preference: Evidence from Panel Data" in *Journal of Political Economy* (1991).

Maclean's Magazine. *Universities: Reading the Rankings.* Toronto, Ontario: Rogers Media, 1994.

----. *Universities: Reading the Rankings.* Toronto, Ontario: Rogers Media, 1995.

----. *Universities: Reading the Rankings.* Toronto, Ontario: Rogers Media, 1996.

----. *Universities: Reading the Rankings.* Toronto, Ontario: Rogers Media, 1997.

Malatest, R. A. and Associates Ltd. *Canadian College Student Finances.* Montreal, Quebec: Canada Millennium Scholarship Foundation, 2003.

Manitoba. Budget estimates 1991–2004.

----. *2003 Inventory of Canada's Youth Employment Programs.* Winnipeg, Manitoba: Government of Manitoba, 2003.

Manitoba Council on Post-Secondary Education. Annual College tuition survey.

Manski, Charles F. "Adolescent econometricians: How do youth infer the returns to schooling?" in *Studies of Supply and Demand in Higher Education.* Charles T. Clotfetter and Michael Rothschild (eds). Chicago: University of Chicago Press, 1990.

Mayer, Susan E. *What Money Can't Buy: Family Income and Children's Life Chances.* Cambridge, Mass: Harvard University Press, 1997.

Michael, Tober. "Education and Consumption." Report Prepared for the Carnegie Commission on Higher Education. Berkeley: Carnegie Foundation for the Advancement of Teaching, and the National Bureau of Economic Research, 1975.

New Brunswick. Budget estimates 1991–2004.

Newfoundland and Labrador. Budget estimates 1991–2004.

Nova Scotia. Budget estimates 1991–2004.

Ontario. Budget estimates 1991–2004.

Organization for Economic Cooperation and Development. Lifelong Learning for All: Meeting of the Education Committee at Ministerial Level, January 16–17, 1996. Paris: OECD, 1996.

---. *Education at a Glance: OECD Indicators.* Paris: OECD, 2003.

Pascarella, Ernest and Patrick Terenzini. *How College Affects Students: Findings and Insights from Twenty Years of Research.* San Francisco: Jossey-Bass Inc., 1991.

Pinker, Steven. *The Blank Slate: The Modern Denial of Human Nature.* New York, NY: Viking, 2002.

Prairie Research Associates. *Canadian College Student Finances: Second Edition.* Montreal, Quebec: Canada Millennium Scholarship Foundation, 2003.

Prairie Research Associates. *Pan-Canadian Secondary School Survey.* Montreal, Quebec: Canada Millennium Scholarship Foundation, forthcoming.

Quebec. Budget estimates 1991–2004.

----. Ministry of Education. *Une Aide à Votre Portée.* Quebec, Quebec: Aide Financière aux Études.

----. Ministry of Education. *Annual Report 1997–98.* Quebec, Quebec: Government of Quebec, 1998.

----. Ministry of Education. *Annual Report 1998–99.* Quebec, Quebec: Government of Quebec, 1999.

----. Ministry of Education. *Annual Report 1999–2000.* Quebec, Quebec: Government of Quebec, 2000.

----. Ministry of Education. *Annual Report 2000–01.* Quebec, Quebec: Government of Quebec, 2001.

----. Ministry of Education. *Annual Report 2001–02.* Quebec, Quebec: Government of Quebec, 2002.

----. Ministry of Education. *Annual Report 2002–03.* Quebec, Quebec: Government of Quebec, 2003.

Rasmussen, Chris. *To Go Or Not To Go: How the Perceived Costs and Benefits of Higher Education Influence College Decision-Making For Low-Income Students.* Center for the Study of Higher and Postsecondary Education: University of Michigan, 2003.

Ryan, Bruce A. and Gerald R. Adams. "How do families affect children's success in school?" in *Statistics Canada Education Quarterly Review* 6.1 (1999)

Saskatchewan. Budget estimates 1991–2004.

Shapiro, Jessie. *Why are the Poor So Hungry? Time Preference, Altruism, and the Food Stamp Nutrition Cycle.* Department of Economics: Harvard University, 2003.

Shipley, Lisa et. al. *Planning and Preparation: First results from the Survey of Approaches to Educational Planning (SAEP)* 2002. Ottawa: Ministry of Industry, 2003.

Snowdon, Ken. *Applicant Data in Canada: Another Perspective on Access.* Montreal, Quebec: Canada Millennium Scholarship Foundation, forthcoming.

Sorensen, Marianne. *The Class of 2000 Two Years after Graduation: results from the 2002 universities and university colleges' graduate employment survey.* Government of Alberta, 2002.

Stager, David. *Returns to Investment in Ontario University Education, 1960–1990 and Implications for Tuition Fee Policy,* Council of Ontario Universities, Ontario, December 1994.

Sturm, Pamela. *The Impact of West Virginia State College on the Kanawha Valley: A Case Study on the Benefits of Higher Education.* Institute: West Virginia State College, 1997.

UNESCO. *1999 UNESCO Statistical Yearbook.* Lanham, MD: Berman Press, 1999.

---. *Global Education Digest 2004: Comparing Education Statistics Across the World.* Montreal, Quebec: UNESCO Institute for Statistics, 2004.

Vaillancourt, François. *The Private and Total Returns to Education in Canada, 1990*, Centre de recherche et développement in économique (CRDE), Université de Montréal, December 1996.

Vaillancourt, François and Sandrine Bourdeau-Primeau. *The Returns to Education in Canada: 1990 and 1995*, Centre de recherche et développement in économique (CRDE), Université de Montréal, 2001.

Wilms, Doug. *Ready or Not: Literacy Skills and Postsecondary Education*. Montreal, Quebec: Canada Millennium Scholarship Foundation, 2003.

Wolf, Alison. *Does Education Matter? Myths About Education and Economic Growth*. London: Penguin Books, 2002.

Zeman, Klarka et. al. *Education and labour market pathways of young Canadians between age 20 and 22: An Overview*. Ottawa, Ontario: Statistics Canada, 2004.

Zhao, John et al. "Brain Drain and Brain Gain: The Migration of Knowledge Workers from and to Canada" in *Statistics Canada Education Quarterly Review* 6.3 (2000).

Appendix A — Additional Data

Supplementary Table 1 — Total Value of Government Loans Issued, 1990–91 to 2002–03 (in 2003$)

	BC	AB	SK	MB	ON	QC	NB	NS
1990–91	$67,980,000	$6,068,538	$55,716,981	$1,432,382	$68,100,326	$372,005,277	$0	$0
1991–92	$73,660,000	$7,587,212	$51,618,152	$1,783,615	$111,629,254	$429,694,042	$0	$0
1992–93	$82,550,000	$8,746,687	$54,279,175	$2,096,399	$132,247,354	$515,895,920	$0	$0
1993–94	$87,664,823	$9,485,796	$51,722,208	$8,336,593	$645,974,851	$563,136,455	$24,300,083	$53,733,129
1994–95	$71,948,992	$11,362,976	$48,252,671	$24,482,463	$666,557,035	$639,391,878	$28,560,936	$38,141,887
1995–96	$81,208,843	$13,152,880	$47,832,557	$25,298,725	$731,662,735	$615,911,139	$28,853,188	$48,233,963
1996–97	$131,048,784	$10,197,462	$51,119,651	$29,203,550	$877,613,802	$657,937,970	$35,013,067	$58,663,319
1997–98	$140,033,270	$11,459,467	$52,086,090	$29,045,233	$829,508,257	$603,099,915	$41,053,466	$66,922,029
1998–99	$153,402,643	$12,738,686	$56,315,394	$27,721,337	$698,844,804	$545,814,975	$51,132,071	$43,604,709
1999–2000	$113,266,648	$11,417,808	$62,932,432	$31,077,803	$482,490,659	$452,303,903	$51,875,371	$43,165,300
2000–01	$93,797,324	$10,714,652	$64,117,197	$27,120,980	$415,277,734	$354,795,480	$47,217,177	$40,441,399
2001–02	$94,897,029	$11,698,674	$62,174,734	$22,216,290	$359,110,526	$355,261,960	$44,198,053	$42,036,294
2002–03	$138,662,130	$9,923,468	$57,651,906	$21,841,857	$368,008,901	$351,702,382	$42,918,636	$43,804,521

	PE	NL	YT	NT	NU	Provinces	CSLP	Total
1990–91	$0	$0	$0	n/a	n/a	$571,303,505	$861,499,525	$1,432,803,030
1991–92	$0	$0	$0	n/a	n/a	$675,972,275	$988,321,092	$1,664,293,367
1992–93	$0	$0	$0	n/a	n/a	$795,815,535	$1,032,889,751	$1,828,705,286
1993–94	$0	$0	$0	$2,868,582	n/a	$1,447,222,519	$1,186,025,006	$2,633,247,525
1994–95	$0	$38,662,374	$0	$4,799,031	n/a	$1,572,160,243	$1,454,197,444	$3,026,357,688
1995–96	$4,582,407	$53,812,745	$0	$5,018,492	n/a	$1,655,567,673	$1,641,062,056	$3,296,629,729
1996–97	$5,567,699	$69,112,639	$0	$4,441,945	n/a	$1,929,919,889	$1,825,172,932	$3,755,092,822
1997–98	$6,989,365	$68,838,199	$0	$4,671,324	n/a	$1,853,706,616	$1,782,470,041	$3,636,176,657
1998–99	$9,177,260	$71,006,744	$0	$4,397,156	n/a	$1,674,155,778	$1,753,906,477	$3,428,062,255
1999–2000	$8,844,393	$61,627,619	$0	$4,289,393	n/a	$1,323,291,328	$1,707,821,949	$3,031,113,277
2000–01	$9,096,192	$52,169,310	$0	$4,338,415	$342,273	$1,119,428,132	$1,658,894,102	$2,778,322,235
2001–02	$9,108,178	$43,933,642	$0	$5,141,121	$429,648	$1,050,206,149	$1,620,082,670	$2,670,288,819
2002–03	$6,273,996	$35,212,411	$0	$5,257,197	$395,831	$1,081,653,236	$1,421,684,543	$2,503,337,779

Supplementary Table 2 — Number of Government Loans Issued, 1990–91 to 2002–03 (in 2003$)

	BC	AB	SK	MB	ON	QC	NB	NS	NL	PE	YT	NT	NU	Total Provinces	CSLP	Total Borrowers
1990–91	n/a	30,806	13,695	434	35,286	114,133	0	0	0	0	0	n/a	n/a	194,354	241,346	355,479
1991–92	n/a	34,869	13,179	490	55,941	131,589	0	0	0	0	0	n/a	n/a	236,068	269,062	400,651
1992–93	n/a	35,813	13,181	580	66,779	147,042	0	0	0	0	0	n/a	n/a	263,395	282,592	429,634
1993–94	38,283	37,816	12,764	2,797	150,349	155,576	8,998	13,991	0	0	0	471	n/a	421,045	306,356	461,932
1994–95	40,836	41,883	14,995	13,304	190,228	162,241	10,295	11,229	13,599	0	0	485	n/a	499,095	317,782	480,023
1995–96	45,561	39,887	14,443	8,624	198,706	160,032	11,180	16,278	16,408	1,822	0	754	n/a	513,695	326,052	486,084
1996–97	50,766	37,148	13,866	9,498	199,288	166,077	12,475	17,993	20,140	2,103	0	685	n/a	530,039	345,083	511,160
1997–98	54,093	40,403	14,338	9,459	189,936	159,956	14,784	18,969	20,899	2,384	0	695	n/a	525,916	353,979	513,935
1998–99	57,909	39,342	14,355	9,648	170,241	149,216	16,078	10,649	20,267	3,032	0	683	n/a	491,420	361,967	511,183
1999–2000	61,890	38,048	16,246	10,288	155,791	139,670	15,985	10,515	18,682	2,998	0	644	n/a	470,757	336,287	475,957
2000–01	63,199	40,318	16,566	9,235	139,570	127,884	14,846	9,932	16,203	3,083	0	649	93	441,578	346,534	474,418
2001–02	65,412	43,002	16,271	7,954	127,964	127,204	13,710	10,137	14,097	3,133	0	468	132	429,484	334052	461,256
2002–03	65,255	38,791	15,663	7,836	132,720	129,523	13,710	10,331	n/a	2,307	0	526	113	416,775	331240	460,763

Supplementary Table 3 — Total Value of Government Grants Issued, 1990–91 to 2002–03 (in 2003$)

	BC	AB	SK	MB	ON	QC	NB	NS
1990–91	n/a	$62,108,707	$0	$7,621,256	$239,933,035	$249,987,546	$19,282,166	$24,584,697
1991–92	$29,560,000	$49,093,722	$0	$8,478,585	$306,232,665	$281,173,136	$21,185,925	$18,844,055
1992–93	$29,013,800	$47,454,129	$0	$10,837,596	$346,787,326	$329,007,164	$21,499,526	$20,128,358
1993–94	$31,997,518	$50,013,827	$0	$1,051,757	$34,125,682	$314,990,929	$5,931,928	$0
1994–95	$27,246,067	$48,014,259	$0	$1,435,638	$32,003,696	$317,660,422	$5,118,727	$0
1995–96	$30,051,164	$26,024,414	$0	$1,473,545	$39,182,025	$306,783,299	$4,461,663	$0
1996–97	$50,089,099	$27,193,233	$0	$1,796,367	$17,652,548	$301,545,301	$8,596,979	$0
1997–98	$51,570,925	$22,850,723	$0	$1,733,699	$14,213,593	$275,004,466	$10,813,735	$0
1998–99	$57,089,932	$11,263,206	$284,885	$1,309,911	$17,968,713	$221,885,163	$6,922,367	$0
1999–2000	$62,398,082	$19,066,417	$5,857,954	$1,686,221	$18,921,401	$128,505,446	$6,250,038	$0
2000–01	$79,764,263	$18,340,395	$4,286,807	$1,822,242	$19,968,452	$144,578,086	$7,605,365	$0
2001–02	$109,724,158	$18,570,988	$4,045,722	$2,035,317	$17,739,455	$189,277,193	$6,705,491	$0
2002–03	$84,335,496	$39,836,510	$4,044,901	$2,131,406	$17,266,676	$227,506,205	$6,705,491	$0

	PE	NL	YT	NT	NU	Provinces	CSLP	Foundation	Canada
1990–91	$3,057,560	n/a	$1,306,871	n/a	n/a	$607,881,838	$0	$0	$607,881,838
1991–92	$3,026,206	n/a	$1,490,540	n/a	n/a	$719,084,834	$0	$0	$719,084,834
1992–93	$2,958,259	$17,534,850	$1,389,467	n/a	n/a	$826,610,475	$0	$0	$826,610,475
1993–94	$2,340,791	$17,922,022	$1,556,921	$3,628,407	n/a	$463,559,783	$0	$0	$463,559,783
1994–95	$1,883,452	$0	$1,655,953	$4,787,058	n/a	$439,805,272		$0	$439,805,272
1995–96	$0	$0	$1,674,003	$4,611,714	n/a	$414,261,827	$4,220,175	$0	$418,482,002
1996–97	$0	$0	$1,731,840	$4,066,310	n/a	$412,671,677	$10,255,075	$0	$422,926,752
1997–98	$0	$0	$1,874,669	$4,398,480	n/a	$382,460,289	$12,732,741	$0	$395,193,030
1998–99	$0	$0	$1,850,545	$4,385,893	n/a	$322,960,614	$83,235,094	$0	$406,195,708
1999–2000	$0	$0	$2,176,657	$4,246,411	n/a	$249,108,626	$91,364,507	$137,939,574	$478,412,707
2000–01	$0	$0	$2,756,422	$4,403,840	$3,606,316	$287,132,186	$86,982,810	$266,448,828	$640,563,824
2001–02	$0	$0	$2,968,211	$7,593,121	$3,312,289	$361,971,945	$73,129,825	$261,053,083	$696,154,853
2002–03	$0	$0	$2,934,249	$8,250,539	$3,863,452	$396,874,925	$85,480,388	$253,496,284	$735,851,596

Notes: 1) Value of Canada Study Grants for 2002–03 is an estimate.

2) Value of grants in Saskatchewan does not include value of grants issued as "Canada/Saskatchewan Study Grants."

3) Value of grants in Nova Scotia for the years 90–91 to 92–93 are an estimate based on figures contained in provincial budgets of these years.

4) Value of grants in New Brunswick for 2003–03 is an estimate.

Supplementary Table 4 — Number of Government Grants Issued, 1990–91 to 2002–03 (in 2003$)

	BC	AB	SK	MB	ON	QC	NB	NS
1990-91	n/a	28,326	0	2,672	63,381	62,319	7,967	n/a
1991-92	8,046	24,171	0	3,466	81,444	68,272	8,467	n/a
1992-93	8,100	22,138	0	4,105	91,691	76,237	8,518	n/a
1993-94	10,190	21,421	0	467	n/a	75,627	5,306	0
1994-95	11,669	21,188	0	537	n/a	73,079	4,671	0
1995-96	13,116	7,673	0	405	n/a	72,040	5,179	0
1996-97	15,024	8,539	0	433	n/a	72,176	7,496	0
1997-98	15,862	9,443	0	354	n/a	69,784	10,397	0
1998-99	17,070	2,936	226	296	n/a	59,050	5,657	0
1999-2000	23,224	12,904	2,467	348	19,033	54,643	5,838	0
2000-01	26,121	12,963	2,166	308	19,708	56,946	6,035	0
2001-02	31,909	13,386	1,955	273	19,111	67,456	6,391	0
2002-03	26,413	16,082	2,023	300	22,545	74,282	6,391	0

	NL	PE	YT	NT	NU	Provinces	CSLP	Foundation	Canada
1990-91	0	1,577	362	n/a	n/a	166,604			166,604
1991-92	0	1,545	424	n/a	n/a	195,835			195,835
1992-93	8,495	1,485	399	n/a	n/a	221,168			221,168
1993-94	9,018	1,228	444	n/a	n/a	123,701			123,701
1994-95	0	1,024	491	n/a	n/a	112,659			112,659
1995-96	0	0	473	n/a	n/a	98,886	1,661		100,547
1996-97	0	0	491	n/a	n/a	104,159	6,273		110,432
1997-98	0	0	548	n/a	n/a	106,388	7,348		113,736
1998-99	0	0	514	n/a	n/a	85,749	56,899		142,648
1999-00	0	0	588	n/a	n/a	119,045	63,793	40,516	223,354
2000-01	0	0	652	1082	388	126,369	55,830	77,123	259,322
2001-02	0	0	696	1065	385	142,627	55,830	76,151	274,608
2002-03	0	0	700	1136	364	150,236	55,830	80,833	286,899

Notes: 1) Number of grants for New Brunswick in 2002–03 is an estimate.

          2) Number of Canada Study Grants in 01–02 and 02–03 are estimates.

Supplementary Table 5 — Total Value of Loan Remission Issued, 1990–91 to 2002–03 (in 2003$)

	BC	AB	SK	MB	ON	QC	NB	NS
1990–91	n/a	$41,147,018	$29,462,912	$3,285,033	$0	$517,573	$429,973	$0
1991–92	n/a	$37,316,188	$16,278,152	$3,927,126	$0	$1,859,611	$553,544	$0
1992–93	n/a	$22,934,129	$17,033,451	$4,058,487	$0	$2,439,801	$608,242	$0
1993–94	$18,736,628	$17,192,253	$14,901,540	$0	$0	$2,765,188	$317,876	$4,348,399
1994–95	$18,195,822	$16,643,347	$14,258,896	$0	$42,409,845	$3,472,353	$0	$11,003,294
1995–96	$1,643,182	$18,404,653	$13,119,815	$0	$80,661,894	$3,751,267	$4,352,759	$11,026,952
1996–97	$15,642,604	$22,008,083	$16,642,199	$0	$181,095,225	$4,724,248	$4,320,383	$7,677,089
1997–98	$16,849,706	$25,579,167	$17,846,903	$0	$329,432,257	$341,056	$4,331,860	$3,547,506
1998–99	$21,109,776	$27,707,487	$20,840,418	$0	$312,386,100	$0	$3,632,609	$2,726,574
1999–2000	$24,764,532	$36,920,518	$22,253,648	$0	$534,195,519	$1,322,526	$3,272,811	$3,299,990
2000–01	$22,163,483	$41,292,702	$23,163,341	$5,435,511	$299,926,515	$1,930,568	$0	$0
2001–02	$17,643,767	$35,987,848	$23,778,056	$5,049,491	$121,472,354	$2,098,417	$36,722	$0
2002–03	$8,809,394	$35,964,931	$18,421,150	$6,280,156	$127,469,907	$1,833,906	$81,507	$0

	PE	NL	YT	NT	NU	Provinces	Foundation	Canada
1990–91	$0	$0	$0	n/a	n/a	$74,842,510		$74,842,510
1991–92	$0	$0	$0	n/a	n/a	$59,934,620		$59,934,620
1992–93	$0	$0	$0	n/a	n/a	$47,074,111		$47,074,111
1993–94	$0	$0	$0	$2,019,789	n/a	$55,933,275		$55,933,275
1994–95	$0	n/a	$0	$3,704,641	n/a	$98,684,905		$98,684,905
1995–96	$0	n/a	$0	$3,652,796	n/a	$125,586,366		$125,586,366
1996–97	$906,825	n/a	$0	$2,627,143	n/a	$247,966,710		$247,966,710
1997–98	$1,172,094	n/a	$0	$2,599,980	n/a	$398,153,023		$398,153,023
1998–99	$723,098	$2,872,116	$0	$2,489,169	n/a	$391,760,772		$391,760,772
1999–2000	$1,469,106	$3,361,557	$0	$2,280,255	n/a	$629,840,474	$162,165,938	$792,006,412
2000–01	$1,396,337	$5,330,500	$0	$2,248,039	$6,542	$402,893,537	$43,686,074	$446,579,611
2001–02	$1,136,293	$5,319,444	$0	$2,605,184	$61,465	$215,189,041	$42,472,204	$257,661,246
2002–03	$1,227,698	$5,674,916	$0	$2,877,194	$31,962	$208,672,721	$41,242,746	$249,915,467

Note : 1) A remission program has existed in Newfoundland since 1994–95; however, no details were available prior to 1998–99.

Supplementary Table 6 — Number of Loans Remitted, 1990–91 to 2002–03 (in 2003$)

	BC	AB	SK	MB	ON	QC	NB	NS
1990–91	n/a	16,093	1,720	2,460	0	214	51	0
1991–92	n/a	14,738	1,458	3,776	0	922	73	0
1992–93	n/a	9,927	1,291	4,478	0	1,175	62	0
1993–94	2,057	7,197	961	0	0	1,238	38	1,876
1994–95	1,982	6,000	700	0	18,639	1,451	0	3,754
1995–96	1,631	5,953	705	0	26,803	1,523	7,426	3,936
1996–97	1,687	5,991	572	0	43,808	1,679	7,499	3,141
1997–98	1,760	5,871	1,025	0	57,765	127	7,621	1,440
1998–99	2,008	5,722	1,663	0	41,210	0	6,450	1,304
1999–2000	2,243	7,176	9,658	0	92,938	847	5,939	2,512
2000–01	1,094	8,152	10,484	1,961	68,444	1,102	0	0
2001–02	709	7,611	10,570	1,936	34,072	1,298	27	0
2002–03	935	7,553	10,170	2,210	58,553	1,235	41	0

	PE	NL	YT	NT	NU	Provinces	Foundation	Total
1990–91	0	0	0	n/a	n/a	20,538		20,538
1991–92	0	0	0	n/a	n/a	20,967		20,967
1992–93	0	0	0	n/a	n/a	16,933		16,933
1993–94	0	0	0	471	n/a	11,962		11,962
1994–95	0	n/a	0	485	n/a	29,257		29,257
1995–96	0	n/a	0	754	n/a	44,795		44,795
1996–97	583	n/a	0	685	n/a	62,504		62,504
1997–98	701	n/a	0	695	n/a	75,565		75,565
1998–99	381	400	0	683	n/a	58,517		58,517
1999–2000	592	404	0	644	n/a	120,441	51,239	171,680
2000–01	488	610	0	649	2	92,986	14,898	107,884
2001–02	365	581	0	468	13	57,650	14,511	72,161
2002–03	438	644	0	526	11	82,316	15,583	97,899

Notes: 1) Saskatchewan has more than one program which reduces debt at the end of studies; the number shown is the sum of recipients of each program. Since it is possible to receive assistance from both programs, this figure likely overstates the true number of recipients of loan remission.

2) Canada Millennium Scholarship Foundation Bursaries are issued as remission in the following provinces: SK, MB, NB, NS, PE and NL. Recipients of millennium bursaries in each of these provinces may also be eligible to receive grants from their province.

Supplementary Table 7 — Total Government Expenditures on Student Assistance 1990–91 to 2002–03 (in 2003$)

	BC	AB	SK	MB	ON	QC	NB	NS
1990-91	$48,063,518	$125,252,559	$54,977,154	$7,621,256	$254,854,941	$258,917,679	$19,712,139	$24,584,697
1991-92	$46,050,577	$108,849,212	$45,078,607	$8,478,585	$327,834,049	$306,996,491	$21,739,469	$18,844,055
1992-93	$38,267,156	$98,323,980	$46,149,737	$10,837,596	$368,779,209	$380,649,178	$22,107,769	$20,128,358
1993-94	$59,734,268	$100,508,556	$43,424,225	$2,494,464	$74,271,621	$340,985,633	$6,432,908	$3,599,867
1994-95	$56,404,800	$99,740,343	$40,047,986	$5,835,109	$148,690,918	$298,338,219	$8,362,503	$2,898,553
1995-96	$43,431,905	$84,872,414	$34,632,737	$5,224,108	$251,726,099	$402,981,448	$12,518,681	$3,658,030
1996-97	$75,404,182	$93,217,481	$33,163,602	$5,622,547	$355,019,283	$452,459,692	$16,976,528	$7,677,089
1997-98	$79,177,666	$90,834,464	$29,538,838	$7,074,061	$567,759,326	$623,270,236	$19,985,174	$10,693,783
1998-99	$95,381,042	$73,436,105	$29,982,171	$7,732,642	$603,671,216	$227,274,756	$22,916,908	$24,838,001
1999-2000	$105,522,908	$86,074,403	$32,156,872	$7,947,830	$706,231,600	$126,650,471	$25,652,486	$18,014,263
2000-01	$125,209,525	$90,414,930	$33,722,541	$13,234,254	$513,896,436	$118,023,771	$22,121,412	$13,592,359
2001-02	$135,218,875	$82,782,542	$34,010,918	$11,120,903	$280,297,391	$83,831,750	$22,721,447	$9,087,511
2002-03	$92,297,701	$95,872,521	$29,445,972	$11,474,695	$234,085,504	$207,537,008	$21,962,550	$8,850,472

	NL	PE	Provinces (Total)	CSL	Foundation	Federal (Total)	Total
1990-91	$27,221,481	$3,057,560	$824,262,983	$525,009,362	0	$525,009,362	$1,349,272,345
1991-92	$27,558,222	$3,026,206	$914,455,473	$470,050,384	0	$470,050,384	$1,384,505,857
1992-93	$24,359,377	$2,958,259	$1,012,560,620	$467,316,990	0	$467,316,990	$1,479,877,610
1993-94	$23,673,064	$2,340,791	$657,465,397	$481,642,318	0	$481,642,318	$1,139,107,715
1994-95	$6,389,757	$1,883,452	$668,591,641	$517,488,728	0	$517,488,728	$1,186,080,369
1995-96	$5,030,522	$112,319	$844,188,264	$873,303,119	0	$873,303,119	$1,717,491,383
1996-97	$5,617,459	$1,417,828	$1,046,575,689	$653,529,413	0	$653,529,413	$1,700,105,102
1997-98	$8,784,497	$1,800,165	$1,438,918,210	$645,571,183	0	$645,571,183	$2,084,489,394
1998-99	$15,620,802	$1,624,400	$1,102,478,041	$704,700,188	0	$704,700,188	$1,807,178,230
1999-2000	$18,816,838	$2,908,205	$1,129,975,877	$617,631,575	$292,054,274	$909,685,850	$2,039,661,726
2000-01	$16,685,469	$3,110,189	$950,010,888	$883,556,579	$310,134,902	$1,193,691,481	$2,143,702,369
2001-02	$14,353,171	$3,228,260	$676,652,767	$855,314,677	$303,525,288	$1,158,839,964	$1,835,492,731
2002-03	$14,649,851	$3,099,889	$719,276,164	$667,337,950	$294,231,113	$961,569,063	$1,680,845,227

Note: 1) Figures represent government own-source expenditures. As a result, expenditure figures for the Government of Quebec exclude any money received from the Government of Canada from the alternative payments on Canada Student Loans.